The Shadow of Selma

UNIVERSITY PRESS OF FLORIDA

Florida A&M University, Tallahassee
Florida Atlantic University, Boca Raton
Florida Gulf Coast University, Ft. Myers
Florida International University, Miami
Florida State University, Tallahassee
New College of Florida, Sarasota
University of Central Florida, Orlando
University of Florida, Gainesville
University of North Florida, Jacksonville
University of South Florida, Tampa
University of West Florida, Pensacola

THE SHADOW OF SELMA

EDITED BY
JOE STREET AND HENRY KNIGHT LOZANO

University Press of Florida
Gainesville · Tallahassee · Tampa · Boca Raton
Pensacola · Orlando · Miami · Jacksonville · Ft. Myers · Sarasota

Copyright 2018 by Joe Street and Henry Knight Lozano
All rights reserved
Published in the United States of America

First cloth printing, 2018
First paperback printing, 2021

26 25 24 23 22 21   6 5 4 3 2 1

Library of Congress Cataloging-in-Publication Data
Names: Street, Joe, editor. | Knight, Henry, 1982– editor.
Title: Shadow of Selma / edited by Joe Street and Henry Knight Lozano.
Description: Gainesville : University Press of Florida, 2018. | Includes
    bibliographical references and index.
Identifiers: LCCN 2017032244 | ISBN 9780813056692 (cloth : alk. paper)
    ISBN 9780813068442 (pbk.)
Subjects: LCSH: African Americans—Civil rights—Alabama—Selma. | Selma
    (Ala.)—Race relations. | Civil rights movements—Alabama—Selma—History.
    | Civil rights workers—Alabama—Selma—History.
Classification: LCC F334.S4 S53 2018 | DDC 323.1196/073076145—dc23
LC record available at https://lccn.loc.gov/2017032244

The University Press of Florida is the scholarly publishing agency for the State University System of Florida, comprising Florida A&M University, Florida Atlantic University, Florida Gulf Coast University, Florida International University, Florida State University, New College of Florida, University of Central Florida, University of Florida, University of North Florida, University of South Florida, and University of West Florida.

University Press of Florida
2046 NE Waldo Road
Suite 2100
Gainesville, FL 32609
http://upress.ufl.edu

CONTENTS

List of Illustrations   vii
Acknowledgments   ix

Introduction   1
   Joe Street and Henry Knight Lozano

Part 1. Selma and the Voting Rights Act

1. Selma: The Bridge and Beyond   15
   Alma Jean Billingslea Brown

2. Before the Bridge: Grassroots Activism in Selma in the Early 1960s   37
   Benjamin Houston

3. Nonviolence Crowned or Dethroned? King's Strategy in Selma and Its Legacy   58
   Peter Ling

4. "The Meat in the Coconut": Lyndon Johnson and the Voting Rights Act of 1965   77
   Mark McLay

5. Backlash or Adjustment? The White South Responds to Selma   96
   Tony Badger

6. "We Cannot Escape the Same Challenge": Britain, France, and the U.S. Voting Rights Act   113
   Clive Webb

Part 2. Media and Memory

7. Mediating Selma: 1965, 2015   133
   Aniko Bodroghkozy

8. "They Couldn't Just Write It the Way It Wasn't Anymore": Mainstream Media Narratives and the 1965 Selma Campaign   150
   Mark Walmsley

9. Sidelining Selma's Segregationists: Memory, Strategy, Ideology, and Agency   171
   George Lewis

10. "Men and Women of God and Goodwill Everywhere": *Selma* and the Role of Religion in Civil Rights Drama   196
    Megan Hunt

Part 3. The Myth of a Color-Blind America

11. The Third Reconstruction: The Racial Wealth Gap in the Post–Civil Rights South   217
    Devin Fergus

12. How the Rise of Color-Blind Racism Opened the Door for the Supreme Court Decision in *Shelby County v. Holder*   240
    Barbara Harris Combs

13. The Racial Laundering of Equality after *Shelby County v. Holder*   264
    Lynn Mie Itagaki

List of Contributors   289
Index   293

ILLUSTRATIONS

Figures

1.1. Selma to Montgomery March   29

7.1. Bloody Sunday 1   135

7.2. Bloody Sunday 2   135

7.3. John Lewis   137

7.4. Amelia Boynton   137

7.5. Hosea Williams   137

7.6. Annie Lee Cooper   145

9.1. State troopers block the way as voters protest   177

9.2. Charles Moore, "State Police form a barricade as they wait for marchers on 'Bloody Sunday'"   177

9.3. Selma to Montgomery protestors   179

9.4. March across Edmund Pettus Bridge   180

9.5. Civil rights marchers kneeling in prayer   180

9.6. Man holding American flag during Selma civil rights march   183

9.7. Onlookers at the Selma to Montgomery march   184

9.8. Selma to Montgomery onlookers   186

11.1. Median net worth by race, 1984–2009   222

11.2. Factors contributing to the wealth gap between whites and blacks   223

11.3. Percent of southern families in top 3 U.S. wealth quintiles by race, 1969 and 1995   224

11.4. Savings and loans return investment in communities per dollar deposited   227

11.5. How much more does a subprime borrower pay compared to a prime rate borrower?   229

Tables

11.1. Net migration into the South 1870–1880 to 2005–2010   219

11.2. White and African American wealth accumulation   223

11.3. Subprime lending as a percentage of state, regional, and U.S. markets by demographics, income, and location, 1998   228

ACKNOWLEDGMENTS

We want to extend our profoundest thanks to the contributors to this collection. We also wish to thank the following institutions for their financial support: Northumbria University and the U.S. Embassy, London. We especially want to thank the embassy for its continued support of academic endeavor in American Studies in the United Kingdom. Professors Sylvia Ellis, Brian Ward, and David Gleeson, offered huge support for this project, for which we are immensely grateful. Brian, in particular, was fundamental to the project's success. We owe a hearty and heartfelt debt of gratitude to our great friends at UPF, Sian Hunter and Meredith Morris-Babb, for their peerless chaperoning of this project. Sian and Meredith have been major cheerleaders for *The Shadow of Selma* since the project's inception and were immensely supportive throughout the writing and editorial process. We are extremely grateful to them and delighted to see this collection published with the finest publishing house that we know. Our heartfelt thanks go to Beth Detwiler, copy editor extraordinaire, for her magnificent work on the manuscript. We also want to thank our families for their support and love while we produced this collection, especially our daughters Carys Street and April Knight Lozano for the joy they bring to our lives. And finally, we do not know any of them, but we wish to thank all the people who fought for racial equality in the Selma campaign for their sense of justice, their courage, indefatigability, and willingness to put their bodies on the line. Each and every one of them is an American hero.

Introduction

JOE STREET AND HENRY KNIGHT LOZANO

The 2014 release of Ava DuVernay's *Selma* movie is widely regarded as a key moment in African American history and culture. The first major motion picture about the life of Dr. Martin Luther King Jr., *Selma* treats a central moment in the civil rights movement with all the sensitivity and rigor that it deserves and earned over $66 million at the box office, over three times its budget.[1] The film was received with almost unanimous critical acclaim. A. O. Scott, of the *New York Times*, was overwhelmed by the movie's "astonishingly rich and nuanced" depiction of the history, predicting that it "will call forth tears of grief, anger, gratitude and hope.... I have rarely seen a historical film that felt so populous and full of life, so alert to the tendrils of narrative that spread beyond the frame," he said.[2] David Denby, writing in the *New Yorker*, considered the film extraordinary and concluded simply, "This is cinema."[3] British reviewers focused on the performance of the British actor David Oyelowo, who portrayed Dr. King. Mark Kermode felt that Oyelowo's performance elevated what might have been a humdrum historical drama "into something genuinely inspiring."[4] David Sexton also praised Oyelowo's moving performance.[5] Ashley Clark, of the British Film Institute's house journal, *Sight and Sound*, felt that King was "complex and alive" in the film, "incarnated wonderfully" by the actor.[6]

Surprisingly, however, *Selma* found Golden Globes and Oscars hard to come by, winning only for the song "Glory," performed by the soul singer John Legend and the rapper Common. This was a sad reflection of white attitudes toward the African American contribution to American history and culture. Once again, African Americans were relegated to "song and dance" men and excluded from the prestigious roles of director, producer, or star. In this sense, one might observe that white America prefers only to remember black America's legacy in terms of song rather than the major contributions African Americans made to the destruction of slavery and then segregation in American political, legal, and, to a certain extent, social life. That Oyelowo was not even nominated for a Best Actor Oscar caused considerable upset, with the actor himself pointing out that this was sadly typical of white attitudes: "We as black people have been celebrated more for when we are subservient, when we are not being leaders, or kings, or at the center of our own narrative driving it forward," he told delegates at the Santa Barbara International Film Festival.[7] The film's director, Ava DuVernay expressed her hurt at Oyelowo's exclusion from the Oscars. When asked about her own absence from the Best Director nominations, she, too, turned to wider issues: "There has been no precedent for a black woman to be nominated for best director, so why was it going to change with me?"[8]

Selma itself is a powerful assertion of the centrality of African Americans to American history. Some white critics might have carped at the sidelining of Lyndon B. Johnson, but in doing so they fell into an artfully created trap. Given the historical marginalizing of black people in America, *Selma*'s mild distortion of the record in suggesting that Johnson had to be convinced by Dr. King of the need for more civil rights legislation was an infinitesimal step in the right direction. In reminding viewers that the Selma campaign was black-organized, black-controlled, and black-staffed, the film was also a profound articulation of African American agency.

Unlike Spike Lee's *Malcolm X*, which famously opened with the 1991 videotape footage of Rodney King being beaten by Los Angeles police, *Selma* made no overt attempt to draw parallels between the past and the present. Common's rap in the theme song featured two references to the uprising in Ferguson, Missouri, in 2014, one explicit and one oblique, but the film itself did not need to.[9] The murder of Michael Brown, an eighteen-year-old African American man, in Ferguson by a white police officer on August 9, 2014, sparked an international outcry. Ferguson soon became a byword for racial tension that emanated from police brutality. It propelled the Black Lives Matter movement, which coalesced in 2013 following the murder of seventeen-year-old Trayvon Martin by a neighborhood watch volunteer, back into the international spotlight. Formed by Alicia Garza, Patrisse Cullors, and Opal Tometi, #BlackLivesMatter started as an online campaign but rapidly outgrew its initial home on the web after helping to organize protests in Ferguson.[10]

The Black Lives Matter movement's engagement with direct action, which included marches, demonstrations, and civil disobedience, inevitably drew comparisons with the celebrated civil rights actions of the 1960s, irrespective of its attempt to subvert the parallels through its decentralized structure, avoidance of a leadership-based hierarchy, explicit focus on marginalized voices, and its often vocal rejection of an older generation of protesters. Nightly vigils in Ferguson took place until the announcement in November that Brown's killer would not be indicted, whereupon tensions erupted amid police gunfire, tear gas, and random violence.[11] By the time of *Selma*'s release on Christmas Day, at least 600 people had been killed by violent police actions in 2014, and two more were to die on that day.[12]

Events following the film's release helped to reinforce the sense that *Selma* spoke across the generations. On January 18, 2015, the film's stars, director, and producers marched across the Edmund Pettus Bridge alongside members of Selma's community in homage to the original march. Selma's mayor welcomed the city's visitors at a vigil in front of the city hall before the marchers set off.[13] The *Selma Times-Journal* was moved enough by the event to offer its thanks to the filmmakers for allowing them to remember the city as a beacon of hope and a place where "great things have happened."[14] This message of conciliation was repeated by Oprah Winfrey, who played Annie Lee Cooper in the film: "Our hearts are saying thank you to Selma," she said. "We thank you for being a symbol of what hope and progress, what grace and goodness can be and do."[15]

The film faded into the background at precisely the moment when the fiftieth anniversary of the original march came into focus. Previous ten year anniversaries of Selma were opportunities for former marchers and civil rights activists to rededicate themselves to the struggle. In 1975, Coretta Scott King led a procession numbering 5,000 across the bridge.[16] Jesse Jackson and 2,500 others joined her in 1985, and Governor George Wallace begged forgiveness for his previous defense of segregation ten years later.[17] Present at all of the marches was John Lewis, civil rights organizer, Selma veteran, and later congressman. By 2005, he was accompanied by five other house representatives.[18] The transformation of Selma commemorations into a moment of triumphal national unity was completed in the fiftieth anniversary celebrations. The march was led this time by the U.S. President, the First Lady, their daughters, and a number of veterans including Lewis, followed by 40,000 Americans. Amid the expected encomiums to American exceptionalism, vitality, and genius, in his address President Barack Obama pointed out that, "The Americans who crossed this bridge, they were not physically imposing. But they gave courage to millions. They held no elected office. But they led a nation.... What they did here will reverberate through the ages. Not because the change they won was preordained; not because their victory was complete; but because they proved that nonviolent change is possible, that love and hope can conquer hate." He cited Ferguson, noting that the horrors experienced there were no longer lawful or customary as they were half a century before.[19]

The 1965 Selma campaign was thus cast as a moment of American transcendence. Yet the 2015 celebrations also remind us of the gulf between memory and history. Obama's speech attempted to memorialize Selma as another moment that is emblematic of the nation's supposed ability to heal its own wounds and look to the future optimistically while glossing over the schisms of the past. A small section of the audience were alive to the problematic nature of such a process, interrupting the speech with chants of "we want change" and "stop the violence" before—somewhat ironically—being removed by the police.[20] These citations of Ferguson, coupled with *Selma*'s unflinching examination of the violence that accompanied the 1965 campaign, remind us that history is far more knotty, troubling, and complicated than (in Abraham Lincoln's peerless phrasing) the mystic chords of memory would like us to believe.

While Obama's presence suggests that history is made by great men (even if his skin color challenges the previous assumption that only white men could be great), *Selma* and the Selma campaign itself remind us that history is very much owned by ordinary people. The pictures of Obama walking over the Edmund Pettus Bridge might have been choreographed to encourage comparisons between him and Dr. King, but the blurred faces of thousands behind him are a reminder that leaders are dependent on their so-called followers whose individualism is often written out of history. Mahatma Gandhi might have told a journalist that he had to leave because his people were moving and he needed to follow them, but few other "great men" make such concessions so readily. The unknown thousands of 2015 were, in this respect, much like the thousands who accompanied Dr. King on his final, triumphant march to Montgomery, Alabama, but they were also reminders of the hundreds who accompanied John Lewis over the bridge on "Bloody Sunday" exactly two weeks before—and on the precise date, March 7, that Obama's speech later took place—and were tear-gassed, beaten, and charged by horses for their trouble. The memory of Obama's speech may well linger, but the history of the thousands must endure.

It was in this spirit that this collection was conceived and produced. The film and the commemorations raised many questions that need answering through historical analysis and debate, including Selma's place both in history and geography. *Selma* reminds its viewers of how small the actual city is, and that such places in relative geographical backwaters can be elevated to sites of historical importance by social movements that descend upon or emerge from them. This volume encourages a rethink of Selma the place as well as "Selma" the event, not to mention *Selma* the movie.

The Shadow of Selma seeks to reconsider the relationship between the "great" individual figures of the Selma campaign and the thousands of other—often equally admirable but unheralded—people who populated the campaign, making it such a historical event. It wants to discuss the networks that undergirded the movement but also the networks that opposed it, in order to undercut the leadership focus that so dominates public discourse about history and historical movements. While the focus on King in *Selma* and Obama in 2015 are part and parcel of popular discourse, this volume calls upon the findings of generations of historians who argue otherwise. As suggested by the collection's title, it shifts focus to consider Selma's long-term impact. Ava DuVernay's film offers a perfect opportunity to reconsider the ways in which contemporary and subsequent media, both fictional and factual, represented, re-represented, and reconfigured Selma.

Finally, the volume contemplates the impact of Selma, and the Voting Rights Act of 1965 that followed it, over the subsequent fifty years of American history. It questions whether the events in Selma during 1965 should be considered a major turning point in American history.

Ultimately, the volume evaluates the nature of Selma's shadow, pointing the way to future assessments of both the civil rights struggle and the Selma campaign itself.

Part 1 of this book, "Selma and the Voting Rights Act," explores the Selma campaign through both a tight chronological focus and by placing it in broader historical, political, and international contexts. Primarily focusing on social and political histories, part 1's chapters reconsider the relationship between the Selma campaign and the historical currents that swirled around it. The section begins with Alma Jean Billingslea Brown's study of Selma as a southern town that holds a significance to the history of U.S. race relations that far outstrips its comparatively small size and population. A significant Confederate base in the American Civil War, by the mid-twentieth century, Selma typified the racial discrimination, segregation, and disfranchisement that reinforced white supremacy in the Jim Crow South. In becoming the site for a coordinated civil rights campaign, however, Selma laid bare the brutality of white law enforcement in the South to countless Americans and non-Americans. In doing so, Selma became a metaphoric "bridge" in the freedom struggle: a crossing that led to the transformative legislation of the Voting Rights Act, yet one which has often been cleansed of its internal conflicts and complexities in popular, triumphal narratives of the civil rights movement.

Benjamin Houston examines how Student Nonviolent Coordinating Committee (SNCC) activists in Selma in the early 1960s, tired of sporadic and largely ineffectual civil rights activity in Lowndes County, worked to develop local leaders in and around Selma in pursuit of enduring racial change. This involved exploring the very meaning of leadership for local African Americans; it contributed toward fruitful alliances with black ministers; and, perhaps most significantly, the growing involvement of local students, including children, in the grassroots activism. SNCC's community organization in Selma laid vital groundwork long before the arrival of Martin Luther King and the Southern Christian Leadership Conference (SCLC) in early 1965.

Martin Luther King, of course, dominates the popular memory of the civil rights movement, and Selma is no exception: as Peter Ling shows in his essay, Selma is often cast as King's greatest victory. Yet King and SCLC confronted and contributed to organizational rivalry. Many SNCC activists were unconvinced both by King's intermittent presence in Selma and by his core strategy of using confrontational nonviolence to force federal intervention to guarantee black voting rights. This strategy worked well enough in the 1963 Birmingham campaign. For King, Sheriff Jim Clark presented an apt substitute for Eugene "Bull" Connor (and more than lived up to the billing by clubbing Annie Lee Cooper in front of a crowd of activists and reporters). Yet King could not fully anticipate the level of violence that would follow: from the untelevised murder of Jimmie Lee Jackson in neighboring Marion to the widely televised attack by armed white police officers of African American marchers on Bloody Sunday.

Famed for his idealism, King showed a calculating pragmatism in using the violent cauldron of Selma to pressure Lyndon B. Johnson into decisive action. Nevertheless, as Ling demonstrates, Selma also widened divisions within the civil rights movement, raising profound doubts among many African Americans about the efficacy of nonviolent direct action and about King himself. If King dominates popular narratives about Selma, Johnson assumes an equally vital position in those surrounding the Voting Rights Act. Yet, as Mark McLay shows in his essay on the Democratic president, perhaps in seeking a corrective to the white-hero stories favored by Hollywood, *Selma* depicts Johnson as a quasi-foe to voting rights, at least until the crisis in Selma forced him into action. Challenging this portrayal, McLay explores Johnson's evolution as a Texas-born pragmatist sensitive both to his white southern electorate and to the racial inequities of mid-twentieth-century America who later presided over the most transformative civil rights legislation since Reconstruction.

Like McLay, Tony Badger's assessment of the responses of white southern politicians to Selma and the Johnson civil rights legislation engages with the apparent culmination of a distinct period in southern history. Badger traces the evolution of politicians' adjustment to the challenges posed by such legislation, noting that many moderate congressmen who voted against the Civil Rights Act of 1964 voted *for* the Voting Rights Act, seeing opposition to the legislation as futile or misguided, particularly in the wake of the violence at Selma. Taking strategic retreats, white southern leaders eschewed the vitriolic defense of Jim Crow in favor of voter-friendly themes relating to constitutionalism, law and order, and the demands of civil rights activists. The white South, Badger shows, thus adjusted to a post-Selma racial climate with a new political language designed to sustain white privilege.

Broadening the focus to incorporate the transatlantic repercussions of

Selma, Clive Webb reveals the response of two of the United States' major diplomatic partners: Britain and France. The Selma campaign heightened British anxieties over the destructive potential of domestic racism. In contrast to this introspection, French coverage made few links to France's own tensions surrounding race, in particular the influx of North Africans into the country. Ironically, as Webb shows, both British and French moral superiority to the United States overlooked their respective stances toward immigration.

Part 2, "Media and Memory," explores the influential role of media representations of the Selma campaign from contemporary newsprint and television coverage to the 2014 Hollywood film. As important, its chapters reveal the power of *mis*representations in shaping popular memory of Selma, and by extension the civil rights movement, calling on readers to remain sensitive to the intricate relationships between the movement, its myths, its memory, and the media. Selma, Aniko Bodroghkozy stresses, must be understood as a media event; one in which the media emphasized certain themes while downplaying others. Network television news and photojournalists told stories about Selma that shaped popular understanding of the campaign, creating images, as in the case of Bloody Sunday, of black victimization facing ferocious white violence. Yet, Bodroghkozy argues, black activists were crucial agents in this narrative, seeking to expose for American audiences the brutality of "law and order" in the Jim Crow South. Media coverage, nonetheless, often prioritized whites. DuVernay's film, however, challenges this "white savior" narrative, placing African Americans center stage as protagonists.

Sharing an interest in how the media portrayed Selma, Mark Walmsley unpacks the role of "race beat" journalists who covered southern civil rights campaigns. These reporters have often been lionized for their frontline coverage; yet the logistics of journalistic production meant they actually reported on the African American community from a distance, both literally and figuratively. As predominantly northern and urban whites who saw racism as a southern problem, their accounts contributed toward white northern conceptions of the black freedom struggle as a regional phenomenon, defined by nonviolent marches rather than a more radical tradition of grassroots organization. Civil rights activists, however, encouraged this image by downplaying for journalists the internal divisions in Selma, presenting instead a unified front that fitted "race beat" visions of the movement.

Echoing the theme of misrepresentation, George Lewis turns the lens onto the media's coverage of Selma's white southern segregationists. Focusing on print media images of white southern police officers, Lewis argues that news photography fed a distorted understanding of the true nature of white opposition to civil rights change. The Alabama highway patrolmen shown defending Jim Crow against the Selma campaigners appeared as faceless, perhaps even totalitarian automatons. Like "race beat" journalism, this framing elided the prevalence of economic intimidation in defending segregation. For Lewis, such simplistic representations helped to fuel a redemptive narrative of the civil rights movement that has shaped popular memory, one that glosses over the nation's ongoing racial problems.

Megan Hunt's essay, meanwhile, focuses on Hollywood's portrayal of southern religion. Hunt argues that, until *Selma*, civil rights cinema presented whites either as southern religious zealots and racists, epitomized by villainous cross-burning Klansmen, or as liberal, secular heroes. Black political activity, meanwhile, is often overlooked in favor of an unthreatening African American spirituality. *Selma*, by contrast, presents a complex landscape of religious thought within the freedom struggle. It suggested to viewers the powerful intersection of spirituality with political demands for racial change, sparking soul-searching, praise, and criticism among different American faiths and denominations.

The final section, "The Myth of a Color-Blind America," considers the limits of the influence of the Voting Rights Act. Its concern is to unpack the act's economic, legal, and democratic consequences for African American citizens, particularly considering the 2013 Supreme Court *Shelby County v. Holder* decision. Together these chapters propose new avenues for examining the legacy not only of Selma but also 1960s liberalism in its entirety.

Devin Fergus examines the evolving economic status of African Americans in the South in terms of wealth inequality. For him, the major legislative breakthroughs of the 1960s were instrumental in improving black political *and* economic conditions, leading to greater income growth among black southerners than their white counterparts. This encouraged a "reverse" Black Migration to the South. Yet Fergus differentiates between income and wealth. Judged according to accumulated economic assets, there is a widening racial gap in the United States. Homeownership is crucial, and Fergus reveals how discriminatory mechanisms in mortgage lending hit African Americans disproportionately hard. It is therefore no coincidence that southern blacks constituted the largest share of the subprime mortgage market at the turn of the twenty-first century. Financial deregulation and ostensibly color-blind laws, Fergus argues, have become a key driver of racial inequality.

Barbara Harris Combs also considers themes of color-blind racism, but with a focus on *Shelby County v. Holder*. The ruling infamously removed Sections 4 and 5 of the Voting Rights Act that guaranteed the federal government's preclearance regulatory powers. These sections were designed to prevent the usage of voting devices and practices that discriminate against minority voters. Combs's essay proposes a theory entitled "Bodies Out of Place" (BOP), designed to engage the ideas behind and the potential ramifications of *Shelby*. BOP suggests a growing white belief that contemporary U.S. social ills are not endemic problems, but isolated incidents, and that color-blind rhetoric masks entrenched white opposition to ethnic and racial minorities achieving heightened status within U.S society—becoming, in effect, *bodies out of place*. As Combs argues, voter discrimination has not disappeared, as demonstrated by post-*Shelby* moves by various states to implement new voter ID and registration laws. The future of voting rights for minorities in the United States cannot be taken for granted.

In the final chapter, Lynn Mie Itagaki explores the Supreme Court's rulings on both campaign finance and voting rights, including *Shelby*, in the context of their restrictive conceptions of citizenship and democratic participation. These decisions reflect a broader strategy of the post–civil rights era that Itagaki terms "racial laundering," or the transformation of illegal and racist intent into race-neutral legal reasoning that purports to deliver ostensibly fair results for all. In recent campaign finance rulings, the Roberts Court privileged the shareholder citizen over the human voter, while the *Shelby* ruling's focus on equal sovereignty resurrects a principle that was used repeatedly in the nineteenth century to justify slavery. Itagaki reminds us not to be blind to forms of racial discrimination and injustice that continue to shape racial inequalities in the United States, from kindergarten education to housing to police targeting and incarceration. Fifty years after Selma and the Voting Rights Act, the obstacles to racial equality may be less formal than a literacy test, less obvious than an Alabama state trooper. They are, however, no less real.

Notes

1. Figures from *Box Office Mojo*, at http://www.boxofficemojo.com/movies/?page=main&id=selma.htm (consulted February 3, 2016).
2. A. O. Scott, "A 50-Mile March, Nearly 50 Years Later" *New York Times*, December 24, 2014, at http://www.nytimes.com/2014/12/25/arts/in-selma-king-is-just-one-of-the-heroes.html?_r=0 (consulted February 2, 2016).
3. David Denby, "Living History," *New Yorker*, December 22 and 29, 2014, at http://www.newyorker.com/magazine/2014/12/22/living-history (consulted February 2, 2016).
4. Mark Kermode, review of *Selma*, *Observer*, February 8, 2015, at http://www.theguardian.com/film/2015/feb/08/selma-observer-film-review (consulted February 3, 2016).
5. David Sexton, *Selma* movie review, *Evening Standard*, February 6, 2015, at http://www.standard.co.uk/goingout/film/selma-film-review-10027864.html (consulted February 3, 2016).
6. Ashley Clark, "Film of the Week: Selma," *Sight and Sound*, March 2015, at http://www.bfi.org.uk/news-opinion/sight-sound-magazine/reviews-recommendations/film-week-selma (consulted February 3, 2016).
7. Linda Ge, "'Selma' Star David Oyelowo on Oscar Snubs," *The Wrap*, February 2, 2015, at http://www.thewrap.com/selma-star-david-oyelowo-on-oscar-snubs-black-people-celebrated-more-when-we-are-subservient/ (consulted February 3, 2016).
8. "Ava DuVernay 'hurt' by David Oyelowo's Oscar Snub," *Contact Music*, February 12, 2015, at http://www.contactmusic.com/ava-duvernay/news/ava-duvernay-hurt-by-david-oyelowo-s-oscar-snub_4580885 (consulted February 3, 2016).
9. Common raps "That's why we walk through Ferguson with our hands up" in his first verse and "Selma is now for every man woman and child" in his second.
10. "About the Black Lives Matter Network," at http://blacklivesmatter.com/about/ (consulted February 3, 2016); "A Herstory of the #BlackLivesMatter Movement," at http://blacklivesmatter.com/herstory/ (consulted February 3, 2016); Herbert Ruffin, "Black Lives Matter: The Growth of a New Social Justice Movement," *BlackPast.org*, at http://www.blackpast.org/perspectives/black-lives-matter-growth-new-social-justice-movement (consulted February 3, 2016); Claudia Rankine, "The Condition of Black Life is Mourning," *New York Times*, June 22, 2015, at http://www.nytimes.com/2015/06/22/magazine/the-condition-of-black-life-is-one-of-mourning.html (consulted February 3, 2016).
11. Ruffin, "Black Lives Matter"; Jelani Cobb, "Chronicle of a Riot Foretold," *New Yorker*, November 25, 2014, at http://www.newyorker.com/news/daily-comment/chronicle-ferguson-riot-michael-brown (consulted February 3, 2016).
12. "Suspect Identified in Deadly Coachella Officer Involved Shooting," at http://www.kesq.com/news/officer-involved-shooting-in-coachella/30399260 (consulted February 3, 2016); "U.S. Citizen Dies After Being Shot with Stun Gun at Border Crossing," at http://latino.foxnews.com/latino/news/2014/12/26/us-citizen-dies-after-being-shot-with-stun-gun-at-border-crossing/ (consulted February 3, 2016); figures from http://www.killedbypolice.net/kbp2014.html (consulted February 3, 2016); Tony Ortega, "Black

Americans Killed by Police in 2014 Outnumbered Those Who Died on 9/11," *Raw Story,* April 8, 2015, at http://www.rawstory.com/2015/04/black-americans-killed-by-police-in-2014-outnumbered-those-who-died-on-911/ (consulted February 3, 2016).

13. Blake DeShazo, "Thousands Come Out for March, Concert on Edmund Pettus," *Selma Times-Journal,* January 18, 2015, at http://www.selmatimesjournal.com/2015/01/18/thousands-come-out-for-march-concert/ (consulted February 3, 2016).

14. "Selma, Paramount job well done," *Selma Times-Journal,* January 19, 2015, at http://www.selmatimesjournal.com/2015/01/19/selma-paramount-job-well-done/ (consulted February 3, 2016)

15. DeShazo, "Thousands Come Out."

16. "Thousands Mark '65 march in Selma, Ala," *New York Times,* March 9, 1965, 50.

17. William E. Schmidt, "Selma Marchers Mark 1965 Clash," *New York Times,* March 4, 1985, A1; Michael Hirsley, "20 Years Later, The Law Joins Marchers in Selma," *Chicago Tribune,* March 4, 1985, 1; Rick Bragg, "Emotional March Gains a Repentant Wallace," *New York Times,* March 11, 1995, 1; "Selma Veterans Get Keys to the City," *Washington Post,* March 6, 1995, A10.

18. "Walking in their Footsteps," *New York Times,* March 7, 2005, A12.

19. Peter Baker and Richard Fausset, "Obama, at Selma Memorial, Says 'We Know the March is Not Yet Over,'" *New York Times,* March 7, 2015, at http://www.nytimes.com/2015/03/08/us/obama-in-selma-for-edmund-pettus-bridge-attack-anniversary.html (consulted February 3, 2016); "Remarks by the President at the 50th Anniversary of the Selma to Montgomery Marches," March 7, 2015, at https://www.whitehouse.gov/the-press-office/2015/03/07/remarks-president-50th-anniversary-selma-montgomery-marches (consulted February 3, 2016).

20. Baker and Fausset, "Obama, at Selma Memorial."

1
SELMA AND THE VOTING RIGHTS ACT

1

Selma

The Bridge and Beyond

ALMA JEAN BILLINGSLEA BROWN

On February 5, 2015, after the premier of Ava DuVernay's controversial film, *Selma*, Diane Nash, leader of the Nashville student sit-ins and field secretary for both the Student Nonviolent Coordinating Committee (SNCC) and the Southern Christian Leadership Conference (SCLC), as guest columnist for the National Newspaper Publishers Association, published a short opinion piece in the *New Journal and Guide*. Responding to a specific critique of the film, the one in which Joseph A. Califano Jr., former assistant for domestic affairs to President Lyndon B. Johnson, stated that Selma was LBJ's idea, Nash entitled her essay, "LBJ Doesn't Deserve Credit for Selma," and writes,

> The impression too often perpetuated in history books and popular culture is that you have to be a president, someone special or White to have an important idea. . . . This is an idea that disempowers citizens and should not be propagated. . . . It was the courage, work, thoughtfulness, sacrifice, discipline and determination of citizens of the United States that obtained our right to vote.[1]

I begin this discussion with the response by Diane Nash in part because it disrupts top-down versions of U.S. history and dominant narratives about the 1960s freedom struggle. But Nash's refutation of Califano's assertion that the original idea of the Selma to Montgomery march was that of President Johnson also demonstrates how both the public and historical memory of the Selma voting rights movement remains a contested terrain.

In a similar vein, comments made by historian, Emilye Crosby about the film also complicate historical interpretations of the Selma movement.

Challenging the great-man paradigm in history as well as the narrative of uncomplicated and uncompromising adherence to nonviolence in Selma, Crosby explains that, while civil rights activists used nonviolent tactics in public demonstrations, at home and in their own communities, they consistently used weapons to defend themselves. Equally important, she clarifies how the televised violence on the Edmund Pettus Bridge and Bloody Sunday, the fifty-four-mile trek from Selma to Montgomery, the images of interracial marchers, and President Johnson's signing the Voting Rights Act of 1965 are all iconic visual representations that reinforce a simplistic version of history described by movement activists as "Rosa sat down, Martin stood up and white folks came south to save the day."[2]

What I want to explore here, however, is how the historic and geopolitical space of Selma, Dallas, and Lowndes County, Alabama, may be seen, like the structure spanning the river, as a threshold space, a symbolic and metaphoric bridge in U.S historical development, one that moves from the Civil War to civil rights, a bridge that connects the end of the first Reconstruction in 1876 to the hope of a second Reconstruction in 1965. Selma and Dallas County, at key moments in time, constituted a critical passageway from an old social, political, and economic order to a new, from law-enforced segregation to black enfranchisement in the South. Moreover, Selma especially in the wake of the fiftieth anniversary commemorative year, can also be seen as a complex "bridge-of-becoming," as a space of transition from the form of democracy to the substance of democracy. At the same time, given some appraisals of Selma as the freedom movement's "finest hour," as one of those moments and places where the "nation's destiny" was decided.[3] I want to also explore mass media's public memory of Selma. This memory, I hypothesize, has not only created a consumable past in which grassroots activism largely disappears but has also fostered a narrative of triumph, one that not only simplifies and leaves out complexities and contradictions, but also one that, as Diane Nash observes, disempowers citizens and discourages critical citizenship practice.

Near the end of this discussion, however, I also consider the memorial landscape of Selma, Dallas, and Lowndes County, Alabama, and how the museums, the institute, the historic trails, and interpretive centers now clustered around the most famous bridge in U.S. constitutional history have become collectively not just a site of memory, but also a symbolic and metaphoric bridge. This bridge connects slavery and the Civil War to civil rights and the vision of civil equality. It also becomes a bridge of human connectivity that journeys from narratives of triumph and consensus memory toward the goal of a society that answers its call to conscience.[4]

The city that has become pivotal in both civil rights historiography and public memory was founded in 1817 on 460 acres near the Alabama River. By 1860, Selma and Dallas County, Alabama, had the third largest per capita income in the United States. Labeled the "queen city" of the Alabama Black Belt, Selma, with its naval foundry, manufacturing center, and military depot, had also been a slave market and was strategic to the defense of the Confederacy.[5] It was also the site of one the last battles fought in the Civil War. Having been routed on April 1, 1865, by Union General James Harrison Wilson, Confederate General Nathan Bedford Forrest retreated to Selma where, on April 2, 1865, three divisions of 13,500 Union soldiers defeated the fewer than 2,000 Confederate soldiers Forrest had mustered to meet them. Lacking formal military training, Forrest had been a slave trader before the war and was associated with the massacre of black and Union prisoners at Fort Pillow, Tennessee. Along with some of his officers and men, Forrest escaped Selma before the Confederates surrendered and later served as the first grand dragon of the Ku Klux Klan but has been praised, nevertheless, by historian Shelby Foote, as one of the "authentic geniuses" of the Civil War.[6] Because so few Civil War battles were fought in the Alabama Black Belt, the battle at Selma became a potent symbol of state pride, honor, and connection to the greater Confederate war effort. The battle also legitimized a place for the city, with its memorial to Nathan Bedford Forrest, in the history of the Confederacy and enabled Selma to become a bastion of resistance to racial change.

A bridge from the world of slave markets, coerced labor, war, prison camps, and emancipation to the era of the Reconstruction, Selma, from 1867 to 1877 experienced viable black political empowerment. With the Union army enforcing the Fifteenth Amendment, black voters helped to elect Benjamin Sterling Turner, who was raised a slave in Selma, to national office. Turner, who had managed to secure some education, had served as Dallas County tax collector and as a member of the Selma City council, before his election to the 42nd Congress. He served from 1871 to 1873. However, between 1868 and 1876, thirteen African Americans from Dallas County also served as members of the Alabama State Legislature.[7]

When Reconstruction and "black rule" ended in 1877, Selma became the locus of what Donald Stone, a Student Nonviolent Coordinating

Committee (SNCC) field secretary during the 1960s, has called the "white leagues": the Knights of the White Camellia and the Ku Klux Klan. Through the lens of biography, Stone recounts in *Fallen Prince* how by 1877 all the black elected officials from Dallas County, "had been driven from the national legislature," and then goes on to describe the domestic terrorism.

> The period of 1868–1871, in the state of Alabama alone, records over 370 cases of violence against Blacks, resulting in 35 murders. The recently freed bondspeople were subject to lynchings, mass murders, beatings, midnight raids, burnings and theft of their livestock and meager land holdings.[8]

With black people being effectively disenfranchised by 1901, the geopolitical space of Selma, Alabama, like the rest of the South, became part of the arc of violence and terror that spanned from the era of Reconstruction into another epoch, the era of segregation and Jim Crow. As Jack O'Dell, advisor to Martin Luther King Jr. and editor of *Freedomways* magazine explains,

> An important fact of history is that the country experienced a period of *retrogression* during the last quarter of the Nineteenth Century in which lynchings, institutionalized segregation and the development of a mass culture of racism became the order of the day.[9]

In Selma, as Emilye Crosby and others have explained, the white power structure used economic, "legal," and extralegal means, including terrorism, to prevent African Americans from accessing their constitutional right to vote. As one law enforcement officer once bragged, the unwritten rule in Alabama was if the mobs don't stop Negroes, the police can; and if the police can't, the courts will. By the time Martin Luther King Jr. and SCLC were invited to launch a campaign in Selma, local organizations, most notably the Dallas County Voters League (DCVL) and field secretaries from the Student Nonviolent Coordinating Committee (SNCC), and especially Bernard and Colia Lafayette, had been at work in the city for more than two years.

But there was a little-known event in 1958 that linked the 1963 arrival of the Lafayettes in Selma to the 1957 Civil Rights Act and ultimately to the 1965 voting rights legislation. Conceptualized as a regional effort for African American enfranchisement and organized by the Southern

Christian Leadership Conference (SCLC), this first phase of what was to become a southern voting rights movement was officially launched in Miami, Florida, on February 12, 1958, and was aptly named the Crusade for Citizenship. The program was launched as a series of simultaneous mass meetings held in twenty-seven cities to stimulate African American voter registration and begin the process of voter education. With the stated purpose of doubling the number of "qualified Negro voters in the South," the Crusade for Citizenship, organized while Ella Baker was still associate director of SCLC, proposed to create registration clinics, leadership workshops, public meetings, and mass print communication "to realize the potential voting strength of the Negro population in the South and to give real meaning to the 1957 Civil Rights Act."[10]

In the speech he delivered to launch the crusade, Martin Luther King Jr. addressed and in some ways attempted to mediate, as did many leaders in the early phases of the civil rights struggle, the politics of regional identity. Near the end of his speech, he appeals to both black and white southerners, asserting that the South could not afford to permit the United States and its heritage to be dishonored "before the world." He goes on to explain finally how ensuring the voting rights of African Americans in the South was not just about exercising constitutional rights. It was about fulfilling a duty and upholding a moral obligation to disrupt the political domination of a small minority that not only crippled the economic and social institutions of the nation but also impoverished and degraded all its citizens.[11]

With the Crusade for Citizenship and the 1957 Civil Rights Act as background, the Selma voting rights movement and the city itself may be seen as a threshold space, as a pivotal moment of transition from early movement efforts at enfranchisement for African Americans in the South to the national legislative victory of the 1965 Voting Rights Act. Interestingly enough, Lyndon B. Johnson had an important role in both moments. Identifying the substantive weakness of the 1957 Civil Rights Act as political victory by southern Democrats, Val J. Washington, then director of minorities for the Republican National Committee sent a letter, issued as a press release, to Texas Senator Johnson. Along with other southern Democratic leaders, Johnson, Val Washington contends, had emasculated the 1957 bill with four "unfriendly votes." In the letter, Washington outlines all of Johnson's votes with emphasis on the last and the most damaging:

> On August 1, you voted for Trial by Jury in voting rights cases which would automatically eliminate any chance for Negroes to be protected in most Southern states. If a Southern jury would not convict confessed kidnappers of Emmett Till after he was found murdered, why would they convict an election official for refusing to give a Negro his right of suffrage?[12]

While a number of scholarly works acknowledge the complexities of Lyndon B. Johnson's role in the long trajectory of the civil rights struggle, mass media representations of Selma and the 1965 Voting Rights Act have emphasized the personalities of President Johnson and Dr. King to construct political and historical meaning. The speeches by both men have been given special historical importance. Two presidential speeches, however, the March 15th speech before Congress in which Johnson closed with the rallying slogan of the movement, "And we shall overcome," and the speech made at the August 6 signing of the Voting Rights Act in which the president named the "outrage of Selma" as the major stimulus for the authorization of federal examiners, inscribe the triumph of U.S. democracy.[13] Most audiences and spectators are thereby led to conclude that the institutional structures of government and political elites ultimately achieved voting rights for African Americans. As Diane Nash discerns in her response to the statement by Califano, the difficult, day-to-day, dangerous work of individuals, local communities, and organizations along with any real attention to or analysis of the complicated interaction between state and citizen are both left out.

Writing just weeks after the August 6, 1965, signing of the Voting Rights Act, Jack O'Dell offers a useful analysis of the Selma campaign in the article, "The Threshold of a New Reconstruction." Observing that the Edmund Pettus Bridge at Selma might suggest that the entire Freedom Movement was "on the bridge"—in this sense, the bridge of historical development—O'Dell goes on to describe that moment in the freedom struggle, not as its "finest hour" but as a threshold moment, a time "more ripe with possibilities for major advances or serious retrogression than any period since the overthrow of the first reconstruction."

> In a very real sense . . . the basic reality is that there are powerful forces who oppose our "crossing the bridge," in our independent way, for they understand, as we must, that once we cross the bridge

into the political epoch, things will never be the same again for us or them.¹⁴

O'Dell identifies the freedom struggle's moving into a new "political epoch" as a bridge crossing, but one that necessitated negotiating a host of conflicts, contradictions, strengths, and weaknesses, which I suggest here might be seen as the flux and drive of a metaphoric river beneath. As he described it, crossing the bridge of historical development in 1965 entailed negotiating a number of issues:

> the barbarism of State police power, especially in the south; contradictions within the Freedom movement itself; the selfless bravery and determination of the grassroots black population prepared to face terror alone while seeking honest allies; the vacillations and maneuverings of a Federal government trying to serve both the forces of racism and democracy at the same time; the personal martyrdom of the Freedom Fighters.¹⁵

With the assertion that Selma as symbol of the freedom struggle as a whole was on "the threshold," O'Dell offers a framework for understanding and evaluating the concrete achievements of the movement at that time. Dismantling public forms of segregation and winning the passage of new legislation that reaffirmed the equal rights principle under the constitution, he explains, were significant concessions. But looking at those achievements as signs of the "great progress" was problematic and had the potential to become one of the great stumbling blocks in the political psychology of well-meaning liberals, both black and white. What Selma represented, O'Dell ultimately concludes, was taking up again where the first Reconstruction had left off.¹⁶

Since 1965, the "great progress" theme has rather consistently undergirded the "consensus memory" of Selma and the civil rights movement in mass culture. Looking at what has been left out of mass media representations over the last several decades, Leigh Raiford and Renee Romano have discerned that consensus memory of the 1960s freedom struggle is now used as a "shining example of the success of democracy." They go on to explain,

> The state has a strong interest in using the memory of the movement as a tool of nation building and of fostering hegemony through

consensus. The movement in this way can become proof of the vitality of America's legal and political institutions and evidence of the nation's ongoing quest to live up to its founding ideals of egalitarianism and justice.[17]

Moreover, representations of the civil rights struggle in mass culture tend to follow, like the consensus memory of the other seminal events in U.S. history, the contours of triumphal narratives. While there may be recognition of brutality, suffering, and loss, narratives of triumph almost always give a sense of completion—that the enemy or the obstacle has been overcome, leaving little to do except celebrate the victory. Because they give audiences and spectators a simple story line—a coherent narrative that we all can enjoy—narratives of triumph do not prompt critical questions. What has been left out? What realities have been obscured? What controversies, complexities, and tensions have been glossed over? More important and perhaps even more problematic, triumphal narratives almost always leave the same power relations intact.[18]

Using the civil rights movement as an example of U.S. democracy in action and as an instrument in the project of nation-building on the contemporary world stage is even more compelling when we consider, as Jelani Cobb informs us, that there are more than 650 streets named for Martin Luther King Jr. in the United States alone. There are also parks, streets, and monuments dedicated to him in Australia, Austria, France, Germany, South Africa, Israel, Italy, Senegal, and Zambia.[19] Given the international exposure of the violence by Dallas County deputies and Alabama state troopers on March 7, 1965, the original protest sites of the Edmund Pettus Bridge and Selma have also become, for activists both in the United States and abroad, sites of memory, heritage, and commemoration. Much like the international legacy of Martin Luther King Jr., Selma now functions as an arc of history and cultural memory, bridging national and transnational events and aspirations into shared perceptions of human rights and social justice.[20]

Skillfully referencing history and cultural memory and linking his election to the presidency of the United States to the successes of the civil rights struggle, President Obama returned to Selma in March 2015 to mark the fiftieth anniversary of the bridge crossing. A reported 20,000 people descended on Selma for two days of public remembrance, for a glimpse of the first family, and a chance to walk across the bridge. After acknowledging the presence of President Bush and his wife, Vice President Joe Biden, Congressman John Lewis, and other elected officials, President Obama began his speech, echoing Lyndon B. Johnson, by noting that, like the historical war sites of Concord, Appomattox, and Gettysburg, and like other sites symbolizing American daring and character, Selma was a place where the nation's destiny had been decided. Obama then went on to explain, "In one afternoon, 50 years ago, so much of our turbulent history—the stain of slavery and the anguish of civil war; the yoke of segregation and tyranny of Jim Crow; the death of four little girls in Birmingham; and the dream of a Baptist preacher—all that history on this bridge."[21]

Affirming—and to some degree expanding—the mass media's public memory of Selma, the violence on the bridge, and the saving grace of the Voting Rights Act, President Obama's speech does the expected work of consensus memory. It reinforces the boundaries of current public discourse by legitimizing national institutions and national identity. As Edward P. Morgan discerns, mass media has created a dominant narrative about the civil rights past that has become a "kind of self-contained media reality," one designed for mass consumption.[22] And the major theme running through that narrative is that the horror of racial oppression occurred in the South but these horrors were erased when civil rights activists appealed to the national conscience and the federal government; that the federal government played a crucial role in righting the wrongs of segregation and Jim Crow; that the country's greatest hypocrisy, or at least its most blatant forms, were then removed.

David Remnick's 2010 biography of President Obama, aptly titled *The Bridge: The Life and Rise of Barack Obama*, affirms and extends, to some degree, the boundaries of consensus memory of Selma and the Edmund Pettus Bridge especially in the 2011 Vintage paperback edition. In that later edition, there are two purposefully sequenced photographs, with a blank page in between, presented as the first three pages of the book. The first photograph is a color image in muted tones of yellow and white that shows Obama scaling the steps of Capitol Hill with the central Capitol dome in the background. The second photograph, coming after the blank page, is Spider Martin's 1965 black-and-white photograph of the marchers at a standstill before attempting to cross the Edmund Pettus Bridge. The leaders of the march, John Lewis, Hosea Williams, Albert Turner, and Bob Mants, stand silently facing Alabama state troopers and Dallas County deputies who are already in motion to begin the attack. Together the photographs offer a purposeful visualization of how President Obama's life and first election may be seen as a bridge from the racial violence of Bloody Sunday in 1965 to the election of the first African American president in 2008. Equally important, the two photographs are also a visual reinforcement of the statement made by John Lewis, on the day before the 2008 inauguration, that "Barack Obama is what comes at the end of that bridge in Selma."[23]

Since the 1980s, there have been annual Jubilee crossings of the Edmund Pettus Bridge, but the fiftieth anniversary celebrations of Selma and the civil rights movement, in many ways constituted another crossing, one that has moved "beyond" what the bridge symbolized in 1965. The difference can be explained in part because fiftieth anniversaries, as John Dower notes, are not like other commemorative observances.[24] The first difference is that people who participated in events that occurred a half century before, in most instances, are still alive and able to share their experiences. The living presence and stories of actual participants connect younger generations who have no recollection or may not have been born at the time of the original event. Second, and more important, after fifty years historians gain access to materials that may have been ignored or not accessible before and can ask new questions and generate new perspectives on the significance of the event.

Selma was different, however. As Martin Luther King Jr. noted in his report to the SCLC convention on August 11 in Birmingham, forty of the "nation's top historians" had participated in the march from Selma to Montgomery.[25] One of those historians, the Harvard-trained African American John Hope Franklin, writes about the specifics of the call for forty historians to participate in the march in his autobiography, *Mirror to America*. After explaining how Walter Johnson from the University of Chicago issued the call, Franklin goes on to list ten of the most prominent scholars and their institutional affiliations at that time. Among the total number were C. Vann Woodward, Richard Hofstadter, and Bernard Weisberg.[26] So there were immediate perceptions and perspectives on the significance of the voting rights campaign, interpretations generated very soon after the movement that were beyond the usual range, process, and time frame for scholarly appraisals of historic events. Given the presence of not just historians but also theologians, educators, and other march participants who went on to create and contribute to the print and visual archive on the civil rights movement, Selma was unique in having encouraged and inspired a generation of "memory creators," activist scholars and documentarians who were actually "on the bridge."

For that reason, scholarship on Selma has generated perspectives that make it possible to see the events of the voting rights campaign and its aftermath as a symbolic "bridge of becoming." Used in 1965 by Jack O'Dell, the phrase, "bridge-of-becoming," referenced how Selma might have represented a shift from a limited protest movement to a full-fledged social movement concerned not just with removing barriers to full opportunity but also with achieving the reality of equality. However, even with new laws, the barriers to black voter participation did not come down without violent resistance. There were several tragic events that occurred in the aftermath of Selma. But because they countered the "great progress" theme of victory and closure, because they pointed not only to the insidious residue of racism but also to the structural violence of poverty and the actual violence of vigilante and police brutality, these events did not affirm permissible media or political viewpoints.

For years, some of these violent events were left out of public memory of Selma. The murder in Hayneville, Alabama, of a twenty-six-year-old seminarian, Jonathan Myrick Daniels, from the Episcopal Theological School in Cambridge, Massachusetts, two weeks after President Johnson signed the Voting Rights Act and the dispossession of sharecropping families in Lowndes County were two such events. After the galvanizing footage of Bloody Sunday and the lofty speeches of Lyndon B. Johnson and Martin Luther King Jr., the dispossession and terror of Lowndes County did not affirm triumphal narratives of closure and final victory. And for those who had envisioned the Selma to Montgomery march and the Voting Rights Act as a bridge to freedom, what the murder and dispossession made clear was that, in the Alabama Black Belt, the bridge from segregation, racial violence, and disenfranchisement to justice and equality was still under construction.

Daniels was murdered in Hayneville, Lowndes County, Alabama, by a construction worker and part-time deputy sheriff, Tom Coleman, on August 20, 1965. He had participated in voter registration activities with the Lowndes County Freedom Organization (LCFO) and was jailed in Lowndes County the week before his death. According to those who had been in jail with him, Daniels had shown a special commitment and strength in demonstrating morale-building support for the other activists.

After his release, along with three other workers, Daniels tried to enter a local store where Coleman pointed a shotgun in the direction of Ruby Sales, an African American teenager. When Daniels jumped in front of Sales to protect her, Coleman fired and killed Daniels. Another minister who was with the group was also wounded. In keeping with the practice of exonerating perpetrators of police and vigilante brutality and murder, Tom Coleman was acquitted by an all-white jury six weeks later.[27]

Within weeks of the signing of the Voting Rights Act, not only did Jonathan Daniels fall victim to violence but also sharecropping farmers who attempted to register to vote or were involved in voter registration activities at any level were systematically thrown off the farms where their families lived and worked by white landowners.[28] Although literacy tests had been suspended and federal agents appointed to monitor elections, newly enfranchised black voters were still vulnerable to extremist violence and terror. To offer some measure of protection, the Student Nonviolent Coordinating Committee (SNCC) and Lowndes County leaders began in December 1965 to help several displaced families remain in the county by setting up Tent City on land owned by Mathew Jackson near U.S. Route 80. SNCC and its Lowndes County partners bought tents, cots, heaters, food, and water and helped several families survive the dispossession by turning Tent City into a community. The National Park Service reports that there were instances of harassment and intimidation, including shots regularly fired into the camp, but residents remained and persevered for nearly two years until organizers helped them to find jobs, permanent housing, and new lives.

With the murder of Jon Daniels and the dispossession of black sharecroppers, the geographic space of Lowndes County in 1965 linked two important markers in the history of the South: the triumph of the 1965 voting rights legislation and the absurd, violent response of southern extremists to changes in race relations. Representing regression or a reverse bridging from civil rights back to the aftermath of the Civil War, the violence, death, and dispossession in Lowndes County also indicated how the "bridge-of-becoming" was still an incomplete structure.

Because of the growing emphasis on civic and public memory, sites in Selma and in Dallas and Lowndes County may be seen as generating another kind of threshold, another kind of bridge, one marked and partly made possible by the U.S. Congress, Congressman John Lewis, and two Alabama attorneys, Rose and Hank Sanders, who met at Harvard Law

School and returned to Selma to work for social justice and social change. Created by Congress in 1996, the Selma to Montgomery National Historic Trail, a combination of heritage trail, historic markers, interpretive center, and museum, operates under the aegis of the National Park Service and the U.S. Department of the Interior. This historic trail, therefore, has not been shaped entirely by market-driven codes and biases. More important, created with and through local partnerships and collaborations, the Selma trail has produced a body of visual and print materials that presents a more complex and inclusive narrative of the history, politics, memory, and grassroots struggle in the Alabama Black Belt during the 1960s.

Eschewing, for the most part, mass media narratives of triumph, victory, and closure, the Lowndes County Interpretative Center of the Selma to Montgomery National Historic Site focuses on the stories of Jonathan Myrick Daniels, Tent City, the teachers and ministers marches, and even SCLC's 1965 Summer Community Organization and Political Education (SCOPE) project that sought to implement voting rights throughout the South. Because its purpose is to interpret and preserve "the important stories of the Selma voting rights movement, inspiring all citizens to be vigilant in protecting their constitutional rights," the Lowndes County Interpretive Center includes a replica of a tent home within the center itself and has created an outdoor site for Tent City situated within the boundaries of the land space of Lowndes County.[29] The replica of the tent home and the story of Tent City are more than just the story of Lowndes County sharecroppers' struggle for citizenship rights. Tent City also tells the story of how human connectivity, effective bridge leadership, ingenuity, and innovation can empower individuals and communities to "cross over" terror and dispossession and sustain a commitment to their goals. Ultimately Tent City is the story of how ordinary citizens, in answering the call to conscience, can bridge the theory of democracy to its implementation.

Fifty years after Tent City, the growing infrastructure of monuments, memorials, and museums throughout the South now includes not only the National Historic Trail but also the National Voting Rights Museum and Institute located at the foot of the Edmund Pettus Bridge and the Slavery and Civil War Museum in downtown Selma, both founded and sustained by two African American civil rights attorneys, one a state legislator. In the same way, another category of visual documents from the civil rights movement—social movement photography—has been retrieved, expanded, and to some degree institutionalized to link the actual events of the Selma marches and voting rights movement to contemporary audiences and spectators. Photographs of women, children, poor and working class families now provide visual evidence of a much wider grassroots participation in the Alabama freedom struggle and move beyond earlier mass media visualizations of prominent personalities, national leaders, and powerful elites. Through exhibitions, documentaries, and print books, these photographs have done the important work of mediating visual images of the movement from corporate controlled print and televisual media with social documentary photography that offers more complicated and inclusive ideas about the past.[30]

The group of activist photographers who helped to create what we now have as social movement photography includes Danny Lyon, Bob Fletcher, Doris Derby, Julius Lester, Joffre Clark, Rufus Hinton, Norris McNamara, Maria Varela, and others. Many of them worked for SNCC. But others like Bob Adelman, Brig Cabe, Bob Fitch, and Elaine Tomlin worked for Congress of Racial Equality (CORE), SCLC, and the National Association for the Advancement of Colored People (NAACP) or independently. Overall the images captured by these photographers moved beyond the ideological and market-driven frames of corporate photo-journalism during the 1960s. Moreover, as Leigh Raiford discerns in her study on the photography produced by the Student Nonviolent Coordinating Committee, documentary photography generated by SNCC and other activist photographers during the 1960s, served two important purposes. First, the images by these photographers helped to create a formidable, independent media structure that influenced the direction and course of the civil rights movement. Second, and equally important, the images captured during that time period now provide cues and clues for contemporary audiences to better understand and incorporate the legacies and lessons of the 1960s freedom struggle, thus potentially bringing them closer to an understanding of Selma and the voting rights movement as a bridge and not a destination.[31]

Several photographs produced by Matt Herron, who was mentored by Dorothea Lange and came south in the early 1960s, are exemplary. Herron, who was never a formal member of SNCC, although his wife Jeanine worked in communications with Julian Bond in the Atlanta SNCC office, has explained how he worked in three different capacities during the 1960s: as a photojournalist on assignment in the South, as a movement

Figure 1.1. Selma to Montgomery March. By permission of © 1978 Matt Herron/Take Stock.

photographer who sometimes covered demonstrations, marches, and jailings, and as a social documentarian. As he explains in his article on the genesis of the Southern Documentary Project, Herron had a two-fold purpose when he worked in Alabama and Mississippi. The first was to assemble a team of photographers to capture southern society—black and white—in transition. The second was to visually document a manner of life, the essence of southern culture and southern institutions. He clarifies more specifically, "As a social activist I was probably looking at what was going on in a slightly different way. . . . I had a conviction that what I was witnessing was history, that things which people saw as everyday events were special and unique."[32]

On the Selma to Montgomery march, Herron photographed what has become one of the most iconic images of the last of the three marches. Reflecting on how he spent five days walking backwards, Herron recalls that although he had already photographed people on the march line, he eventually realized that he had not captured marchers positioned against the horizon. So, once the line moved into a rural area, he dropped into a ditch and waited for the right moment. That frame, in which, according to Herron, "every foot, every arm, every gesture is separately articulated," has been used in exhibitions, print books, documentaries, and most recently by the National Park Service in a commemorative button.[33]

With two flags at the center of the composition, the visibly integrated line of marchers with several people at the front pointing to an airplane overhead, the photograph may be interpreted as envisioning utopian democracy, justice, and racial progress, an interpretation that would have most readily been accepted in 1965. The image, however, also conveys motion, movement, and transition, from the formally dressed black man in hat, suit, and tie, to the black woman in a dress and heels, to the teenager in bib overalls. Moreover, as Herron explained at a March 2015 exhibition of his work in Syracuse, all the motion seems to move toward the flags and up toward the single airplane in the sky, a government plane looking out for any ambush attempts by the Ku Klux Klan. As a visual representation of racial diversity and harmony, of collective movement and social action—in particular place and time, Herron's photograph, much like that of photojournalist, James Karales, is a "view from the trenches." And in the context of Selma, the marches, the Voting Rights Act, and its fiftieth commemoration, that view, metaphorically a view that includes repressed histories of marginalized groups, or the view from grassroots and working-class citizens, has generated political and cultural meanings that have shifted over time and remain in flux. Nevertheless, those meanings have become, as Leigh Raiford observes, integral to the processes of national, racial, and political identity formation.[34]

Another iconic photograph from the Selma to Montgomery march, the one by James Karales, has been used recently by the NAACP's Legal Defense and Educational Fund (LDF) as cover for a commemorative booklet entitled "The Voting Rights Act @50." In the Karales photograph, instead of an airplane overhead, there is a huge mass of dark clouds, a visual foreshadowing, perhaps, of the certain tragic events that would come after the end of the march. Inside the booklet, the opening essay cautions the reader that while it is useful to reflect on the tremendous progress toward equality made since the 1965 Voting Rights Act, it is perhaps more important to remember that the march toward equality in the United States continues. The essay declares more specifically,

> The work of advancing and protecting the right to vote is not self-executing. It requires our eternal vigilance. Indeed the U.S. Supreme Court's devastating ruling in the 2013 *Shelby County, Alabama v Holder*, which struck a core provision of the Voting Rights Act and

the recent assault on voting rights across our nation, are salient reminders of this reality.³⁵

The booklet goes on to explain how the 2014 Voting Rights Amendment Act (VRAA) bill has been introduced to restore key provisions and protections to millions of voters who have been effectively disenfranchised by the *Shelby County* decision. For the NAACP Legal Defense Fund, as illustrated by both image and text, the geopolitical space of Selma may be seen as bridging the promise of the Voting Rights Act of 1965 to the potential of the Voting Rights Amendment Act of 2014 and as a call to end voter intimidation and voter suppression in the United States today.

Conclusion

This chapter, beginning with analyses of comments on the fiftieth anniversary celebrations of the 1965 Voting Rights Act, examines how the geopolitical space of Selma and Lowndes County, Alabama, has functioned as a complex "bridge of becoming" from its founding in 1817 to the present. Owing to its unique place in confederate history, as the birthplace of the White Citizens Council, as a bastion of resistance to racial change, and as a sociopolitical site rift with potential for both advancement and retrogression, Selma has been and remains a threshold space in U.S. historical development and in public memory.

From the March 1965 television footage of Bloody Sunday to the 2015 anniversary speech by President Barack Obama, mass media's public memory of Selma and the 1960s freedom struggle has functioned to create a consumable past and a national narrative of triumph. Glossing over instances of extremist violence like the murder of Jonathan Myrick Daniels in Lowndes County two weeks after the signing of the Voting Rights Act of 1965 and the eviction of sharecropping farmers who attempted to register to vote after the bill was passed, the triumphal narrative of Selma not only leaves out contradictions and complexities but ultimately discourages critical citizenship practice. The memorial landscape around Selma, however, the museum, the institute, the historic trails, and interpretive centers, mediates to some degree the consensus memory of Selma and the Voting Rights Act. Much like the social movement photography that emerged during the 1960s, Selma's museums and historic trails not only complicate narratives of victory, triumph, and completion but also begin the process of transforming Alabama's long and regretful history of racial violence and discrimination into a bridge of human solidarity and connectivity.

Notes

1. Diane Nash, "LBJ Doesn't Deserve Credit for Selma," *New Journal and Guide*, February 2, 2015, at http://www.crmvet.org/comm/selma-dn.htm (consulted February 15, 2016).

Though generally recognized for her leadership in the Nashville student sit-ins and the 1960–1961 Freedom Rides, Diane Nash is rarely acknowledged as one of the first field staff members for SNCC and SCLC. Recruited by Martin Luther King Jr. because she functioned effectively as bridge leader between SCLC and SNCC, Nash made substantive contributions to movement strategies in Rock Hill, South Carolina, Albany, Georgia, Birmingham, and Selma, Alabama.

2. Emilye Crosby, "Ten Things You Should Know About Selma Before You See the Film," *Zinn Education Project: Teaching People's History*, January 3 2015, at http://zinnedproject.org/2015/01/selma-ten-things/ (consulted February 15, 2016).

3. The phrase, "bridge-of-becoming" is used by Jack H. O'Dell in "The Threshold of a New Reconstruction," *Freedomways: A Quarterly Review of the Negro Freedom Movement* (1965): 5, 9.

Historian Stephen B. Oates identifies the Selma campaign as the civil rights movement's "finest hour" in "Trumpet of Conscience: Martin Luther King, Jr.," *Portrait of America, Vol. II: From 1865*, ed. Stephen Oates (Boston: Houghton Mifflin, 1999), 318–31.

David J. Garrow makes a similar assessment, writing that Selma marked both the end and the "culmination . . . of the movement's successful employment of direct action tactics," in Garrow, *Protest at Selma: Martin Luther King, Jr. and the Voting Rights Act of 1965* (New Haven: Yale University Press, 1978), 231.

President Barack Obama identifies Selma as a site at which "the nation's destiny" was decided in his speech at the fiftieth anniversary Jubilee celebration in Selma in March 2015. "Remarks by the President at the 50th Anniversary of the Selma to Montgomery Marches," March 7, 2015, at https://www.whitehouse.gov/the-press-office/2015/03/07/remarks-president-50th-anniversary-selma-montgomery-marches (consulted February 15, 2016).

4. Pamela S. Karlan proposes that the Edmund Pettus Bridge is "the most famous bridge in American constitutional history" in her essay, "The Alabama Foundations of the Law of Democracy," *Alabama Law Review* 67 (2016): 415. In the speech at the conclusion of the Selma to Montgomery march, Martin Luther King Jr. explained how the nonviolence, sacrifices, and determination of the civil rights struggle, particularly in Birmingham and Selma, had stirred the conscience of the nation. He concludes the speech with the vision of a society able to live with its conscience. King, "Address at the Conclusion of the Selma to Montgomery March," in *A Call to Conscience: The Landmark*

Speeches of Dr. Martin Luther King, Jr.," ed. Clayborne Carson and Kris Shepard (New York: Grand Central Publishing, 2001).

5. The first chapter of Sharon Jackson's book *Images of America: Selma* (Charleston, SC: Arcadia Publishing, 2014), is titled, "The Early Years of the Queen City." The 1989 publication commissioned by the Selma City Council and written by Alston Fitts III, former director of information for the Edmundite Southern Missions, is also entitled, *Selma: Queen City of the Black Belt* (Selma, AL: Clairmont Press, 1989).

6. Michael Beschloss, "Foote and Lincoln" in *American Homer,* ed. John Meacham (New York: Random House, 2011).

7. See Richard Bailey, *Neither Carpetbaggers Nor Scalawags: Black Officeholders during the Reconstruction of Alabama 1867-1878,* (Montgomery: Richard Bailey Publishers, 1997), 311-15. See also Sarah Woolfolk Wiggins, *The Scalawag in Alabama Politics, 1865-1881* (Tuscaloosa: University of Alabama Press, 1977), 63, 139. From Dallas County, Richard Bailey identifies two African Americans, Jordan Hatcher and Alfred Strother, as participants in the 1867 Alabama Constitutional Convention. The thirteen African Americans from Dallas County who held state office were Joseph Drawn, Spencer Weaver, Henry A. Cochran, Edward Gee, R. L. Johnson, Jeremiah Haralson, Joseph H. Goldsby, Thomas H. Walker, William H. Blevins, Charles E. Harris, Jacob Martin, Green T. Johnson, and William J. Stevens. Without identifying officeholders by name, J. L. Chestnut Jr., and Julia Cass also provide information on African American elected officials in Selma and Dallas County during Reconstruction in Chestnut and Cass, *Black in Selma: The Uncommon Life of J. L. Chestnut, Jr.* (New York: Farrar, Straus and Giroux, 1990), 5; O'Dell, "Threshold of a New Reconstruction," 497.

8. Donald Stone, *Fallen Prince: William James Edwards, Black Education, and the Quest for Afro-American Nationality* (Snow Hill, AL: Snow Hill Press, 1990), 44-45. Interpretations of the era of Reconstruction in U.S. historical development have been varying. Just two years after the Voting Rights Act, Thomas D. Clark and Albert D. Kirwan published *The South Since Appomattox: A Century of Regional Change* (New York: Oxford University Press, 1967), which offers an incomplete and traditionally partisan perspective on Reconstruction. Joel Williamson, examining Reconstruction within the wider context of U.S. race relations, offers a more original interpretation in his *The Crucible of Race: Black-White Relations in the American South Since Emancipation* (New York: Oxford University Press, 1984). W.E.B. DuBois's *Black Reconstruction in America: An Essay Toward a History of the Part Which Black Folk Played in the Attempt to Reconstruct Democracy in America 1860-1880* (New York: Atheneum, 1969) first published in 1935, remains foundational scholarship for the period. J. Mills Thornton III devotes considerable attention to the "white leagues" and the singular, statewide role of Selma's White Citizens' Councils during the 1950s and 1960s in Thornton, *Dividing Lines: Municipal Politics and the Struggle for Civil Rights in Montgomery, Birmingham and Selma* (Tuscaloosa: University of Alabama Press, 2002), 392-499.

9. O'Dell, "Threshold of a New Reconstruction," 496-97. The arc of violence and terror in the Georgia Black Belt, marked most notably by the 1868 Camilla massacre, is chronicled by Susan Eva Donovan in *Becoming Free in the Cotton South* (Cambridge: Harvard University Press, 2007), 261-63. Hassan Kwame Jeffries uses the "bleak

assessment" made by W.E.B. DuBois, who lived in Lowndes County in 1906, to describe early twentieth-century manifestations of violence and terror in the county. "'The white element was lawless,' explained DuBois, 'and up until recent times the body of a dead Negro did not even call for an arrest.'" Jeffries, *Bloody Lowndes: Civil Rights and Black Power in Alabama's Black Belt* (New York: New York University Press, 2009), 9.

10. The text of the 1958 brochure, "Crusade for Citizenship," January 20, 1958, at http://www.crmvet.org/docs/5801_sclc_cfc.pdf (consulted February 24, 2016).

11. Martin Luther King Jr., "Address Delivered at a Meeting Launching the SCLC Crusade for Citizenship at Greater Bethel AME Church," in *The Papers of Martin Luther King, Jr.*, vol. 4, ed. Clayborne Carson et al. (Berkeley: University of California Press, 2000), 367–71.

12. Val J. Washington, "Republican National Committee News Release," August 7, 1957, at www.cicerosystems.com/history/unit/cold-war/content/1510/7886 (consulted February 24, 2016).

13. Lyndon B. Johnson, "Special Message to the Congress: The American Promise," March 15, 1965. Online by Gerhard Peters and John T. Woolley, *The American Presidency Project*, at http://www.presidency.ucsb.edu/ws/?pid=26805 (consulted June 21, 2016); Johnson, "Remarks in the Capitol Rotunda at the Signing of the Voting Rights Act.," August 6, 1965. Online by Peters and Woolley, *The American Presidency Project*, at http://www.presidency.ucsb.edu/ws/?pid=27140 (consulted June 21, 2016).

14. O'Dell, "Threshold of a New Reconstruction," 495–96.

15. Ibid.

16. Ibid.

17. Renee C. Romano and Leigh Raiford, "Introduction: The Struggle Over Memory," in their edited, *The Civil Rights Movement in American Memory* (Athens: University of Georgia Press, 2006), xvii.

18. I am grateful to Patricia Davis, author of *Laying Claim: African American Cultural Memory and Southern Identity*, for sharing her insights on narratives of triumph. I want to also express appreciation to Vera Rorie who provided very useful 50th Commemoration material on Selma.

19. Jelani Cobb, "A President and a King," *New Yorker*, January 26, 2015, 21.

20. This perspective derives in part from theorizing by Sharon Monteith, "A Tale of Three Bridges: Pont Saint-Michel, Paris, 1961; Trefechan Bridge, Aberystwyth, Wales, 1963; Edmund Pettus Bridge, Selma, Alabama, 1965," in *The Transatlantic Sixties: Europe and the United States in the Counterculture Decade*, ed. Grzegorz Kosc, Clara Juncker, Sharon Monteith, and Britta Waldschmidt-Nelson (Washington, DC: German Historical Institute, 2013), 283. Monteith notes the bridge in all three sites "as an arc of history and cultural memory, drawing the separate episodes together in a shared perception of social justice."

21. Obama, "Remarks by the President at the 50th Anniversary of the Selma to Montgomery Marches."

22. Edward P. Morgan, "The Good, the Bad, the Forgotten: Media Culture and Public Memory of the Civil Rights Movement," in *The Civil Rights Movement in American Memory*, ed. Romano and Raiford, 153.

23. David Remnick, *The Bridge: The Life and Rise of Barack Obama* (New York: Vintage Books, 2011), 575.

24. John W. Dower, "Triumphal and Tragic Narratives of the War in Asia," *Journal of American History* 82 (1995): 1124.

25. Martin Luther King Jr., "Annual Report," in *Summary of Ninth Annual Convention,* Southern Christian Leadership Conference, ed. Edward T. Clayton, Junius Griffin, Van Hall, August 11, 1965, at http://www.thekingcenter.org/archive/document/sclc-summary-ninth-annual-convention (consulted February 24, 2016). Juanita Terry Williams, wife of Hosea Williams, was among the participants in the march and completed a master's thesis on the Selma to Montgomery march soon after her participation.

26. John Hope Franklin, *Mirror to America: The Autobiography of John Hope Franklin* (New York: Farrar, Straus and Giroux, 2005), 237–39.

27. See William J. Schneider, *The Jon Daniels Story: With His Letters and Papers* (New York: Seabury Press, 1967). The definitive treatment is Charles W. Eagles, *Outside Agitator: Jon Daniels and the Civil Rights Movement in Alabama* (Chapel Hill: University of North Carolina Press, 1993).

28. John Hulett who was Chairman of the Lowndes County Freedom Organization (LCFO) provides brief, first-hand information on the eviction of sharecropping farmers and the creation of Tent City. See Hulett, "How the Black Panther Party Was Organized" in *The Black Panther Party: Speech by John Hulett, Interview with Stokely Carmichael, Report from Lowndes County* (New York: Merit Publishers, c. 1966), at https://www.freedomarchives.org/Documents/Finder/DOC513_scans/Lowndes_Co/513.LowndesCO.bpp.6.1966.pdf (consulted February 14, 2017). See also Interview with John Hulett, *Eyes on the Prize II Interviews,* October 18, 1988, at http://digital.wustl.edu/e/eii/eiiweb/hul5427.0553.068marc_record_interviewee_process.html (consulted August 21, 2016); National Park Service, Selma-to-Montgomery National Historic Trail, "Tent City," at https://www.nps.gov/semo/planyourvisit/brochures.htm (consulted April 25, 2016).

In addition to the main brochure for the National Historic Trail, the site includes twelve additional shorter brochures, at https://www.nps.gov/semo/planyourvisit/brochures.htm (consulted April 25, 2016). For information on literacy tests, see Bruce Hartford, *The Selma Voting Rights Struggle and March to Montgomery* (San Francisco: Westwind Writers, 2014), 175–88.

29. U.S. National Park Service, Selma to Montgomery National Historic Trail, "Foundation Document Overview Selma to Montgomery National Historic Trail." Print copy in author's collection.

30. See Owen Dwyer, "Interpreting the Civil Rights Movement: Place, Memory, Conflict," *Professional Geographer* 52 (2000): 660–71. See also Leigh Raiford, "'Come Let Us Build a New World Together': SNCC and Photography of the Civil Rights Movement," *American Quarterly* 59 (2007): 1129–56.

31. Raiford, "'Come Let Us Build a New World Together,'" 1133.

32. Sean Kirst, "Photographer Matt Herron, today at ArtRage: Iconic images of Selma—and why Tuesday marked his first 'selfie,'" at http://www.syracuse.com/kirst/index.ssf/2015/03/matt_herron_photographer_of_the_selma_march_today_at_artrage_an_iconic_image_and.html (consulted February 15, 2016). Matt Herron, "The

Civil Rights Movement and the Southern Documentary Project," in *Witness in Our Time: Working Lives of Documentary Photographers*, ed. Ken Light (Washington, DC: Smithsonian Books, 2000), 64.

33. Kirst, "Photographer Matt Herron, today at ArtRage."

34. Raiford, "'Come Let Us Build a New World Together,'" 1130.

35. NAACP Legal Defense and Educational Fund, "Selma: Defending Democracy in the 50th Anniversary Year of the Voting Rights Act," at http://www.naacpldf.org/files/publications/The%20Voting%20Rights%20Act%20at%2050%20brochure.pdf (consulted February 24, 2016), 1.

2

Before the Bridge

Grassroots Activism in Selma in the Early 1960s

BENJAMIN HOUSTON

When Student Nonviolent Coordinating Committee (SNCC) worker Bernard Lafayette initially scouted Selma in 1962, he was alert to two interrelated issues: how to develop local leadership and how to directly confront the fear ruling the local Black Belt. His organization advised that Selma was futile to organize—that his predecessors had found black fright rampant and white resistance daunting. Informants in the black community quickly notified the police about his arrival, and he recalled hearing that "the place was just so backwards, the people were just not ready, the blacks were not ready." The town had a large X through it on maps at SNCC headquarters based on these judgments, even as the U.S. Department of Justice was beginning to probe local voting irregularities. Lafayette remained undeterred. His presence was a small but critical step in the painstakingly slow "opening up" of the Alabama Black Belt to civil rights activism.[1]

It is well established that the civil rights movement is sanitized too readily in contemporary discussions and historical memory. With historical context weakly rendered in most popular accounts, the effect is to dramatically downplay the vision and radicalism of the black freedom struggle and purge the complexities of the era in favor of stories more comforting and heroic. The problem is especially manifest in dealing with a place like Selma, which holds an undeniably substantive and iconic place in the civil rights canon. Here, the resultant importance of the local struggle's role in national debates foregrounds Martin Luther King Jr. and Lyndon B. Johnson, plus highlights the images of Bloody Sunday and the Selma to Montgomery March that filled TV screens across the world.

Historians sounding any dissonant note to the triumph associated with Selma's role in the Voting Rights Act of 1965 results can often be misheard. The building sounds of Black Power radicalism, disaffected anger with classic civil rights activity, and bleaker racial interaction to come were top notes to more downbeat realities, as obstacles to eradicating the interlocking vestiges of Jim Crow endured.

Given this, civil rights scholars have a two-fold task: not only to highlight what the "master narrative" on Selma misses entirely but also to more meaningfully describe and contextualize what *is* included in this flawed master narrative. There is a lot more work to be done but, rather than an exhaustive overview, this essay serves this scholarly task by drawing from Lafayette's own instincts. By understanding how he worked to nurture that process of cultivating leadership and confronting fear, and how his work bore fruit with other constituents and communities, scholars can recalibrate Selma as a fuller and richer case study of what the black freedom struggle entailed and move toward the fuller "people's history" of Selma that scholar Emilye Crosby advocates.[2]

Historians have sketched some general antecedents of Selma's black activism and its ebb and flow over the generations, which will only be treated briefly here. Some evidence indicates the presence of Garveyite chapters in Selma and Neenah (Camden, in nearby Wilcox County) although that sentiment was not always channeled into organized activity. Selma's local National Association for the Advancement of Colored People (NAACP) chapter was formed in 1918, one of the two earliest in the state, although the group was later banned by the State of Alabama. Throughout the 1920s and 1930s, the work of Charles J. Adams and the famous Boyntons, Amelia and Sam, was particularly noteworthy. The breadth of their labors constituted critical groundwork serving black aspirations in a variety of arenas. Some of their activities were federally focused—helping veterans with assistance programs, for example. Others were more locally based, organizing fertilizer purchases as suppliers tried to force foreclosures among independent black landowners, or buying land for the black community that served as a site for camping, recreation, and community gatherings. Reactivated in the Great Depression, their Dallas County Voters League (DCVL), despite pronounced ups and downs, at least tenaciously kept an activist presence in Selma that was revitalized upon Lafayette's arrival.

Local black attorney and civil rights figure J. L. Chestnut Jr. called SNCC a "confidence builder" despite his pessimism about racial possibility more generally. (Chestnut himself benefitted from black institutions, as the local Elks club loaned him money to open his legal practice after the bar association told local banks not to finance him.) By the 1960s, isolated pockets of activist work had resumed. Lafayette's formal remit was to help Mrs. Marie Foster (herself trained by the Southern Christian Leadership Conference [SCLC] in Beaufort, South Carolina) with her registration work, armed with a Voter Education Project grant. A quiet parallel development, fostered by Catholic activists, included the Fathers of St. Edmund in town and Maria Varela's literacy programs.[3]

In the 1950s, Dallas County experienced fear and apathy—the latter perhaps better understood as calculated inaction. Both were understandable. And yet, even when continually met with varied and cruel repression from whites, there was activity. Several local blacks had testified before the U.S. Civil Rights Commission in the late 1950s. Although those teachers who signed a petition calling for integrated schools after the *Brown v. Board of Education of Topeka, Kansas* decision were threatened or run out of town, their silencing by whites was answered by a quiet black boycott against Cloverleaf Creamery, where one of the petitioners worked and which had customers of both races. Before that, the William Earl Fikes case had electrified the town with its racial subtexts, as a black defendant stood accused of raping the white mayor's daughter. During the trials, the forthright testimonies of black leaders were powerful attestations to a new day coming. J. L. Chestnut noted that NAACP memberships increased dramatically after this trial. The three black candidates for city council in May 1964 provide more evidence of independent assertiveness, as did the 240 black votes that were decisive in electing Joseph Smitherman as mayor in that same election. All of these efforts garnered intense white responses. The tension that deadlocked racial progress was born not just from considerable repression but also from the very civil rights activity that persisted nonetheless—even when disaggregated rather than fully realized collectively. By the 1960s, on-again/off-again boycotts found occasional success, but the episodic nature of those boycotts signaled part of the problem.[4]

If nothing else, Lafayette's focus on developing leadership commingled elements of the classic "community mobilizing" and "community organizing" dichotomy highlighted by Bob Moses and explored by scholar Charles M. Payne. The young activist indicated that his philosophy was, generally speaking, consistent with SNCC's inclination to nurture local leadership. Yet he also maintained a logistical preference for organizing with some structure in place. Technically he was also working for the American Friends Service Committee while in Selma, and that group allowed him opportunities to work locally and also connect different groups from different communities. In coming years, he served as a conduit between SNCC and SCLC as the two wrangled about the direction of Black Belt organizing. He understood how, as he later expressed, SNCC's inconsistency in staffing often led to a lack of continuity in supporting local projects, but that SCLC's ability to inspire activity was not always parlayed into sustained longer-term considerations. So Lafayette's dilemma in Selma was how to cultivate that activism but translate it into something more enduring. If his answer was indeed to "develop the leadership," the strategy to do so was rather unlike the reputation of his fellow Nashville-trained brethren, supposedly obsessed with direct action and nonviolent spectacle. Rather, Lafayette was attracted to Selma because "I wouldn't have the pressure on me to start some kind of confrontative [sic] activities." (Only later would the SCLC adapt for the Selma campaign an abridged version of Diane Nash's plan to have a nonviolent army besiege Alabama.) The fact that the DCVL remained visible but stagnant as Samuel Boynton's health declined was a problem, Lafayette thought; people were not committed to the organization's mission as a whole when they unduly deferred to Boynton. They "didn't know what to do." Moreover, he noted the acute sense of insecurity in both white and black Selma: the latter called the town "the worst place in the world" with "some of the most backward people in the world." And as far as black leaders: "Man, they aren't going to do anything." So, with the support of Marie Foster and Amelia Boynton, whom he saw as "open to change," he focused on revitalizing that group rather than starting another.[5]

Lafayette's strategies in responding to these insecurities and lack of collective faith were strikingly simple yet profound. In talking with blacks in Selma, he stressed the positive—not about segregated realities, but about individuals specifically. In identifying problems and solutions, he conferred about what "would or wouldn't work," but was sure to stress "all the good things that someone else said about them." This began the first signs of "people having different attitudes about each other" and cultivated, he later recounted, the first signs of hope. He cited Frederick Reese as an important influence in this regard; he was the visible representative of someone with "hope that we could win." In Lafayette's interpretation, hope inferred that there was a way toward racial progress, which spoke to those worried about jail and/or death. He also disapproved openly of the term "Uncle Tom," preferring to take each person at their professed level of commitment without judging their motivations. He understood that fear came from worry about the unknown and as a symptom of hopelessness rather than apathy.[6]

Part of this process, he also suggested, was exploring "attitudes towards leadership," which he thought crucial: "If I can identify the key characteristics of leadership, then I can get a sense of what kind of movement we can put together based on that leadership." He explained that the answers to this, in his experience, varied widely from town to town. From his vantage, the presence of Selma University and other smaller denominational schools helped. Similarly, the number of ministers (and here he stressed seminary-trained ministers in particular) was important; although activities had to be planned carefully, they could also be "more sophisticated" once the ministers committed to action. He used what he called "the interview approach" in getting people to voice their interpretation of "the problem in Selma," then asking "How can it be changed?" As the answers inevitably mentioned black leadership, his response was: "OK, so will you come to meetings and change it?" In this manner he gradually coaxed people toward activism, parlaying their criticism from the sidelines into something more fully engaged. As he put it, the people "will teach you how to educate them and organize them."[7]

Lafayette also initiated what he termed "a deliberate leadership role reversal" where, with the use of a silent partner, he steered those black ministers uneasy with Lafayette's visible role (and outsider status) into alliance with each other. Eventually they took the next step forward in claiming the leadership mantle themselves. This was vital: leaders of groups who could encourage their own members toward activism could have a multiplying effect. Previously, the reverse was true and compounding, as Lafayette saw it: there were not enough leaders with specific programs of action, and those who were supposedly in leadership roles were not "ready for a mass movement."[8]

J. Mills Thornton suggests that Lafayette's visit initially produced a division between black leaders regarding their tolerance for direct action and that this conflict was willingly downplayed by black moderates. While Thornton cleverly excavates how this dynamic tied into municipal political shifts for whites and blacks, the fact that these divisions within the black community were easily submerged when necessary for tactical considerations suggests that we should be wary about overly schematic interpretations of these perceived divisions. J. L. Chestnut described Edwin Moss, for example, as always a moderate but always helpful to the movement due to his "power base different from that of black preachers and school principals," which was, in effect, "a unique leadership role in Selma." With a broader base of activism in Selma growing, with more scope for individual action, and as these groups merged into a collective, Lafayette understood this unity among them as steeling their "growing sense of power." Now channels for action existed, especially when white repression energized blacks toward activism instead of cowing them.[9]

Lafayette also led by example. The failed assassination attempt on him, the same evening as Medgar Evers's murder, is the oft-cited example, as Lafayette wore his bloody shirt around for days, testifying to his purpose and drive. But perhaps the more telling example came when he went to Sheriff Jim Clark's office, with a youngster whom Clark had scolded, to confront the officer directly. It was a two-fold reminder: (1) that voter registration, as a constitutionally legitimate act, should be protected by the sheriff and (2) that it was possible "to act with courage and to act normal" in standing up to the sheriff. Interacting with Clark not only underscored how the latter "used this political position for political reasons in terms of his authority as policeman," as Lafayette later recounted, which "doesn't eliminate fear" but also meant that there would be "no surprises as a result." The sheriff was not after you, he counseled his young charge; "you are after the sheriff."[10] The modeling of this psychological shift—to inculcate leadership, to facilitate moral righteousness rather than fear, and to spur action—facilitated Selma's transformation.

A more expansive view of leadership leads to another critical issue that needs fuller exploration: the importance of children, particularly high-schoolers from R. B. Hudson High School, but often even younger. Well before the celebrated events of Bloody Sunday, young activists in Selma were at the vanguard of activism, and their sustained efforts consistently marked moments pivotal to the broader campaign. This theme is emphatically stressed by many of Selma's citizens and civil rights workers, but often ends up ignored by the dominant focus on themes such as Martin Luther King's role in Selma, the divisiveness between SCLC and SNCC, and the callousness of Jim Clark.[11]

Scholars have underscored how children's activism pushed the envelope of racial change for generations. Lafayette himself remembered his early boyhood as an eleven-year-old member of the Parish Street gang in North Philadelphia organizing a boycott of the Tastykakes baking company for unfair hiring practices. In Selma, Lafayette—along with fellow organizer and wife Colia plus activist Frank Holloway, both of whom remain under-documented in Selma's story—initially recruited some students from the universities in town. But they ran into some resistance (both tactical and philosophical), especially from the administration at Selma University. Still, students from that institution were staging sit-ins at downtown drugstores as early as May 1963, plus setting up places where voter registration forms could be completed.[12]

But the Lafayettes wanted more numbers, so they cultivated students at R. B. Hudson High School. Chuck Bonner tells the story of pushing a broken-down 1954 Ford with his friend Cleophus Hobbs when Lafayette appeared and began to help them out, talking all the while about canvassing, voter registration, and direct action as the students peppered him with more questions. Bonner recalled, "We were totally primed to take some action, against what my friend Cleo and I both saw as tremendous unfairness in the world." Lafayette at that point was only a mere five or six years older than these high-schoolers. As a SNCC report read:

> As with many SNCC projects, one of the most successful aspects of the project has been work with young people. Building on an already existing gang structure, the staff has developed a democratically controlled group of high school age students who have aided with registration and held their own weekly citizenship training meetings. With the help of these students and a group of interested adults, the entire town of Selma has almost been canvassed for the first time. Several of the students came to the SNCC conference for their first interracial group experience, an experience which in itself developed new leadership and new expectation.[13]

This was only months before Lafayette's Nashville compatriot James Bevel was pilloried for the famed Children's Crusade in Birmingham. In fact, James Orange, a popular organizer in Selma and former Birmingham gang member, helped Bevel facilitate contacts with Birmingham children. And, of course, it was Orange's later arrest in Perry County for contributing to the delinquency of minors (in encouraging freedom songs at the courthouse) that inspired the night march in 1965 that culminated in Jimmie Lee Jackson's murder. Colia Lafayette's reports showed how Birmingham children were used to further recruit their Selma counterparts into the movement when high-schooler Alex Brown traveled to speak in Selma, stating simply, "In Birmingham we went to jail for you, now register to vote for us." Similarly, Lafayette talked frequently about the Nashville movement, what it had accomplished, and how it helped birth SNCC. The message: You are not alone, and there is a way.[14]

Birmingham events provoked intense reaction in Selma as elsewhere. On September 16, 1963, sparked by Birmingham's 16th Street Baptist Church bombing and led by SNCC's Worth Long, local students staged sit-ins. Willie C. Robinson had his head cracked open after being attacked by the owner of Carter's drugstore, bus boycotting and picketing began in force, four students were arrested, and more students were mobilized and sat in at lunch counters and libraries, with some Birmingham students driven in by John Lewis to help. It was at that point that contemporaries noted "a degree of unity in the black community that would otherwise have been inconceivable." Historian J. Mills Thornton records that "during this period about 350 blacks were arrested, of whom about 250 were under the age of sixteen."[15] The similarities and differences among Selma's black community, united against white cruelties if divided over activist responses, would have been moot had youth activism not kept civil rights issues alive.

This activism was not mere childish rebellion but rather sustained, committed work by a sophisticated cadre on behalf of the movement. One SNCC observer noted at the time that Hudson High School, with a normal attendance of about 1,500 students, had only a third of that number in school—the rest were working for the movement. When a 10:00 p.m. curfew was put in place, kids posted lookouts and hid under houses on raised stilts to dodge the mandate. While in jail, the young girls removed their slips, tore them in half, and draped them through cell bars to preserve some privacy and reclaim their dignity. Activist Bruce Hartford remembers how, later in 1965, when in charge of arranging Saturday pickets to support the boycott of stores in town, students comprised the teams. With discipline and organization, they dodged the police, snuck into the local funeral home where signs were kept, and picketed along assigned routes—in constant rotation with other groups—before being arrested.[16]

The degree that student commitment outpaced the community's was such that, in 1964, SNCC worker John A. Love warned that the Selma movement was "in very bad need of revision" and needed a broadening of participation. He called it a student movement that needed to be a community movement. Just a week later, activists at the Selma Literacy Project decided to test the Civil Rights Act at the Thirsty Boy restaurant. (SNCC worker Silas Norman noted that this contradicted some explicit instructions from director Maria Varela to avoid jail. That, he explained, lasted about two and a half weeks.) On this day, their arrest triggered hundreds more as students joined in, finding an outlet for their sentiment after mounting frustrations. With tensions heightening as Clark's troops blocked African Americans from testing access to public accommodations, the result was the harsh injunction limiting meetings of black leaders that put a chill on activism for months.[17]

By the time of the demonstrations in 1965, after SCLC had zeroed in on Selma, students were again central. Taylor Branch describes how, after viewing an NBC documentary on the 1960 Nashville sit-ins, Hosea Williams challenged participants at a youth rally about voting: "If you can't vote, then you're not free . . . and if you ain't free, children, then you are a slave." Wrote Branch, "Eight-year old children went home to ask their parents whether they were slaves." On February 1, the fifth anniversary of the lunch counter sit-ins, students demonstrated by the hundreds, some of them using crayon for their signs, and were rounded up for detention in Camp Selma. In Marion, Perry County, hundreds more marched to test public accommodations there; they were rewarded with jailing in a concrete stockade and only a water trough for hydration. Most powerfully, the commitment of the young activists was tested on February 10, at a moment when civil rights activity was ebbing: 160 students going to the courthouse were literally run out of town by Sheriff Jim Clark and his posse, chasing on horseback and jabbing with electric cattle prods, all while blocking off the area to prevent media from witnessing the event. Children as young as nine were forced like animals to run for miles, beaten as their bodies shook from fear and exhaustion as they vomited, then forced to run even more. One account recounted a teen challenging a deputy by saying "God sees you"; he was clubbed across the face in response.[18]

The appalling attacks revitalized a movement that had been "sagging." Thornton notes that this came precisely at the juncture where the SCLC and DCVL were rather at odds. The nominal issue was whether to cooperate with the "appearance book" used as a stalling maneuver against those trying to register to vote. The former group wanted dramatic confrontations to instigate federal legislation; the latter was preoccupied with boosting registration numbers locally. With the attack on the children, then, those issues were muted. On February 15, the SCLC focused on helping the kids encourage adults to attempt to register: "The result was that more than twelve hundred blacks were in line when the board opened for business." Annie Lee Cooper called this "the turning point" for Selma; for many locals, it had equal or more significance than the famed teachers march in January 1965.[19]

The point is that these students were not merely symbolically effective: they did real organizing work. They canvassed the city for voters; they directly "aided with registration and held their own weekly citizenship training meetings." SNCC workers remarked that "they were shocked at the answers their neighbors were giving to the voter question. They watched doors close in their faces and men tell them they were afraid." Said one, "I show [sic] didn't know there were so many scared Negroes in Selma, it's a shame." In short, Selma's youngsters (like Lafayette himself) enthusiastically participated in both the grassroots canvassing and the symbolically potent coercive nonviolence that SNCC and SCLC would soon clash over in Selma.[20]

To be sure, the students were quietly supported by a few teachers. Margaret Moore is frequently cited, but Reverend Reese, Mrs. Carter, and Mr. Perry Anderson were also key. One observer described at least one teacher who registered students present at attendance-taking and promptly looked the other way when students left school to canvass or rally. These were generational "bridge leaders," but the actualization of activism went two ways. The adults nurtured student courage, which in turn convinced a wider swath of teachers to underscore their growing commitment with the teachers march on January 22, 1965, followed by later marches from other elite professional groups. This was justly celebrated as an important shift, a new sector of black elites moving publicly to make a stand. But consider the rapturous reception of students who witnessed this march. In Sheyann Webb's words: "Kids were shaking hands with their teachers and hugging them. I had never seen anything like that before." Webb described some teachers "crying, they were so elated" and embracing one of her teachers who confessed to some tiredness. Said Webb in response, "You did real good." It is powerful evidence about who exactly was leading whom by example. As J. L. Chestnut put it, "To see young students willing to get their heads whipped gave a depth of meaning to the Constitution I could never feel in the sterile atmosphere of the courtroom."[21]

Webb's anecdote lends credence to historian Rebecca de Schweinitz's argument that civil rights historians need to understand children as independent political actors. Young people of this era, dubbed the Emmett Till generation, came of age in an era marked by that atrocity and the false hope of the *Brown v. Board of Education* ruling. Not only were they profoundly shaped by that specific historical context but also those events underscored how children were, consciously or unconsciously, at the forefront of racial change. De Schweinitz notes that children were not only moved to act in protest to segregation but also specifically in reaction to the perceived inadequacies of older generations' responses. Lula Belle Williams King emphasized instead that there "were a lot of classmates who didn't see it at the time. They were the ones we called the elite. We weren't part of the elite. I guess when you had parents who had "positions" you needed to stay out of the limelight." High-schooler Bettie Mae Fikes admitted to leading a rather sheltered life as a young girl in a relatively safe middle-class existence; but she also described how segregation cultivated that cocooning sense of self-protection. "We were taught that we didn't want to be anywhere we weren't wanted," she said—and yet she also underscored how she and like-minded students were "already radical and militant at Hudson High, but we didn't know it." She credited SNCC. The group, in her words, "saved us and kept us from going too far, in expressing those feelings." Fikes stresses unequivocally that "From 1961 to 1965 youth carried the full load of the Selma Movement and had to make adult decisions" and further added that later, after their stand, black adults "pushed them out of the way." Bernice Savage Mutuku added that "there was no credit given to the students who were the ones to get it all started. And they were left out of the official history."[22]

Reflections from Sheyann Webb, eight years old in 1965, are particularly revealing about her embrace of the movement. Her curiosity piqued by an interracial gathering at Brown Chapel AME, she went into the church instead of going to school. "I didn't know anything about any of these things, but it was something that seemed exciting. It was like something was about to happen." When scolded by teachers and her parents, sensing the fear that these activities provoked "made it even more interesting to me." Indeed, seeing the "fear factor" in her parents made her "motivated more and more." As she attended mass meetings, "the more I began to learn 'equality' and 'justice.'" Webb said, "I put all those pieces together just with those words. I may not have understood it well, but I understood enough." The result was that "I became a very disobedient child. That's how deep I got into it."[23]

The activism of these young people cannot be dismissed only as youthful exuberance, although that was certainly part of it, or chalked up to merely being free of adult commitments or responsibilities that often led to punishing repercussions from whites. Annie Laura Williams said that "Selma would kill practically any dream a black child had." And yet, it did not, as she later describes: "At the time we marched on the courthouse, I knew that one of our classmates had already been hit in the head, and people had already been cattle-prodded and clubbed, but I was still gonna go." Similarly, Webb stated pointedly that "There were a number of situations that I knew of as a kid where death actually happened." She recalled attending Jimmie Lee Jackson's funeral with her father and, shaken after the events of Bloody Sunday, writing down her impressions and even detailing her requests for funeral arrangements in the event of her death, because "I still wanted to go out and fight." For several months, seniors at Hudson had no diplomas after graduating, ostensibly because their school attendance had flagged with their commitment to the movement and disqualified them from graduating. This was interpreted by most as a further sign of intimidation. And, of course, the harassment from Sheriff Jim Clark during the forced children's march was equal to the worst that white Selma devised.[24]

No one, no matter what age, could remain unaware of the racial terrorism that menaced adults and children alike. These children knew precisely what the stakes were, and they responded with unwavering commitment. As activist Jean Wiley remarked, it is a misnomer to use the term apathy when talking about galvanizing activism in black Selma, but nonetheless it "did need the spark. I think it did need it from the outside. And I think it did need young people. I don't think it could have happened without young people, or it would have happened very, very, very differently, and more slowly. It needed all of that coming together." More simply, Gloria House, who came to Selma in 1965, called the children "bright, spunky muses of revolution."[25] The purity of that absolute belief, the embodiment of black aspirations for a future generation, and the energy of their activism meant that children led the way.

A third way of exploring how Black Belt leadership and activism developed during the civil rights era is to understand that the stock Selma story flattens the fullest scope of historical events by confining the narrative to city limits. Rather the story should be recalled, as earlier observers noted, with Selma as a nexus for a wider periphery of activism in surrounding counties, each with its own risks and challenges. Before Lafayette even set foot in Selma, he had conferred with Rufus Lewis, black politico and Alabama voting mastermind, and obtained contacts in the counties surrounding Dallas County. Lewis had praised the activities in Macon and Perry counties in particular, where some racial dynamics mirrored Selma's example with early activism and white repression on full display. Dotted throughout the Black Belt were places where black landownership was higher; these citizens had a keen desire for reclaiming voting rights with an eye toward obtaining more economic power. From 1963, SNCC "had made some forays" both in the rural sections of Dallas County and also these surrounding counties.[26]

The SNCC papers are littered with these accounts. Worth Long and Prathia Hall, after replacing Lafayette, directed outreach to Selma's surrounding towns of "Sardis, Orrville, Hayen, Bogue Chitto, and Beloit." Plantersville, a town with some rugged backcountry, had a particularly active Klan presence, and despite some "encouraging" results, activists there found a lot of fear among African Americans, which they tried to counter by bringing other African Americans into Selma for registration. More promising was the Bogue Chitto area, where twenty-five people joined a meeting with their "undivided attention." Attorney Chestnut observed that the more rural Bogue Chitto folks were brought into Selma to embarrass locals into joining forces.[27]

Orrville, a larger town of which Bogue Chitto was a part, manifested similar fear from African Americans: "When one drives into Orrville (of course being a Negro) he will feel and see the coldness of fear in every 'Black Brothers' eyes. If he speaks of registering to Vote, he might as well be speaking to a 'Stone Wall.' Sometimes you might find an individual who will say in a whispering voice, 'Shh! Not here, come to my house or to a certain Box number on a certain road.'"[28] Nonetheless, led by Reverend Ceborn Powell, who persisted despite rumors of threats to his life, small numbers of blacks began the process of registering. Powell also lobbied SNCC for help addressing the various ways that whites were suppressing black initiative. He described one agent who refused to assist African Americans with federal loans unless the black applicant agreed to a 25 percent interest rate that the agent himself pocketed. Reverend Powell lobbied SNCC folks instead for a "branch office" or an informal banking cooperative with the black landowners in the area.[29]

But the activism had been spreading farther afield too. Cynthia Griggs Fleming, historian of civil rights in Wilcox County, has recounted Lafayette's excursions there, particularly in the black community of Boykin (better-known as Gee's Bend, famed for its quilting) where he found skeptical teachers but eager students. He also found other locals who had taken first tentative steps and only needed further facilitating. Some small attempts claiming the right to vote had occurred in the late 1950s, led by Reverend Lonnie Brown, a force behind the Wilcox County Civic and Progressive League. In late March 1963, SNCC workers joined six applicants, including Monroe Pettway and Reverend Brown, to register in Camden, Wilcox County, after black citizens there reached out to the activists for assistance. SNCC's proud proclamation that it was "the first time Negroes had tried to register in this county in fifty years" thus was more self-promotional than accurate. The six were denied because of the local requirement that a white person had to vouch for each new registrant. From that point, however, in Camden as in Selma, children set the pace; "The children were the real leaders," said one local, "they got the adults involved." Some accounts have James Orange going into Hale County and others to Marengo County. James Bevel attempted to crack notoriously rigid Lowndes County, although he had trouble finding a host. Later, in 1964, the activism in surrounding areas surpassed that of Dallas County after Judge James Hare's infamous injunction requiring county voter applicants to use a register book.[30]

Before the tensions that later beset SNCC and SCLC erupted, both were actually working in teams out in these surrounding counties across the Black Belt, along with Tuskegee Institute Advancement League, the Tuskegee State student group. And, of course, it was a march in neighboring Perry County that led to the tragic shooting of Jimmie Lee Jackson and the resultant March to Montgomery. Similar protests occurred in Wilcox County. The troopers had been called in precisely because of this widening of dissent in counties with small sheriffs' departments; unlike in Selma with Jim Clark's posse, these counties relied on these troopers and as such movement activists deliberately fanned out more widely across the region to "scatter the resources of the State." As the sequence of events with Jimmie Lee Jackson's and later Reverend James Reeb's deaths showed, Selma centered a regional movement.[31]

The celebrated shift of SNCC to Lowndes County was preceded by activist work across several counties, but even as organizers became enamored with the organic black nationalism and self-sufficiency of farmers in the area, black leaders in Selma and elsewhere remained equally willing to draw upon external authorities—the federal government, judges, SCLC—for their benefit. Similarly, this Black Belt activism also overlaps with developments derived from Justice Department efforts. Brian Landsberg traced the evolution of case law in Elmore, Perry, and Sumter counties, with three different judges "who followed strikingly different paths" in responding to Justice Department lawsuits, each culminating in verdicts that had pronounced influences on the final shape of the Voting Rights Act. While Landsberg is keen to emphasize the federal role in this story, he firmly stresses how black activism in these local counties was the only way that these rulings and legislation would gain firm traction.[32]

It should also be remembered that activist focus was diverse, not just geographically: some activists note unionizing projects that happened in Selma, at the local soft drink bottling plant, for example. SCLC tried to leverage pressure on a national scale for the companies behind the Hammermill Paper plant and the Dan River textile mill, responding directly to the impulse of Selma's white moderates who were keen to lure industry to the city for jobs. This was part of a bigger story about Sun Belt economic development at the expense of local citizens and especially African Americans, as Brenda Gayle Plummer observes. At the Selma Literacy Project, as James W. Wiley remembered, there was the "Frederick Douglass Free Press" that circulated details of "movement news and activities across the Black Belt," and, as part of voter registration and education, they showed "borrowed movies about the new black nations of Africa." There are reminders that the movement was at once intensely local and broadly global in perspective, to say nothing of its keenly strategic fusing of moral authority and economic leverage.[33]

Civil rights activists are correct to demand recognition of a decades-long struggle in Selma well before the cameras and the celebrities flocked to town. And yet the fact that most know Selma because of the latter shows how the movement is best understood as a confluence of events at many levels, but especially as those events transmuted to a wider audience via national media. The reality that a cornerstone civil rights victory was identified with Selma should not obscure the range of approaches and tactics that converged (sometimes messily, sometimes effectively) in this one place. Scholars need to explore these fits and starts to civil rights activism to detail more accurately how the movement functioned and succeeded. We need to write more complex multifaceted narratives that resist oversimplified distillations pitting a few justly celebrated heroes against supposed indifference and apathy. Instead, exploring the broader spectrum of attitudes and activity that took place in the harsh racial climate of Black Belt Alabama will help us understand, as Lafayette instinctively did, how people can embrace their own leadership qualities and become alive to the alchemy of building a movement.

In sum, then, the story of activism in Selma "before the bridge" is not just comprised of those individuals finding themselves stirred by the civil rights movement in singular ways, from a child's moral certainty to the powerful liberating public steps forward from black ministers and teachers. Nor is this merely a collective story of how that commitment coalesced into something greater. Rather it is both of those intermeshed. Activism had its own dynamics and cadence from town to town, county to county, person to person. Not only was the assertion of a basic American right at stake but also the freeing of oneself from the choking effects of segregated legacies in all their grim power. With those individual stands, sometimes mobilized and sometimes organized, pathways to a new spirit began to form, and it showed in internal and external ways. Bettie Mae Fikes stressed the sense of self-worth and closeness forged by the children and leaders across the Black Belt who tested their commitment well before the rest of America was listening.[34]

The candid observations of Selma attorney J. L. Chestnut noted that, by 1965, there was a genuine "transformation" or what he called "a subtle revision of the power arrangement" inherent in Jim Crow, as "black public opinion began to hold a little weight." In his estimation, black leaders now found themselves preoccupied with how well they were thought of by black people in addition to white. In these ways did some measure of change come to Selma. As Lafayette said, "The seeds of resistance were there before. It was a matter of rearranging those and replanting those in a way that would cause new life to grow." Exploring how these various elements should be joined to the story of the movement may be the best bridge to understanding Selma's legacy of all.[35]

Notes

1. Prathia Hall, in Faith S. Holsaert, Martha Prescod Norman Noonan, Judy Richardson, Betty Garman Robinson, Jean Smith Young, and Dorothy M. Zellner, eds., *Hands on the Freedom Plow: Personal Accounts by Women in SNCC* (Urbana: University of Illinois Press, 2012), 470–71; Lafayette interview, UNC-SHC, Taylor Branch Papers, Series 4, Box 99, Folder 711, 15–16; J. L. Chestnut Jr. and Julia Cass, *Black in Selma, The Uncommon Life of J. L. Chestnut Jr.* (New York: Farrar, Strauss and Giroux, 1990), 149; James Forman, *The Making of Black Revolutionaries* (New York: Macmillan Co., 1972), 316–26; Rufus Burrow, *A Child Shall Lead Them, Martin Luther King Jr., Young People, and the Movement* (Minneapolis: Augsburg Fortress Press, 2014), 219.

2. Emilye Crosby, "The Selma Voting Rights Struggle: 15 Key Points from Bottom-Up History," at http://www.teachingforchange.org/selma-bottom-up-history (consulted March 21, 2017).

3. Lafayette interview, UNC-SHC, Taylor Branch Papers, Series 4, Box 99, Folder 711, 17, 20; Lafayette, Field Report, February 11–15, 1963, at http://www.crmvet.org/lets/630215_sncc_selma-r.pdf (consulted March 21, 2017); J. Mills Thornton, *Dividing Lines: Municipal Politics and the Struggle for Civil Rights in Montgomery, Birmingham, and Selma*, (Tuscaloosa: University of Alabama Press, 2002), 449–50; Carroll Van West, "The Civil Rights Movement in Selma, Alabama, 1865–1972" (2013), 27–28, at https://www.nps.gov/nr/feature/places/pdfs/64501182.pdf (consulted March 21, 2017); Wayne Greenhaw, *Fighting the Devil in Dixie: How Civil Rights Activists Took on the Ku Klux Klan in Alabama* (Zephyr Press, 2011), 161–80 (87 on Elks); Taylor Branch, *Pillar of Fire: America in the King Years, 1963-1964* (New York: Touchstone, 1999), 63–64; Chestnut and Cass, *Black in Selma*, 51–52, 74; 132–37 (on early black activism), 134 ("confidence builder"), 41, 184–85 (on Catholic activism). NAACP chapters had also been outlawed in Wilcox and Marengo counties—see Mary Gitin, *This Bright Light of Ours: Stories from the Voting Rights Fight* (Tuscaloosa: University of Alabama Press, 2014), 50. On Garvey, see Mary G. Rolinson, *Grassroots Garveyism: The Universal Negro Improvement Association in the Rural South, 1920-1927* (Chapel Hill: University of North Carolina Press, 2007), 197.

4. Thornton, *Dividing Lines*, 386–92, 395–98, 433–34. On "calculated inaction,"—one scholar preferred "nonparticipation"—see Thomas R. Frazier, "An Analysis of Nonviolent Coercion as Used by the Sit-In Movement," *Phylon* 29, no. 1 (1968): 27–40; Chestnut and Cass, *Black in Selma*, 78. On the Civil Rights Commission, Richie Jean Sherrod Jackson, *The House by the Side of the Road: The Selma Civil Rights Movement* (Tuscaloosa: University of Alabama Press, 2011), 26, 31; Thornton, *Dividing Lines*, 440; Charles

M. Payne, *I've Got the Light of Freedom: The Organizing Tradition and the Mississippi Freedom Struggle* (Berkeley: University of California Press, 1995), 3–4.

5. Lafayette interview, UNC-SHC, Taylor Branch Papers, Series 4, Box 99, Folder 711, 17, 40–41, 43, 48; Bernard Lafayette, interview part 5 with James Findlay (2002), at http://webarchives.apps.uri.edu/xml/Guide%20to%20the%20Bernard%20LaFayette%20Oral%20History%20Project.xml (consulted March 21, 2017), 13–15, 18, 34; Bernard Lafayette Jr., and Kathryn Lee Johnson, *In Peace and Freedom: My Journey in Selma* (University Press of Kentucky, 2013), 33–34; Branch, *Pillar of Fire*, 553; Chestnut and Cass, *Black in Selma*, 148.

6. Lafayette interview by Robert Weisbrot, July 25, 1984, in Robert W. Woodruff Library, Emory University, David Garrow Papers, Box 1.9 SCLC aides, 34; Lafayette interview, UNC-SHC, Taylor Branch Papers, Series 4, Box 99, Folder 711, 24; Lafayette and Lee Johnson, *In Peace and Freedom*, 28; Thornton, *Dividing Lines*, 448, 482; Chestnut and Cass, *Black in Selma*, 154. On the propensity for using "Uncle Tom," see also Gitin, *This Bright Light of Ours*, 244–45.

7. Lafayette interview by Robert Weisbrot, July 25, 1984, in Robert W. Woodruff Library, Emory University, David Garrow Papers, Box 1.9 SCLC aides, 13, 15, 18–19; Cheryl Lynn Greenberg, ed., *A Circle of Trust: Remembering SNCC* (Rutgers University Press, 1998), 90.

8. Lafayette and Lee Johnson, *In Peace and Freedom*, 29, 50, 61.

9. Thornton, *Dividing Lines*, 448; on Moss, see Chestnut and Cass, *Black in Selma*, 91–92. Lafayette interview, UNC-SHC, Taylor Branch Papers, Series 4, Box 99, Folder 711, 17.

10. Lafayette and Lee Johnson, *In Peace and Freedom*, 38–40; Lafayette interview by Robert Weisbrot, July 25, 1984, in Robert W. Woodruff Library, Emory University, David Garrow Papers, Box 1.9 SCLC aides, 20–21; Chestnut and Cass, *Black in Selma*, 91–92. See also Burrow, *A Child Shall Lead Them*, 232.

11. Bruce Hartford, *The Selma Voting Rights Struggle and the March to Montgomery* (Westwind Writers, 2014), 15; Wally G. Vaughn, ed., *The Selma Campaign, 1963–1965: The Decisive Battle of the Civil Rights Movement* (Majority Press, 2008), 135; Bettie Mae Fikes in Holsaert et al., *Hands on the Freedom Plow*, 467–68; Chestnut and Cass, *Black in Selma*, 160. Specific names are in Colia Lafayette, Dallas County Field Report, April 6, 1963, at http://www.crmvet.org/lets/630406_sncc_selma_colia-r.pdf (consulted March 21, 2017); Silas Norman in Greenberg, *Circle of Trust*, 95–97.

12. Rebecca de Schweinitz, *If We Could Change the World: Young People and America's Long Struggle for Racial Equality* (University of North Carolina Press, 2011), 218, 236, 245, 248; Lafayette and Lee Johnson, *In Peace and Freedom*, 97–98; Van West, "The Civil Rights Movement in Selma, Alabama, 1865–1972," 28–30; Thornton, *Dividing Lines*, 448–49; Chestnut and Cass, *Black in Selma*, 153–59.

13. Various authors, "Survey: Current Field Work Spring 1963," at http://www.crmvet.org/docs/sncc50_field-reports.pdf; Alex Brown in "Report on Student Canvassing, May 1963," at http://www.crmvet.org/docs/6305_sncc_selma_convas-r.pdf (both consulted March 21, 2017).

14. de Schweinitz, *If We Could Change the World*, 134, 234, 239; David Halberstam, *The Children* (New York: Random House, 1999), 439; account of Lafayette and Hobbs

meeting in Bruce Gordon, November 9, 1963, Field Report, at http://www.crmvet.org/lets/631109_sncc_selma_gordon.pdf (consulted March 21, 2017); interview with Chuck Bonner and Bettie Mae Fikes (2005), at http://crmvet/org/nars/chuckbet.htm (consulted March 21, 2017); "Field Report—Mrs. Colia Lafayette, April 6, 1963," at http://www.teachingforchange.org/wp-content/uploads/2014/12/CL_1963Report.pdf (consulted March 21, 2017); Sherrod Jackson, *The House by the Side of the Road*, 82; Gitin, *This Bright Light of Ours*, 76–77, on Chuck Bonner recruitment and expulsion.

15. Thornton, *Dividing Lines*, 454–55; Branch, *Pillar of Fire*, 144; Chestnut and Cass, *Black in Selma*, 168–69; Cynthia Griggs Fleming, *In the Shadow of Selma: The Continuing Struggle for Civil Rights in the Rural South* (New York: Rowman and Littlefield, 2004), 152.

16. Reverend B. L. Tucker memo, September 16–24, 1963, at http://www.crmvet.org/lets/630916_selma_tucker.pdf (consulted March 21, 2017); Bettie Mae Fikes in Holsaert et al., *Hands on the Freedom Plow*, 465–67; Vaughn, *The Selma Campaign, 1963–1965*, 80; "The Selma Pickets" in roundtable interview, "Selma & the March to Montgomery: A Discussion" (November–June, 2004–2005), at http://www.crmvet.org/disc/selma.htm#ala65pickets (consulted March 21, 2017).

17. Thornton, *Dividing Lines*, 451–53, 461–64; John A. Love, June 28, 1964, "Project—Selma, Alabama," at http://www.crmvet.org/lets/6406_sncc_selma_love.pdf (consulted March 21, 2017); Chestnut and Cass, *Black in Selma*, 173–74. See also journalist Jerry DeMuth's account of his assault in August 1964: "Brown Uniforms in Selma, Alabama," at http://www.crmvet.org/info/6408_demuth_selma.pdf (consulted March 21, 2017).

18. Branch, *Pillar of Fire*, 559; Hartford, *The Selma Voting Rights Struggle and the March to Montgomery*, 53–55, 60–62; Vaughn, *The Selma Campaign, 1963–1965*, 90; Lafayette and Lee Johnson, *In Peace and Freedom*, 35.

19. Thornton, *Dividing Lines*, 484–86; Burrow, *A Child Shall Lead Them*, 237.

20. Van West, "The Civil Rights Movement in Selma, Alabama, 1865–1972," 29; "shame" quotation: Colia Lafayette, Dallas County Field Report, April 6, 1963, at http://www.crmvet.org/lets/630406_sncc_selma_colia-r.pdf (consulted March 21, 2017).

21. Bettie Mae Fikes in Holsaert et al., *Hands on the Freedom Plow*, 467; Ellen S. Levine, *Freedom's Children: Young Civil Rights Activists Tell Their Own Stories* (New York: Putnam, 1993), 125–26; interview with Chuck Bonner and Bettie Mae Fikes (2005), at http://www.crmvet.org/nars/chuckbet.htm (consulted March 21, 2017); Hartford, *The Selma Voting Rights Struggle and the March to Montgomery*, 48; Vaughn, *The Selma Campaign, 1963–1965*, 129; Burrow, *A Child Shall Lead Them*, 247–48; Sherrod Jackson, *The House by the Side of the Road*, 65; Sheyann Webb and Rachel West Nelson, *Selma, Lord, Selma: Girlhood Memories of the Civil Rights Days* (New York: William Morrow, 1980), 64–65; Chestnut and Cass, *Black in Selma*, 183, 201.

22. de Schweinitz, *If We Could Change th World*, 193, 196, 211, 203–4, 239; Bettie Mae Fikes in Holsaert et al., *Hands on the Freedom Plow*, 464–65; reminiscence from Bernice Savage Mutuku (2015), at http://www.crmvet.org/nars/mutuku.htm; reminiscence from Lula Belle Williams King (2016), at http://www.crmvet.org/nars/lulaking.htm (both consulted March 21, 2017).

23. Levine, *Freedom's Children*, 126; de Schweinitz, *If We Could Change the World*, 211; Burrow, *A Child Shall Lead Them*, 238–65.

24. Account from Annie Laura Williams (2016), at http://www.crmvet.org/nars/anniewms.htm (consulted March 21, 2017); Levine, *Freedom's Children*, 126–27.

25. Wiley in Selma and the March to Montgomery: A Discussion (November–June 2004–2005), at http://www.crmvet.org/disc/selma.htm (consulted March 21, 2017); Gloria House in Holsaert et al., *Hands on the Freedom Plow*, 506.

26. Lafayette interview, UNC-SHC, Branch Papers, Series 4, Box 99, Folder 711, 18–19, 26; "forays" quote, Holsaert et al., *Hands on the Freedom Plow*, 449.

27. Bruce Gordon, Field Report, Selma, Alabama, November 9, 1963, at http://www.crmvet.org/lets/631109_sncc_selma_gordon.pdf (consulted March 21, 2017); William Robertson and Tom Brown, "Official Report: Plantersville," November 6, 1963, at http://www.crmvet.org/lets/631106_sncc_dallasco.pdf (consulted March 21, 2017); "The Selma Report" by Alvery Lee Williams, November 6, 1963, at http://www.crmvet.org/lets/631106_sncc_selma_alw.pdf (consulted March 21, 2017); Chestnut and Cass, *Black in Selma*, 166–67.

28. "Official report of Orrville," November 7, 1963, at http://www.crmvet.org/lets/631107_sncc_dallasco2.pdf (consulted March 21, 2017).

29. Ibid.

30. Fleming, *In the Shadow of Selma*, 111, 135, 142–44, 152–53, 166; Taylor Branch, *At Canaan's Edge: America in the King Years, 1965–1968* (New York: Simon and Schuster, 2007), 10; Gitin, *This Bright Light of Ours*, 242 (quotation), see also 69, 93, 98, 230–33, 241, 245); Hassan Kwame Jeffries, "SNCC, Black Power, and Independent Political Party Organizing in Alabama, 1964–1966," *Journal of African American History* 91 (2006): 180–81. On Gee's Bend, see Gitin, *This Bright Light of Ours*, 51, 53–54, 131, 165. "Fifty years" quotation, "Appendix A: Survey: Current Field Work, Spring 1963," at http://www.crmvet.org/docs/6305_sncc_cong_fieldwork.pdf (consulted March 21, 2017); Hartford, *The Selma Voting Rights Struggle and the March to Montgomery*, 73.

31. Lafayette interview, UNC-SHC, Branch Papers, Series 4, Box 99, Folder 711, 21–24, 35, 37–42; Fay Bellamy Powell in Holsaert et al., *Hands on the Freedom Plow*, 477; Martha Prescod Norman Noonan in Holsaert et al., *Hands on the Freedom Plow*, 497; Fleming, *In the Shadow of Selma*, 153–54; Hasan Kwame Jeffries, *Bloody Lowndes: Civil Rights and Black Power in Alabama's Black Belt* (New York: New York University Press, 2009), 54–55. Subsequent links with white Presbyterians and Camden Academy are discussed in Dwain Epps's recollections at http://www.crmvet.org/nars/epps16.pdf (consulted March 21, 2017). See also James Bevel report from Perry County, post-Bloody Sunday, in SCLC: Series 4: Reel 8, frame 0161.

32. Hartford, *The Selma Voting Rights Struggle and the March to Montgomery*, 110–11; Lafayette interview, UNC-SHC, Branch Papers, Series 4, Box 99, Folder 711, 41, 49; Fleming, *In the Shadow of Selma*, 154; Jeffries, "SNCC, Black Power, and Independent Political Party Organizing in Alabama, 1964–1966," 176, 179, 182–83; Brian K. Landsberg, *Free at Last to Vote: The Alabama Origins of the 1965 Voting Rights Act* (Lawrence: University Press of Kansas, 2007). For Justice Department and Selma, see David J. Garrow, *Protest*

at Selma: Martin Luther King Jr. and the Voting Rights Act of 1965 (New Haven: Yale University Press, 1978), 31–35.

33. Martha Prescod Norman Noonan in Holsaert et al., *Hands on the Freedom Plow*, 496; Silas Norman in Greenberg, *Circle of Trust*, 97; Brenda Gayle Plummer, *In Search of Power: African Americans in the Era of Decolonization* (Cambridge: Cambridge University Press, 2013).

34. Bettie Mae Fikes in Holsaert et al., *Hands on the Freedom Plow*, 470.

35. Chestnut and Cass, *Black in Selma*, 198; Jeffries, *Bloody Lowndes*, 73, 256n13; Lafayette in Greenberg, *Circle of Trust*, 92.

3

Nonviolence Crowned or Dethroned?

King's Strategy in Selma and Its Legacy

PETER LING

The Selma campaign stands as a watershed moment in Martin Luther King Jr.'s career. It is part of a series of campaigns from 1961 to 1965 in which King's success as a nonviolent protest leader emerged: thus, Albany is portrayed as a failure from which King learned, Birmingham as a breakthrough victory, St. Augustine as a brave application of Birmingham's tactics to ensure passage of the Civil Rights Act of 1964, and Selma as the capstone—the most effective campaign—that forced a reluctant President Lyndon B. Johnson to introduce what became the Voting Rights Act of 1965. After Selma, come the later campaigns positioned along an arc of declension: namely, the Chicago campaign with its lack of clear gains and the Meredith March Against Fear with its Black Power call in 1966; a year later King came out against the Vietnam War and was widely denounced; and finally, in 1968 the Poor People's Campaign, unimplemented, but struggling, at the time of King's death, and of course, the Memphis sanitation workers' strike, during which King was assassinated after returning to the city to lead a nonviolent march after a previous protest had been marred by violence. Thus, Selma seems to be Martin Luther King's crowning moment as a nonviolent activist: his greatest victory. But success for King was always partial, transient, or ambiguous.[1]

Scholars of King's nonviolent practice, such as James Colaiaco, have written of the "paradox of nonviolence" and emphasized how King's tactics seemed to depend for their success on eliciting a violent response from his segregationist adversaries.[2] In Selma, success seemed to flow from King's adversaries' need to put on a show of brutal intimidation for their own, local supporters at the expense of their reputation nationally and among the nonaligned public. Thus, Sheriff Jim Clark in Selma stepped into the role previously played by Birmingham Police Commissioner Eugene "Bull" Connor, as the segregationist defender who blindly damaged his own cause. The moral ambiguity here lies in Martin Luther King's calculated exploitation not only of his opponents but also of his followers. Did he treat them in some sense as "cannon fodder?"

David Garrow's *Protest at Selma* (1978) was the first major study to analyze how King's nonviolence had shifted by 1965. When Martin Luther King first came to prominence in 1956 as the young leader of the Montgomery Bus Boycott, he tended to meld Gandhian nonviolence with the Christian gospel's faith in the power of redemptive suffering. In early 1959 in an address to the War Resisters League, he declared: "Suffering, the nonviolent resister realizes, has tremendous educational and transforming possibilities." Having cited Gandhi's claim that it could open the ears of the oppressor, King specifically pointed to its impact on the uncommitted, but he also claimed that such undeserved suffering boosted recruitment and solidarity inside the movement.[3] Events in Selma would test that claim in key respects since tensions within the Southern Christian Leadership Conference (SCLC) and between King's organization and other civil rights groups became still more evident in the aftermath.

A more assured aspect of nonviolence's effectiveness was its impact on the legitimacy of the regimes it contested. Its ability to call them into question and thus erode the consent of the governed rested significantly on its own moral standing. Accordingly, in his many statements, King tended to stress the idealism of nonviolence rather than its tactical astuteness.[4] This was not done out of cynicism since King's faith was real and he had embraced nonviolence as a way of life, but nor was it naïve. Here, one should acknowledge that throughout his career, Martin Luther King was a principled practitioner of nonviolence as a way of life and a pragmatic leader who appreciated that power yields nothing willingly. Nevertheless, King's position as the leading spokesman for the movement in the eyes of the white media rested at least partly on his mastery of the moral discourse that framed race as a matter of personal prejudice during this period. Thus, the scenario of "converting" the prejudiced by revealing to them the immorality of their stance continued to circulate as a prominent part of the rationale for the movement's nonviolence, and thereby aggravated internal tensions. To black militants, African American suffering was too high a price to pay for white redemption.

By 1965, King's philosophy of nonviolence was probably best known through the "Letter from Birmingham Jail," which had been reprinted in his bestselling volume *Why We Can't Wait* (1964).[5] Here, King had explained that nonviolence had a psychologically therapeutic function, providing a "creative outlet" for the pent-up resentments of African Americans. Using the same logic, he had argued that the August 1963 March on Washington should go ahead, despite President John F. Kennedy's acute misgivings, because if it did not, African American grievances might otherwise find expression in violence. Kennedy himself in his June television address on civil rights had conceded this possibility by arguing that legislation was needed to give African Americans a means of securing equal treatment via the courts rather than having to take their grievances to the streets.

Implicit within Martin Luther King's defense of nonviolence was the assumption that feelings can only be repressed for a finite period and will always seek an outlet. If the creative outlet of nonviolence is not available, mass frustration at injustice will readily erupt into violent disorder. Violence and nonviolence could thus spring from the same source.[6] In his original "Letter," King had also spoken of the therapeutic benefits of the "creative tension" that a nonviolently induced crisis could bring by dramatizing an issue "so that it can no longer be ignored."[7] This outlook was also reflected in his references to nonviolence as "the sword that heals," although the underlying truth that it was white America that needed to be healed was only implied.[8] In Selma, King was in search of creative tension.

By the time King's SCLC joined the protests for voting rights in Selma, white officials were well aware of its approach. While the stereotypical figure of Sheriff Clark made Selma seem like an obvious site for a staged confrontation, in reality Clark's jurisdiction there was confined to the county courthouse. The city of Selma had recently elected a moderate, business-orientated mayor, Joseph Smitherman, whose plans to revive the local economy by attracting new investment implied shrewder public relations: the city should appear a calm and progressive community. By hiring Wilson Baker, who had taught criminal law at the University of Alabama, as his director of public safety, Smitherman had signaled that he wanted a modern approach to policing that favored subtler policies than those employed by Clark and his posse beyond the city limits. Baker's different approach was evident when he phoned assistant attorney general Burke

Marshall in late 1964 to see if Marshall could dissuade King from coming to Selma. At the federal level, the 1964 Civil Rights Act had established the Community Relations Service (CRS), part of whose job was to manage local situations so that they did not escalate into the crisis that in key respects King's strategy required. Continuing segregationist violence—symbolized by the 1964 Freedom Summer murder of James Chaney, Andrew Goodman, and Michael Schwerner—underlined the need for the CRS to diffuse local tensions before they reached a potentially lethal climax. Aware that both local and federal officials might prevent the campaign in Selma from becoming a full-scale confrontation between King's nonviolent army and Governor George Wallace's hardline segregationists, the SCLC had already scouted the possibility of moving from Selma to the neighboring county seats of Camden and Marion. Nevertheless, on January 18, 1965, when King first became actively engaged in Selma, the local, white newspaper editor Arthur Capell still believed that if they could avoid arresting King and thereby avoid media attention, "we'll have them whipped."[9]

The recognition that police violence redounded to Martin Luther King's benefit meant that moderate segregationists like Baker, Capell, and Smitherman watched with dismay when Sheriff Clark roughly manhandled the leader of the local Dallas County Voters League, Mrs. Amelia Boynton, in front of the press on January 19. King sought to underline the desired message by describing the incident to journalists as "one of the most brutal and unlawful acts I have ever seen an officer commit." One suspects that by this stage he had actually seen worse. Attempting to limit the damage, Baker and Smitherman told reporters sadly that Sheriff Clark was obviously "out of control." A few days later, Clark provided a more graphic example of his brutality when he brought his billy club down on the head of Mrs. Annie Lee Cooper "with a whack," as John Herbers wrote in the *New York Times*, "that was heard throughout the crowd gathered in the street." As Aniko Bodroghkozy has shown, this second incident was covered much more ambiguously on television than in the *Times*. A CBS news report was edited in a way that seemed to offer a sympathetic account of a hard-pressed sheriff struggling to keep order amidst an unstable black crowd. In contrast, the image in the *Times* (showing Cooper pinned to the ground by two deputies while Clark hit her) was much more supportive of King's line. Such divergent interpretations usefully remind us that the mass media was not unfailingly on the movement's side in Selma by any means. Even Herbers's article had a headline—"Woman Punches Alabama Sheriff"—that identified Cooper as striking the first blow.[10]

It is in this context of a media predisposed to privilege the forces of order over those of protest that one has to place reports that King had prevented several black men from rushing to Mrs. Cooper's aid.[11] If true, they may perhaps reinforce the impression that Martin Luther King's nonviolence was manipulative, and irreconcilable with the generally accepted rules of self-defense. King's lieutenant, James Bevel, a key source of tactical innovation and advice within SCLC, explained why such restraint was necessary. Any recourse to violence, he warned movement followers, would allow the local authorities "to call you a mob, and beat you to death."[12] When asked directly whether nonviolence worked only if it elicited violence, Bevel demurred, but added that the contrast offered by a violent oppressor provided "a better means of showing and revealing and bringing out the contradiction."[13] Again Bodroghkozy's analysis of CBS news reinforces the view that protesters walked a fine line in retaining media sympathy. She notes that youthful protesters were regarded cynically as "not serious but rather engaged in high jinks and antics to get out of school."[14]

It has become the orthodox, scholarly view that King's campaigns were strongly shaped by their predecessors. The lessons Martin Luther King had taken from Birmingham centered largely on the use of mass demonstration as a media spectacle to elicit federal intervention. At the same time, there was a growing belief in government circles that King's actions were also shaped by the rivalry that had developed between different civil rights groups. Over the course of 1964, the SCLC had been involved in both the St. Augustine desegregation protests and the lobbying efforts that secured the Civil Rights Act's passage, and King's global standing had been confirmed by the award of the Nobel Peace Prize. Yet over the same period, other organizations had become more influential in key respects. The Student Nonviolent Coordinating Committee (SNCC) may have rejected the tainted compromise seating plan offered by President Johnson to its protégés in the Mississippi Freedom Democratic Party at the national convention in Atlantic City, but overall its Freedom Summer project had raised its organizational profile to a level not seen since the 1961 Freedom Rides.[15]

The successful effort to pass the Civil Rights Act and the triumphant defeat of Barry Goldwater in the autumn of 1964 had renewed the confidence of more established groups like the National Association for the Advancement of Colored People (NAACP). On the basis of very different assumptions, both SNCC and NAACP were becoming convinced that Martin Luther King's preeminence, rooted in his advocacy of nonviolent direct action, might be passing. SNCC's political organizing focus in the Deep South had diminished the place of nonviolence in its repertoire and deepened its skepticism of the federal government. The NAACP's lobbying and engagement with the Johnson White House, in contrast, had sharpened its leaders' belief that the coalition with Johnson and the liberals was valuable. Accordingly, Roy Wilkins had supported President Johnson's proposal that civil rights groups accept a moratorium on protest activity in the run-up to the November election—an idea that SNCC strongly rejected. In view of these developments, King's strategy in Selma was a re-assertion of his position that nonviolent protest could mobilize a potent coalition of conscience that could secure meaningful gains.[16]

Shortly before President Johnson's landslide election victory in November, King told reporters that demonstrations around the right to vote in either Alabama or Mississippi were imminent in order to secure more effective federal intervention. In doing so, King reflected not only the reality that previous measures to protect African American voting rights had not secured re-enfranchisement in areas like Selma but also his determination to demonstrate that SCLC remained a force. After the stunning electoral victory, the Johnson administration was considering its legislative strategy. U. S. Department of Justice officials were well aware that additional protection of the right to vote was needed, but were undecided as to whether it could be found without a constitutional amendment. They were also mindful that key Republican figures like Congressman William McCulloch and Senator Everett Dirksen had been opposed to proposals to extend oversight of the electoral process by federal judges that had been floated in 1963 and 1964.

Even though the liberal complexion of Congress had improved as a result of the 1964 elections, President Johnson was wary. He had his War on Poverty to launch and the old alliance of southern Democrats and Republicans might be rekindled by returning to the vexed civil rights issue before the 1964 Civil Rights Act had been fully implemented and tested. For Johnson, given this political outlook, King's Selma campaign was as ill-timed as his 1963 Birmingham campaign had been in the eyes of Jack and Bobby Kennedy. This made it essential that King's tactics generate the "creative tension" that would force the president to act.

King's vital role as the chief fundraiser and publicist for the SCLC meant that his presence in Selma was intermittent. On February 1, he and Ralph Abernathy led a march to the county courthouse and were duly arrested with 260 others. Drawing on Birmingham's example, 500 children marched that afternoon. They, too, were arrested, and SCLC had its "Letter from Martin Luther King, Jr., from Selma, Alabama Jail" in the *New York Times* on February 5 to appeal to a coalition of conscience and to ratchet up the fundraising appeal. Smitherman and Baker had been forced to abandon their initial policy of not arresting King due to growing pressure from ardent segregationists.[17]

From jail, King issued detailed instructions designed to entangle the Johnson administration in the unfolding campaign and to maximize support. SCLC board member Joseph Lowery was tasked with liaising with the CRS about the continued recalcitrance of Dallas County voter registrars in processing applicants and with lobbying the White House for a public statement. SCLC's Washington-based lobbyist, Walter Fauntroy, was told to line up a sympathetic congressional delegation to visit Selma, and Abernathy was to make a personal call on his release from prison to entertainer Sammy Davis Jr. to press him to do a benefit concert. "I find these guys respond better when I'm in jail," King noted sanguinely.[18]

King's periods in jail had to be limited because SCLC could not function indefinitely without him in the public eye. Poised to post bail on February 5, he seemed to have made progress since federal judge Daniel Thomas had enjoined the county registrars to process one hundred applicants a day. President Johnson had told a press conference that all Americans should share his indignation "over the loss of any American's right to vote," and a liberal congressional delegation was waiting to meet King at Brown Chapel A.M.E. Church. These positive developments prompted the SCLC's Andrew Young Jr. to announce a suspension of demonstrations, an order that King immediately rescinded since the objective was not to improve local registration in a piecemeal fashion, but to compel the federal government to act as guarantor of African American voting rights everywhere. A further 500 schoolchildren marched and were arrested. Later press reports indicated that Sheriff Clark had taken 165 teenage demonstrators on a forced march through Dallas County with his posse ensuring the pace never slackened through the use of electric cattle prods.[19]

Media coverage that helped King's plans also proved problematic. If nonviolence worked by inducing nonaligned spectators to identify positively with the protesters and feel alienated from the actions of law enforcement officers, then it was vital that images of police brutality reached the national audience via TV news. At the same time, television coverage in particular exaggerated King's personal role by relying on him as the spokesman for the movement.[20] This touched a sore point with SNCC activists, some of whom had been critical of King's nonviolent practice ever since he refused to join them on the Freedom Ride bus from Montgomery to Jackson, Mississippi, in 1961. Whereas SNCC's vanguard at that time had taken pride in the slogan "Jail, not Bail," King customarily filed bail as soon as he was needed to meet prior engagements. Sharpening the sense of grievance was the realization that donations tended to flow to SCLC whenever King's name was associated with a campaign, even though those most intensely and dangerously engaged in the protest might be SNCC workers, or more often, local people. In black Selma, as in Birmingham, people had begun to question the value of having Dr. King in town as the arrest tally mounted. Local leader Frederick Reese, for instance, readily accepted the idea of an appearance book that would allow prospective registrants to prebook their appointment with the county registrars, a move that potentially eliminated the need for marches to, and lines outside, the courthouse.[21]

King had already discussed new tactics with his lieutenants if the demonstrations began to lose their hold on the media. One risky option that had been developed in St. Augustine was the night march. Judging by events there, darkness emboldened segregationist violence, which sometimes spilled over into attacks on the press, an outcome that increased media sympathy for the movement. King had held confidential discussions with the White House and learned from President Johnson himself that voting rights legislation was being prepared. He recognized that black Selma was already growing weary, and so he asked the campaign organizers, including local leaders and SNCC representatives, to help him stage a dignified exit in the context of concessions that gave people a sense of tangible gains. Pointedly, he told SNCC: "You should not only know how to start a good Movement, [you] should also know when to stop."[22]

In reflecting on the role of nonviolence in Selma, it is worth recalling, therefore, that before Jimmie Lee Jackson's death, before the Bloody Sunday attack on marchers, before King's "Tuesday Turnaround"—in short, before the whole Selma-to-Montgomery spectacle that claimed two further lives—King was thinking in terms of ending the Selma campaign because he felt that its key objective of forcing voting rights legislation up the Johnson administration's list of priorities had been achieved. Thus, the symbolic moments for which Selma is remembered were not solely the outcome of King's nonviolent principles in action, but contingent events that grew out of the internal politics of the Wallace regime and of the movement itself.[23] King's sense that black Selma was feeling the pressure by mid-February and his desire to demonstrate that Selma was not the only example of segregationist oppression prompted him to authorize a switch of protest activity to Marion in neighboring Perry County. Local police promptly arrested SCLC's James Orange, and a subsequent night march to the jailhouse on February 18 was broken up violently by local whites and a detachment of Alabama state troopers under Colonel Al Lingo. Jimmie Lee Jackson had taken refuge in a small café and was shot at close range while he tried to protect his mother when the troopers burst in. Eight others, including three white reporters, were hospitalized and 826 were arrested for unlawful assembly. Governor Wallace blamed "career and professional agitators with pro-Communist affiliations." Jackson died in a Selma hospital on February 26.[24]

What happened in Marion sprang primarily from a combination of local segregationist anger at black defiance crucially emboldened by the arrival of external segregationist sympathizers in the form of the state troopers (out of uniform, Sheriff Clark, was spotted too). There was certainly an intent to intimidate the incipient Perry County protest movement through brutality, and the deliberate extinguishing of street lighting and targeting of media cameras, suggests that this was meant to happen beyond the eyes of the outside world. Jackson's fatal shooting was probably an unplanned step too far, and in combination with the national media's outrage at the attacks on their own reporters, this ensured intensive coverage.

Emotions were running understandably high inside the movement after Jimmie Lee Jackson's death. Memories of black retaliation after the Gaston Motel bombing in May 1963 made King fear that the distinction between segregationist brutality and African American protest, which his demonstrations had placed so candidly before the American public, might blur once the media had stories to tell of black violence and white victims. As James Bevel explains it,

> When you have a great violation of the people and there's a great sense of injury, you have to give people an honorable means and context in which to express and eliminate the grief and speak decisively and succinctly back to the issue.[25]

In proposing a mass march to Montgomery, Bevel and others realized that the time spent in the fifty-mile trek "would give you time to discuss in the nation, through papers, radio and television and going around speaking, what the real issues were."[26]

With the exception of John Lewis, SNCC spokesmen condemned this SCLC proposal as a publicity stunt and a distraction. As a sign that its tactics were not intrinsically limited to nonviolence, SNCC had already hosted Malcolm X in Selma on February 4 while King was in prison. Now, as they waited to see whether Jimmie Lee Jackson survived, news came of Malcolm's assassination in New York on February 21. Four days later arsonists torched SNCC's offices in Selma. Charles Cobb has written about how the gun culture of the rural South meant that SNCC fieldworkers lived routinely in homes with guns and with people who did not hesitate to shoot if their homes were attacked. He reports that fieldworker Bernard Lafayette was saved from possible assassination in Selma in 1963 by an armed neighbor, "Red," a Korean War veteran who scared off two white men who attacked as Lafayette was entering his apartment. Hasan Kwame Jeffries has similarly written about how the Lowndes County Freedom Party emerged in 1966 within a preexisting tradition of armed self-defense, and others have documented the presence of self-defense groups elsewhere in Alabama.[27] In short, as white violence intensified, the likelihood of black retaliation increased, and the difficulty of maintaining the spectacle of nonviolence intensified.

At the same time, the killing in Marion reflected and reinforced the factionalism within segregationist ranks that also generated a barely contained fury against renegade whites. Forty white Selmians organized the National Great Society of White People on February 25 as a gesture against Lyndon B. Johnson's treachery. A proposed march by sixty white Alabamians in support of the black cause was blocked at the last minute on March 5 to prevent it walking into the hands of an incensed five-hundred-strong crowd bent on beating these race traitors. Meanwhile, Governor Wallace considered allowing the hastily assembled SCLC march to proceed along the highway but was warned that once it reached Lowndes County there would be further potentially lethal attacks. He instructed Lingo and other highway patrol officers to stop the march and personally assured Mayor Smitherman that there would be no undue use of force. Anticipating that the march would be quickly halted and warned by the Justice Department that King's participation risked an assassination attempt, SCLC gave Hosea Williams the job of leading the marchers while King remained in Atlanta ready to rally support. Acting as an individual rather than as an SNCC spokesman, John Lewis fatefully joined Williams in the front rank.

The infamous televised scenes of Bloody Sunday certainly reflected the violence intrinsic to an unjust racial system but they were not ordered by Governor Wallace nor anticipated by Martin Luther King. If reporters' claims that Colonel Lingo invited them to what he termed a "ringside seat" are accurate, the initiative was taken by others eager to win favor with hardline racist opinion. As the battered marchers sought safety and medical assistance back at Brown Chapel, SCLC leaders like Andrew Young scrambled to stifle the urge for violent retaliation. Young never forgot how he dissuaded local men from getting their guns by being as grimly specific as possible about the firepower that the white authorities could muster and what their high velocity rifles could do. He appealed as much to their instinct for self-preservation as to nonviolent principle.

At the same time, the televised images of the attack on the Edmund Pettus Bridge triggered a political reaction in the movement's favor. Here, too, serendipity rather than planning was crucial. Sunday evening was the ultimate prime time for TV audiences in the mid-1960s, and the premiere of a star-studded, award-winning movie, *Judgment at Nuremberg* on *ABC Sunday Night Movie* ensured high viewing figures, far higher than for regular newscasts. After interrupting the movie with a special report that showed Sheriff Clark's posse on horseback and eerily gas-masked state troopers, beating the fleeing black demonstrators, the station returned viewers to a movie about Nazi war criminals.[28]

This jaw-dropping footage and universal press coverage on Monday provided the context for Martin Luther King's appeal for men and women of good will, especially clergy, to come to Selma for a new march on Tuesday. At the same time, it was reported that Republican leader Senator Everett Dirksen was reviewing a draft administration bill with a view to introducing a bipartisan measure on voting rights reform. In Alabama itself, Wallace allegedly rebuked Lingo and Clark for their actions, and SCLC attorneys applied to federal judge Frank Johnson for an injunction against state interference with the planned Tuesday march, a move that showed that SCLC did not seek any further dramatic confrontations. There were already suggestions that King would call off the march if he got clear signs of federal intervention.[29]

Judge Johnson indicated that his priority was no repetition of Sunday's events and that he would issue a federal injunction against Tuesday's march since its safety could not be assured. This placed King in a quandary. On the one hand, CRS chief LeRoy Collins had arrived in Selma to mediate, and he stressed to King that breaking a federal court order would be extremely damaging for a movement that wanted to use federal law to enforce racial reform. On the other hand, SNCC's James Forman was insistent that white judges should not be allowed to timetable movement actions and saw King's reluctance as confirmation that he valued his White House alliance more than he did the wishes of the movement's rank-and-file.

Court orders had been used in the past to block movement forces, and the associated delays weakened momentum and incurred legal costs. SNCC warned that if King did not march, they would proceed unilaterally and thus make the split with Martin Luther King highly visible. Thus, going ahead seemed essential, despite the risk of prosecution for breaching Judge Johnson's order. Another compelling yet mundane concern for SCLC organizers was that King's call for sympathizers had brought an influx from across the country, and it was clear that there was no time to position adequate support services along the fifty-mile route. Johnson had scheduled hearings for Thursday, and a postponement would provide time to rectify this situation. In the early hours of Tuesday, March 9, discussions broke up with King indicating that the march would go ahead.

Nevertheless, CRS Director Collins sensed that King would welcome a compromise and privately told him that he would seek assurances from Alabama authorities that a token march would not be attacked, and he would also try to ensure that King was not liable to federal prosecution. While a weary King continued to confer indecisively with advisors by phone, Collins extracted a promise from Lingo and Clark that they would not use force as long as King limited the march to a set route. Their map had the added benefit of keeping the march largely in the city limits and off the federal highway and thus gave a basis for arguing that King had complied with Judge Johnson's order. As King set off at the head of 2,000 marchers, many of them white sympathizers responding to his call, Collins thrust the map into his hand and quietly explained that if he kept to the route, all would be well.

To underline King's predicament, as the group reached the Edmund Pettus Bridge, a federal marshal read Judge Johnson's order to ensure that King's contempt would be readily proven if he proceeded. Guided by the map, King stopped the marchers fifty yards from the ranks of state troopers. Keen to accentuate King's dilemma, Lingo had ordered his troopers to withdraw to the roadside at this point, leaving Highway 80 open and clear. After a short pause for prayer, King turned the march around and returned to Brown Chapel where angry SNCC workers and local teenagers demanded an explanation. King failed to respond but told the press that he had acted to prevent further injuries. Only under oath on Thursday did he confess that he had reached "a tacit agreement" with LeRoy Collins.[30]

Among the clergy who had responded to Martin Luther King's appeal was a Boston Unitarian minister, James Reeb, who was attacked that evening by segregationists with a baseball bat blow that shattered his skull. Reeb's severe injuries predictably mesmerized the national press, deflecting their attention and the nation's from the angry recriminations that King's Tuesday Turnaround had caused inside the movement. Hostility to King was so strong that he temporarily withdrew to a friend's house in Montgomery. Reeb's death on Friday March 12 not only escalated national calls for President Johnson and Congress to act to end the Alabama crisis, but also redirected the anger circulating inside the movement away from King and toward LBJ. Press reports indicated that the president had immediately phoned Reeb's family to offer his condolences, a gesture that he had signally failed to make when Jimmie Lee Jackson died. Not for the last time, African Americans wondered aloud why black lives seemingly did not matter.

On March 15, President Johnson addressed a special joint session of Congress and likened Selma to the hallowed battlegrounds of the Revolution and the Civil War as "a turning point in man's unending search for freedom." Demanding voting rights legislation and calling upon the nation to confront its "crippling legacy of bigotry and injustice," an unusually eloquent Johnson signaled his own alignment with the movement by pointedly stating: "And We Shall Overcome."[31] By this stage, however, the president's public commitment and the likelihood that Congress would pass voting rights legislation on a bipartisan basis was not enough to heal the rifts inside the movement or to improve the immediate state of race relations in Alabama. The day after President Johnson's speech, SNCC protesters were beaten in Montgomery in scenes reminiscent of Bloody Sunday. The images were so harrowing that Stokely Carmichael, trapped in an upstairs room, experienced a breakdown, and was hurried away from the city by colleagues so he could receive medical help.[32] An incensed James Forman, who had been dealing with issues arising from tensions between SNCC, SCLC, and the Montgomery Improvement Association, told a church mass meeting that if black people were not to be allowed to sit at "the table of government," then they should "blow the fucking legs off." His intemperate outburst sharpened King's fears over the growing likelihood of black retaliatory violence, which he believed would quickly swamp the nation's shallow commitment to reform.[33]

On March 21, with Judge Johnson's sanction and President Johnson's federalization of the Alabama National Guard (instructed to provide protection), the Selma to Montgomery March set off again. Martin Luther King walked with them for the first three days, left for fundraising events for a day, and then rejoined the front rank on the outskirts of Montgomery. Returning to the Alabama capital at the head of an interracial demonstration at least 25,000 strong, King strode past Dexter Avenue Baptist Church from which he led the Bus Boycott less than a decade earlier. Addressing the crowd, he promised that if they marched on the ballot boxes, the "Wallaces of our nation" would have to "tremble away in silence." Building to a signature climax, he created a call-and-response crescendo around the recurring question of "how long would the struggle for justice take?" and capped the sequence with a quotation: "Not long. Because the arc of the moral universe is long, but it bends towards justice." He concluded with the familiar words of the "Battle Hymn of the Republic," declaring not only that his "eyes had seen the glory of the coming of the Lord" but also that "His Truth is marching on."[34]

It was a declaration of faith that was true to the euphoria of the moment and the integrity of King's vision. The murder of a white volunteer, Viola Liuzzo, as she helped to ferry marchers back to Selma that evening, underscored the sacrifices the struggle still demanded. Liuzzo's Klan killers were acquitted by a local jury in Lowndes County as were the murderers of a white Episcopal seminarian, Jonathan Daniels, shot in the county seat Hayneville during the SNCC-led summer voter registration campaign that accompanied passage of the Voting Rights Act. A Perry County grand jury also refused to indict the state trooper who shot Jimmie Lee Jackson, and no indictments flowed from the Edmund Pettus Bridge attack. The length of the moral arc of the universe in the summer of 1965 seemed more conspicuous than its curve. In Selma, a boycott of white merchants eroded support for concessions and sparked further recriminations. King's unsuccessful attempts to organize a national boycott of Alabama businesses intensified white resentment since it punished innocent and guilty alike. Teacher Frederick Reese, who had become prominent in the Voters Leagues during the protests, was fired by the school board in June and within a year was facing trial for misuse of donations to the league. Nationally, the Watts uprising in Los Angeles within days of the Voting Rights Act's passage confirmed that the ghetto grievances that had flared and festered in the postwar decades would dominate the African American freedom struggle for the rest of Martin Luther King's career. The nonviolent sword that heals was elusive.[35]

A close examination of King's nonviolence in Selma confirms that the idealism with which his credo is rightly associated was inextricably mixed with a calculating pragmatism. A shift to nonviolent coercion, already evident in Birmingham was conspicuous in terms of King's assessment of assets and management of the evolving campaign. It was also clear that Martin Luther King's mistrust of white liberals and moderates of all persuasions was profound. He could not truly trust the president's promises that voting rights measures would be sought at what Johnson judged to be the right time nor assume that the national media would champion his cause without the contrast of undeniable injustice. On March 17, he summarized a key part of SCLC's hard-nosed strategy when he declared: "We will no longer let [white men] use their clubs on us in dark corners. We are going to make them do it in the glaring light of television."[36] It was an observation that made explicit his tactical use of the media, but he was already aware of the media's shortcomings. Media attention increased the challenges of maintaining discipline and unity by its readiness to present protest as the source of disorder and by its positioning of King as the movement's one great leader.

The death of Jimmie Lee Jackson, the attack on the Edmund Pettus Bridge, and ultimately the fury stirred by the Tuesday Turnaround, crystalized the resentments that had been incipient within the movement from the moment in 1956 when King was catapulted onto the national stage at the same time as the established NAACP was reeling from the blows of massive resistance. By 1965, the NAACP's conviction that King had siphoned away the support (and particularly the money and kudos) that Roy Wilkins believed was rightly the NAACP's had been supplemented by SNCC's critique that the SCLC was a "hit-and-run" organization that exploited local campaigns to promote itself nationally and that King had become more anxious to cultivate his White House alliance than to honor his local commitments. Neither charge was entirely baseless, but nor was either accusation fair or really true. Such raw feelings made unity increasingly fragile.

It is ironic that the nonviolence that Black Power advocates would shortly reject was the pure philosophical act of witness that was actually more evident in the sit-ins and Freedom Rides in which King was a peripheral player than in the mass protest campaigns for which he is famed. Had Sheriff Clark or Governor Wallace shown remorse when confronted by nonviolent protesters, Martin Luther King would have been astonished. He might have welcomed the miracle but his experiences had led him to conclude that nonviolence's strength lay in its vital denial of legitimacy, that veil of reassuring hypocrisy beneath which the majority of whites in a racist society were happy to live their lives. To the extent that the Selma campaign rent that veil asunder, it was a crowning triumph. But it was not solely nor enduringly so. King had warned in his "Letter from Birmingham Jail" that a bigger obstacle to justice than the brutal Klansman was the moderate white of ostensible good will.

In the wake of Freedom Summer especially, SNCC was poised to abandon efforts to elicit better white behavior through greater African American sacrifices. In their view, Selma proved that the liberals from the president down reacted to disorder and the threat of disorder—and gave as little as they could. Legislation worked not to give African Americans rights (they had those already) but to restore the legitimacy of a system that still did not wish to share power. To the extent that Selma was a campaign that used nonviolence to court white allies, it represented for SNCC militants the wrong path, and in Lowndes County, and in Mississippi the next summer, they would popularize a different course focused on African Americans and aimed explicitly at Black Power. Thus, in Selma, nonviolence was simultaneously crowned and dethroned.

Notes

1. Peter J. Ling, *Martin Luther King* (New York: Routledge, 2015), 180.

2. Colaiaco, "Martin Luther King, Jr., and the Paradox of Nonviolent Direct Action," *Phylon* 47 (1986): 16–28. There is a rich literature on nonviolence that stresses the tension between moral persuasion and coercion: for example Lakshmi K. Bharadwaj, "Principled versus Pragmatic Nonviolence," *Peace Review* 10.1 (1998): 79–81; John J. Ansbro, *Martin Luther King, Jr.: Nonviolent Strategies and Tactics for Social Change* (Maryknoll, NY: Orbis, 1984); Kurt Schock, "Nonviolent Action and its Misconceptions: Insights for Social Scientists," *PS, Political Science and Politics* 36 (2003): 705–12; and of course Gene Sharp's three volumes, *The Politics of Nonviolent Action* (Boston: Porter Sargent, 1973). On the other hand, Greg Moses, *Revolution of Conscience: Martin Luther King, Jr. and the Philosophy of Nonviolence* (New York: Guildford Press, 1997); James P. Hanigan, *Martin Luther King, Jr. and the Foundations of Nonviolence* (Lanham, MD: University Press of America, 1984) stress King's philosophical devotion to nonviolence as a way of life throughout his career.

3. Clayborne Carson et al., eds., *The Papers of Martin Luther King Jr. Volume V: Threshold of a New Decade*, (Berkeley: University of California Press, 2005), 124.

4. See for example his sermon "The American Dream" (delivered July 4, 1965) in Clayborne Carson and Peter Halloran, eds., *A Knock at Midnight: The Great Sermons of Martin Luther King, Jr.* (London: Little, Brown, 1998), 96–97.

5. Martin Luther King, *Why We Can't Wait* (New York: New American Library, 1964).

6. For the relationship between nonviolence and self-defense in the civil rights movement, Timothy B. Tyson, *Radio Free Dixie: Robert F. Williams and the Roots of Black Power* (Chapel Hill: University of North Carolina Press, 1999); Jenny Louise Walker, "Black violence and nonviolence in the civil rights and black power eras," PhD diss., University of Newcastle upon Tyne, 2000; Jenny Walker, "A Media-Made Movement?: Black Violence and Nonviolence in the Historiography of the Civil Rights Movement," in *Media, Culture and the Modern African American Freedom Struggle*, ed. Brian Ward, (Gainesville: University Press of Florida, 2001); Lance Hill, *The Deacons for Defense: Armed Resistance and the Civil Rights Movement* (Chapel Hill: University of North Carolina Press, 2004); Christopher Strain, *Pure Fire: Self-Defense as Activism in the Civil Rights Era* (Athens: University of Georgia Press, 2005); Simon Wendt, *The Spirit and the Shotgun: Armed Resistance and the Struggle for Civil Rights* (Gainesville: University Press of Florida, 2007); Akinyele Omowale Umoja, *We Will Shoot Back: Armed Resistance in the Mississippi Freedom Movement* (New York: New York University Press, 2013); Charles E. Cobb, *This Nonviolent Stuff'll Get You Killed: How Guns Made the Civil Rights Movement Possible* (Durham: Duke University Press, 2014).

7. "Letter from Birmingham Jail" (original text) in *The Autobiography of Martin Luther King*, ed. Clayborne Carson (New York: Warner Books, 1998), 188–204.

8. King, *Why We Can't Wait*, 21.

9. David J. Garrow, *Bearing the Cross: Martin Luther King and the Southern Christian Leadership Conference* (London: Jonathan Cape 1988), 378–79; Charles Fager, *Selma 1965* (New York: Scribner's, 1974), 6–7; Adam Fairclough, *To Redeem the Soul of America: The*

Southern Christian Leadership Conference and Martin Luther King (Athens: University of Georgia Press, 1987), 231.

10. Gene Roberts and Hank Klibanoff, *The Race Beat: The Press, the Civil Rights Struggle, and the Awakening of a Nation*, (New York: Vintage, 2007), 380; Herbers, "Woman Punches Alabama Sheriff," *New York Times*, January 26, 1965, 1; Aniko Bodroghkozy, *Equal Time: Television and the Civil Rights Movement* (Urbana: University of Illinois Press, 2013), 120–21.

11. "Negro Woman Strikes Selma Sheriff in Face: Attack Occurs at Start of Second Week of All-Out Voter Registration Campaign," *Los Angeles Times*, January 26, 1965, 3.

12. Taylor Branch, *At Canaan's Edge: America in the King Years, 1965–1968* (New York: Simon and Schuster, 2006), 64.

13. Interview with James Bevel, conducted by Blackside, Inc. on November 13, 1985, for *Eyes on the Prize: America's Civil Rights Years (1954–1965)*. Washington University Libraries, Film and Media Archive, Henry Hampton Collection, at http://repository.wustl.edu/concern/videos/2n49t3322 (consulted March 21, 2017).

14. Stephen Oates, *Let the Trumpet Sound: A life of Martin Luther King* (New York: HarperCollins, 1994), 336–37; Bodroghkozy, *Equal Time*, 122.

15. Bruce Watson, *Freedom Summer: The Savage Season of 1964 that Made Mississippi Burn and Made America a Democracy* (New York: Penguin Books, 2014).

16. The divergent assessment of President Johnson is evident in studies of SNCC's emerging radicals and the older established NAACP leadership; see Peniel E. Joseph, *Stokely: A Life* (New York: Basic Civitas, 2014); Yvonne Ryan, *Roy Wilkins: The Quiet Revolutionary and the NAACP* (Lexington: University Press of Kentucky, 2013).

17. David J. Garrow, *Protest at Selma: Martin Luther King Jr. and the Voting Rights Act of 1965* (Kindle Edition, Open Media 2015) Locations 1164–65; 1188–84.

18. Garrow, *Bearing the Cross*, 384; Ling, *Martin Luther King*, 188–89.

19. Fairclough, *To Redeem the Soul of America*, 234; Roy Reed, "165 Selma Negro Youths Taken on Forced March," *New York Times*, February 11, 1965, 1.

20. Bodroghkozy, *Equal Time*, 122.

21. Garrow, *Bearing the Cross*, 387–88.

22. "2/10/65 Wednesday Night at the Torch Motel," notes in Student Nonviolent Coordinating Committee Papers, 7. Ling, *Martin Luther King*, 192.

23. King was not the only key player in the Selma campaign. Others included federal judge Frank Johnson, see Jack Bass, *Taming the Storm: The Life and Times of Judge Frank M. Johnson, Jr., and the South's Fight Over Civil Rights* (New York: Doubleday 1993); Alabama Governor George Wallace, see Dan T. Carter, *The Politics of Rage: George Wallace, the Origins of the New Conservatism, and the Transformation of American Politics* (New York: Simon and Schuster 1995); Justice Department officials like Nicholas Katzenbach, see his memoir *Some of It Was Fun: Working with RFK and LBJ* (New York: Norton, 2008); and LeRoy Collins, see Bertram Levine, *Resolving Racial Conflict: The Community Relations Service and Civil Rights, 1964–1989* (Columbia: University of Missouri Press, 2005). For a summary of LBJ's evolving position on the Voting Rights Act, see Nick Kotz, *Judgment Days: Lyndon Baines Johnson, Martin Luther King, Jr., and the Laws that Changed America* (Boston: Houghton Mifflin, 2005) and Sylvia Ellis, *Freedom's*

Pragmatist: Lyndon Johnson and Civil Rights (Gainesville: University Press of Florida, 2013).

24. J. Mills Thornton III, *Dividing Lines: Municipal Politics and the Struggle for Civil Rights in Montgomery, Birmingham, and Selma* (Tuscaloosa: University of Alabama Press, 2002), 486.

25. Interview with James Bevel, conducted by Blackside, Inc. on November 13, 1985, for *Eyes on the Prize: America's Civil Rights Years (1954-1965)*. Washington University Libraries, Film and Media Archive, Henry Hampton Collection, at http://repository.wustl.edu/concern/videos/2n49t3322 (consulted March 21, 2017).

26. Ibid.

27. Ling, *Martin Luther King*, 195; Cobb, *This Nonviolent Stuff'll Get You Killed*, 182; Hasan Kwame Jeffries, *Bloody Lowndes: Civil Rights and Black Power in the Alabama Black Belt* (New York: New York University Press, 2010); see also Simon Wendt, "God, Gandhi, and Guns: The African American Freedom Struggle in Tuscaloosa, 1964-65," *Journal of African American History* 89 (2004): 35-56.

28. Ling, *Martin Luther King*, 196; Bodroghkozy, *Equal Time*, 115-16.

29. Garrow, *Protest at Selma*, chap. 3 covers the reaction to Bloody Sunday.

30. For King's reluctant admission, see his response to Judge Johnson's questions in his testimony in Williams v. Wallace C.A. #2181-N, M D. Ala., 1965; 240 F. Supp. 100, 25-110 on March 1, 1965. Ling, *Martin Luther King*, 198-200; Garrow, *Bearing the Cross*, 404.

31. Robert Dallek, *Flawed Giant: Lyndon Johnson and His Times, 1961-1973* (New York: Oxford University Press, 1998), 218-19.

32. Joseph, *Stokely*, 83.

33. Garrow, *Bearing the Cross*, 409.

34. Ling, *Martin Luther King*, 205-6.

35. Thornton, *Dividing Lines*, 489-92.

36. Garrow, *Protest at Selma*, 111; William M. Kunstler, *Deep in My Heart* (New York: William Morrow, 1966), 354-55; Ling, *Martin Luther King*, 203.

4

"The Meat in the Coconut"

Lyndon Johnson and the Voting Rights Act of 1965

MARK MCLAY

Upon its release in December 2014, Ava DuVernay's film *Selma* quickly generated a storm of controversy over the movie's portrayal of President Lyndon B. Johnson and his role during the civil rights struggle. To many, including the director herself, the criticism that the film received for its depiction of the thirty-seventh president was misguided. As DuVernay noted, the film was not about Lyndon Johnson, but rather about Dr. Martin Luther King Jr., civil rights activists, and local residents who together bravely highlighted the racial injustices of Selma, Alabama, and subsequently awakened the conscience of a nation.[1] Indeed, there is a marked irony that a film that celebrates the heroic endeavors of African Americans as they strove to overcome white-imposed segregation, became caught up in a dispute over its depiction of a powerful white man.

With that being said, it is also true that *Selma* presents an inaccurate and misleading portrayal of LBJ's role in the effort to secure the Voting Rights Act of 1965. President Johnson, played by actor Tom Wilkinson, is presented as an almost sinister foe of voting rights until events in Selma force his hand. A man who, so angered at the Selma protest, would stoop to the level of FBI Director J. Edgar Hoover—a clear enemy of the civil rights movement—and sanction an attempt to ruin King's marriage.[2] While it is important to remember that *Selma* is a work of fiction, not a documentary, artistic license does not preclude criticism for this blatant misrepresentation. Films that seek to recapture a moment in history, may distort the sequence of historical events, but should at least seek to present essential truths about the era and the figures whom they are depicting. Regrettably, *Selma*'s representation of Johnson is largely false.

Lyndon Johnson was, and arguably remains, the greatest ally that African Americans have had in the White House. It is also true, however, that Johnson has faced depressingly little competition among his peers for this prize. Admittedly, the Texan sometimes talked about black Americans using racist language, but nevertheless, during his time in residence at 1600 Pennsylvania Avenue, LBJ was instrumental in the passage of the Civil Rights Act of 1964, the Voting Rights Act of 1965, the Civil Rights Act of 1968, and a host of "Great Society" legislation that, he hoped, would go some way to alleviating the poverty and ghetto conditions that afflicted many black communities across America. LBJ was also one of the only modern U.S. presidents to explicitly tie African American struggles to the legacy of slavery.[3] Weighing up these achievements and sentiments, many black leaders in the 1960s were overwhelmingly positive about Johnson's record. Indeed, one recent study showed that of thirty-four editorials in five major African American owned newspapers that discussed Johnson's civil rights record, every single one was positive.[4]

While acknowledging that King and those involved in the civil rights movement were the primary actors in driving racial progress, there is broad agreement among historians that the struggle for the Voting Rights Act represents Johnson's finest hour and the zenith of his presidency.[5] In addition to the effective voting legislation that LBJ would sign into law, Johnson also delivered the most eloquent and powerful speech of his presidency as he sought to capitalize on events in Selma and push Congress to decisive action on guaranteeing African Americans the franchise. For Johnson, voting rights was *the* greatest weapon for black Americans. "The right to vote is the meat in the coconut," he explained to one aide, "They [African Americans] can get the rest themselves if they've got this—and can get it on their own terms, not as a gift from the white man."[6]

The Voting Rights Act was not a gift from the white man either. It was earned by those who had been part of the decades long civil rights movement. Without their sacrifice, politicians in Washington would likely have continued to ignore the problem of southern segregation as the majority of elected leaders had done for decades. With regards to the Voting Rights Act specifically, those who took part in the protest at Selma during the early months of 1965 undoubtedly sped up the timetable of legislation. As this article will outline, however, they had the benefit of a president who largely shared their goals.

The Texan Scalawag

On October 9, 1964, LBJ made a seemingly innocuous appearance at a fundraising event hosted by the local Democratic party in downtown New Orleans. Holding a comfortable lead in the national presidential election polls, the Big Easy was an apt venue for the Johnson campaign as it made inexorable progress toward a thumping November victory. Yet, in the Deep South, nothing was easy for LBJ in 1964. Polls also showed that the first avowedly Southern president since Woodrow Wilson was lagging in his native region.[7] Johnson's high-profile role in passing and signing the Civil Rights Act earlier in the year had earned him the enmity of large swathes of the white South. Moreover, his Republican opponent, Senator Barry Goldwater (R-AZ), was drawing support across the South following his "nay" vote on the civil rights bill. As such, the event that Johnson was attending may have been a Democratic party fundraiser, but the president—raised in neighboring Texas—was far from guaranteed a warm welcome in Louisiana that October evening.

With respect to race, it had been a long and meandering road to this point for Lyndon Johnson. Growing up in the Texas Hill Country, not far from the state capitol in Austin, Johnson rarely encountered African Americans. He later recalled to biographer Doris Kearns Goodwin that "I never had any bigotry in me. My daddy wouldn't let me. He was a strong anti-Klansman. . . . They threatened to kill him several times."[8] Furthermore, whenever discussing his desire to advance minority rights, Johnson almost always harked back to when, as a young man, he spent a year in Cotulla, Texas teaching poor Mexican American children. Of the experience, Johnson, in a speech made during the height of the struggle for the Voting Rights Act, said, "They knew even in their youth the pain of prejudice. They never seemed to know why people disliked them. But they knew it was so, because I saw it in their eyes. I often walked home late in the afternoon, after the classes were finished, wishing there was more that I could do."[9]

While LBJ was often prone to exaggeration and sentimentality when speaking of his youth, his early career in politics would seem to bear out his assertion that he lacked the racial bigotry that was endemic in the South at that time. In 1935, Franklin Roosevelt's administration appointed him to run the National Youth Administration (NYA) in Texas. The NYA, which was supposed to provide work and education for all Americans between sixteen and twenty-five, often functioned—particularly in the South—as yet another way to provide white Americans with preferential treatment. Johnson stood out as the exception in this regard, as Kearns Goodwin explains:

> "In the middle thirties we didn't know Lyndon Johnson from Adam," recounted a venerable and distinguished Negro leader, describing the period when Johnson had directed the NYA in Texas. "We began to get word up here that there was one NYA director who wasn't like the others. He was looking after Negroes and poor folks and most NYA people weren't doing that."[10]

While it is possible to view Johnson's later embrace of civil rights in the mid-1950s as a political calculation to appeal to a national electorate, Johnson's NYA record and his experience in Cotulla suggest that there was more to his commitment than mere cynicism.

Johnson, however, was no wide-eyed savior who was willing to sacrifice his political career to make a stand for racial justice. Between 1937 and 1956, when Johnson served first as a congressman before becoming senator in 1949, LBJ voted against every single civil rights bill—including those that sought to categorize lynching as a federal crime. Johnson, who abhorred impractical idealism, later justified this stance by pointing out—almost certainly correctly—that, as a member of the Texas delegation and the wider Southern bloc, he would have quickly been voted out of office if he had "come out" for civil rights at that time. Or, as Johnson put it, "That'd be nonsense, like swimming one-half the way across a lake or going to Dallas with one-half a tank of gas left, so you'd be left floating in the water or stranded on the road."[11] Nevertheless, had Johnson died from the near-fatal heart attack that struck him in 1955, there would have been few civil rights advocates that would have mourned his passing.

Returning from his sick bed, Johnson's subsequent career showed a strong commitment to racial justice, particularly when it came to dismantling the Jim Crow laws in his native South. Two years after the Supreme Court's landmark *Brown v Board of Education of Topeka, Kansas* decision in 1954 that outlawed segregation in education, most southerners in Congress had signed up to the Southern Manifesto of 1956—a document that reaffirmed Dixie's opposition to racial integration in public places. Johnson was one of only four Southern Senate Democrats not to affix his name to the manifesto. Then, in 1957 and in 1960, LBJ—in his role as Senate majority leader, and also with an eye on running for president in the upcoming election—shepherded the first two civil rights bills to pass Congress since Reconstruction. The legislation was largely symbolic—Johnson received much criticism for gutting those bills of effective mechanisms of enforcement so that they would pass without intense Southern filibustering—but nevertheless it was another sign of how LBJ would behave if he achieved national office. And in his role as vice president to John F. Kennedy, Johnson showed further signs that he was a firm advocate of civil rights. During a Memorial Day speech at Gettysburg on May 30, 1963, Johnson, reflecting on the slavery that had been ended by the civil war, declared: "One hundred years later, the Negro remains in bondage to the color of his skin." He then signaled his agreement with Dr. King's recent "Letter from Birmingham Jail," in which King had made it clear that African Americans were no longer willing to be patient in their pursuit of equality under the law.[12]

The assassination of Kennedy on November 22, 1963, thrust Johnson into a position that would make clear his sincere desire to see the main goals of the civil rights movement achieved. Skillfully making the fallen president a martyr for civil rights—despite Kennedy's own questionable commitment to the cause—Johnson urged Congress to pass his predecessor's stalled civil rights bill as a fitting tribute to JFK. The new president then, in combination with civil rights leaders and congressional supporters, mobilized effectively to ensure passage of the landmark Civil Rights Act of 1964 that, among other examples of progress, wiped away the "white" and "colored" signs from southern life. Before the summer was out, Johnson had also begun the War on Poverty, which he envisaged would function in a similar fashion to the NYA and provide jobs and training to Americans of all races. He thus pursued the dual goals of civil rights leaders who had marched on Washington the previous year for freedom *and* jobs.

The president, however, blotted his copybook with many civil rights activists during the struggle between two dueling Mississippi delegations at the Democratic National Convention in August 1964. Having been illegally barred from the regular lily-white Mississippi Democratic party, civil rights activists had elected their own multiracial Mississippi Freedom Democratic Party (MFDP) delegates and demanded to be seated ahead of the regulars. While sympathetic to their cause, Johnson was more concerned with keeping the party as united as possible and was convinced that if he agreed to MFDP demands, it would trigger a walk out from large sections of the Southern delegations.[13] Ultimately, a compromise was reached that gave the MFDP two delegates-at-large with full voting rights, while the Mississippi regulars were seated in full.

In protest, despite Martin Luther King's own urgings to accept the compromise, many MFDP activists left the New Jersey convention disillusioned with the Democratic party and the entire political process. At the same time, many in the all-white Mississippi delegation, angered at any compromise with the MFDP, also bolted the convention. Moreover, many Southerners were infuriated by Johnson's announcement that Hubert Humphrey was his pick for vice president. Humphrey, after all, remained a bête noire for segregationists following his electrifying call for the Democratic party to fully embrace civil rights back during the 1948 convention.[14] As such, while the Democratic convention showed the limits of Johnson's willingness to accede to the demands of activists when they directly challenged his political interests, he had demonstrated in his selection of Humphrey and through his role during the struggle for the Civil Rights Act that he was a pragmatic ally of racial progress.

Johnson, then, was likely viewed by many present in the Jung Hotel that October night in Louisiana, as a Texan scalawag—a Southerner gone rogue. Some of the president's advisers had cautioned him to avoid the issue of civil rights during the speech, and if he had to mention it, then he should refer to "constitutional rights" instead.[15] Johnson, speaking in pronounced Southern tones, began by lavishing praise on the two senators and four congressmen—all Democrats—with whom he shared the stage; all six had voted against the Civil Rights Act. After nearly thirty minutes of a typical stump speech, Johnson discarded his notes and spoke to his audience directly about civil rights. Of the act itself, LBJ declared "I signed it, and I am going to enforce it, and I am going to observe it, and I think any man that is worthy of the high office of President is going to do the same thing."[16]

He warned his audience that the South had been held back by politicians who had campaigned on racial bigotry rather on economic justice. To illustrate the point, Johnson told one of his favorite anecdotes about an old Texas senator, Joseph Weldon Bailey, who had been born in Mississippi. Bailey, nearing retirement, and in conversation with the former

Speaker of the House, Sam Rayburn (D-TX), wistfully mused on what it would be like to go back to Mississippi for one more speech. In Johnson's telling that night, he never mentioned Bailey's name or that the old senator came from Mississippi. Instead, the anecdote was to serve as a lesson for the whole South:

> [Bailey] was talking about the economy and what a great future we could have in the South, if we could just meet our economic problems, if we could just take a look at the resources of the South and develop them. And he said, "Sammy, I wish I felt a little better. . . . I would like to go back down there and make them one more Democratic speech. I just feel like I have one in me. The poor old State, they haven't heard a Democratic speech in 30 years. All they ever hear at election time is 'Negro, Negro, Negro!'"

Johnson ended his remarks on race by hinting that his civil rights agenda was not yet complete without further economic progress for minorities, declaring that he would seek "equal opportunity for all, special privileges for none."[17] LBJ, in contrast to what *Selma* suggests, did not need to tread a redemptive path on racial progress in 1965; the giant Texan was already trying to pave the way for his fellow Southerners to follow him.

Selma and the Voting Rights Act

After the polls closed on November 3, 1964, Johnson did not win Louisiana, nor did he win the Deep South, but he won just about everywhere else. Moreover, the Democrats won sweeping victories in congressional races—freeing the president from the normal confines of the unofficial "conservative coalition" between northern Republicans and southern Democrats that often blocked liberal legislation from reaching the president's desk. Johnson had his mandate, and he intended to use it to build the Great Society.

While voting rights were part of LBJ's larger vision, he believed that he should get two hugely consequential bills—Medicare and federal aid to education—passed first, before moving onto another contentious civil rights battle. As such, Johnson envisaged proposing voting rights legislation toward the end of 1965, or the beginning of 1966.[18] Unsurprisingly, civil rights leaders, hoping to build on the momentum generated by the passage of the Civil Rights Act, and also seeking recompense for the eye-watering 94 percent of black votes that LBJ had received, held other ideas.[19] The protest at Selma would ultimately throw LBJ's timetable out of the window, ensure a muscular voting rights act, and push Johnson into making one of the most important speeches in American history.

In the wake of his victory, Johnson quickly set the ball rolling on voting rights. In November, he charged Attorney General Nicholas Katzenbach with preparing the "toughest voting rights act you can devise."[20] Always sensitive to how Congress would react, LBJ also instructed Katzenbach to keep Republican Senate Minority Leader Everett Dirksen (R-IL) informed throughout the process—a decision that later paid dividends when Dirksen jointly proposed voting rights legislation with his Democratic opposite number in a show of bipartisan unity.[21] While Johnson was undoubtedly motivated to push voting rights for moral reasons, he also would not have failed to notice that African American voters had provided his winning margins in "Rim South" states, such as Arkansas, Florida, Tennessee, and Virginia—an outcome of which Martin Luther King was savvy enough to remind LBJ during one of their many discussions in the months after the election.[22]

The relationship between LBJ and MLK has featured prominently in the historiography of the Voting Rights Act—as it does in *Selma*. While accounts vary about how harmonious the relationship was, most scholars agree that Johnson and King were skilled political operators who, while harboring suspicions of the other, ultimately enjoyed a healthy dose of mutual respect.[23] From Johnson's perspective, King's belief in nonviolence was eminently preferable to alternative forms of black protest, but LBJ was keen to not appear too close to the civil rights leader, for fear that it alienate white southern voters and also scare southern Democrats from working with him on any of his other Great Society legislation. As such, in July 1964, Johnson had upbraided his press secretary, George Reedy, for telling reporters that LBJ was continuously in touch with Dr. King.[24] According to civil rights historian Taylor Branch, "[Johnson] was intensely personal but unpredictable—treating King variously to a Texas bear hug of shared dreams or a towering, wounded snit."[25] Such a description, however, could probably be applied to every single person who ever had a relationship with LBJ.[26] While their understanding would later shatter on the rocks of the Vietnam War, Johnson and King would work closely—and successfully—in pursuit of voting rights.

Following his electoral landslide, Johnson placed a call to King two days after the election to praise the "wisdom" of African Americans in voting overwhelmingly for the Democrats and to indirectly thank the civil rights leader for his support. In addition, LBJ stressed his desire for King to help make the War on Poverty a success for African Americans. There was no mention of voting rights, even though King had already announced his plans to lead a campaign on the issue.[27] LBJ, as per usual, chose to play his cards close to his chest until it was absolutely necessary to show his hand.

Voting rights did come up, however, when Martin Luther King and his wife, Coretta, visited the White House on December 18 following King's appearance in Oslo to accept the Nobel Peace Prize. Of the meeting, King later recalled that, after outlining voting rights abuses to Johnson, the president replied, "Martin, you're right about that. I'm going to do it eventually, but I can't get a voting rights bill through in this session of Congress."[28] In *Selma*, this scene is depicted as confrontational and sees Johnson giving King the cold shoulder—"this voting thing will just have to wait"—despite the latter's protestations that people were being murdered across the South.[29] Yet, according to Andrew Young, a young aide of King's who was later appointed ambassador to the United Nations, the meeting "was not very tense at all. We were very much welcomed by President Johnson. He and Martin never had that kind of confrontation."[30]

Nevertheless, the meeting also illustrated that Johnson and King were adhering to different timetables. Johnson, who had witnessed conservatives block federal intervention in health care and education for three decades, was acutely conscious of the small window available to pass large-scale reform on those two issues. Meanwhile, King must have sensed the urgency to maintain the momentum garnered from that year's Civil Rights Act. Shortly after the meeting, King departed to join forces with the Student Nonviolent Coordinating Committee (SNCC) and their effort to highlight voting rights abuses in Selma.

On January 15—only eleven days after Johnson had called for Congress to "eliminate every remaining obstacle to the right and the opportunity to vote" during his State of the Union address—the two men spoke again, this time on the telephone. During the conversation, LBJ advised that Katzenbach was still working out the details on voting rights, before imparting to King some unsolicited advice for how to generate the public's support behind voting rights legislation:

If you can find the worst condition that you run into in Alabama, Mississippi, or Louisiana, or South Carolina where—well, I think one of the worst I ever heard of is the president of the school at Tuskegee [Institute], or the head of the Government Department there, or something, being denied the right to cast a vote, and if you just take that one illustration and get it on radio, and get it on television, and get it on ... in the pulpits, and get it in the meetings, get it every place you can, pretty soon the fellow that didn't do anything but follow—drive a tractor, he'll say, "Well, that's not right, that's not fair."[31]

Joseph A. Califano Jr., a key Johnson legislative aide, who was upset at the portrayal of his former boss in *Selma*, argues that this conversation shows that the protest at Selma was actually LBJ's idea.[32] Such an assertion is patently false—the Selma protest was already under way. Moreover, King—a key figure in the civil rights movement for almost ten years—did not need Lyndon Johnson to give him lessons in how to successfully arouse the American conscience with nonviolent protest. The conversation does, however, once again, demonstrate both Johnson's commitment to voting rights and also his acute understanding of why the civil rights movement was so successful.

As events in Selma escalated in early February, Johnson appears to have quickly shifted his own timetable after realizing that voting rights would not wait until late 1965. On February 2, King was locked up in a Selma jail having been arrested by officers under the command of Jim Clark, whom historian Mark Updegrove describes as "a villainous sheriff of almost cartoon-like proportions."[33] Two days later, Johnson appeared before the media to condemn the behavior of the Selma authorities in restricting African American voter registration. Instinctively appealing for consensus on the issue, the president urged that "all Americans should be indignant when one American is denied the right to vote."[34]

On February 9, Martin Luther King, having been released from jail, arrived in Washington to meet with Attorney General Katzenbach and Vice President Hubert Humphrey to discuss the specifics of voting rights legislation. During the visit, LBJ and King had a short, clandestine meeting, with the latter emerging to tell the press that he was confident Johnson would act very soon on voting rights. Less than a month later, King was again at the White House, this time in a ninety-minute consultation with the president over the specifics of voting rights legislation.[35] These interactions amply illustrate the fruitful nature of their relationship during this fraught period.

Still, as the violence in Selma escalated during February, the president faced increasing calls from civil rights leaders and sympathetic voices in Congress to present a voting rights bill immediately. On February 18, black activist and military veteran, Jimmie Lee Jackson was murdered by an Alabama state trooper in nearby Marion. In the wake of his slaying, King and other activists proposed a march from Selma to the state capitol Montgomery to give more attention to the violence and denial of voting rights taking place in the Yellowhammer State. The end result was Bloody Sunday, when the marchers (with King absent for safety reasons) were met by state troopers and Sheriff Clark's horse-mounted deputies, who violently drove the protestors back across the Edmund Pettus Bridge. Amelia Boynton, a protestor who was present on the march, succinctly and horrifyingly sums up the carnage of the events of March 7: "The horses . . . were more humane than the troopers; they stepped over the fallen victims."[36]

On March 9, President Johnson attempted to regain control of the situation, appearing before the press to condemn the brutality and urge the passage of a voting rights act, but events were now hurtling forward at a furious speed.[37] On the same day, King led another defiant march across the Edmund Pettus Bridge, before turning back to avoid further violence. Then, in the evening, the white Unitarian minister James Reeb was murdered in Selma by residents who took exception to his support for the African American cause. The president would then face justifiable criticism for calling Reeb's family having not extended the same courtesy to Jimmie Lee Jackson's relatives. Moreover, Johnson's attempts to expedite voting rights legislation in response were complicated by the fact that Katzenbach still had not provided the president with a bill. As Hugh Davis Graham notes, "The Selma crisis accelerated the Justice Department's already hurried efforts to draft a bill radical enough to be quickly effective, yet still reasonably respectful of the long traditions of due process and federalism that had made all its predecessors both passable and yet largely ineffective."[38]

LBJ was also now under increasing pressure to send federal troops into Alabama to protect the marchers, especially when it became clear that activists in Selma were determined to successfully complete the long march to Montgomery that had been stopped so abruptly on Bloody Sunday. Alabama's governor, George Wallace, who had famously declared "segregation now, segregation tomorrow, segregation forever" during his 1963 inaugural address, was proving as unhelpful in preserving the peace as would be expected. Wallace was unwilling to protect the marchers with his own troops and against asking for federal help, leaving Johnson in a bind. The president demurred on dispatching the National Guard uninvited to protect the swelling numbers of activists for fear that it would "look like Reconstruction all over again. I will lose every moderate, not just in Alabama but all over the South." Johnson argued convincingly that such a move "will make a martyr of Wallace. And that's not going to help the Negroes."[39] As historian Sylvia Ellis notes, Johnson was also wary of disrupting the progress being made in implementing the Civil Rights Act across the South.[40] It was therefore much to LBJ's relief, when, on March 12, Wallace sent him a telegram requesting an urgent meeting at the White House to discuss the situation. Unwittingly, Wallace had just secured a starring role in one of American history's great "fly on the wall" moments.

When Wallace—a former middleweight boxer—arrived at the White House the following day, he was treated to the full fifteen rounds from his president. Ushering the governor into the Oval Office, Johnson sat him down in a low-sprung chair that meant LBJ, perched in his favorite rocking chair, towered over the man he considered "a runty little bastard."[41] Johnson then let his visitor say his piece. Predictably, Wallace protested that there was no culture of brutality in his state—the trouble was merely a result of outside agitators—and, as governor, he did not have the power to force local registrars to allow black Alabamans to register to vote. After listening like an unimpressed school teacher who had heard all of the excuses for his students' failure to submit their homework, the president pounced: "Don't you shit me about your persuasive power, George. Why, just this morning I was watching you on television. . . . you were so damn persuasive that I had to turn off the set before you had me changing my mind."[42] The tone for the rest of the meeting was set.

After two hours, President Johnson got to the crux of the matter, asking Wallace, "Why are you off on this black thing?"[43] And he finished by appealing to the governor's sense of history: "Now listen, George, don't think about 1968; you think about 1988. You and me, we'll be dead and gone then." Wallace, who was only forty-five years old at the time of the meeting, was probably somewhat perturbed to hear this, but Johnson continued, "Now you've got a lot of poor people down there in Alabama, a lot of ignorant people. You can do a lot for them George. Your president will help you, what do you want left after you die? Do you want a Great . . . Big . . . Marble monument that reads, 'George Wallace—He Built'? . . . Or do you want a little piece of scrawny pine board lying across that harsh, caliche soil, that reads, 'George Wallace—He Hated?'" Wallace left shortly after, memorably telling reporters, "Hell, if I'd stayed in there much longer, he'd have had me coming out for civil rights."[44] Nevertheless, before he departed, Wallace agreed that at some point he would request President Johnson send in the National Guard to protect the peace in Alabama. Attorney General Katzenbach, who was present at the meeting, reflected on Johnson's role: "I have never seen a political performance to compare with it. It was like a violin concert by a virtuoso, with every note perfection."[45]

Two days later, in front of a national television audience of seventy million, LBJ arguably went one better. Appearing before both houses of Congress to address the issue of voting rights and the violence in Selma, Johnson delivered what biographer, Robert Dallek, deems his "greatest speech and one of the most moving and memorable presidential addresses in the country's history."[46] Martin Luther King described it as "an address that will live in history as one of the most passionate pleas for human rights ever made."[47] Furthermore, as the scholar Jorge Chapa points out, while the speech was on one hand an eloquent emotive response to Bloody Sunday, it was on the other hand also substantial because, by now, Johnson was armed with voting rights legislation that he would submit to Congress two days later.[48]

During the speech, entitled "The American Promise," Johnson laid bare the United States' original sin of racism. Placing the violence at Selma in the pantheon of American mythology along with Lexington, Concord, and Appomattox, he made the issue of equal rights for African Americans central to the nation's future progress: "Should we defeat every enemy, should we double our wealth and conquer the stars, and still be unequal to this issue, then we will have failed as a people and as a nation." Preaching an ecumenical message—searching for the consensus that he always sought—Johnson argued that "There is no Negro problem. There is no Southern problem. There is no Northern problem. There is only an American problem."[49]

The line for which the speech is most remembered once again sought to bind Americans in common endeavor: "Because it is not just Negroes, but really it is all of us, who must overcome the crippling legacy of bigotry and injustice. And we shall overcome."[50] By embracing the words of the well-known civil rights anthem, Johnson triggered a variety of responses that suggested consensus would ultimately prove elusive. King supposedly wept while watching on television, one southern governor felt "sick," and Nicholas Katzenbach—sitting in the audience—almost fell off of his chair.[51] Meanwhile, SNCC activist, James Forman, decried that Lyndon Johnson "spoiled a good song that day."[52] Forman's fellow SNCC activist, John Lewis, was less cynical, saying: "I was deeply moved. Lyndon Johnson was no politician that night. He was a man who spoke from his heart. His were the words of a statesman and more; they were the words of a poet."[53]

During the speech, President Johnson, a very egotistical man, was careful to confer primary praise for civil rights progress on the activists who had driven change with their often heroic actions. Far from being the agitators that white racists had denounced, LBJ declared that "The real hero of this struggle is the American Negro. His actions and protests, his courage to risk safety and even to risk his life, have awakened the conscience of this Nation."[54] On the way home from the speech, King called to congratulate, and Johnson reiterated what he had said in the speech, "Thank you, Reverend, but you're the leader who's making it all possible, I'm just following along trying to do what's right."[55] Nonetheless, it was still personally satisfying to Johnson, as positive responses to the speech flooded into the White House over the coming days. The vast majority of mail received indicated that most Americans were solidly in support of voting rights for southern blacks.[56] From that point onward, the momentum behind the voting rights legislation was never seriously in question.

Still, there was the small matter of the third attempted march from Selma to Montgomery that would take place over the five days between March 21 and 25. Yet, with the exception of the horrific Klan-related murder of Viola Liuzzo, a white mother of five from Michigan who had volunteered to help drive participants to Montgomery airport, the march was largely peaceful. President Johnson had eventually been forced to federalize the National Guard when Wallace claimed Alabama could not afford to protect the marchers. Such circumstances meant that, much to Johnson's relief, there was little whiff of Reconstruction in the deployment. At the end of the march, Martin Luther King, speaking from the

Capitol steps in Montgomery, praised Johnson who he acclaimed as: "A president born in the South [who] had the sensitivity to feel the will of the country."[57]

Back in Washington, when small roadblocks appeared in the voting rights bill's path—such as a liberal attempt to go beyond the scope of the original bill to implement a blanket ban on poll taxes—Johnson and King worked in tandem to head off any impasse.[58] LBJ, in a glimpse of the future, briefly sulked over comments King had made with regards to Vietnam, but overall their temporary partnership proved strong.[59] The southern filibuster was meek compared to previous efforts to block civil rights measures, and the eventual bill easily passed both houses of Congress with overwhelming margins. Ultimately, the final legislation, "except for some technical changes," civil rights scholar Steven Lawson argues, "closely resembled the administration's original proposal."[60] In signing the bill on August 6, President Johnson—recalling that African Americans had first arrived in North America in chains—pronounced that "today we strike away the last major shackle of those fierce and ancient bonds. Today the Negro story and the American story fuse and blend."[61]

The Voting Rights Act of 1965 proved an incredibly effective piece of legislation. By the time of the next presidential election, all southern states had black registration far surpassing 50 percent—including Mississippi, which, before the act, only had 6.7 percent of African Americans registered.[62] Lyndon Johnson would not be part of that election, however, as the signing of the Voting Rights Act proved the high-water mark of his presidency. Five days after the ceremony, the Watts area of Los Angeles—a majority black neighborhood—erupted in violence and endured six days of arson and looting, which resulted in thirty-four deaths. Polls quickly showed white Americans turning against further legislative gains for African Americans.

A bereft Johnson oscillated between self-pity and an acute understanding of why Watts—and the hundreds of other riots that would occur during his presidency—had happened. On the one hand, showing his ignorance of history, he recalled southern stereotypes of Reconstruction and worried that "Negroes will end up pissing in the aisles of the Senate."[63] On the other hand, in his more reflective moments, Johnson conceded, "I have moved the Negro from D+ TO C-. He's still nowhere. He knows it. And that's why he's out on the streets. Hell, I'd be there, too."[64] As race riots and an unpopular war exposed stark fissures in the country, the president who dreamed of racial harmony and consensus would leave America divided. The influence of the Voting Rights Act, however, would endure long after LBJ had departed the political scene.

Conclusion

Selma remains an incredibly important film, not least for its bracing depiction of the violence that was perpetrated against Americans who merely wanted to vote. Nevertheless, in rewriting the original script to make Lyndon B. Johnson's role more controversial, Ava DuVernay created a needless sideshow. As historian David Kaiser argues, "There was no shortage of real white villains in the Selma controversy, but LBJ was not one of them."[65] DuVernay, who, for understandable reasons, was not interested in making a "white-savior movie"—Hollywood has previously made enough of those films—did not have to alter LBJ's role to avoid this outcome.[66] For Johnson was not a white savior. He was merely the right president, at the right time, who performed admirably in the struggle for voting rights. During his final press conference as president, he reflected with pride that the Voting Rights Act was the greatest accomplishment of his administration.[67] But for the sacrifices of generations of civil rights activists, it is unimaginable that he would ever have had the chance to sign it.

Notes

1. Ava DuVernay, "The Sounds, Space and Spirit of 'Selma': A Director's Take," *NPR Fresh Air*, January 8, 2015, at http://www.npr.org/2015/01/08/375756377/the-sounds-space-and-spirit-of-selma-a-director-s-take (consulted June 20, 2016).

2. While Johnson was aware of the bugging of King that had originally been sanctioned by Attorney General Robert F. Kennedy, there is no evidence to suggest LBJ made any attempt to sabotage King's affairs. Indeed, as Johnson favored King over other, more radical black leaders, it would have been a counterproductive step for the president.

3. Alvin B. Tillery Jr., "Who disagrees with 'Selma's' portrayal of LBJ? Blacks in the civil rights era," *Washington Post*, January 5, 2015, at https://www.washingtonpost.com/blogs/monkey-cage/wp/2015/01/05/who-disagrees-with-selmas-portrayal-of-lbj-blacks-in-the-civil-rights-era/ (consulted June 20, 2016).

4. Ibid.

5. Kent B. Germany, "African-American Civil Rights," in *A Companion to Lyndon B. Johnson*, ed. Mitchell B. Lerner (Malden, MA: Wiley-Blackwell, 2012), 123.

6. LBJ quoted in Richard N. Goodwin, *Remembering America: A Voice from the Sixties* (Boston: Little, Brown and Co., 1988), 318.

7. President Dwight D. Eisenhower (1953–1961) was born in Texas, but is more associated with Abilene, Kansas.

8. LBJ quoted in Doris Kearns Goodwin, *Lyndon Johnson and the American Dream* (New York: Harper and Row, 1976), 230.

9. LBJ, "Special Message to Congress: The American Promise," March 15, 1965, at http://www.presidency.ucsb.edu/ws/?pid=26805 (consulted June 20, 2016).

10. Kearns Goodwin, *Lyndon Johnson and the American Dream*, 231.

11. LBJ quoted, ibid., 231.

12. LBJ quoted in David M, Shribman, "L.B.J.'s Gettysburg Address," *New York Times*, May 24, 2013, at *LBJ Presidential Library* http://www.lbjlibrary.org/press/lbj-in-the-news/lbjs-gettysburg-address (consulted March 22, 2017).

13. Robert Dallek, *Flawed Giant: Lyndon Johnson and His Times* (New York: Oxford University Press, 1998), 163.

14. Sylvia Ellis, *Freedom's Pragmatist: Lyndon Johnson and Civil Rights* (Gainesville: University Press of Florida, 2013), 186–92.

15. Roman Heleniak, "Lyndon Johnson in New Orleans," *Louisiana History* 21 (Summer 1980): 272.

16. LBJ, "Remarks at Fundraising Dinner in New Orleans," October 9, 1964, at http://www.presidency.ucsb.edu/ws/index.php?pid=26585&st=new+orleans&st1 (consulted June 10, 2016).

17. Ibid.

18. Dallek, *Flawed Giant*, 212; Randall Woods, *LBJ: Architect of American Ambition* (New York: Free Press, 2006), 578.

19. Julian Zelizer, *The Fierce Urgency of Now: Lyndon Johnson, Congress, and the Battle for the Great Society* (New York: Penguin Press, 2015), 202.

20. Jorge Chapa, "Expansion and Contraction in LBJ's Voting Rights Legacy," in *LBJ's Neglected Legacy: How Lyndon Johnson Reshaped Domestic Policy and Government*, ed. Glickman et al. (Austin: University of Texas Press, 2015), 100.

21. Byron Hulsey, *Everett Dirksen and His Presidents: How a Senate Giant Shaped American Politics* (Lawrence: University Press of Kansas), 211–12.

22. Hugh Davis Graham, *The Civil Rights Era: Origins and Development of National Policy, 1960–1972* (New York: Oxford University Press, 1990), 163; Lyndon Johnson and Martin Luther King Jr., Conversation WH6501-04-6736-6737m, January 15, 1965, at https://millercenter.org/the-presidency/secret-white-house-tapes/conversation-martin-luther-king-january-15-1965 (consulted March 22, 2017).

23. The most detailed discussion of the relationship between Johnson and King is Nick Kotz, *Judgment Days: Lyndon Baines Johnson, Martin Luther King Jr., and the Laws That Changed America* (Boston: Houghton Mifflin, 2005).

24. LBJ and George Reedy, Conversation WH6407-04-4155, July 4, 1964, at https://millercenter.org/the-presidency/secret-white-house-tapes/conversation-george-reedy-july-4-1964-0 (consulted March 22, 2017).

25. Taylor Branch, *At Canaan's Edge: America in the King Years, 1965–1968* (New York, Simon and Schuster), 14.

26. John Connally, a long-time Johnson ally, recalled of his friend: "There is no adjective in the dictionary to describe him. He was cruel and kind, generous and greedy, sensitive and insensitive, crafty and naive, ruthless and thoughtful, simple in many ways and yet extremely complex, caring and totally not caring. . . . he knew how to use people in politics in the way nobody else could." John A. Andrew, *Lyndon Johnson and the Great Society* (Chicago: I. R. Dee, 1998), 9.

27. LBJ and Martin Luther King Jr., Conversation WH6411-05-6239, November 5, 1964, at https://millercenter.org/the-presidency/secret-white-house-tapes/conversation-martin-luther-king-november-5-1964 (consulted March 22, 2017).

28. MLK quoted in Irving Bernstein, *Guns or Butter: The Presidency of Lyndon Johnson* (New York: Oxford University Press, 1996), 218.

29. *Selma*, dir. Ava DuVernay (2014).

30. Andrew Young quoted in "'Selma' sets off a controversy amid Oscar buzz," *Washington Post*, December 31, 2014.

31. LBJ Conversation with Martin Luther King Jr., January 15, 1965, at https://millercenter.org/the-presidency/secret-white-house-tapes/conversation-martin-luther-king-january-15-1965 (consulted March 22, 2017).

32. Joseph A. Califano Jr., "The movie 'Selma' has a glaring flaw," *Washington Post*, December 26, 2014.

33. Mark Updegrove, *Indomitable Will: LBJ in the Presidency* (New York: Crown Publishers, 2012), 135.

34. LBJ, "The President's News Conference," February 4, 1965, at http://www.presidency.ucsb.edu/ws/?pid=27196 (consulted June 20, 2016).

35. Kent Germany, "Selma, Martin Luther King Jr., and the Lyndon Johnson Tapes," at http://millercenter.org/presidentialclassroom/exhibits/selma (consulted June 10, 2016), archived at http://web.archive.org/web/20161020161028/http://millercenter.org/presidentialclassroom/exhibits/selma (consulted March 22, 2017).

36. Amelia Boynton quoted in Juan Williams, *Eyes on the Prize: America's Civil Rights Years, 1954–1965* (New York: Viking Press, 1987), 269.

37. LBJ, "Statement by the President on the Situation in Selma, Alabama," March 9, 1965, at http://www.presidency.ucsb.edu/ws/index.php?pid=26802&st=&st1= (consulted June 20, 2016).

38. Graham, *The Civil Rights Era*, 163.

39. Kearns Goodwin, *Lyndon Johnson and the American Dream*, 319.

40. Ellis, *Freedom's Pragmatist*, 199.

41. Joseph A. Califano, *The Triumph and Tragedy of Lyndon Johnson: The White House Years* (New York: Simon and Schuster, 1991), 56.

42. Kearns Goodwin, *Lyndon Johnson and the American Dream*, 323.

43. Branch, *At Canaan's Edge*, 96.

44. Kearns Goodwin, *Lyndon Johnson and the American Dream*, 323.

45. Nicholas deB. Katzenbach, *Some of It Was Fun: Working with RFK and LBJ* (New York: W. W. Norton and Company, 2008), 167.

46. Dallek, *Flawed Giant*, 218.
47. King quoted in Ellis, *Freedom's Pragmatist*, 206.
48. Chapa, "Expansion and Contraction in LBJ's Voting Rights Legacy," 100.
49. LBJ, "Special Message to the Congress: The American Promise," March 15, 1965, at http://www.presidency.ucsb.edu/ws/index.php?pid=26805&st=&stl= (consulted June 20, 2016).
50. Ibid.
51. William E. Leuchtenburg, *The White House Looks South: Franklin D. Roosevelt, Harry S. Truman, and Lyndon B. Johnson* (Baton Rouge: Louisiana State University Press, 2005), 332; Katzenbach, *Some of It Was Fun*, 167.
52. James Forman quoted in Leuchtenburg, *The White House Looks South*, 333.
53. John Lewis quoted, ibid., 328.
54. LBJ, "The American Promise."
55. Kearns Goodwin, *Lyndon Johnson and the American Dream*, 310.
56. Branch, *At Canaan's Edge*, 117.
57. King quoted in Ellis, *Freedom's Pragmatist*, 206.
58. Branch, *At Canaan's Edge*, 254.
59. LBJ and MLK, Conversation WH6507-02-8311-8312-8313, July 7, 1965, at https://millercenter.org/the-presidency/secret-white-house-tapes/conversation-martin-luther-king-july-8-1965-0 (consulted March 22, 2017). The website inaccurately dates this conversation as July 8.
60. Steven Lawson, *Black Ballots: Voting Rights in the South, 1944–1969* (New York: Columbia University Press, 1976), 321.
61. LBJ, "Remarks in the Capitol Rotunda at the Signing of the Voting Rights Act," August 6, 1965, at http://www.presidency.ucsb.edu/ws/index.php?pid=27140&st=&stl= (consulted June 20, 1965).
62. Updegrove, *Indomitable Will*, 144; Ellis, *Freedom's Pragmatist*, 209.
63. LBJ quoted in Kotz, *Judgment Days*, 341.
64. LBJ quoted in James T. Patterson, *The Eve of Destruction: How 1965 Transformed America* (New York: Basic Books, 2012), 186.
65. David Kaiser, "Why You Should Care That *Selma* Gets LBJ Wrong," *Time*, January 9, 2015.
66. Ava DuVernay quoted in Adolph Reed Jr., "The Strange Career of the Voting Rights Act: Selma in Fact and Fiction," *New Labor Forum* 24 (2015): 33.
67. Chapa, "Expansion and Contraction in LBJ's Voting Rights Legacy," 98.

5

Backlash or Adjustment?

The White South Responds to Selma

TONY BADGER

For almost fifty years I have been studying white southerners from Huey Long to North Carolina politicians and tobacco farmers in the 1930s, to those southerners who did not sign the Southern Manifesto, to Louisiana and South Carolina governors as they coped with Massive Resistance and racial protest, to the career of Albert Gore Sr. Much of my approach has been shaped by two comments from the early 1980s. The first was a statement made to the distinguished southern historian Dan T. Carter by the former South Carolina congressman, William Jennings Bryan Dorn, whose comment captured the ambiguity of white southern perceptions of what had happened since 1945 in the South. Of course, Dorn interpreted, we did not really believe what we said back then in the days of Massive Resistance, we said what we had to say to get re-elected and satisfy our constituents. But at the same time, the reflective Dorn also noted that at times, looking back, he could not really believe that he had actually said the apocalyptic statements he had made back in the 1950s.[1]

The second comment was made by John Shelton Reed in an underappreciated essay in the *Virginia Quarterly Review* in 1984. Reed was making a characteristically clear-headed and measured attempt to flesh out what had and had not changed in the South. He catalogued poll data on white attitudes to desegregation and noted the number of elected African American officials, especially in Mississippi, which had in 1981 more elected black officials than any other state in the nation. He summed up his on-the-whole-positive view of white adjustment: "On a day to day basis . . . in places like courthouses and stores and schools, Southern whites seem disposed to treat black Southerners as sort of honorary white folks—and by and large, whatever their private opinions of one another, white Southerners treat each other with courtesy and at least the appearance of good-natured respect."[2]

I have wrestled with two common adaptations of these observations by Dorn and Reed. The first is what I have described as the self-exculpatory model of backlash: the fault for segregationist lawless defiance of civil rights protest and the courts lies with everyone except the white political leaders of the state, particularly irresponsible outside forces and the racism of lower-income whites. The second, notably in Louisiana, Tennessee, North Carolina, and South Carolina, is the self-congratulatory model of adjustment: racial change, white leaders say with satisfaction, was in the end accepted surprisingly peacefully, without the violent confrontations that wracked Mississippi and Alabama.[3] Over the past twenty-five years in various ways, my writing has been raising questions about both those interpretations. Where does the white South of 1965 fit into these two models?

It is possible to produce two compelling but very different narratives from the events of 1965. The first is the final, albeit belated, acceptance by white southerners of inevitable racial changes imposed from below by civil rights protest and from outside by the federal government. The second is the persistent backlash and opposition to what whites saw as these unwarranted changes. First, I'll discuss the positive picture of adjustment.

Selma liberated some white southern moderate politicians. As Hodding Carter III, the battling Mississippi journalist recalled, the civil rights acts and the civil rights movement freed a lot of white people "to quit being closet moderates."[4] White moderate politicians had struggled with the consequences of the civil rights movement. The pincer movement of African American protest and the judicial and legislative response of the federal government dashed the hopes of white moderates that change would be gradual, impelled by economic modernization, that segregation would not be abandoned but slowly softened, and that the timetable of change would be dictated by southern whites. For example, Albert Gore, an archetypal southern moderate, refused to sign the Southern Manifesto and supported both the 1957 and 1960 civil rights acts. In both cases, he withheld judgment on the laws, then stressed that they were voting rights acts, rather than attacks on segregation, and that compromises had been won that enabled him to support the legislation.[5] Gore hoped to go through the same process in 1964. He withheld judgment on the Kennedy proposals in 1963, and in 1964 he clearly hoped there would be compromises, especially on Title VI, that might enable him to support the bill. He acknowledged that more needed to be done in Tennessee and that the federal government "properly has a role in eliminating discrimination." The objectives of the bill were "laudable," but he believed that amendments would be helpful. If they were made, he would be "glad to support it."[6]

The problem was that when President Lyndon B. Johnson worked to secure the passage of the Civil Rights Act in 1957 (and indeed again in 1960), the president's tactics and Gore's needs meshed perfectly. In order to prevent a southern filibuster, which would have killed the bill, Johnson worked to secure concessions from northern and western Democrats to make the bill moderate enough for southern conservatives to keep their powder dry for more threatening legislation in the future. The concessions Johnson won enabled Gore to vote for the bills. But in 1964, unlike 1957 and 1960, the imperative for LBJ was not to compromise, and nothing was done to ease Gore's path.

In 1964, Gore simply was not a factor for President Johnson and Hubert Humphrey, who was leading in the Senate, as they sought to secure enough votes for cloture and break the filibuster by conservative southern senators. Johnson and Humphrey knew that Gore would not be part of the teams of southern senators organized to prolong debates on the Senate floor. But there was no incentive for them to win Gore over. It was the Republicans, and not southern moderates like Gore, that Johnson needed in the summer of 1964. There has been an assumption that Gore would have been a southerner who might have been persuaded "to do a Vandenberg" and move over to support a cloture vote to end the filibuster and to support the act. There is no evidence that Johnson reached out to Gore. Indeed, Johnson made few attempts to win over individual senators that summer. Instead he kept himself meticulously informed about the Mansfield-Humphrey strategy for bringing the bill to the Senate floor but did not involve himself individually with senators, except Republican Minority Leader Everett Dirksen. Stephen Horn, Minority Whip Thomas H. Kuchel's assistant, kept very detailed minutes of the bipartisan daily strategy meetings of the staffers of the Senate leadership. Gore is clearly identified in the "no" camp in vote tallies for possible cloture votes. There is no evidence to suggest that the strategy team thought he could be tempted over to the civil rights side. For Johnson and Humphrey, Gore was largely an irrelevance in the fight for the civil rights bill. If he voted for the bill, so much the better, but if he did not, it would not affect the outcome that they struggled so hard to achieve.[7]

What would Al Gore do? His mail ran overwhelmingly against the legislation. Correspondents spent most time asserting that the sections desegregating public accommodations grossly assaulted rights of private property and would impose great burdens on business. Others, of course, posted dire warnings of communism, black violence, and intermarriage. Unlike 1956, when many correspondents praised his stand against the Southern Manifesto, few encouraged Gore to vote for the 1964 Civil Rights Act.

Gore himself focused on what he saw as the arbitrary power of the attorney general in the act and, particularly on Title VI, which provided for the cutting off of federal funds to state and local programs that discriminated. Gore complained that there were no guidelines, no standards, by which local school boards, for example, could be judged. Instead, power appeared to reside solely with unelected and unaccountable bureaucrats. He feared, for example, that a school district desegregating under court order would still find itself punished by the loss of federal funds if administrators, not the court, deemed its compliance insufficient. He feared that the token school desegregation, which white Tennesseans appeared to accept, would fall foul of zealous bureaucrats and that he would find it even harder to contain white anger. According to Clarence Mitchell from the Leadership Conference on Civil Rights, Gore worried that all the funds for a state would be cut off if some programs in the state were not in compliance. Burke Marshall of the U.S. Department of Justice thought that Gore was simply wrong.

No one felt the need to alleviate Gore's concerns. His amendment to strike Title VI from the bill failed easily. Then on the morning of the final vote, Gore received unanimous consent to introduce a motion to recommit the whole bill to the Senate Judiciary Committee on the grounds that Title VI was so onerous and needed further legal scrutiny. Although the motion was overwhelmingly defeated seventy-four votes to twenty-five, the amendment infuriated Hubert Humphrey, the bill's manager. According to aide John G. Stewart, Humphrey regarded Gore's move as "the highest breach of senatorial ethics." Gore had gone behind the floor leaders' backs the night before to secure unanimous consent without informing Humphrey. Stewart interpreted the scale of Gore's defeat as Senate displeasure at the "rather shoddy way" he had gone about securing the vote. It was difficult to avoid historian Todd S. Purdom's analysis that Gore was "yet again trying to have it both ways" seeking kudos for opposing Title VI, but not blocking in any real way the eventual passage of the bill.[8]

There is little doubt that Gore was aware of the challenge he faced in his own Senate race from a western Tennessee Barry Goldwater supporter and from the disaffection of white supporters in Tennessee. John Seigenthaler believed that Pauline Gore, alerted by brother Whit LaFon in Jackson, was fearful of the political fallout in western Tennessee in the election. His administrative assistant, Bill Allen, would have been cautious as well. In the past, the presence of Estes Kefauver alongside Gore in the Senate had given him a measure of protection. Kefauver was a lightning rod for segregationist criticism. Kefauver was no longer there. Herbert S. Walters, appointed to Kefauver's seat, was a state party war horse who routinely voted with the other southerners against the Civil Rights Act. Conversely, Gore's closest senate friends, Mike Monroney and Ralph Yarborough, voted for the act. In his own state, Gore had seen two young congressmen, Ross Bass and Richard Fulton, vote for it in the House.[9]

With the election out of the way, Gore did not need to be so defensive. He was in a position to act more freely on civil rights. In addition, compliance with the 1964 Civil Rights Act turned out to be largely uncontroversial in Tennessee, and token compliance with school desegregation continued peacefully across the state. At this point, only a small number of African Americans were attending previously white schools. The violence at Selma in March 1965 and the proposals for voting rights legislation were much easier for Gore to support than the 1964 act had been.

Many of Gore's constituents blamed Martin Luther King and the protesters for the violence at Selma and feared that Johnson's voting rights bill in 1965 would create a "watered down replica of the Russian monstrosity." Whites in western Tennessee expressed their disillusionment. The specter of Communism loomed large. "The Communists are our most deadly enemies, our boys died by the 1000s in Korea and now over 400 in South Vietnam so far, why let these boys down by letting these Communist agitators create chaotic conditions as exist in Selma today." A repeated refrain was the double standard applied to whites and to civil rights protesters.

King was a lawbreaker "who violates any law he wishes, according to his conscience, while no one else is allowed to." Welfare mothers loomed large as well. Is it right "for us to be taxed to support the negs to raise bastards. Negro preacher's daughter down here has six bastards. And the US News shows that Washington is full of bastards."[10]

By contrast, Al Gore found President Johnson's address to Congress "inspiring" and from the start indicated that he would support the Voting Rights Act. "Freedom of the ballot box is the very essence of democracy," he proclaimed. It was a relatively easy step for a man who had supported the 1957 Civil Rights Act as a voting rights measure. Gore went further. As someone who had supported anti-poll tax legislation in 1942, he supported Ted Kennedy's efforts to add the abolition of the poll tax in state elections to the bill. Gore received a modicum of support from newspapers and constituents appalled by the vivid televised footage of Bloody Sunday. Young southern historian Bruce Clayton wrote him from Bristol, Tennessee, that the "moral and constitutional issue is clear: we Americans must act if we believe in democracy."[11]

Gore was unmoved by the white backlash that continued in response to the urban riots of 1965–1967. When Johnson called for legislation in 1966 eliminating discrimination in the sale and rental of housing, real estate interests deluged Gore with mail opposing a fair housing bill. Gore's defection on the one cloture vote did not stop the Senate, including Gore, passing the bill on the day that Martin Luther King was assassinated in April 1968. The House passed the bill shortly afterward. Later, he opposed Richard Nixon's nominations of southern judges, Clement Haynsworth and G. Harrold Carswell, to the Supreme Court.[12]

Gore's fellow senator, Ross Bass, who, as a congressman had voted for the 1964 Civil Rights Act, joined him in support of the 1965 Voting Rights Act, as did Ralph Yarborough, Gore's friend, who had cast the only southern Senate vote for the 1964 act. The change from 1964 to 1965 could be seen in the House votes. Seven Tennessee congressmen, compared to two in 1964, voted for the 1965 act. Seven, rather than one, out of twelve Florida congressmen, and eleven rather than four Texas congressmen supported the legislation. From the Deep South, James Mackay joined Charles Weltner to double the Georgia vote for change. Hale Boggs and Jimmy Morrison breached the unity of the Louisiana delegation. Gore's succession of civil rights stances—refusing to sign the Southern Manifesto, voting for the 1957 and 1960 civil rights acts, against the 1964 act but for the Voting Rights Act—was a stance common to a number of southern moderates like Dante Fascell and future speaker, Jim Wright.[13]

If southern moderates felt liberated, southern conservatives felt trapped. There was a sense that, after the great battle by the southern caucus to stop the 1964 Civil Rights Act, there was resignation about the inevitability of defeat in 1965. The southern senators were old and frail. Their leader Richard Russell had gone into hospital for surgery for pulmonary edema. The success of the closure votes in 1964 had to be recognized—and the southerners were in a weaker position now. Veteran sponsor of the Southern Manifesto Harry Byrd resignedly said, "Yes, I'll do my part but you know we can't stop this bill. We can't deny the Negroes a basic constitutional right to vote." Russell Long, recently elected Senate Whip, said that he had had to adjust to a changing world, and "all southerners will have to do that." He continued, "The southern Senators will not be able to defeat a voting rights bill by taking the attitude that nothing is wrong and that no action is needed." Similarly, William Fulbright said that he was for voting rights. African Americans should have the vote. "These are the last gasps of the opposition, I think it is nearing the end of the very active opposition." The southerners dutifully went through the motions in their filibuster, but when Richard Russell returned to the Senate the day before the final vote, he admitted on May 24th "if there is anything I could do, I would do it, but I assume the die is cast."[14]

Parallel to the fatalism of the southern senators was the eventual, albeit belated, acceptance of southern business leaders that continued white resistance was costly economically and that they needed to take the lead in enabling their communities to take the first tentative steps toward racial change. In some ways, what was striking was how much damage southern businessmen accepted before they decided to take a leadership role. For the longest time, they seemed to believe that they could secure economic growth and maintain traditional patterns of race relations. In Alabama, the realization that these hopes were chimerical was slow in coming. If the Freedom Rides gave some segregationists like Sid Smyer pause, Birmingham and the confrontation at the school house door in 1963 brought it home more sharply. Selma and the threatened boycott of Alabama goods finally rammed the message home. Alabama businessmen took a full-page ad in local papers and in the *Wall Street Journal* announcing their intention to comply with Title VII of the 1964 Civil Rights Act, which was just going into effect, and to eliminate discrimination in job hires.[15]

By and large, southern businesses complied with the 1964 desegregation of public accommodations. As the Voting Rights Act went into operation, so emerged the cross-class biracial political coalition first delineated by Numan Bartley and Hugh David Graham. Upper-income whites and lower-income African Americans elected politicians who combined support for civil rights and stability with economic moderation and voted against politicians representing lower- and middle-income whites. Nowhere was this clearer than in Selma, of course, where Public Safety Commissioner Wilson Baker, Selma's white business leaders, and newly enfranchised black voters drove Sheriff Jim Clark from office.[16]

The Voting Rights Act knocked out the final brick in the cornerstone of white supremacy and conservative domination that V. O. Key had identified in the 1940s. Conservative elite control, according to Key, rested on four devices—segregation, black disfranchisement, the one-party system, and malapportionment of state legislatures. Eliminate those devices, Key optimistically believed, and the forces of liberalism in the South would be immeasurably strengthened. Enfranchising African Americans should, according to Key, have been the final nail in the coffin of conservative segregationist control.[17]

Mississippi in 1965 seemed to confirm this optimism. It initially appeared that the crisis at Ole Miss and Freedom Summer had simply reinforced the closed society in Mississippi, or what Jessica Mitford described as a concentration camp of the mind. But in retrospect, they had opened cracks in the edifice of the fanatical defense of segregation in the Magnolia State. A Yazoo City businessmen told Willie Morris that the Ole Miss crisis had shown that whites were "whistling in the wind"—that they were trying to fight cannons with a pea shooter. The same metaphor was used by Clarence Mitchell in Neshoba County in 1970. He told a northern reporter whom he had threatened in 1964, "We resent this forcing but there's no way to resist. It's like looking down a barrel of a cannon—you can't fight back with a peashooter."[18]

Sally Belfrage lamented that the Freedom Summer volunteers had totally failed to open up dialogue with the white community. But Belfrage never returned to Mississippi after she left in 1964. Volunteer Tracy Sugarman did return the following year. He met, again, the mayor of the local town with whom he had a futile attempt at a meeting of minds in 1964. A year later the mayor welcomed him warmly. The mayor was contemplating change that had seemed impossible to envisage a year earlier. He told Sugarman that the community was eagerly applying for federal grants—and, as a condition of the grant application, he had to demonstrate they had consulted with the African American community and enlist their support.[19]

Governor Paul Johnson Jr., son of the closest Mississippi came to a New Deal governor, had been part of the elaborate plans to defy the federal government on the Oxford campus in 1962. In 1965 he told Mississippians that they had to realize that they were part of the rest of the world. As he recalled, as governor "we changed everything that we could think of to change." This news undoubtedly surprised many Mississippi whites, but as the Mississippi Economic Development Council worked hard to attract outside investment, so the language of resistance changed remarkably quickly. In Neshoba County where the three civil rights workers were murdered in 1964, the Philadelphia high school desegregated under freedom of choice in September 1965. Although the black students faced hostility, they did not face violence. The Klansman who harassed the superintendent of schools was stopped in December 1966 by an ultimatum from the town's leaders. Within fifteen years, African Americans and whites in Philadelphia were filling the high school stadium stands on Friday nights to watch and cheer African American student, Marcus Dupree attempt to beat Herschel Walker's record for touchdowns in a season. Cecil Price Jr., son of the deputy sheriff who had been convicted in federal court for his role in the civil rights murders, was a teammate of Dupree's. When Dupree broke Walker's record, no one celebrated more wildly than Cecil Price Sr.[20]

As John Dollard had observed of Mississippi half a century earlier, voting was not an honorific function. It had real consequences in law enforcement and the lack of physical protection for African Americans. Patricia "Patt" Derian, member of the Democratic National Committee recalled in 1974, "I think you know that when we first moved here [1959], no black person was safe walking the streets anywhere in this state, not in this town or any other place. The system of justice did not apply to black people." She acknowledged the persistent poverty and the terrible jails, "but that absolute iron control has gone." As for politics in 1971, according to Adam Nossiter, "for the first time since Reconstruction, major candidates for governor in Mississippi did not use racial appeals." Politics had certainly changed when in 1983 a white Democrat could be elected governor despite sworn affidavits that he had slept with three black transvestites.[21]

But the alternative defiance narrative is also compelling. The moderates were not the political force of the future. Bass, Gore, and Yarborough were all defeated the next time they faced the electorate. Bass was defeated in the Democratic primary in 1966 by the forces of established Democrats in Tennessee. In turn, Frank Clement was defeated comfortably by the rising star of the southern Republican Party, Howard Baker Jr. Baker won the Senate seat that he believed he could have won two years earlier if Barry Goldwater had not reaffirmed his desire to sell the TVA.[22] Both Yarborough and Gore were defeated in 1970, Yarborough in the Democratic primary by Lloyd Bentsen, Gore by conservative Republican congressman, William Brock. Gore especially was a target of the Nixon White House.

George Grider, elected on LBJ's coattails from Memphis, was defeated in 1966 by Goldwater Republican Dan Kuykendall. Charles Weltner did not stand again in 1966 because of Lester Maddox's nomination as Democratic candidate for governor in Georgia. James Mackay was defeated for renomination. The moderate politicians moved uneasily to the next phase of southern politics. Despite African American support, Gore, in particular, never dealt with the black community in Tennessee directly. He worked, as moderates of that generation tended to, through identified intermediaries. He had always been more attuned to the passion of his white constituents than to the impatience of African Americans. He was more aware of black demands in his final term in office, but in the new politics of cross-class, biracial alliances he was unlikely to win the allegiance of upper-income whites. Similarly, upper-income whites in Texas disliked Yarborough's unapologetic support of organized labor.[23] Significantly, for all their skepticism about blanket opposition to the Voting Rights Act, Russell Long, William Fulbright and George Smathers all voted against the final act. So, older southern moderates were not the driving force of a New South. The New South governors elected from 1970 were a new generation of politicians largely unencumbered by a past track record. The other forces of the future were Strom Thurmond, John Stennis, and James Eastland, who adjusted to a black electorate by providing constituency services, backed by their committee seniority, that they had once provided just for whites.

But it was more than just pork and patronage that explained their conservative success. The southern caucus may have gone through the motions in their 1965 filibuster, but they were carving out an argument that would have powerful resonances after 1965, North and South. Whereas the civil rights movement won the culture war in the court of northern public opinion against the white segregationists before 1965, after 1965, they lost it. The rhetoric of the southerners avoided talk of Jim Crow or the defense of the southern way of life. Instead they talked of constitutionalism, taxpayers' rights, the threat of lawlessness, the likelihood of never-ending demands by civil rights protesters and the way in which the legislation seemed to punish the South.

The historian Anders Walker has shown how apparently moderate southern governors of the 1950s, LeRoy Collins, Luther Hodges, and J. P. Coleman fashioned a strategic constitutionalism that eschewed racism and violence, would appeal to northern whites, but would also limit African American gains. "Modifications in welfare law, adoption law, marriage law, police jurisdiction and judicial administration," he observed, "formed interlocking pieces of a complex puzzle aimed at preventing violence, preserving as much segregation as possible, and complying formally with the Supreme Court." Emphasis on African American shortcomings, assembling statistics on illegitimacy, crime, and venereal disease, could elicit a sympathetic response from the North after 1965. In 1965, Collins was at Selma to try to deflect Martin Luther King's protests and Coleman was appointed by Lyndon Johnson to the fifth circuit court of appeals. There, in Walker's words "he used pro-law enforcement arguments to limit the contours of civil rights protest, even as he used facially neutral color-blind arguments to deny black claims in educational, economic and voting contexts."[24]

As William P. Hustwit has shown, the cultured ideologue of Massive Resistance, James J. Kilpatrick, changed his tune. When Martin Luther King was assassinated, Kilpatrick praised him not only as one of the few black leaders who could control the militants but also as "the bravest man I ever knew in public life. During the terrible days that followed upon the school desegregation ruling, no white southerner ever matched a fraction of his courage. To watch one of his marches was to sense the awesome power of string character, combined with high purpose. That is the way it must have been . . . when the early Christians braved the hate and ridicule of Rome."[25] Kilpatrick, Hustwit showed, "renounced racism and acknowledged the rightness and permanence of the Brown ruling." Sam Ervin, one of the drafters of the Southern Manifesto made the same move. He accepted the rightness of Brown and praised King, in retrospect. These were, of course, strategic retreats. Kilpatrick knew that his success as a nationally syndicated columnist demanded this adjustment. Ervin, as Karl Campbell shows, embraced Brown and championed Martin Luther King because he could portray King as an advocate of color-blind policies that would be used to attack affirmative action and busing.[26]

But the white conservative reaction to Selma also took a more visceral form. Virginia Durr memorably captured that reaction in Alabama. As she wrote to Carl and Anne Braden:

> I have seen the country, or at least Alabama, and that is the vantage point I have, take on the same attitudes that Germany did, self-pity, race hatred, conformity and I really cannot see where it is going to end, as I see absolutely no signs in the white community of any change of heart or mind, simply a furious and rebellious consent to making a token compliance.[27]

She explained to Jessica Mitford the reality behind the wild statements on the floor of the House of Representatives of Congressman William Dickinson:

> More and more I see this society as really crazy, they have lost all sense of reality. Dickinson's crazy speeches about sexual orgies are quoted and BELIEVED all over town. I heard the story about rapes so much that I called St. Margaret's Hospital and they said not a word of truth. The only sensible remark I have heard is one old lady who was told the story of a white girl that got raped 47 times in the Ben Moore Hotel (where SNCC had headquarters when they first came) and she said in a mild way "I wonder why she didn't holler instead of counting." But no one laughed except me.[28]

She wrote gloomily to her sister-in-law Elizabeth and her husband Supreme Court Justice Hugo Black: "George Wallace expresses their feelings of persecution and gets stronger all the time, and I do not see any signs of repentance on his part or on the part of the white population."[29]

Arguably the backlash in token compliance states was worse than in Deep South Massive Resistance states. The hitherto dormant Ku Klux Klan dramatically increased its membership in eastern North Carolina between 1965 and 1967, for example. Only Alabama and Mississippi had larger Klan membership. In token compliance states like Tennessee and East North Carolina, there had been an informal political arrangement: the Black Belt politicians in eastern North Carolina and western Tennessee tolerated token compliance at the state level in return for a small amount of school desegregation in the urban Piedmont in order to preserve maximum segregation in the black majority areas. By 1965 it was clear that this grand bargain was breaking down.

Segregation could not be protected in the Black Belt—first the 1964 Civil Rights Act, then school desegregation, and now the prospect of large numbers of African Americans voting. Here was the white backlash that would support George Wallace and in eastern North Carolina propel Jesse Helms to victory in 1972. It is telling that, when the Southern Christian Leadership Conference decided which community to organize in 1965, they chose to accept the invitation from Selma. But they had also received an invitation from Williamston, eastern North Carolina. In Deep South states, arguably there was more chance of a positive change because the number of black voters would increase dramatically. The increased importance of black voting in Mississippi and South Carolina would be far greater than in states like Tennessee.[30]

In the summer of 2008, veteran Raleigh political commentator Rob Christensen mused on Barack Obama's chances of winning North Carolina in the presidential election. It was possible, noted Christensen, for African Americans to win state-wide Democratic primaries. Obama and Howard Gantt had proved that. But the general election was another matter. Not only was Obama black, but he had a funny name, was Ivy League educated, and "had absolutely no good ole-boy credentials." Obama, Christensen concluded, would have a hard time winning North Carolina if he was white.[31]

Yet Obama did win North Carolina in 2008, just as he did Virginia and Florida. National commentators made much of the changing demographics of those states: the influx of affluent, cosmopolitan northern white migrants. But the results were still remarkable. An African American had won North Carolina, something two southern-born white Democrats had failed to do—Bill Clinton and Al Gore. Virginia had not even voted for Jimmy Carter and had not voted Democratic in a presidential election since 1964.

But the balance sheet of a biracial politics in the South is not clear-cut, just as it was not for John Shelton Reed thirty years ago. One the one hand, the success of an African American presidential candidate, African American office holders right across the South, visible positions of authority for African Americans in a society that would not have contemplated such a situation fifty years ago, a successful African American middle class. On the other hand, there exists African American mayors of communities that do not have the tax base to provide services for their constituents, rural African American communities with no hope of economic growth, and rising inequality between black and white and within the African American community. Above all there is a polarized politics in which a lily-white Republican party has replaced the Democratic Party as the regional majority party. In 2017, 19 of 22 southern senators are Republican, and 8 of the 11 governors. The GOP holds 119 of the 159 House seats. It controls every state legislature.

For a time, white Democrats in the South were able to mitigate the effect of a Republican "Southern Strategy" that aimed to win over former segregationists. Veteran senators banked on their seniority to deliver unequalled benefits to their states. New South governors put together growth-oriented biracial coalitions. Republican success was often a top-down phenomenon. At the local level, both in congressional races and in state legislatures, the GOP was not a promising career path for an ambitious young white politician in the 1970s.

But by the 1990s it was becoming increasingly difficult for Democrats to maximize the African American vote and to gain the 35 to 40 percent of the white vote necessary to win statewide. The generation of senior white conservative Democrats who had successfully adjusted to black voting was replaced by white Republicans who tapped into both the social conservatism of the Religious Right and the anti-government tax-cutting appeal of Ronald Reagan and George Bush.[32]

How important has race been to this Republican success? As political scientists and historians of the suburban South have argued, the move of southern whites can be linked to the class interests of upper-income voters and a middle-class sense of entitlement on the part of white suburban taxpayers who resented their tax dollars being spent on government programs and welfare. But, it is nevertheless true that racial exclusivity is at the heart of the GOP success. There is no incentive for Republicans to pursue policies designed to appeal to African Americans. The party bolsters its position by sophisticated control of redistricting to maximize the strength of white GOP voters and support of voter registration laws designed to depress or suppress the African American vote in state after state.[33] The white South adjusted to Selma, but the South in 2017 shows that adjustment did not mean surrender.

Notes

1. Dan T. Carter to the author, 25 May 1984; William Jennings Bryan and Scott Derks, *Dorn: Of the People, A Political Way of Life* (Columbia and Orangeburg, SC: Bruccoli Clark Layman/Sandlapper Publishing, 1988). Anyone consulting the Dorn papers for the years 1953–1956 in South Carolina Political Collections, Ernest F. Hollings Special Collections Library, University of South Carolina, would find it difficult to doubt that Dorn was fully committed to the defense of segregation.

2. John Shelton Reed, "Up from Segregation," *Virginia Quarterly Review* 60 (summer 1984): 373–93, at http://www.vqronline.org/essay/segregation (consulted February 16, 2016).

3. Tony Badger, "From Defiance to Moderation: South Carolina Governors and Racial Change," *New Deal/New South: An Anthony J. Badger Reader* (Fayetteville: University of Arkansas Press, 2007), 142–43.

4. Interview with Hodding Carter III by Jack Bass and Walter De Vries, April 1, 1974, A-0100 in the Southern Oral History Program Collection #4007 Southern Historical Collection, Wilson Library, University of North Carolina at Chapel Hill.

5. Tony Badger, "Southerners Who Refused to Sign the Southern Manifesto," in Badger, *New Deal/New South: An Anthony J. Badger Reader*, 79–80, 87.

6. Copy of statement for campaign announcement, Senate Papers of Albert Gore, Albert Gore Research Center, Middle Tennessee State University, Murfreesboro, TN.

7. Periodic Log Maintained during the Discussions Concerning the Passage of the Civil Rights Act of 1964 by Stephen Horn, Carl Albert Congressional Research and Studies Center, Congressional Archives, University of Oklahoma.

8. Periodic Log Maintained during the Discussions Concerning the Passage of the Civil Rights Act of 1964 by Stephen Horn, Carl Albert Congressional Research and Studies Center, Congressional Archives, University of Oklahoma, 143. Todd S. Purdom, *An Idea Whose Time Has Come: Two presidents, Two Parties, and the Battle for the Civil Rights Act of 1964* (New York: Henry Holt, 2014), 305, 309; John G. Stewart, "Thoughts on the Civil Rights Bill and Independence and Control," in Robert D. Loevy, *The Civil Rights Act of 1964: The Passage of the Law That Ended Racial Segregation* (Albany: State University Press of New York, 2011), 146, 311–12.

9. John Seigenthaler interview with the author, February 27, 2003; James Sasser interview with the author, December 10, 2003.

10. M. W. Allen to Albert Gore, March 10, 1965; James J. Justice to Albert Gore, March 15, 1965, Gore Senate Papers.

11. M. W. Allen to Albert Gore March 10, 1965, Albert Gore to Allen, March 25, 1965,

Gore Senate Papers; Ted Kennedy interview with the author, December 10, 2003; Bruce L. Clayton to Albert Gore, March 15, 1965, Gore Senate Papers.

12. Walter Mondale with David Hage, *The Last Good Fight: A Life in Liberal Politics* (New York: Scribner, 2010), 66.

13. Charles L. Weltner, *Southerner* (Philadelphia: B. Lippincott, 1966), 55–82; Badger, "Southerners Who Refused to Sign the Southern Manifesto," in Badger, *New Deal/New South*, 87; Jim Wright interview with the author, November 18, 1996; Dante Fascell interview with the author February 27, 1997,

14. Keith M. Finley, *Delaying the Dream: Southern Senators and the Fight against Civil Rights, 1938–1965* (Baton Rouge: Louisiana State University Press, 2008) 284–305; Gary May, *Bending Toward Justice: The Voting Rights Act and the Transformation of American Democracy* (Durham, NC: Duke University Press, 2014).

15. Subsequent community studies have done little to challenge the conclusions of the authors of case studies in Elizabeth Jacoway and David Colburn, *Southern Businessmen and Desegregation* (Baton Rouge: Louisiana State University Press, 1982); J. Mills Thornton, *Dividing Lines: Municipal Politics and the Struggle for Civil Rights in Montgomery, Birmingham, and Selma* (Tuscaloosa: University of Alabama Press, 2002), 494.

16. Thornton, *Dividing Lines*, 498–99. Numan V. Bartley and Hugh D. Graham, *Southern Politics and the Second Reconstruction* (College Park, MD: Johns Hopkins, 1975).

17. V. O. Key Jr., *Southern Politics in State and Nation* (New York: Knopf, 1949).

18. Jessica Mitford, *A Fine Old Conflict* (London: Michael Joseph, 1977), 145. Willie Morris, *Yazoo: Integration in a Deep-Southern Town* (New York: Ballantine Books, 1972), 55; Florence Mars, *Witness in Philadelphia* (Baton Rouge: Louisiana State University Press, 1977), 272.

19. Sally Belfrage, obituary, *Independent*, April 3, 1994. Tracy Sugarman, *Stranger at the Gates: A Summer in Mississippi* (New York: Hill and Wang, 1966).

20. Paul B. Johnson Jr., interview, Southern Oral History Program; W. F. "Bill" Minor, interview, Southern Oral History Program; Mars, *Witness in Philadelphia*, 217–19; Willie Morris, *The Courting of Marcus Dupree* (Jackson: University of Mississippi Press, 1992).

21. Interview with Patricia M. Derian by Jack Bass and Walter De Vries, March 25, 1974, A-0105 in the Southern Oral History Program Collection #4007 Southern Historical Collection, Wilson Library, University of North Carolina at Chapel Hill; Adam Nossiter, *Of Long Memory: Mississippi and the Murder of Medgar Evers* (New York: Addison Wesley, 1994), 161.

22. Howard Baker interview with the author, April 7, 2008.

23. Tony Badger (with Michael Martin), "The Anti-Gore Campaign of 1970," in Badger, *New Deal/New South*, 201–12.

24. Anders Walker, *The Ghost of Jim Crow: How Southern Moderates Used Brown v. Board of Education to Stall Civil Rights* (New York: Oxford University Press, 2009), 4, 8.

25. William P. Hustwit, *James J. Kilpatrick: Salesman for Segregation* (Chapel Hill: University of North Carolina Press, 2013), 159.

26. Ibid., 160; Karl Campbell, *Senator Sam Ervin: Last of the Founding Fathers* (Chapel Hill: University of North Carolina Press: Chapel Hill, 2007), 158–60.

27. Virginia Foster Durr, letter to Carl and Anne Braden, April 19, 1965, in Patricia

Sullivan, ed., *Freedom Writer: Virginia Foster Durr, Letters from the Civil Rights Years* (Athens: University of Georgia Press, 2006), 327.

28. Durr letter to "Dec" (Jessica Mitford), April 28, 1965, in Sullivan, *Freedom Writer*, 327.

29. Durr letter to Elizabeth and Hugo, March 18, 1965, in Sullivan, *Freedom Writer*, 321–22.

30. Tony Badger, "Closet Moderates: Why White Southern Liberals Failed, 1940–1970," in Badger, *New Deal/New South*, 123–25; David Cecelski, *Along Freedom Road: Hyde County, North Carolina and the Fate of Black Schools in the South* (Chapel Hill: University of North Carolina Press, 1994), 39, 155–58; David C. Carter, "The Williamston Freedom Movement: Civil Rights at the Grass Roots in Eastern North Carolina, 1957–1964," *North Carolina Historical Review* 76, no. 1 (January 1999): 1–42.

31. Rob Christensen to the author, May 28, 2008.

32. Anthony J. Badger, "The Dilemmas of Biracial Politics in the South since 1965," in Badger, *New Deal/New South*, 168–80.

33. Dan T. Carter, "More than Race: Conservatism in the White South since V. O. Key Jr," and Byron Shafer and Richard Johnston, "Partisan Change in the Post-Key South," in Angie Maxwell and Todd G. Shields, eds., *Unlocking V. O. Key Jr.: Southern Politics in the Twenty-first Century* (Fayetteville: University of Arkansas Press, 2011), 129–84; D. T. Carter, *From George Wallace to Newt Gingrich: Race in the Conservative Counterrevolution, 1963–1994* (Baton Rouge: Louisiana State University Press, 1999); Byron Shafer and Richard Johnston, *The End of Southern Exceptionalism: Class, Race, and Partisan Change in the Postwar South* (Cambridge: Harvard University Press, 2006), 2; Matthew D. Lassiter, *The Silent Majority: Politics in the Sunbelt South* (Princeton, NJ: Princeton University Press, 2006), 1–19; Glenn Feldman, ed., *Painting Dixie Red: When, Where, Why, and How the South became Republican* (Gainesville: University Press of Florida, 2011), 79–197.

6

"We Cannot Escape the Same Challenge"

Britain, France, and the U.S. Voting Rights Act

CLIVE WEBB

During the middle of the twentieth century, the world media bore witness to the dramatic struggle of African Americans to secure their constitutional rights. Print and broadcast journalists dispatched from overseas to the front lines of the American civil rights conflict conveyed to their home countries an emphatic support for black protesters, moral outrage at white racists, and mounting impatience with the federal government for failing to enact reform that would resolve the United States' greatest domestic dilemma. From the Montgomery bus boycott that first brought Martin Luther King Jr. to international attention to the more radical phase of nonviolent direct action initiated by the student sit-ins to the dramatic scenes of police brutality on the streets of Birmingham, Alabama, foreign reporters mobilized global pressure on the United States to make good on its rhetorical commitment as leader of the free world.

The Selma campaign of 1965 was no exception. In particular, the appalling events of Bloody Sunday, in which black marchers on the Edmund Pettus Bridge suffered teargassing and beatings, evoked international condemnation. The tone of that coverage had nonetheless started to shift.

This essay compares political reaction to Selma on the part of two of the United States' most important diplomatic partners, Britain and France. In assessing the international dynamics of the civil rights struggle, historians focus their concentration on the United States' Cold War adversaries or the nonaligned nations of Africa and Asia. The United States' military and diplomatic allies, by contrast, receive far less attention.[1] An assessment of the impact that the Selma campaign had on the domestic race and immigration policies of Britain and France reveals how the African American freedom struggle aggravated the fault lines within the Atlantic alliance.

Until the recent past, the British and French had both conveyed a sense of moral superiority over the United States on the issue of race. The two countries had robustly defended themselves against American criticism of their colonial policies by pointing to the persistence of racial discrimination, particularly in the southern states. Far from accepting their own culpability for compromising international allegiance to western capitalist democracy, they accused the United States of recklessly ceding global influence to the communist forces of the East because of the failure to effect civil rights reform.

While moral smugness and self-protectiveness were still evident in 1965, racial troubles closer to home led the British press, in particular, to temper its tone and content when reporting on the Selma campaign. The upsurge of domestic racism in Britain resulted not only in a new caution when reporting on civil rights struggles in the United States but also an appreciation that African American activism could serve as an inspiring example on the other side of the Atlantic. By contrast, racial conflict in the United States remained a source of tension in its diplomatic relationship with Gaullist France. Simmering racial tensions in the Fifth Republic did not induce the same degree of self-reflection when the French media commented on the political drama in Alabama.

In 1956, a survey of western European countries conducted by the United States Information Agency found that, along with the Netherlands, Britain was the harshest critic of American race relations.[2] The British press provided extensive coverage of the civil rights struggle that emphasized the moral integrity and physical bravery of black activists. Joyce Egginton, Hella Pick, and William J. Weatherby were among the many journalists whose reporting from the other side of the Atlantic aroused the political consciousness of British readers. British criticism of the federal government's failure to enforce civil rights reform came not despite, but because of the supposed "special relationship" between London and Washington. Politicians and the press stressed not only the ethical dimension of the situation but also a strategic concern that the United States had compromised the global containment of communism by allowing the problem of racial inequality to tarnish its status as leader of the free world. As the *Manchester Guardian* asserted, the resolution of the race problem would mean that "the United States will rest on firmer foundations than it did, and will face the world with the happy consciousness of having put behind it what has long been its worst reproach."[3]

Events during the late 1950s nonetheless shook some political commentators from their complacent use of the United States as a convenient foil to emphasize the comparatively progressive state of British race relations. Postwar migration from the Caribbean to Britain had resulted by 1958 in the permanent settlement of around 125,000 West Indians.[4] The racist backlash to the arrival of the Windrush generation (named after the vessel whose arrival from Jamaica to Tilbury Docks in June 1948 heralded the new era of migration from the colonies to the metropole) shook sanctimonious assumptions about Britain being a liberal and progressive society. Racial disorders in Liverpool in August 1948 and in Deptford in July 1949 prefaced the riots that erupted on the streets of Nottingham and London's Notting Hill district during August and September 1958.[5] Reporters and pundits in both Britain and the United States drew discomforting analogies between the rioting and the Little Rock crisis of 1957, suggesting that racism was a communicable disease swept by westerly winds across the Atlantic. According to historian Arnold Toynbee, the adverse publicity provoked by Britain's racial troubles was "a punishment for self-righteousness."[6]

The tone of moral condescension that characterized British political commentary on American race relations nonetheless endured. British policymakers and political observers conceded that black migrants faced problems such as inadequate housing and restricted employment opportunities. They nonetheless retorted that racial discrimination had no basis in British law and, being less deeply rooted in history, would not prove as intractable as was the case in the United States. Racial disturbances on the other side of the Atlantic continued to elicit what historian Mike Sewell describes as a "post-Suez Schadenfreude" on the part of many Britons.[7]

Throughout the 1950s, the British press interpreted the civil rights movement as an important but essentially domestic matter for the United States. When reporters did contextualize events within a broader global framework, their concern was with the negative impact on the newly decolonized and nonaligned nations of Africa and Asia. The notion that what was happening on the other side of the Atlantic had any direct relevance to Britain was seldom articulated. That was to change during the early 1960s.

The turn of the decade witnessed an increasingly intolerant attitude toward racial and ethnic minorities in Britain. Following the race riots of the late 1950s, there were increasingly clamorous calls for immigration restrictions. Almost 80 percent of respondents to a poll conducted by the reactionary *Daily Express* essentially blamed the Afro-Caribbean community for the rioting by agreeing that Britain's mounting racial problems could only be resolved through tighter immigration controls.[8] In response to public pressure, politicians formed a cross-party consensus in support of restrictions. According to Robert Miles and Annie Phizacklea, "The central division between the two main political parties was not whether the 'coloureds' should be kept out, but over how few should be allowed in."[9] The result was the Commonwealth Immigrants Act of 1962, which introduced a work voucher scheme in an attempt to restrict the number of nonwhite migrants admitted to Britain, a move regarded by liberal activists as institutionalizing racism.[10]

The awareness that Britain was not entirely different from the United States owed not only to declining race relations but also to the efforts of black activists to emulate the tactics used by African Americans to protect and promote their rights. Inspired by the new phase of radical nonviolent direction led by black students in the southern states, British demonstrators launched their own sit-ins at pubs that refused them service.[11] The Montgomery bus boycott served as a similar catalyst to black youth worker Paul Stephenson. In 1963, Stephenson organized a boycott of buses in Bristol in protest at the operating company's refusal to employ nonwhite drivers and conductors.[12]

These attempts to adapt American protest tactics to a British political context faced insurmountable obstacles. In contrast to Montgomery, the absence of either a written constitution or law prohibiting racial discrimination in employment rendered it impossible to mount a legal challenge against the bus company. The black population of Britain was also much smaller in real and proportionate terms than in Montgomery and therefore had far less economic leverage over the bus company. Although the business did eventually accede to the demands of the protesters—by happy coincidence on August 28, the same day as the March on Washington—it owed less to economic pressure than to adverse publicity both in Britain and the Commonwealth.[13]

Although political conditions with the United States proved far from analogous, the rise of white racism and black resistance demonstrated that Britain had become one of the battlefronts in a larger world struggle. A cartoon published by the *Daily Mail* in May 1963 depicted three figures trying to force a lid down on a black man whose fury could barely be contained: South African Prime Minister Hendrick Verwoerd, the "architect of apartheid;" an Alabama police officer, and a representative of the Bristol Omnibus Company. The message was clear. How could Britain condemn the racism of South Africa and the United States when it, too, discriminated against its black population?[14]

It was in this climate of increasing soul-searching that the British press reacted to the Selma campaign. British reporters united across the political divide in their support of African American demonstrators. Leader writers emphasized what the *Economist* declared was the "glaringly obvious" need for federal voting rights legislation.[15] They also expressed complete support for the tactics employed by the Southern Christian Leadership Conference (SCLC). While unsparing in their condemnation of the brutal assault of black activists by Alabama state troopers and local posse men on Bloody Sunday, the newspapers applauded the SCLC for successfully dramatizing the plight of disenfranchised African Americans to a complacent administration in Washington.

Some reporting represented African Americans as passive victims who needed liberation from political disempowerment and racial violence by a benevolent Lyndon B. Johnson. William Papas, whose South African origins sensitized him to the struggle against racial discrimination, produced a cartoon for the *Guardian* that depicted a black man forced onto all fours by an Alabama state trooper as he crawls painfully toward the elusive destination of equality.[16] Leslie Illingworth also emphasized black victimhood in a cartoon for the *Daily Mail* that featured a prostrate black figure liberated from the stakes that bound him to the ground by a knife-wielding Lyndon Johnson.[17]

The more recurrent representation of African Americans was nonetheless of brave and resilient demonstrators whose confrontation with racist southern whites had mobilized a national consensus in support of voting rights.[18] Black disenfranchisement had been one of the United States' most shameful problems for decades, observed the *New Statesman*, so why was reform finally happening now? "What touched the conscience was the resolve and restraint of the Negroes whose rightful claim could neither be ignored or denied."[19] The pained but determined features of the black activist drawn by cartoonist Victor Weisz for the *Evening Standard* emphasized African Americans' role in securing their own liberation. Weisz filtered his interpretation of the civil rights struggle in the United States through his personal experience as a German-born Jew who fled Nazism during the 1930s. His ironic usage of the Declaration of Independence underlined the moral condemnation of American racism that featured prominently in his cartoons from the 1940s to his death in the 1960s.[20]

While the British press applauded President Johnson for his announcing to Congress his intention to enact federal voting rights legislation, it also criticized him for having forced black activists into dangerous confrontation with white southern racists by not taking preventive action much sooner. The president had done the right thing, but only because his hand had been forced by others. In an editorial that combined sincere praise with sarcasm, the *Spectator* concluded that "Mr. Johnson had, to his surprise and ours, been fed with that spirit which comes from below. Of all diets he has avoided it most, and, of all diets, none would seem to have agreed with him more."[21]

The pious tone that had long typified British press coverage of American race relations was still evident in much of the editorializing about the Selma campaign. Some of the sharpest finger-pointing came from the *Daily Mail*, which applauded the prospect of a federal voting rights law but ridiculed the United States for taking a century since the abolition of slavery to secure the full rights of citizenship for its black population: "The United States, which tore itself to pieces a century ago on the issue of human dignity, has been extraordinarily slow in honouring the guarantees established by the Civil War."[22] The *Sunday Citizen* ran a cartoon featuring a black astronaut hanging precariously to a thin safety line and with a placard demanding equal rights slipping from his hands as he falls from a space rocket labeled "World Progress." The vessel served as both metaphor and a literal criticism of the United States for investing millions in its attempt to land a man on the moon while the efforts of its own black population to secure equal rights struggled to take flight.[23] Stanley Franklin in the *Daily Mirror* represented the Selma campaign as plaster falling from the ceiling of an operating theater in which President Johnson is the chief surgeon wielding a knife against the disease of communism that afflicts Vietnam. The collapsing ceiling implied that the United States needed to repair its own society before intervening in others.[24]

Media coverage of Selma nonetheless accelerated the shift away from much of its earlier treatment of the civil rights struggle. The Selma campaign induced troubled self-reflection on the part of an increasing number of white Britons who had once claimed moral superiority over the United States in terms of their own country's treatment of racial and ethnic minorities.

Events in the months before the SCLC demonstrations, meanwhile, further elided the differences between Britain and the United States. The general election of October 1964 witnessed the unprecedented exploitation of antiwhite prejudice, specifically the stunning upset in the West Midlands constituency of Smethwick, where Conservative candidate Peter Griffiths exploited racial tensions over housing and employment to defeat sitting MP Patrick Gordon Walker. Griffiths successfully manipulated white working-class fears by tacitly endorsing the slogan "If you want a nigger for a neighbour, vote Labour."[25]

The narrowing of the transatlantic owed not only to the rise of race-baiting politicians but also to the much-publicized visits to Britain of African American leaders who warned that the country could be headed in the same direction as the United States. In December 1964, Martin Luther King traveled to London en route to receiving the Nobel Peace Prize in Oslo. Addressing an audience that crowded the aisles of St. Paul's Cathedral, King warned that unless the British government took measures to address racial discrimination in housing and education, "festering sores of bitterness" on the part of the black community would precipitate a racial crisis comparable to the United States.[26] Malcolm X also undertook two trips to Britain, the first in December 1964 when he addressed the Oxford Union, and the second two months later when he toured Smethwick.[27]

The arrival on British shores of African American civil rights activists suggested more than ever the interconnectedness of the global struggle against racism. Although the British press did not refrain from condemning the violence in Selma, it largely refrained from the condescending and censorious anti-Americanism of old. As the *Guardian* affirmed, given recent events, Britain was in no position to moralize to the United States: "From our island, where multiracialism is still a word and not a reality, we are not in a position to condemn or to offer guide-lines for the future."[28] The *Times* expressed similar sentiments in response to President Johnson's address to Congress in which he called for the enactment of a new Voting Rights Act: "No one, least of all in Britain today, can feel complacent or detached about the issue of race. We have felt the breath of the problem now ourselves and have yet to face it with honesty. The President has put his own nation on trial in the name of its own Constitution and of the cause that made the United States. We cannot escape the same challenge."[29]

The influence of the United States was most apparent in Britain's first Race Relations Act, which came into force on December 8, 1965. Modeled on the Civil Rights Act enacted in the United States seventeen months earlier, the new law outlawed racial discrimination in "places of public resort," although not in housing or employment, and made the incitement of racial hatred a criminal offense.[30] During the House of Lords debate on the bill, Labour's Peter Ritchie Calder underlined how an increased awareness of the interconnectedness of anti-racist struggles around the globe informed British policymaking. "My concern," he informed his fellow peers, "is with international relations and with the world, which has now become a neighbourhood—a neighbourhood where what happens in Smethwick or Selma . . . reverberates everywhere."[31]

While the African American freedom struggle had a clear impact on governmental policy, the reaction of Britain's own racial and ethnic minorities to the Selma campaign is difficult to determine. Black activists in Britain certainly saw their domestic struggle for racial equality as a local front in a larger global campaign against white supremacy. One expression of this was a march on the U.S. Embassy in Grosvenor Square staged by the Committee of Afro-Asian and Caribbean Associations in solidarity with the March on Washington on August 28, 1963. The leader of that organization, Trinidadian born activist Claudia Jones, died in December 1964, and her pioneering newspaper the *West Indian Gazette* folded two months later just as the events on the Edmund Pettus Bridge were about to play out. The last issue of that newspaper announced the formation of a Committee for Democratic Rights in the United States but further details are elusive.

Nonetheless, the Selma campaign had a direct impact on one of the most serious conflicts in the British Isles, the Troubles in Northern Ireland. In January 1969, Michael Farrell of the radical republican People's Democracy organized a four-day protest march from Belfast to Derry that in methods and aims explicitly emulated the Selma to Montgomery march. The parallel that Farrell drew between Northern Ireland and the American South lacked precision, particularly in terms of his modelling People's Democracy on the Student Nonviolent Coordinating Committee given the latter organization's reluctance to support the Selma march. Farrell nonetheless anticipated that People's Democracy could incite a similar confrontation to the one that had occurred on the Edmund Pettus Bridge, the Royal Ulster Constabulary substituting for the Alabama state troopers and Dallas County posse men who had brutally assaulted black activists.

As had been the case in Selma where the resultant public outrage had compelled federal government intervention, so Farrell believed that the British government would be forced to act over the heads of officials in Stormont to implement "one man, one vote" in local government elections. In scenes that evoked the bloody confrontation on the Edmund Pettus Bridge, a loyalist mob supported by police who were supposed to protect the marchers launched an assault on the Burntollet Bridge in Belfast that resulted in hospital treatment for eighty-seven injured people. The marchers were unprepared for the scale of the assault, lacking the training in nonviolent direct action received by black activists on the other side of the Atlantic, and the march had a less decisive outcome.

The transnational influence of the civil rights movement is nonetheless indisputable.[32] An area for future research is to determine how the British press and political establishment reacted to the analogies Irish republican activists drew between themselves and the African American freedom struggle. The parallels between the two protest movements appear to have troubled at least some politicians. Speaking in the House of Commons, Labour MP Paul Rose responded to the violence on the Burntollet Bridge by stating that,

> It is a responsibility which we in this House must accept to ensure that all our citizens, of all religions and of all races on both sides of the Irish Sea, are accorded the same rights, privileges and responsibilities which we must accept in a great democracy. Let not our good name be tarnished by a Selma . . . in the mother of democracy.[33]

The lens through which the British viewed American race relations had become a mirror reflecting back on their own domestic problems.

By contrast, the lens used by the French was more like part of a riflescope. It may not have always been possible in the mid-1960s to determine what was special about the supposed special relationship between Britain and the United States, but France was the coldest of America's Cold War allies. Like Britain, France had a strong sense of itself as a liberal and progressive nation untainted by the racial prejudice that plagued the United

States. Paris was the focus of this national self-mythologizing, since its cosmopolitan culture had long served as a migratory magnet to African Americans including the emergence of a sizeable community founded by former GIs after the First World War. The presence in the city of so many African American artistic luminaries such as Josephine Baker, Richard Wright, and James Baldwin further sharpened the contrast between progressive France and the racially repressive United States.[34]

French media reporting of the United States during the 1950s and 1960s conveyed a condescending sense of moral outrage at the continued mistreatment of African Americans. Press coverage of the civil rights struggle turned fiercer still following the death of Agence France-Presse journalist Paul Guihard, shot dead during the riot caused by the admission of black student James Meredith to the University of Mississippi in September 1962.[35] French novelists and playwrights also focused their scorn on American race relations. While some, such as Simone de Beauvoir, wrote from first-hand experience following her tour of the United States, others drew on the imagination, including Marcel Aymé, whose play *Louisiane*, staged in 1961, featured a black man murdered for attempting to marry a white woman.[36] While the French usually watched the evolving civil rights struggle from afar, racist discrimination at U.S. air bases within their own borders was a more direct affront.[37]

It is important to place French reaction to the civil rights movement in the broader context of its testy diplomatic relationship with the United States. France bristled at American censure of its efforts to suppress the Algerian nationalist insurgency that led to the long and bloody war of independence between 1956 and 1962. French commentators turned on American critics, accusing them of hypocrisy for claiming the moral high ground while their own country continued to tolerate violence and discrimination against its own black population. Alluding to the Little Rock school crisis where President Dwight D. Eisenhower had dispatched troops to enforce desegregation, the French press asserted that under benevolent colonial rule, Arab children in Algeria attended school without need of military protection.[38] The escalation of American intervention in Vietnam fueled further tensions between the two nations. Stung by American criticism of French foreign policy in North Africa, the De Gaulle government accused Washington of blatant double standards for itself using military force to impose an unpopular government on a foreign nation.

According to the French president, his country was "violently opposed to the blatant American imperialism now rampant in the world."[39]

These diplomatic tensions provided the setting for French press coverage of the Selma campaign. The muted tone of British media analysis contrasted with the sharp criticism of the United States from the other side of the English Channel. This was despite the fact that, by the 1960s, France was similarly experiencing racial and ethnic difficulties of its own. Decolonization resulted in unprecedented numbers of North African migrants resettling in France, enticed by opportunities to assist in the country's postwar economic reconstruction. The largest cohort came from Algeria, 111,000 relocating to France in the three years following the end of the War of Independence.[40] Although legally accorded the full rights of citizenship, migrants suffered economic marginalization and social exclusion, working the poorest jobs and living in the slum conditions of "bidonvilles," shantytowns on the periphery of urban centers. The state refused to recognize the reality of institutional racism, diminishing the migrants' plight by dealing only with individual acts of discrimination.[41]

Surveying the situation, the *Chicago Defender* concluded that "France, which prides itself on being one of the least-conscious nations of the world, is being hit by [a] mounting racial problem."[42] Unlike the British press, however, French newspapers did not analyze the Selma campaign through the interpretive lens of their country's own recent experiences. French newspapers saw themselves as not only bearing witness to events but also actively contributing to the civil rights cause. By covering the unfolding drama, one publication asserted that "Alabama's African-Americans know they are no longer alone" because of "international public sympathy" for their plight.[43] In contrast to Britain, the French media divided along political lines as to the legitimacy of direct action as a means to further racial equality in the United States. Both left and right nonetheless condemned the violence on the Edmund Pettus Bridge and applauded the Johnson administration for forcing passage of the Voting Rights Act.

Leftist newspapers in particular lauded black activists for forcing the hand of a complacent federal government. The leading voice of the left, *Le Monde*, asserted that African Americans had no choice but to stage the dramatic showdown with racist authorities in Selma since "far from decreasing, the apathy of the majority of the white population with regard to their struggle seems to get worse."[44] Although the leftist press applauded the federal government's intervention in Selma following the events of Bloody Sunday—*La Nation* going so far as to compare Lyndon Johnson, following his address to Congress on voting rights, to Abraham Lincoln—it was critical of its failure to act sooner.[45] *Le Monde* criticized Johnson for his initial reliance on intermediaries including Vice President Hubert Humphrey and Attorney General Nicholas Katzenbach to negotiate with Martin Luther King. Turning its sights on American foreign policy, the newspaper argued that without the leadership of King, "who was able to channel the indignation of his brothers of color and whites from the north," the White House would have been content to focus its energies on the escalating war in Vietnam.[46] With the Johnson administration under pressure to federalize the Alabama National Guard in order to protect marchers en route from Selma to Montgomery, *Le Monde* wondered disbelievingly: "Why the government that does not hesitate to send American troops to protect the freedom of South Vietnam, does not send troops to conquer freedom in Alabama?"[47]

France's right-wing press was more equivocal about the demonstrations in Selma. Conservative publications accepted the need for the direct-action tactics deployed by the SCLC and attributed blame for the events of Bloody Sunday entirely to state troopers and local posse men. *Le Figaro*, the foremost newspaper of the right, graphically described the brutality and mayhem of that day, emphasizing that among those seriously injured were female, elderly, and young activists.[48] The newspaper was, however, skeptical of the need for further protests after Bloody Sunday had forced the federal government into pushing for legislative reform. *Le Figaro* dismissed the self-righteousness of "fanatic and irresponsible" white northern liberals who responded to King's call to join the second march.[49] Correspondent Nicolas Chatelain espoused a gradualist position, claiming that while it was "possible" progress was impossible without persistent pressure on federal authorities, "the fact remains that the social and material conditions of African Americans regularly improve year by year, notably in the southern states." This, he concluded, had occurred "without uproar and awaking much curiosity, because there are no wounds and bumps to be counted or advertising speeches to be broadcasted. Yet, only a simple photograph of a police officer with a truncheon is sufficient for us to forget all this."[50]

Newspapers on both the left and right commended President Johnson on securing passage of the Voting Rights Act in August 1965. They nonetheless cautioned that it was not simply the enactment of new legislation that mattered, but its implementation. On the left, *Le Monde* published an article pointedly titled "Eighty-Five Years Later," which stated that the Voting Rights Act finally promised to fulfil the intentions of the Fifteenth Amendment. This would only occur, however, if Washington protected African Americans from segregationists who would either try to intimidate them from casting their ballots or mobilize otherwise politically apathetic white southerners into an unbeatable electoral bloc.[51] On the right, *Le Figaro* journalist Léo Sauvage commented that the federal government had passed laws with voting rights measures in 1957, 1960, and 1964, but all were inadequate and ineffectually enforced. "They gave nothing," he concluded, "and this experience ended up convincing the African-Americans that it is not the voting of these laws that counts. Indeed, what counts is the will to apply them, and when necessary, impose them."[52]

Unlike the increasingly troubled consciences of the British, the French do not appear to have seen events across the Atlantic as having any implications closer to home. News coverage of the Selma campaign contained no references to the plight of North African immigrants in France. Implicit in these reports was the self-righteous assumption that France remained a more racially enlightened nation. Compounding this sense of moral superiority, in the spring of 1965, Paris theatergoers flocked to a stage production in which the actors read from the United States government's own official documents to tell the story of racial discrimination from the transportation of African slaves along the Middle Passage to the Selma campaign.[53]

The civil rights struggle in the United States may have provoked little self-reflection on the part of the French about their own increasingly troubled racial and ethnic relations, but this is not surprising when even African American activists who visited Paris gave them no reason to consider the transnational connection. In October 1965, Martin Luther King traveled to Paris on a whirlwind two-day trip during which he addressed audiences at the American Church and the Palais de la Mutualité. Neither in these speeches nor in press interviews did King reflect on the condition of North African migrants in France. Instead, he spoke exclusively about the civil rights struggle in his own country with one brief exception when he encouraged world leaders to impose economic sanctions against the white supremacist government of Rhodesia.[54]

"All of America has its eyes turned towards Alabama," observed President Johnson as civil rights demonstrators embarked on the seventy-mile journey from Selma to Montgomery, "the entire world has its eyes turned towards the United States."[55] What the world saw, however, was not always the same. For the British press, racial conflict in the United States was a disturbing portent of their country's own potential future. British reaction was emblematic of a broader shift by many western Europeans from the moral certainty that had characterized earlier coverage of the American civil rights struggle. The Dutch newspaper *Nieuwe Rotterdamse Courant* similarly concluded that "the West [of Europe] should not indulge in a feeling of superiority. We should not say that it can happen only over here."[56] The reaction of the French press, which drew no instructive lessons from the American experience, was therefore atypical.

Britain and France could nonetheless both still delude themselves that they did not share any of the racial and ethnic problems that beset the United States. The SCLC campaign in Selma focused on voting rights, but denial of the franchise was not an issue for minorities in either France or Britain. Press coverage of the racial violence overseas carried an implicit, and sometimes explicit, message about the more enlightened and harmonious state of race relations back home.

In concentrating so much attention on events in Alabama, the French and British almost entirely ignored another development in the United States that inverted the story told to their readers. On October 3, 1965, President Johnson signed into law a new Immigration and Nationality Act, which eliminated the national origin quotas used to restrict the number of foreigners admitted to the United States from outside northern and western Europe.[57] The French and British media overlooked the new law, perhaps because it contradicted their presumption of the greater liberalism of their own countries compared with the United States. At the same time as the Johnson administration opened the United States' doors to the world, the governments of Britain and France set about closing theirs. In 1963 and 1964, France signed bilateral agreements with Algeria, Mali, Mauritania, Morocco, Senegal, and Tunisia to restrict the number of migrants it accepted from those countries.[58] On its return to power in 1964, the British Labour Party reneged on its commitment to repeal the Commonwealth Immigrants Act. The following year, the new government released a white paper, which proposed tighter controls on the number of former colonial subjects admitted to Britain.[59] Drawing misleading parallels between racial conflict in the United States and their own nations allowed the British and French media to construct a narrative contradicted by the more analogous issue of immigration policy.

Within months of the Selma campaign, another civil rights incident would in any case force further reevaluation by both nations. While black people in Britain and France had the right to vote, the Watts Rebellion of August 1965 demonstrated the need for firmer action to promote equality of opportunity. The lesson of Watts that both countries would have to learn was that serious racial unrest could occur in any society where minorities found themselves restricted to underpaid jobs and crowded into what the French, for the first time drawing analogies between their own country and the United States, would come to label "Harlem-Sur-Seine."[60]

Notes

1. Works that place the civil rights movement in a broader world context include: Thomas Borstelmann, *The Cold War and the Color Line: American Race Relations in the Global Arena* (Cambridge: Harvard University Press, 2001); Mary L. Dudziak, *Cold War Civil Rights: Race and the Image of American Democracy* (Princeton, NJ: Princeton University Press, 2000); Azza Salama Layton, *International Politics and Civil Rights Policies in the United States, 1941–1960* (New York: Cambridge University Press, 2000). One study that does focus on the United States' relationship with one of its Cold War allies is Maria Höhn and Martin A. Klimke, *A Breath of Freedom: The Civil Rights Struggle, African American GIs, and Germany* (New York: Palgrave Macmillan, 2010).

2. Hazel Erskine, "The Polls: World Opinion of U.S. Racial Problems," in *Race and the U.S. Foreign Policy from the Colonial Period to the Present: A Collection of Essays*, ed. Michael L. Krenn (New York: Garland, 1998), 275–88.

3. "The Supreme Court," *Manchester Guardian*, May 18, 1954, 6.

4. Peter Fryer, *Staying Power: The History of Black People in Britain* (London: Pluto Press, 1984), 372.

5. Edward Pilkington, *Beyond the Mother Country: West Indians and the Notting Hill White Riots* (London: I. B. Tauris, 1988).

6. Arnold Toynbee, *New York Times*, August 7, 1960.

7. Mike Sewell, "British Responses to Martin Luther King Jr and the Civil Rights Movement, 1954–68," in *The Making of Martin Luther King and the Civil Rights Movement*, ed. Brian Ward and Tony Badger (Houndmills, Basingstoke: Macmillan, 1996), 202.

8. Peter Alexander, *Racism, resistance and revolution* (London: Bookmarks, 1987), 33.

9. Robert Miles and Annie Phizacklea, *White Man's Country: Racism in British Politics* (London: Pluto Press, 1984), 53.

10. For details of public protest against the law, see *West Indian Gazette & Afro-Asian-Caribbean News*, February 1962.

11. Stephen Tuck, "From Greensboro to Notting Hill: The Sit-Ins in England," in *From Sit-Ins to SNCC: The Student Civil Rights Movement in the 1960s*, ed. Iwan Morgan and Philip Davies (Gainesville: University Press of Florida, 2012), 153–70.

12. Madge Dresser, *Black and White on the Buses: The 1963 Colour Bar Dispute in Bristol* (Bristol: Bristol Broadsides, 1989); Paul Stephenson and Lilleith Morrison, *Memoirs of a Black Englishman* (Bristol: Tangent Books, 2011).

13. "Bus Bar—Bristol Fashion," *Race Today,* June 1963), 5–6; "Bristol—After the Bus Dispute," *Race Today,* July 1963), 13–16.

14. *Daily Mail*, May 7, 1963.

15. "America's Unkept Promise," *Economist,* March 20, 1965), 1267.

16. Willian Papas, political cartoon, *Guardian,* March 9, 1965.

17. Leslie Illingworth, political cartoon, *Daily Mail,* March 22, 1965.

18. *Economist,* March 20, 1965. See also *Times,* February 17, 1965; *Guardian,* March 26, 1965.

19. *New Statesman,* March 19, 1965.

20. *Evening Standard,* March 22, 1965.

21. Editorial, *Spectator,* March 19, 1965.

22. *Daily Mail,* March 17, 1965.

23. *Sunday Citizen,* March 21, 1965.

24. *Daily Mirror,* March 15, 1965.

25. Erik Bleich, *Race Politics in Britain and France: Ideas and Policymaking since the 1960s* (Cambridge: Cambridge University Press, 2003), 48–50.

26. *Guardian,* December 7, 1964; *Times,* December 7, 1964; *Jet,* December 24, 1964.

27. Saladin M. Ambar, *Malcolm X at Oxford Union: Racial Politics in a Global Era* (New York: Oxford University Press, 2014); Stephen Tuck, *The Night Malcolm X Spoke at the Oxford Union: A Transatlantic Story of Antiracist Protest* (Berkeley: University of California Press, 2014); Joe Street, "Malcolm X, Smethwick, and the Influence of the African American Freedom Struggle on British Race Relations in the 1960s," *Journal of Black Studies* 38 (2008): 932–50.

28. *Guardian,* March 11, 1965.

29. *Times,* March 17, 1965.

30. Rob Witte, *Racist Violence and the State: A Comparative Analysis of Britain, France and the Netherlands* (London and New York: Routledge, 1996), 37.

31. HC Deb., December 19, 1966, vol. 279, col. 1867.

32. Brian Dooley, *Black and Green: The Fight for Civil Rights in Northern Ireland and Black America* (London: Pluto Press, 1998), 54–57; Simon Prince, *Northern Ireland's '68: Civil Rights, Global Revolt and the Origins of The Troubles* (Dublin: Irish Academic Press, 2007), 206–8.

33. HC Deb., April 22, 1969, vol. 782 col. 271.

34. For further detail on Paris as a haven for African Americans, see Michel Fabre, *From Harlem to Paris: Black Writers in France, 1840–1980* (Urbana: University of Illinois Press, 1991); Tyler Stovall, *Paris Noir: African Americans in the City of Light* (Boston: Houghton Mifflin, 1990).

35. Reported in the *Guardian,* October 3, 1962.

36. Simone de Beauvoir, *America Day by Day* (1954. Reprint, London: Phoenix, 1999), 229–46; Marcel Aymé, *Louisiane: Pièce en Quatre Actes* (Paris: Gallimard, 1961).
37. *Chicago Defender*, December 4, 1963.
38. Frank Costigliola, *France and the United States: The Cold Alliance Since World War II* (New York: Twayne, 1992), 111–12.
39. Max Paul Friedman, *Rethinking Anti-Americanism: The History of an Exceptional Concept in American Foreign Relations* (New York: Cambridge University Press, 2012), 169.
40. Maxim Silverman, *Deconstructing the Nation: Immigration, Racism and Citizenship in Modern France* (London and New York: Routledge, 1992), 42.
41. Silverman, *Deconstructing the Nation*, 46; Emily Marker, "Obscuring Race: Franco-African Conversations about Colonial Reform and Racism after World War II and the Making of Colorblind France, 1945–1950," *French Politics, Culture, and Society* 33 (2015): 18–19.
42. *Chicago Defender*, March 28, 1964.
43. *Le Figaro*, March 9, 1965.
44. *Le Monde*, February 11, 1965.
45. Richard Lentz and Karla K. Gower, *The Opinions of Mankind: Racial Issues, Press, and Propaganda in the Cold War* (Columbia: University of Missouri Press, 2010), 195–96.
46. *Le Monde*, March 19, 1965.
47. *Le Monde*, March 11, 1965.
48. *Le Figaro*, March 9, 1965.
49. Ibid., March 16, 1965.
50. Ibid.
51. "Eighty-Five Years Later," *Le Monde*, August 9, 1965.
52. *Le Figaro*, March 14–15, 1965.
53. *Le Monde*, May 28, 1965.
54. Interview with Martin Luther King for "Présence Protestante," November 7, 1965, at http://martin-luther-king.protestants.org/index.php?id=31468 (consulted December 24, 2015); *Le Christianisme aux XX Siècle*, November 4, 1965; *Le Figaro*, October 23, 1965; *New York Times*, September 30, October 25, 1965.
55. *Le Figaro*, March 22, 1965.
56. Cited in *New York Times*, March 12, 1965.
57. Gabriel J. Chin and Rose Cuizon Villazor, eds., *The Immigration and Nationality Act of 1965* (New York: Cambridge University Press, 1965).
58. Silverman, *Deconstructing the Nation*, 42.
59. Randall Hansen, *Citizenship and Immigration in Postwar Britain* (Oxford: Oxford University Press, 2000), chap. 6.
60. *Le Figaro*, cited in *Chicago Defender*, September 10, 1966.

2
MEDIA AND MEMORY

7

Mediating Selma

1965, 2015

ANIKO BODROGHKOZY

The Selma campaign of 1965 and its enduring significance can be understood in a variety of different ways, as the contributors of this volume make clear. I want to suggest we also need to understand the Selma campaign as fundamentally and crucially a media event. It functioned as a particular kind of media event in 1965 and then, fifty years later, Selma became a new kind of media event in 2015, largely because of the success and controversy around Ava DuVernay's Hollywood film *Selma*.

In 1965 network television news and photojournalism, the two forms of media I will focus on in this paper, had particular stories they wanted to tell about Selma, emphasizing particular themes, along with visual and narrative tropes while ignoring other ways to present the Selma story. Fifty years later, Hollywood cinema, in the hands of an African American female director, has a different story to tell about the Selma campaign. The much celebrated, discussed, and debated film also emphasizes certain things, while ignoring or downplaying others. It gives a very different rendering of the Selma campaign than audiences saw fifty years ago on television screens and in newsmagazines. What is significant about this new "media event" of Selma? How has Selma been "mediated" and why did it matter in 1965? Why and how does it matter in 2015?

I want to start with Bloody Sunday, the confrontation between nonviolent voting rights marchers and Alabama state troopers on the Edmund Pettus Bridge, March 7, 1965, and its representation to the nation in 1965. As I will argue, those iconic images differ in important ways from the representations that DuVernay's film gives audiences in 2015. Bloody Sunday is the most famous and galvanizing event of the Selma campaign and one of the iconic moments of the civil rights movement. Why is it famous? Why is it so consequential? Its momentousness and its impact rest largely on the fact that it was a television phenomenon.

Certainly, Bloody Sunday received front-page newspaper coverage. In his pioneering analysis of the Selma protests and the passage of the Voting Rights Act, David Garrow notes how congressional members referenced newspaper coverage in their call for legislative action. Nevertheless, Garrow points out that the television coverage of Bloody Sunday seemed to have "a more intense impact" on them and that this form of media was "extremely influential" in raising awareness and concern in the general population.[1] Television coverage functioned in a fundamentally different manner from that of print media—and how the footage got to the American public is crucial to its galvanizing power.

On that Sunday night, the news division of ABC, one of the country's three television networks, made the decision to break into its prime-time programming to show the Pettus Bridge brutality. Sunday night, then and now, was the biggest night for TV watching, and ABC had a very special draw for viewers: a premiere broadcast of the blockbuster 1961 motion picture *Judgment at Nuremberg* with a star-studded cast of Hollywood luminaries, including the perennially popular Spencer Tracy. The film dealt with the Holocaust and the moral culpability of Germans in the genocide of Europe's Jews. Approximately forty-eight million people tuned in.[2] Even in those days of only three networks, news programming did not generate those kinds of viewer numbers. Shortly after the film started, ABC interrupted the film with its report from Selma. The juxtaposing of a narrative about Nazi brutality toward victimized Jews with footage of southern segregationist brutality against victimized blacks was incredibly powerful.

The news division's decision to break in to that particular program resulted in a remarkable moment of televisual "flow." Within the field of media and cultural studies, Raymond Williams, in the 1970s, developed this concept he coined "flow." He argued that television was not experienced as discrete units of programming; rather, the entirety of programs, promos, and ads all flowed together and meanings likewise flowed across different bits of programming.[3] In this case, the meanings from *Judgment at Nuremberg* flowed into the Bloody Sunday footage amplifying its already nascent signification. Numerous commentators made the inevitable

Figure 7.1. Bloody Sunday 1.

Figure 7.2. Bloody Sunday 2.

comparisons between Nazi storm troopers and Alabama state troopers in the following days. David Garrow, in his study of congressional response, noted that a dozen speakers "drew parallels between the Alabama action and the official conduct typical of totalitarian regimes such as Nazi Germany."[4] Ordinary people made similar connections. One young man from Auburn, Alabama, wrote to the *Birmingham News* observing, "I have just witnessed on television the new sequel to Adolf Hitler's brown shirts. They are George Wallace's blue shirts."[5]

Beyond the juxtaposing of the Nazi Holocaust motion picture and the Selma news report, what was going on with the news footage itself, outside of the elements of flow, to elicit such powerful responses? News cameras had been cordoned off to the side of the road at the foot of the bridge as the marchers encountered the cordon of troopers blocking their way down the highway. With troopers to the left and marchers to the right, the television cameras were able to record with great clarity a showdown between opposing forces: troopers with gasmasks and billy clubs plowing over a line of stationary and peaceful marchers and beating the marchers mercilessly off in the distance as the gas explodes and troopers on horseback attack. Viewers seem to have a ringside seat, but it is from a distance. Once tear gas explodes, it is hard to see very much. The footage becomes like a horror film as viewers can only imagine what is going on behind the plumes of smoke. One can hear coughing, screaming, and beating, but the monstrousness is obscured. Viewers may be encouraged to pity and sympathize with the often-hidden victims of this news film, but not to feel as if one with them. This is one way to narrate the story: pity at a distance.

Ava DuVernay, in her retelling and reenacting of Bloody Sunday, makes some very different representational choices. Rather than attempt to recreate the iconic news footage, she shifts the vantage point by putting her camera on the bridge in the midst of the beatings. With a visual dynamism that only cinema can provide, we get individualized shots of characters we have come to know—John Lewis, Hosea Williams, Amelia Boynton—being bludgeoned. But we also see unnamed marchers cut down, whipped, chased by mounted troopers, and overcome by the tear gas. The assault is literally up close and personal. The camera follows John Lewis attempting to get up and assist the unconscious Boynton. We track in to a close-up on Hosea Williams in the thick soup of tear gas and are encouraged not only to witness his anguished expression but also to share in it.

Figure 7.3. John Lewis.

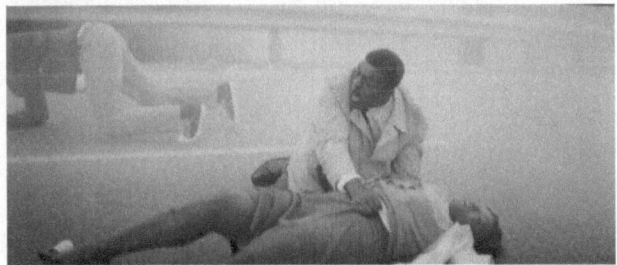

Figure 7.4. Amelia Boynton.

Figure 7.5. Hosea Williams.

DuVernay is putting viewers right in the center of the violence. By bringing her camera close, viewers are encouraged to feel the blows of the billy clubs and the sting of the tear gas. The film asks viewers to *be with* the marchers, sharing and partaking in their brutalization. This is not something the iconic Bloody Sunday news film necessarily invites its viewers to do. DuVernay is not trying to elicit pity, but rather emotional participation.

This distinction gets at a crucial theme of civil rights–era media coverage, both in TV news and in photojournalism: How are African

Americans represented and portrayed for mass media audiences? In my book, *Equal Time: Television and the Civil Rights Movement*, I suggested that the mainstream media, television in particular, provided a limited range of representations: individualized "worthy" black victims who were typically educated, articulate, middle-class-appearing, and not seen to be part of organized activism or, when in a group (such as the March on Washington), seen as silenced, dignified, scrupulously nonviolent and spoken for by either Dr. Martin Luther King Jr. or by a white newsman.[6]

Martin A. Berger makes some similar observations about photojournalism in his book, *Seeing through Race: A Reinterpretation of Civil Rights Photography*. Mainstream news organizations chose particular images to illustrate their stories: photographs of blacks as powerless, supine, supplicating, images that he argues would elicit white viewers' sympathy without provoking any white anxieties. Berger argues that iconic civil rights photography typically gives us white segregationists as empowered—they're the active ones—making bad things happen. The implication of these photographic choices is to encourage good white people who encounter these images to come to the rescue of the power*less* blacks being brutalized by power*ful* bad whites.[7]

The imagery of black victimization and white brutality was crucial to how and why the Bloody Sunday news film moved audiences the way it did in 1965 and continues to do so fifty years later. For instance, we can compare the iconic photograph that ran in *Life* magazine from the 1963 Birmingham campaign. In the foreground, we see a trio of white firemen pointing the powerful blast of water from their hose. Their stance, with jutting arms and bodies leaning into the spray, puts them in the active position: they are in charge of this narrative. Further into the middle ground are seated, crumpled, and huddled black protesters on the sidewalk suffering the explosion of the water against their bodies. They are the objects, passively and helplessly enduring this brutal treatment.[8]

Likewise, the Bloody Sunday footage shows us blacks knocked over and sprawled to the ground as the state troopers plow over them and then bludgeon them with billy clubs. The ultimate message is that whites are always in control and that good white people, seeing these images, need to take control away from bad white people to ameliorate the condition of victimized but powerless black people. Berger criticizes this impulse in civil rights iconography as it discounts the agency of African Americans;

its short-term benefits (passage of legislation) undermines attention to more long-term structural issues around racism and white supremacy.

Martin Berger's argument is compelling but, I would suggest, it discounts the agency among civil rights activists in orchestrating these confrontations. During the Selma campaign, Dr. Martin Luther King Jr. publicly proclaimed, "We are here to say to the white men that we no longer will let them use clubs on us in the dark corners. We're going to make them do it in the glaring light of television."[9] Rather than hapless, docile, pathetically suffering objects, civil rights activists knowingly embraced the redemptive value of "unmerited suffering," as King put it, and the iconography of white violence.[10] They were active agents in these narratives, whether or not white audiences grasped that fact or not. Ironically, the white racists were less in charge than they or the white journalists may have thought. On Bloody Sunday, probably none of the marchers expected they were heading to Montgomery that day. Marching to Montgomery wasn't really the narrative. Segregationist oppression and obstruction was the story the marchers expected to tell.

None of those marchers, however, expected the degree of the brutality they encountered. And that is why the footage is so shocking: the white violence is so out of control, so excessive. The sheer hyperbolic, disproportionate response of white power at the Edmund Pettus Bridge calls to mind another set of images that galvanized the attention of the nation more recently: Ferguson, Missouri. Compare iconic images of the August 2014 confrontations between the militarized Ferguson police force against the unarmed mostly black Ferguson citizens protesting the police killing of an unarmed, young black man, Michael Brown. In one image that graced the pages of the *New York Times* and was heavily circulated elsewhere, a young black man with knitted cap, long dreadlocks, and arms raised faces a trio of battle-ready police officers, decked out in gas masks, body armor, and the accouterments of warfare and brandishing automatic weapons as they race toward this clearly unarmed and solitary figure.[11] Another now iconic image that appeared on the cover of *Time* magazine featured a lone black protester kneeling on the ground with arm raised while a convoy of military vehicles, obscured by haze and, perhaps, tear gas advances on the lone figure.[12]

The now-famous "hands-up, don't-shoot" stance by the protesters (and the accompanying Twitter #handsupdontshoot hashtag that went viral) seen in these images and countless others suggests victimization and a docile subjugation. However, it is anything but docile or passive. Reverend Al Sharpton both encouraged and explained Ferguson protesters' use of the gesture, by proclaiming, "If you're angry, throw your arms up. If you want justice, throw your arms up."[13] In solidarity with Michael Brown, protesters mimicked his final (now disputed) gesture. Kate Drazner Hoyt argues that they used it to keep Brown's imperiled body and subjectivity affectively alive via their own embodied standing-in for him: not merely standing *with* Brown, but rather standing *within* his victimized position.[14] The stance, thus, subversively talked back to police power and made defiantly visible the power relations between white law enforcement and black communities.

The protesters, using this seemingly submissive gesture, actually empowered themselves—at least within the realm of image politics—eventually leading to action by the U.S. Department of Justice and the forced resignations of key Ferguson white judicial and police officials, in part by the dissemination of media imagery that suggested black powerlessness. In the end, the protesters commanded more power, ironically, than the police with their 2014 body armor and Humvees or the 1965 troopers with their billy clubs and tear gas. In both cases, they made the federal government take action. In both cases, they understood the power of media imagery to tell narratives that at key moments they at least partially controlled.

I want to switch my focus now to the emphasis on white people in the Selma campaign in the media coverage in 1965. While Berger argues that civil rights photojournalism emphasizes empowered (and malevolent) whites, television coverage typically took somewhat different approaches. Generally, network television news tried to avoid giving segregationists a platform, but rather elevated "the Southern white moderate" and white allies to black civil rights activists. White "moderates" or white activists were more likely to be interviewed than blacks (with the exception of King, of course). For instance, white clergymen and students who descended on Selma following Bloody Sunday were far more likely to be interviewed than were black clergy or students—or any black activist involved in the Selma campaign who was not Martin Luther King. In order both to make civil rights activity unthreatening and to provide identification points for white viewers, network television news tended to overemphasize the significance of white supporters and white participants.[15]

We see something similar in *Life* magazine's coverage of the Selma campaign following Bloody Sunday after King called on clergy and other supporters to come to Selma. In an eight-page spread, one entire full-color page is devoted to two photos featuring Mrs. Paul Douglas, the wife of an Illinois senator, who has come to Selma to lend her support. One photo shows the pearl-bedecked and elegant elderly lady in close-up patting Martin Luther King's shoulder approvingly with a white-gloved hand. In another on the same page Mrs. Douglas is center-framed looking off with a concerned expression with black Selmians walking behind her. Despite the visual attention paid to her presence by *Life* magazine, Mrs. Douglas was in no way important to the Selma campaign, but she was white. Another two-page spread is dominated by a large photo of kneeling clergymen and others under the looming figure of a club-wielding Alabama trooper. Their importance: they, also, are all white.[16]

The media in 1965 took a similar approach in privileging whites in their coverage of Selma's three martyrs: Jimmie Lee Jackson, the Reverend James Reeb, and Viola Liuzzo. Jackson and his family received practically no coverage. The lack of media attention to Jackson's killing was an issue that DuVernay's film points out in a scene between Martin Luther King and President Lyndon B. Johnson following Reverend Reeb's murder. King notes that LBJ called Reeb's widow—and that this gesture got a lot of press attention—but he never thought to contact Jackson's family who received no national media coverage. In television news, neither Jackson nor his family were interviewed, portrayed as individuals, or spotlighted in any way.[17] A CBS reporter, in a most unfortunate use of words, merely described the twenty-six-year-old Jackson as a "farm boy" as well as "a deacon of his church, mason, and activist." Conversely, Reeb, a white Unitarian minister from Boston, and Liuzzo, a wife and mother of five from Detroit, were white. Their deaths received a great deal of poignant coverage and interviews with family members. The media attention to Liuzzo was massive, focusing on her status as a wife and mother. In melodramatic poignancy, unusual for network news at this time, a CBS news story highlighted Liuzzo's grief-stricken widower impulsively trying to call Alabama governor George Wallace.[18]

Ava DuVernay provides a very different narrative; in fact, *Selma* flips the script completely. Jackson, his mother, and his eighty-two-year-old grandfather, Cager Lee, are significant side characters, and the film (not quite accurately) portrays them as activists in Selma confronting Sheriff

Jim Clark, being beaten by him, and (equally inaccurately) having Annie Lee Cooper come to their defense by walloping Clark.[19] The film provides a tender and poignant scene with King attempting to comfort the grieving Cager Lee at the morgue. Reeb and Liuzzo are briefly introduced and acknowledged but, unlike the Jackson family, are not given privileged narrative positions.

Ava DuVernay has said that she wasn't interested in doing a "white savior" film.[20] She said this in response to the criticism that the film misrepresented Lyndon Johnson's role in pushing for voting rights legislation. The "white hero" narrative, which, as we will see, has been until recently the dominant trope in Hollywood films dealing with the civil rights era, also factors quite centrally in news media coverage of the movement and in the ways the period has been remembered. White journalists become saviors to the movement by heroically facing the same brutality from racist segregationists that movement activists face.[21] In the Selma campaign, NBC's Richard Valeriani was clubbed in the head while covering a nighttime march in Marion—this was the march that resulted in Jimmie Lee Jackson's death. Valeriani famously delivers his news report from his hospital bed with bandaged head and slurred speech.[22] His heroism and the brutality meted out to him become the story, not Jackson's death at the hands of state troopers. Memoirs by network television star reporters such as Dan Rather make much of the violence they encountered in trying to cover the civil rights story. Because segregationist mobs tended to single out TV news reporters and cameramen, one can detect a latent self-glorification in these narratives.[23] Gene Roberts and Hank Klibanoff's definitive volume on the media and the civil rights era (which focuses largely on print journalism), *The Race Beat*, continues to privilege the role of reporters in the civil rights movement's success.[24]

Hollywood took up the "white savior" narrative trope beginning in the 1980s in the first attempts by major motion pictures to chronicle the civil rights era. In 1988, the blockbuster film *Mississippi Burning* provided the Hollywood narrative template for telling the civil rights story. Two white FBI agents come to the rescue of brutalized black victims of segregationist racism in the Magnolia State following the 1964 murder of civil rights workers based on James Chaney, Andrew Goodman, and Michael Schwerner. Using the conventions of the "cop action" genre film like *Die Hard* (1988) and *Lethal Weapon* (1987), the film focuses on two antagonistic lawmen, one an older, crusty, and southern agent played by

Gene Hackman; the other a young, idealistic, by-the-book agent played by Willem DeFoe who allies himself with the civil rights struggle and tries to persuade his partner that he should, too.[25] Blacks are presented only as victims and objects of racist brutality. The film provides powerful and wrenching scenes of white violence against the black community, but beyond a scene with a King-like preacher telling his congregation about how tired he is of the brutality, we see no evidence of black activism or organizing.[26]

As Martin Berger would argue, blacks are presented as objects of pity and white active agents (in the world of the film and in the film audience) are beseeched to come to their aid. In 1996, *Ghosts of Mississippi* gives us a heroic white district attorney who finally brings the assassin of Medgar Evers to trial and conviction. *The Help*, in 2011, provides another white savior in the civil rights years, also in Mississippi, who affords the means by which black domestics can give voice to their oppressive conditions. The representational field has gotten somewhat better since the black maids are also protagonists, not just victims; the film, nevertheless, emphasizes Skeeter, the white writer, as the central heroine. More so than in the book on which the film is based, the narrative and the film's publicity campaign revolve entirely around Skeeter, played by rising star Emma Stone, her relationship with her white girlfriends from their days at Ole Miss, Skeeter's desire to be a writer, and her struggles in gaining the trust of Jackson's maids. Stone is the film's star, not Viola Davis's Aibileen or Octavia Spencer's Minny. The film's poster emphasizes this by placing Stone's Skeeter in the center of the picture looking out and engaging the viewer, while Davis and Spencer's characters are off to the side looking at each other while the film's evil nemesis, Skeeter's racist sorority sister, Hilly, sits opposite, absorbed narcissistically in her manicure.

Selma, following on the success of another major Hollywood film tackling the civil rights era, Lee Daniels' *The Butler* in 2013, departs dramatically from the previous Hollywood template. Like the Daniels film, blacks in *Selma* are not only subjects of their own stories but also the main protagonists. DuVernay is not interested in finding whites to privilege or in giving white audiences the white heroes they presumably need to identify with. President Johnson is the only major white character in the film, and DuVernay reduced his role from what it was in the original script because she felt it slanted the story too much toward him.[27]

It is obviously no accident that we get Hollywood stories focused on blacks as narrative agents and protagonists when we have films directed and under the control of African Americans as is the case with both these films. The industry power of Oprah Winfrey in helping green light both projects, which she also acts in, is obviously significant. In 1988 when white filmmaker Alan Parker put together *Mississippi Burning*, he publicly admitted that "the film would probably have never been made" if he did not have white heroes.[28] *The Butler* and *Selma* suggest something in the cultural environment has changed significantly. Hollywood executives may be realizing that a nation that twice elected an African American president could handle major cinematic offerings with black-themed narratives and central protagonists—at least if they are relegated to historical periods such as the civil rights movement and the era of American slavery, with the box office hits *Twelve Years a Slave* (2013) and *Django Unchained* (2012).

Conversely, the major criticism that Ava DuVernay's film has received is its somewhat negative treatment of President Lyndon Johnson.[29] In fact, for a while the LBJ controversy crowded out almost any other media discussion of the film. In an ironic twist, the media was putting a white man back at the center of the Selma story. For instance, former LBJ aide, Joseph Califano took to the *Washington Post* to claim that Selma was essentially LBJ's idea.[30] And then the media jumped aboard this new story of just how central the president was or was not. I have no desire to carry on the debate about whether or not the film is wholly accurate in its portrayal of LBJ.[31] Rather, I want to note that even in a narrative that insists on the primacy and centrality of black subjects in the civil rights story, there is still a residual push to reassert the centrality of a white subject.

If *Selma* emphasizes black protagonists, one of the ways it does so is by highlighting various leaders and individuals associated with the Selma campaign, especially women such as Amelia Boynton, Diane Nash, and especially Annie Lee Cooper. While the film, as I will discuss further below, focuses on King, it doesn't do so to the exclusion of these and other key figures like John Lewis and Hosea Williams. Annie Lee Cooper, a foot soldier in the Selma struggle and largely unknown before DuVernay's film, became almost a household name mostly because Oprah Winfrey portrays her. In one of the film's opening scenes, we see Cooper calmly and with tired dignity attempt to register to vote, answering increasingly difficult questions by a hostile white registrar only to be summarily denied when she cannot name all sixty-seven Alabama county judges.

Figure 7.6. Annie Lee Cooper.

Cooper became momentarily famous following her January 25, 1965, scuffle with Sheriff Clark. A news photo of Cooper on the ground as two sheriffs pin her down and Clark wields a billy club over her splashed across the front pages of newspapers around the country. While the *New York Times*' caption noted that Cooper had hit the sheriff, the image conveys a message of white violence, police brutality, and black victimization. DuVernay's film, as we have seen, portrays Cooper retaliating against Clark because he has been brutalizing the Jimmie Lee Jackson family, including Jackson's elderly grandfather. Taking creative license, DuVernay gives viewers a protective, matriarchal Cooper coming to the defense of her people.

In 1965 CBS news provided its viewers a very different image of Mrs. Cooper. In a story broadcast on the Cronkite *Evening News,* Cooper is shown as disruptive and suspicious even before her confrontation with Clark. The CBS camera zooms in on her standing on the courthouse steps in a line of would-be registrants; yet she is wearing no shoes. The news film zooms in on her dishabille and pans over to show her footwear on the next step. In close-up, she appears shifty-eyed. In the struggle with Clark and his men, CBS shows her being rolled over and hauled up to her shoe-less feet very inelegantly. Everything about the CBS portrayal of Mrs. Cooper suggests that she is deviant, out of control, and responsible for the manhandling she receives. Clark is interviewed, out of breath, explaining how he and his men were attempting to create order. Mrs. Cooper is never given the opportunity to speak.[32]

Annie Lee Cooper's clobbering of Sheriff Clark obviously defied the Martin Luther King–led nonviolent strategies of the movement. But perhaps more important, she defied a media script: civil rights activists were supposed to be objects of pity, abject and powerless, requiring help. The iconic images of the 1963 Birmingham campaign that Berger analyses in his work exemplify the theme. In her film, DuVernay had to give Cooper's action a suitable motivation, raise it to a noble and heroic status.

If DuVernay gives us portraits of Selma's female leaders and foot soldiers, nevertheless, the film, ultimately, is mostly about Martin Luther King Jr. In its privileging of King in telling the civil rights story, the 2014 film echoes the 1965 media coverage of Selma. Certainly for television news, Selma was King and King was Selma. For instance, CBS in its coverage of the Bloody Sunday melee, insisted on inserting King (as well as Alabama governor George Wallace) into the confrontation even though neither one was anywhere near Selma that Sunday. Describing King and Wallace as "two determined men," the CBS anchor made sense of the event by observing: "Yesterday their determination turned the streets of Alabama into a battleground as Wallace's state troopers broke up a march order by King." Set up this way, the marchers were little more than pawns for King's grudge match with Wallace. This framing denied any agency to the activists on the bridge: they were only stand-ins for King, the important political player.[33]

More generally, in CBS's coverage of the campaign, King was the only "go-to" African American spokesperson reporters turned to for on-camera explanations or reactions. Turnaround Tuesday, the aborted second march following Bloody Sunday—which King led—is noteworthy for the extremes to which cameramen went to try to keep King always in the center as marchers proceeded to the foot of the bridge, kneeled to pray, and then abruptly turned around and retreated. Even when, as in the case of CBS's aired report, the footage was bobbled, occasionally out-of-focus, and visually chaotic, the story of the march was about King—what he would do, what he would say. The marchers around him were mostly extras.

DuVernay's film obviously corrects this narrative of King-and-only-King, but *Selma* does not fundamentally undermine this traditional way of telling the civil rights story. The publicity poster for the film visually reenacts CBS's presentation of a King-led Bloody Sunday. The poster presents us with King's head and shoulders from behind as he confronts Alabama state troopers in the background arrayed before him. The poster shows no marchers: we, as viewers along with the marchers are imaginatively supposed to be lined up behind him. Here again, "Selma" is about King, his leadership, his heroism, his individuality, his centrality.

Ultimately why does it matter how the media, then and now, represented the Selma voting rights campaign? In 1965, the media's focus on abject black victimization and on white participation may have helped to galvanize the country (at least outside the Deep South) in supporting voting rights. But it did so perhaps at the cost of seeing black people as fully human and in control of their own political movement and destiny.

Fifty years later, *Selma*, the movie, asks audiences to embrace African Americans as active agents, not victims to be rescued by privileged whites. And it favors black protagonists rather than white "moderates" and supporters. It shatters the long-standing Hollywood way of telling the civil rights story and the assumption that mass (read: white) audiences will only see film dramas if they have white main characters. The film also implicitly challenges the sentiment encapsulated in Hillary Clinton's much discussed declaration in 2008 that "Dr. King's dream began to be realized when President Johnson passed the Civil Rights Act. It took a president to get it done."[34] LBJ was certainly important to the passage of the legislation, but Clinton's quote suggests King was merely a dreamer and that there were no activists organizing and pushing and demanding and forcing change.

Selma provides a powerful corrective to fifty years of media representations that, while well-meaning, have given Americans a rather limited understanding of who made the civil rights revolution. The film has its own limitations, of course. It continues the over-emphasis on King, even as it recognizes other activists and even the tensions within the movement, especially between the SCLC and the Student Nonviolent Coordinating Committee. In correcting the "white savior" theme, it perhaps stumbles in its portrayal of LBJ. Television news and photojournalism got a partial version of Selma's significance, largely through a whitened lens; *Selma*, with an African American lens, also tells a partial story, but it is a necessary and corrective partial story.

Notes

1. David J. Garrow, *Protest at Selma: Martin Luther King Jr. and the Voting Rights Act of 1965* (New Haven: Yale University Press, 1978), 163.

2. Dan T. Carter, *The Politics of Rage: George Wallace, the Origins of the New Conservatism, and the Transformation of American Politics* (New York: Simon and Schuster, 1995), 248.

3. Raymond Williams, *Television: Technology and Cultural Form* (London: Fontana, 1974).

4. Garrow, *Protest at Selma*, 146.

5. Aniko Bodroghkozy, *Equal Time: Television and the Civil Rights Movement* (Urbana: University of Illinois Press, 2013), 142.

6. Ibid.

7. Martin A. Berger, *Seeing through Race: A Reinterpretation of Civil Rights Photography* (Berkeley: University of California Press, 2011).

8. "They Fight a Fire That Won't Go Out," *Life,* May 11, 1963, 26–27. *Life* magazine is fully scanned and publicly accessible in Google Books. The rest of the magazine's coverage of Birmingham features numerous other pictures of blacks being brutalized. Only one image shows blacks as empowered and active: a picture of a crowd of protesters, including a center-framed image of a women with a raised, clenched fist (34).

9. Bodroghkozy, *Equal Time*, 2. King said this on March 18, 1965, in Montgomery following the beating of students protesting disenfranchisement in the Alabama capital. They were beaten and whipped by mounted sheriff's posse men. Television cameras did, indeed, record the melee.

10. King, "Suffering and Faith," *Christian Century* 77 (27 April 1960): 510, at http://kingencyclopedia.stanford.edu/encyclopedia/documentsentry/suffering_and_faith.1.html (consulted March 23, 2017).

11. Randall Kennedy and Jennifer Schuessler, "Ferguson Images Evoke Civil Rights Era," *New York Times,* August 14, 2014, A14.

12. *Time*, September 1, 2014.

13. Matt Pearce, "Protesters use hands-up gesture defiantly after Michael Brown shooting," *Los Angeles Times,* August 12, 2014, at http://www.latimes.com/nation/la-na-hands-up-20140813-story.html (consulted March 23, 2017).

14. Kate Drazner Hoyt, "The Effect of the Hashtag: #HandsUpDontShoot and the Body in Peril," *Explorations in Media Ecology* 15, no. 1 (March 2016): 33–54.

15. I discuss these strategies in more detail in *Equal Time*.

16. "The Savage Season Begins," *Life,* March 19, 1965, 30–37.

17. That is the case at least for CBS whose nightly coverage of the Selma story for *The Evening News with Walter Cronkite* I was able to study at the CBS News Archive. NBC did not preserve its nightly news programming, and ABC did not inaugurate a half hour nightly news program until 1967.

18. Bodroghkozy, *Equal Time*, 132–35.

19. Jimmie Lee Jackson was active in neighboring Perry County. Annie Lee Cooper (who is discussed more below) did famously strike Clark, but not in retaliation for his violence toward other voting rights activists.

20. Gavin Edwards, "We Shall Overcome: Ava DuVernay on Making 'Selma,'" *Rolling Stone,* January 5, 2015, at http://www.rollingstone.com/movies/features/ava-duvernay-on-making-selma-20150105 (consulted March 23, 2017).

21. Mark Joseph Walmsley notes the lionizing of civil rights–era journalists in "Tell It Like It Isn't: SNCC and the Media, 1960–1965," *Journal of American Studies* 48, no. 1 (February 2014): 294.

22. Juan Williams, *Eyes on the Prize: America's Civil Rights Years, 1954–1965* (New York: Viking Press, 1987), 265. See also Nancy Doyle Palmer, "Selma and Richard Valeriani: A Reporter's Story," *Huffington Post,* January 5, 2015, updated March 7, 2015, at http://www.huffingtonpost.com/nancy-doyle-palmer-/selma-and-richard-valeria_b_6414664.html (consulted March 23, 2017).

23. Dan Rather with Mickey Hershkowitz, *The Camera Never Blinks: Adventures of a TV Journalist* (New York: William Morrow, 1977).

24. Gene Roberts and Hank Klibanoff, *The Race Beat: The Press, the Civil Rights Struggle, and the Awakening of a Nation* (New York: Vintage, 2007).

25. The film perverts civil rights history in that the FBI were at best neutral and often quite hostile to civil rights activism and individual organizers—the wiretapping and blackmailing of Martin Luther King being the most well-known instance of FBI attempts to derail the movement. *Mississippi Burning* took a significant amount of flak for its portrayal of FBI agents as crusaders for racial justice.

26. For a fine analysis of the film and how Hollywood remembers civil rights, see Kristen Hoerl, "Burning Mississippi into Memory? Cinematic Amnesia as a Resource for Remembering Civil Rights," *Critical Studies in Media Communication* 26, no. 1 (March 2009): 54–79.

27. Gavin Edwards, "We Shall Overcome."

28. Kristen Hoerl, "Burning Mississippi into Memory," 59.

29. DuVernay also received some chiding for not developing the film's black female characters more fully.

30. Joseph A. Califano Jr. "The Movie 'Selma' Has a Glaring Flaw," *Washington Post,* December 26, 2014, at https://www.washingtonpost.com/opinions/the-movie-selma-has-a-glaring-historical-inaccuracy/2014/12/26/70ad3ea2-8aa4-11e4-a085-34e9b9f09a58_story.html?utm_term=.08145adc85b5 (consulted March 23, 2017).

31. See for instance: David Kaiser, "Why You Should Care That *Selma* Gets LBJ Wrong," *Time,* January 9, 2015, at http://time.com/3658593/selma-lbj-history/ (consulted March 23, 2017); Amy Davidson, "Why 'Selma' Is More Than Fair to L.B.J.," *New Yorker,* January 22, 2015, at http://www.newyorker.com/news/amy-davidson/selma-fair-l-b-j (consulted March 23, 2017); Kent Germany, "When History Is Not Good Enough for Hollywood: Selma, Lyndon B. Johnson, and Martin Luther King, Jr.," *AHA Today: A Blog of the American Historical Association,* February 25, 2015, at http://blog.historians.org/2015/02/history-good-enough-hollywood-selma-lyndon-b-johnson-martin-luther-king-jr/ (consulted March 23, 2017).

32. Bodroghkozy, *Equal Time,* 120–21.

33. Ibid., 126–27.

34. Sarah Wheaton, "Clinton's Civil Rights Lesson," *New York Times,* January 7, 2008, at https://thecaucus.blogs.nytimes.com/2008/01/07/civilrights/ (consulted March 23, 2017).

8

"They Couldn't Just Write It the Way It Wasn't Anymore"

Mainstream Media Narratives and the 1965 Selma Campaign

MARK WALMSLEY

In one of the most iconic scenes in Ava DuVernay's 2014 film *Selma*, *New York Times* reporter Roy Reed narrates his story down a telephone as the screen cuts from images of brutal violence on the Edmund Pettus Bridge to the reaction of men and women from all walks of life sitting around their televisions in shock and anger.[1] Reproducing sections of Reed's actual front-page article on the March verbatim—and clearly staging certain shots to resemble photos published in various national newspapers—this scene mirrors historical scholarship that emphasizes the role that media coverage played in the success of the civil rights movement, and particularly the Selma campaign.[2] By choosing to highlight Reed as the only journalist with a named speaking role, *Selma* also consciously or unconsciously promotes the notion that "mainstream" northern outlets took the lead in this coverage. In the process, the film echoes narratives produced by journalists such as Richard Valeriani of NBC news, who pit a dishonest southern establishment against the burning white light of mainstream media scrutiny. Indeed, claiming at a commemorative event in 2004 that northern coverage meant that racists in the South "couldn't just write it the way it wasn't anymore," Valeriani exemplifies the self-congratulatory mood within media circles that allowed Hedley Donovan of *TIME* magazine to claim in 1968 that his corporation had "very possibly . . . done as much for the cause of civil rights as any private organization in the United States."[3]

This celebration of the mainstream media's impact on the southern movement is not confined to Hollywood. In what historian Gordon Mantler argues is the "virtual lionization of journalists," reporters who covered the civil rights movement have been valorized as having "stared down shotgun barrels and crawled out of ditches under gunfire to get stories."[4] Indeed, popular narratives—such as actor and filmmaker Jim Carrier's *A Traveler's Guide to the Civil Rights Movement*—claim it was, "ultimately, pictures and stories of police states trying to deny citizens their rights [that] brought down the walls of segregation."[5] Credited with awakening a spirit of liberalism that allowed social movements to break down discriminatory laws and practices that had stood for decades, mainstream coverage of the civil rights movement has been described by communication scholars as a "classic example" of the way in which journalists performed their roles as "a voice for the voiceless."[6] Former Student Nonviolent Coordinating Committee (SNCC) chairman John Lewis even put this praise on Congressional Record, claiming that "without the media, the civil rights movement would have been like a bird without wings."[7]

However, as this chapter will demonstrate, race beat reporting was not above the logistical, social, and commercial processes that dominated news production in the 1960s. Indeed, while race beat reporters may have claimed that their coverage held up a mirror to the brutalities of the South, it is important to remember that:

> It is a fact of optics that the shape, composition, location and angle of a mirror affect the image it reflects. So even if we do think of the media as a mirror, we should examine its structure, check its position, and always remember who is holding it, and at what angle.[8]

Using the Selma campaign as a case study, this chapter demonstrates how processes common to reporting—such as sourcing and legitimizing information and framing stories—influence the image produced by this "mirror" and can lead to serious misconceptions in both popular and scholarly understandings of the past. Before doing so, however, it is important to understand how the racial and geographical composition of the "mainstream" press influenced what newspapers such as the *New York Times* believed was "Fit to Print." For instance, while the *Times* expressed mild alarm when a survey revealed that 31 percent of white New Yorkers did not know a single African American by name in 1964, the picture within the nation's most powerful newsrooms was not much different.⁹ *Newsweek* editor, Osborne "Oz" Elliott, for example, was born to an affluent New York family who purposely recruited Irish servants to avoid having African Americans in their home. He recalled that, while his parents were certainly bigoted, "by the simple force of isolation, everyone in their set was."¹⁰ Indeed, born and raised in highly segregated northern cities, editors such as Max Frankel, who joined the *New York Times* in 1952 and became its executive editor in 1986, "did not live or play close enough to blacks in early life to grow up genuinely color-blind."¹¹

While the impact of this racial divide on coverage could have been ameliorated by the contribution of African American reporters, even liberal publications such as *Newsweek* had attached a low priority to the recruitment of African Americans. Recalling that *Newsweek* only integrated its newsroom in the late 1960s, Peter Goldman states that "in a way that was the shame of *Newsweek*. . . . We were out there on the street preaching and our own house was not in order."¹² *Newsweek* was by no means alone. While the *New York Times* hired its first African American reporter, George Streator, in 1945, it would be more than a decade before black journalists outnumbered the lift attendants hired to give the office a southern plantation aesthetic.¹³ Indeed, one study by Lincoln University found that only twenty-one African Americans were working as reporters for white-owned newspapers in 1955—an apparent increase on just five in 1950.¹⁴ While the urban rioting of the mid-to-late 1960s hastened moves to employ journalists of color—a key recommendation of the Kerner Commission—there were still less than two hundred African American men and women working in the newsrooms of America's 1,740 daily newspapers in 1968.¹⁵

This lack of diversity had a detrimental impact on the nature of mainstream coverage, with *New York Times* editor Max Frankel recalling that "too often, we found ourselves discussing articles about racial strife without a single black face in the room."¹⁶ Raised in fundamentally different circumstances than the men and women whom they covered in the rural South, race beat journalists were therefore liable to produce and reinforce a narrative that prioritized a particular understanding of what the civil rights movement actually was. Indeed, despite being referred to in contemporary and modern discourses as the race beat, this coverage did not represent a long-standing commitment to news events relating to men and women of color in America.¹⁷ Instead, the race beat was a temporary phenomenon among the mainstream northern press that confined itself to the African American civil rights movement of the 1950s and 1960s. Concentrating on the increasingly vocal and dangerous protests against southern segregation, the race beat also had a limited geographical focus that tended to ignore northern racism until the ghettoes of cities like Los Angeles, Newark, and Detroit erupted in flames during the mid-to-late 1960s.

Consequently, mainstream narratives often bore little resemblance to what many in the movement—or activist circles in the 1960s in general—witnessed and experienced. Indeed, former Students for a Democratic Society member, Todd Gitlin, claims that:

> I worked in a movement and watched it construed as something quite other than what I thought it was. Living with the discrepancy became one characteristic experience of my generation; we had, after all, grown up to take on faith what was in the newspapers, and to believe with Walter Cronkite that "that's the way it is."[18]

This disjunction between media narratives and lived experience is a common feature of memoirs and testimonies from civil rights activists, especially those who espoused Black Power.[19]

More recently, revisionist historians have also blamed superficial media coverage for producing simplistic accounts of the movement that distort the nature of postwar civil rights activism. The historian Brian Ward, for instance, argues that media coverage and retrospective portrayals of the movement have helped create a "master narrative" that has reduced a complex history into a "reductive and brittle formulation."[20] Indeed, critiquing what he argues is the designation of the decade between the *Brown v. Board of Education of Topeka, Kansas,* decision and the Selma campaign as the "heroic period" of civil rights activism, Peniel Joseph argues that initial histories of the decade took their cues from the "bully pulpit" of the national media and "differed . . . only in the degree to which they condemned the black power movement and its legacy."[21]

Unfortunately, however, whether scholars choose to laud or condemn media narratives, few have actively engaged with the people and institutions that created this "first rough draft of history."[22] Indeed, communications scholar and former journalist Barbie Zelizer argues that historians have "mined the press for data without sufficiently considering the processes by which news came to be."[23] As David Ortiz and others argue, "newspaper content is not created for the purpose of conducting social scientific research nor is it intended to capture or sample all protests or other political events, even in a limited geographic area."[24] Indeed, while often viewed as a mirror to society, the press could more accurately be compared to, in Godfrey Hodgson's words, "a gigantic stereo system" that plays "the sound that the men at the controls think the audience want to hear."[25] This more interactive conception of media production not only hints at the interplay between the press and its audience but also acknowledges the power that editors and publishers had over the direction and content of their publications.

Studies that take a more qualitative approach to the process of news construction, however, are often written by former journalists, with media history relegated to "a stepchild within a number of largely indifferent family set-ups."[26] The understandable tendency for self-reflection in such narratives can provide a useful window into the minds and lives of those actively involved in covering social movements.[27] However, this self-reflection can also obscure the macro processes that guide the actions of their subjects as well as exclude or diminish narratives that fall outside of the white, heteronormative male experience so common in this literature. As Zelizer argues, "The predominance of white, privileged, and male perspectives defining so much of the field has created an aura by which its givens appear natural and commonsensical."[28]

This self-aggrandizement also risks ignoring how protest movements of the 1960s were active participants in the creation of media coverage. Indeed, while arguing that journalists "composed versions of reality," Gitlin is careful to demonstrate how this "composition was entering into our own deliberations" and creating symbiotic links between media narratives and the nature and tenor of movement activism.[29] As a result, more recent scholarship has demonstrated the need for civil rights historiography to abandon binary conceptions of the media that either valorize "heroic" allies of the movement or condemn the diktats of its "bully pulpit." Jane Rhodes and Edward P. Morgan, for example, focus on how the Black Panther Party sought to challenge incomplete and often hostile contemporary media images, while simultaneously relying on these images for exposure.[30]

Nowhere was this symbiosis, and the tensions it brought to the movement, clearer than in the Selma campaign of 1965. Viewing media attention—and subsequent public support—as a major bargaining chip in local and federal negotiations, the Southern Christian Leadership Conference's (SCLC) strategy differed sharply from groups such as SNCC that were dedicated to developing grassroots leadership. Indeed, the relationship that the SCLC forged with the media is central to an important scene in DuVernay's biopic, *Selma*, in which King instructs the "hot-headed" leaders of SNCC that victory required "being on the front page of the national press every morning and . . . being on the TV news every night." Consequently, and in stark contrast to the long and repetitive process of door-to-door canvassing and local meetings that typified the work of SNCC as well as the Congress of Racial Equality (CORE), the large-scale demonstrations organized by SCLC in Selma were designed to fit neatly into the process of mainstream news construction.

However, by focusing on these large-scale mobilizations, including those in earlier campaigns in Albany and Birmingham, this interest in the spectacular obscured the everyday activity of millions of Americans who fought for equality outside of the media spotlight. Indeed, with the mobilization efforts of the SCLC often focused on specific changes to local or national legislation, media coverage obscured the work that SNCC, CORE, and local National Association for the Advancement of Color People (NAACP) groups were doing to cultivate indigenous leadership that could pursue a more radical social, political, and economic vision of the future. In the process, this focus associates the Selma campaign—and the southern movement more broadly—with nonviolent marches against segregation, rather than a longer and more radical tradition of grassroots organization for economic and political liberty. Indeed, the sociologist Doug McAdam warns that accepting this "stylized image of social movements . . . threatens to distort our understanding of popular contention."[31]

As King and others found in Albany, however, getting on the front page was not always easy for African Americans. Indeed, civil rights activists often found that their appeals to outlets produced for and by white northerners would go unanswered unless they could provide almost unparalleled levels of social unrest and violence for these outlets to cover. SNCC communication director Julian Bond, for instance, lamented in 1963 that "activity has increased in the South to the point that only the crises—killings, really outrageous brutality or shootings—get any national attention."[32] By 1965, fatigue with the daily brutalities and injustices faced by activists in the South had an important impact on the strategies deployed by groups like the SCLC who relied on national attention to force local or federal officials into action. As David Garrow's investigation of the 1965 Selma campaign demonstrates, King and the SCLC perfected mobilization techniques that exploited the barbarism of white segregationists to elicit sympathy and action from white liberals and federal officials in the North.[33] Clarifying his strategy at a later rally in Montgomery, King declared that "we are here today to say to the white men that we will no longer let them use their clubs on us in dark corners. We are going to make them do it in the glaring light of television."[34]

In reality, however, the SCLC and the civil rights movement more widely had been utilizing such violence to frame their activism for over half a decade. Indeed, by consciously feeding the sensationalist impulses of the mainstream media, the SCLC and others were active participants in the lens of escalation that accompanied much civil rights coverage. In other words, as *Newsweek*'s chief writer Peter Goldman argues:

> The media were part of the strategy, it was sort of one hand washes the other. We had an interest in getting the story obviously, and they had an interest in getting the story framed as a struggle between peaceful petitioners and ... a recalcitrant and often violent Southern resistance.[35]

More important, with mainstream journalists writing for predominantly white audiences in the urban North, the direction and tenor of this coverage continued to reflect white, northern conceptions of the black freedom struggle that, Martin Berger argues, "routinely cast black ... protestors as the hapless victims of violent whites."[36] Similarly, contemporary print media narratives that focused on white involvement presented local black activists as the passive recipients of enlightened (and often northern) white aid, detailing white volunteers while often failing to even name African American activists.[37] Indeed, as Peter Ling argues, for those not versed in the nuances and practicalities of the tactic, the focus on nonviolent direct action fed into the notion that activists in the South were submissive; acted *upon* rather than being active themselves.[38] For instance, calling Martin Luther King Jr. the "passive resistance hero of the embattled Southern Negro," *Newsweek* presented the SCLC leader and southern activists as meekly resisting the brutalities of an un-American and unfamiliar southern enemy.[39]

However, while this simplistic framing of southern activism "worked as long as there was Jim Crow and as long as there were Jim Clarks and

Bull Connors," as Goldman recalls, it failed to comprehend urban rebellions that were "not clearly good-versus-evil" and required journalists to "strain to see them that way."[40] In other words, while dramatic pictures of violence against churchgoing demonstrators "fed the media's need for the drama of good against evil, the morality play," the move to cover urban unrest in cities like Los Angeles meant that "the plot became extremely subtle."[41] Once again, however, civil rights activists were complicit in the creation of these myths. During the Selma campaign, for example, the SCLC used images taken on Bloody Sunday in a full-page fundraising advertisement for the organization in the *New York Times*, promoting the notion that embattled black southerners were reliant on the aid and liberalism of enlightened white liberal northerners.[42] Similarly, while SNCC's style of activism did not lend itself to these large-scale mobilizations, the emphasis that the organization's Communication Section placed on segregationist violence within its press releases also acted to encourage a vision of the South that centered on violence being actively inflicted on passive black bodies.

This idea of a battle between a satanic enemy and nonviolent angels not only created an impossible standard against which protesters were measured but also helped caricature southerners as violent rednecks, ignoring the larger structural and institutional factors that helped to perpetuate Jim Crow. Indeed, as *Newsweek* correspondent Karl Fleming argues, many race beat reporters felt that framing stories about the police in the South was simple: "We all knew that Bull Connor was the bad guy, Martin Luther King the good guy. It was like a western movie.... And we wrote our stories like western movie scenarios."[43] Once again, activists played a key role in cementing such frames. As King and the SCLC found to their cost in Albany, the morality play required a villain who was unrestrained and unthinking in their denial of equality. Consequently, activists who were invested in this narrative purposefully tried to select cities and officials that they thought were most likely to generate the kind of violence that made newspaper headlines.

As Kenneth Crawford argued in *Newsweek* during the Selma campaign, Martin Luther King had "a way of picking the right opponents. With the kind of enemies he makes, he scarcely needs friends."[44] While tactically effective, this concentration on Selma and other flashpoints presented a one-dimensional view of segregationist resistance that focused almost exclusively on images of police officials rather than documenting and humanizing the array of oppositional forces in the South.[45] Indeed, profiles of Sheriff Clark in the mainstream press that dubbed him Selma's "symbol of racism" were indicative of articles that painted southern resistance as a distant, unusual, and easily defeated aberration.[46] This distortion not only exacerbated tensions between local southerners and journalists working for mainstream press outlets but also presented oppression as a line of helmeted officers under the command of tyrannical officials, rather than a systematic and institutionalized program of discrimination that had as much strength in the urban North as the more rural South.[47]

Responsibility for this geographic distinction, however, does not just lie with northern journalists. It is also important to recognize how the rhetoric of civil rights organizations helped to encourage the notion that activism in the South was aimed at a fundamentally different and peculiarly southern problem. Describing itself in various press releases throughout 1962 as "an independent southwide movement" that worked "in hard-core areas of the South," SNCC clearly projected a southern image that was made more explicit by the Southern Christian Leadership Conference.[48] Indeed, in March 1964, Communication Section worker Mary King told a potential northern recruit that an upcoming SNCC conference was "geared to southern students and is not national in scope at all."[49] This is not to argue that SNCC or the SCLC ignored the problems of northern racism, but the emergence of both organizations out of particular waves of southern protest meant that they were often willing to confine their limited financial and human resources to the Deep South. Although tactically sound on many levels, this meant that activists failed to challenge conceptions of the black freedom struggle that affirmed white northern conceptions of what that struggle meant. Consequently, when profiling SNCC in the run up to the Selma campaign of 1965, *Rolling Stone* founder Ralph J. Gleason felt able to characterize the South as "an America unknown to the rest of us," thus distancing readers from the brutality and institutionalized racism he described and framing SNCC's activism as taking place in some foreign land.[50] These tactics were not only important in forming narratives around the Selma campaign but also informed the perception of later struggles such as the Black Power movement when commentators felt that rhetoric that alienated northern white audiences signified that "the public relations element [had] virtually disappeared from the civil rights movement."[51]

The celebratory attitude toward press coverage of the "heroic" period of civil rights activity also risks portraying race beat coverage as somehow above the logistical processes that dominate news production.[52] In an age where anyone with a cell phone can become a photo or video journalist, it is easy to forget just how hard it was for reporters to adequately cover the thousands of square miles that made up the southern race beat. Reliant on a certain standard of infrastructure that enabled them to report stories over the phone or via teletype to their respective news desks, journalists were rarely able to dictate events live. Indeed, even live video would have to be shot by early afternoon to ensure it could be processed and sent to studios in the North before the evening news bulletins aired.[53] With such facilities often hard to find in rural African American neighborhoods, reporters would have to stay in white-owned hotels where phone lines, although sometimes tapped by local officials, were at least provided as standard.[54]

As David Ortiz and others demonstrate, these logistical details are crucial to understanding the nature of southern coverage, because journalistic routine acts to "place certain events in [journalist's] paths, while others escape their attention because they are too far removed from the usual ways of conducting reporters' jobs."[55] For instance, while sympathy for the movement can explain why some journalists overlooked minor lapses of nonviolent discipline, it is clear that the physical separation between white reporters and African American communities also meant that they were viewing the southern movement through a particular—and well-choreographed—window; observing and reporting on the heroic displays of tactical nonviolence by demonstrators on Main Street while missing the widespread use of armed self-defense against Ku Klux Klan night riders and other white vigilantes.

More important, even if reporters were later made aware of these events, coverage was much more muted and lacked the visceral impact that accompanied live footage or photographs of segregationist violence. For example, while Roy Reed's front-page article after Bloody Sunday talked briefly about the bricks and bottles hurled at Selma possemen, the physical separation of reporters from the crowd meant that accusations of African American violence were preceded by modifiers such as "reportedly."[56] In contrast, the violence of white state troopers, witnessed and photographed first-hand by a number of journalists, required no such qualification. Consequently, while the framing of the marchers on Bloody Sunday as helpless victims of white violence was a well-used and favored media trope, it is important to note the role that media logistics could play in sustaining these narratives.

Indeed, this distance from the African American community meant that reporters often relied on second-hand evidence for particular events, or else were entirely unaware of their existence. For instance, during the Selma to Montgomery March, *Newsweek*'s Joe Cumming claims that while he saw instances of men and women sharing the same tent, such acts "couldn't have been more innocent" and were a far cry from the orgies described in the segregationist press.[57] However, with few journalists joining Cumming in the special press tents that March organizers had arranged, first-hand accounts of these sleeping arrangements were absent from much mainstream coverage. Instead, papers such as the *New York Times* first carried the accusations by the Alabama State Legislature that there had been "evidence of much fornication" on the march and then relied on the erroneous assertion by march leaders that "the sexes were required to sleep in separate tents" to dispute the story the following day.[58]

While a relatively trivial detail, this episode demonstrates how dependent race beat journalists were on sources that had their own motives for providing the media with information. Describing SNCC executive secretary James Forman as "a contact I needed to cultivate" in his recent memoir, *Newsweek* correspondent Karl Fleming highlights the unusual emphasis many race beat reporters placed on building positive relationships with key civil rights activists.[59] As previously discussed, this reliance was partly the result of popular movement frames that undermined the traditional model of "balanced" reporting, which saw neutrality as the presentation of two opposing but equal views. Indeed, Fred Powledge of the *New York Times* claims that the race beat was "a new one for the newsgatherers of the South and the nation" because it cast "traditional centers of respectability and power," such as the governor's office, "in the role of lawbreaker and arrogant defier of the law of the land."[60] However, it is also clear that many among the growing press cadre in the South held personal sympathy for African American demonstrators that often manifested itself in a protective instinct. Associated Press reporter Don McKee, for instance, was soon nicknamed "Fink McKee" by some race beat journalists after he informed local officials of a demonstration that was later broken up by the police. Explaining the ill-feeling toward McKee, William Cook claimed that "ratting on a news source is always bad. Ratting on Negroes is unforgivable to the generally liberal press corps."[61]

While journalistic conventions of neutrality and objectivity would seemingly prohibit such bias, Peter Goldman states that his coverage for *Newsweek* was "totally *journalisme engagé* from the top down."[62] In fact, at the same time as the publication was running an advertising campaign claiming that "this magazine separates fact from opinion," Goldman admits that he was practicing a form of journalism "that doesn't pretend to be strictly 'objective,' viewing events from a neutral distance. Instead, it actively takes sides—not uncritically, but with an undisguised preference for one side of the story."[63] When justifying this approach, he remarks that balanced reporting was impossible when "the injustices were so clear . . . as clear as white only and colored only signs over water fountains or restrooms."[64] These feelings were mirrored by Powledge who argues that "it was hard to adopt the reporters' fake sense of objectivity . . . [because] it was so clear as to who the good guys were and who the bad guys were."[65] This symbiosis, Jenny Walker argues, can explain why certain media outlets, including *Newsweek* and the *New York Times* were willing to overlook or downplay public lapses in nonviolent discipline.[66] For example, when Selma activist Annie Lee Cooper struck Sheriff Clark across the face in January 1965, the story was carried on the *Times*' front page. However, while the headline did not excuse or ignore Cooper's violent actions, the accompanying picture of her brutal arrest encouraged the reader to view the incident through the familiar frame of helpless African Americans at the mercy of violent southern law enforcement.[67]

If journalists covering the southern movement were increasingly wary of collaboration with southern officialdom, the feeling was mutual. Following the Little Rock crisis of 1957, which saw more than 225 reporters from across the globe descend on the town, Bob Allison of CBS news claimed that "the northern newspaper reporter has been definitely tied in with the machinery of enforcing integration. . . . Apparently now there is a solidified conviction in the South that the reporter from the North is going to do everything wrong."[68] By 1962, UPI reporter John Herbers thought that this feeling even extended to wire service operators, with distinctions between outlets becoming blurred in the face of growing hostility to news reporters in general.[69] Indeed, Birmingham's Commissioner of Public Safety Eugene "Bull" Connor spoke for many in the South when he argued that "the trouble with this country is communism, socialism, and journalism."[70]

It was no coincidence, for example, that of the two people killed during the Ole Miss riots in 1962, one was journalist Paul Guihard, a reporter for the French *Agence France-Presse*. By 1965, these tensions were clearly visible and had an important impact on key elements of the Selma campaign. For instance, while the violence on the Edmund Pettus Bridge came to symbolize the brutality of the segregated South for millions of Americans, witnesses at an earlier march in Marion in February have described far more chaotic and bloody scenes.[71] Despite claiming the life of activist Jimmie Lee Jackson, this brutality would never be depicted on the nation's TV screens or presented at its breakfast tables. While racism certainly played a part in the relative absence of coverage—especially when compared to that given to the deaths of two white activists later in the campaign—local resident and SCLC activist Albert Turner argued that "the story of Marion was never told because the news media was not allowed to picture it."[72] Indeed, in what witnesses described as a calculated move, state troopers first attacked journalists and broke their lighting rigs and cameras, before turning on the large, predominantly African American crowd.[73] In contrast, efforts to restrain journalists at the Edmund Pettus Bridge not only failed to hide the extent of segregationist brutality from the lenses of TV and photo journalists but also had the unintended consequence of hiding the retaliatory violence aimed at possemen and troopers who advanced into black neighborhoods on the opposite bank of the Alabama River.

This did not mean that race beat journalists were unaware of some of the less public tensions and problems within the movement. However, since these occurred off the record or consisted of unsubstantiated rumor, reporters were not able to put much of this "unwriteable discourse" into their articles without fear of libel charges or alienating important contacts.[74] Indeed, instances where movement public relations downplayed, obscured, or simply did not recognize what white journalists viewed as growing trends—were common. In such cases, reporters would often look for particular kinds of events—known as "news pegs"—upon which these trends or ideas could be hung.[75] These events would then act as a vehicle through which publications could report evolutions in ideas or tactics that actually had a much longer genesis. In the process, news coverage transformed these events from the mundane to the significant, imbuing them with a symbolic importance that often emerged from journalistic protocol rather than social activism.

Pointing to the importance of definable and reportable breaks in the movement, for example, Fred Powledge argued in 1972 that "it never really was news that all the big civil rights leaders distrusted one another. It is news only when one of them acknowledges the frictions and tries to explain what caused them."[76] However, while division was "sure to arise," because civil rights organizations were "downright poor and competing for contributions," it was often denied by civil rights organizations, thereby starving these stories of publishable material.[77] Indeed, this pattern had an important impact on coverage of the Selma campaign. *Newsweek* correspondent Joe Cumming told his New York office that during preparations for the march there was "a sub-theme that ran almost unnoticed through the week—a rivalry between SCLC in Selma with its clergy and SNCC in Montgomery with [its] students."[78] However, Cumming also claimed that this division was "hard to prove because on the surface they present a solid front."[79] Consequently, while Cumming felt that there was "enough evidence to make the assertion," division in Selma was not made the major peg of *Newsweek*'s coverage.[80] Instead, for many northern publications, the first opportunity to expose these divisions fully was the enunciation of Black Power on the Meredith March Against Fear in June 1966, when accusations could be backed up by quotes taken from Roy Wilkins of the NAACP, who dismissed SNCC's program as "[offering] a disadvantaged minority little except the chance to shrivel and die."[81] More important, this delay allowed the media to portray movement unity as having been "shattered by the rising cry of 'Black Power,'" rather than the result of longstanding tensions that had solidified during the Mississippi Summer Project in 1964 and threatened to boil over in Selma a year before the Black Power slogan was popularized.[82]

Therefore, when analyzing media coverage of the Selma campaign, it is important to consider how the equation of movement success with popularity in the mainstream media fails to examine how securing this coverage could mask growing disillusionment with central movement tenets. Even accounts that challenge theories of media hegemony in news production by foregrounding the efforts of civil rights activists do not adequately critique the notion that movement strategies were, and should have been, aimed at gaining legitimacy in the eyes of mainstream society.[83] For instance, while tactically effective in the short term, the disavowal of genuine and deep disagreements within the movement would influence how subsequent divisions—in particular over the March Against Fear a year later—would be portrayed by the press. Indeed, when Black Power activists began openly and forcefully to critique the systematic and institutionalized racism of the urban North as well as the rural South—and did so in a way that challenged the passive role that African Americans had been seen to occupy in the morality plays of Selma and Birmingham—they were greeted with surprise and alarm. While not wanting to deny Jeanne Theoharis's characterization of this mood as "the surprise of intransigence—a willful shock," it is important to note how encouraging a good versus evil narrative in the South fed into white, northern conceptions of the freedom struggle that emphasized the role of whites, downplayed African American agency, sanctified nonviolent direct action, and focused attention on a small number of places, organizations, and individuals.[84]

Consequently, while the Watts Rebellion and Black Power were always likely to draw hostile criticism, dichotomous histories that continue to see Selma as a watershed moment in the civil rights movement are not simply the result of Black Power activists "fumbling the ball" of public relations, as John Lewis claimed in 1966.[85] Instead, civil rights organizations—often with very good reason—pursued a strategy that placed short-term gains above an honest and open dialogue about America's racial problems and the necessary solutions it required. For their part, the media actively encouraged and shaped a narrative that placed spectacle and drama above honest discussion and debate. In doing so, they aimed to please a predominantly white audience that were insulated from, and had little interest in, the problems faced by African Americans in the North or South.

That this coverage has received praise from veterans and modern-day scholars alike, does not mean that journalists stopped writing it "the way it wasn't," or that they don't continue doing so in the present day with many of the same consequences.[86] Indeed, given the unparalleled access journalists now have to the lives and experiences of people all across the world, the "shape, composition, location and angle" of the mainstream media's "mirror" is perhaps of more importance than ever before.[87] Unfortunately, while Stuart Hall commented in the 1970s that "even the best news stories have only a brief half-life," the modern-day news cycle has only increased the tendency among national media to jump from crisis to crisis with little attempt to embed journalism within a local context or to report on these communities once violence has dissipated.[88]

Consequently, while protest in Ferguson, Missouri, in 2014 may have caused some commentators to remark that "little has changed" since the 1960s, the same could be said of mainstream media outlets that only cover institutionalized racism when it presents itself as armed policemen standing over the bodies of dead African Americans.[89] Similarly, while this chapter has critiqued the simplistic good-versus-evil narrative that this style of coverage produced in the 1960s, the same can be seen in articles, such as that written by Professor John McWhorter in *TIME* in November 2014, that worried the events leading up to Michael Brown's death were "too knotted to coax a critical mass of America into seeing *a civil rights icon* in Brown and an *institutionally racist devil* in [Darren] Wilson."[90] Indeed, with McWhorter claiming that Brown's death did not "qualify as a Selma-style—or even Trayvon [Martin]-style—teaching moment," it is clear that deconstructing the media's coverage of the 1965 Selma campaign is as relevant and as necessary today as it was over fifty years ago.[91]

Notes

1. Ava DuVernay, dir., *Selma*, 2014.

2. Roy Reed, "Alabama Police Use Gas and Clubs to Rout Negroes," *New York Times*, March 8, 1965; Daniel J. Myers and Beth Schaefer Caniglia, "All the Rioting That's Fit to Print: Selection Effects in National Newspaper Coverage of Civil Disorders, 1968–1969," *American Sociological Review* 69 (2004): 519–43; Doug McAdam et al., "'There Will Be Fighting in the Streets': The Distorting Lens of Social Movement Theory," *Mobilization: An International Quarterly* 10, no. 1 (2005): 1–18.

3. Richard Valeriani, interview by Mary Morin, April 2004, at http://knightpolitical reporting.syr.edu/wp-content/uploads/2012/05/richard_valeriani_oral_essay.pdf (consulted March 22, 2017); Hedley Donovan, as cited in Curtis Prendergast and Geoffrey Colvin, *The World of Time Inc.: The Intimate History of a Changing Enterprise, 1960–1980* (New York: Atheneum, 1986), 449.

4. Gordon Mantler, "'The Press Did You In': The Poor People's Campaign and the Mass Media," *The Sixties: A Journal of History, Politics, and Culture* 3 (2010): 34; Melvin N. Coffee in Charlotte Grimes, "Debate: Civil Rights and the Press," *Journalism Studies* 6 (2005): 126.

5. Jim Carrier, *A Traveler's Guide to the Civil Rights Movement* (Orlando: Harcourt, 2004), 71.

6. Grimes, "Debate," 117.

7. John Lewis, "Congressional Record: On the Contribution of the Press to the Civil Rights Movement," *Federation of American Scientists*, September 8, 2005, at http://www.fas.org/sgp/congress/2005/h090805.html (consulted March 22, 2017).

8. Godfrey Hodgson, *America in Our Time* (New York: Doubleday, 1976), 134–35. As well as being a common title for news publications, "mirror" was also applied to new media: Sig Mickelson, *The Electric Mirror: Politics in an Age of Television* (New York: Dodd, Mead, 1972).

9. "Results of Key Questions on Whites' Attitudes," *New York Times*, September 21, 1964. See also Fred Powledge, "Poll Shows Whites in City Resent Civil Rights Drive," *New York Times*, September 21, 1964.

10. Osborn Elliott, *The World of Oz* (New York: Viking Press, 1980), 70.

11. Max Frankel, *The Times of My Life and My Life with "The Times"* (New York: Dell, 2000), 463.

12. Peter Goldman, interview by Mark Joseph Walmsley, telephone, May 24, 2013. Hereafter Goldman interview.

13. Gay Talese, *The Kingdom and the Power* (New York: World Pub. Co, 1969), 113, 326; Richard F. Shepard, *The Paper's Papers: A Reporter's Journey through the Archives of "The New York Times"* (New York: Times Books, 1996), 299–300.

14. David R. Davies, *The Postwar Decline of American Newspapers, 1945–1965*, The History of American Journalism Vol. 6 (Westport: Praeger, 2006), 65; Carl T. Rowan, *Breaking Barriers: A Memoir* (Boston: Little, Brown, 1991), 97–98.

15. James Brian McPherson, *Journalism at the End of the American Century, 1965-Present*, The History of American Journalism Vol. 7 (Westport: Praeger, 2006), 8; Davies, *The Postwar Decline of American Newspapers, 1945–1965*, 65.

16. Frankel, *The Times of My Life and My Life with "The Times,"* 465.

17. "The Race Beat," *Newsweek*, June 15, 1964; Gene Roberts and Hank Klibanoff, *Race Beat: The Press, the Civil Rights Struggle, and the Awakening of a Nation* (New York: Vintage, 2007).

18. Todd Gitlin, *The Whole World Is Watching: Mass Media in the Making and Unmaking of the New Left* (Berkeley: University of California Press, 1980), 17.

19. Stokely Carmichael and Ekwueme Michael Thelwell, *Ready for Revolution: The Life and Struggles of Stokely Carmichael (Kwame Ture)* (New York: Scribner's, 2003), 226, 254, 306, 427, 501; Casey Hayden in *Circle of Trust: Remembering SNCC*, ed. Cheryl Lynn Greenberg (New Brunswick, NJ: Rutgers University Press, 2003), 134.

20. Brian Ward, introduction to *Media, Culture, and the Modern African American Freedom Struggle*, ed. Brian Ward (Gainesville: University Press of Florida, 2001), 3, 8. See also: Jacquelyn Dowd Hall, "The Long Civil Rights Movement and the Political Uses of the Past," *Journal of American History* 91, no. 4 (2005): 1233–63.

21. Peniel E. Joseph, "The Black Power Movement: A State of the Field," *Journal of American History* 96 (2009): 755–56, 758, 756.

22. Philip Graham, as cited in Katharine Graham, *Personal History* (New York: A. A. Knopf, 1997), 324.

23. Barbie Zelizer, *Taking Journalism Seriously: News and the Academy* (Thousand Oaks, CA: Sage Publications, Inc., 2004), 85.

24. David G. Ortiz et al., "Where Do We Stand with Newspaper Data?," *Mobilization: An International Journal* 10, no. 3 (2005): 397.

25. Hodgson, *America in Our Time*, 134–35.

26. Zelizer, *Taking Journalism Seriously*, 86.

27. Roberts and Klibanoff, *Race Beat*.

28. Zelizer, *Taking Journalism Seriously*, 91.

29. Gitlin, *The Whole World Is Watching*, xiv–xv.

30. Jane Rhodes, *Framing the Black Panthers: The Spectacular Rise of a Black Power Icon* (New York: New Press, 2007); Edward P. Morgan, "Media Culture and the Public Memory of the Black Panther Party," in *In Search of the Black Panther Party: New Perspectives on a Revolutionary Movement*, ed. Jama Lazerow and Yohuru R. Williams (Durham, NC: Duke University Press, 2006), 324–74.

31. McAdam et al., "'There Will Be Fighting in the Streets.'"

32. Julian Bond to Steven Roberts, August 1, 1963, Series A.VII.1, Reel 13 Slide 45, The Student Nonviolent Coordinating Committee Papers, 1959–1972 (Ann Arbor, MI: United Microfilms International, 1994). Hereafter referred to as SNCC Papers.

33. David J. Garrow, *Protest at Selma: Martin Luther King, Jr., and the Voting Rights Act of 1965* (New Haven: Yale University Press, 1978).

34. Martin Luther King Jr., as cited in ibid., 111.

35. Goldman interview.

36. Martin A. Berger, *Seeing through Race: A Reinterpretation of Civil Rights Photography* (Berkeley: University of California Press, 2011), 15. See also: Aniko Bodroghkozy, *Equal Time: Television and the Civil Rights Movement* (Urbana: University of Illinois Press, 2012).

37. "Mississippi: The Attack on Bigotry," *Look*, September 8, 1964, Series A.IX.4A, Reel 23 Slide 1167–76, SNCC Papers; Associated Press, "10 Indicted in Virginia," *New York Times*, June 22, 1963.

38. Peter J. Ling, "Gender and Generation: Manhood at the Southern Christian Leadership Conference," in *Gender and the Civil Rights Movement*, ed. Peter J. Ling and Sharon Monteith (New Brunswick: Rutgers University Press, 2004), 112.

39. "Georgia: The Wall," *Newsweek*, January 14, 1963, 27.

40. Goldman interview.

41. Ibid. See also, Karl Fleming, "Comment By Karl Fleming," in *The Black American and the Press*, ed. Jack Lyle (Los Angeles: Ward Ritchie, 1968), 32.

42. Howell Raines, *My Soul Is Rested: Movement Days in the Deep South Remembered* (New York: Penguin, 1983), 213.

43. Fleming, "Comment By Karl Fleming," 32.

44. Kenneth Crawford, "Washington: Right to Vote," *Newsweek*, March 1, 1965, 39.

45. George Lewis, "Sidelining Selma's Segregationists: Memory, Strategy, Ideology, and Agency," in *The Shadow of Selma*, ed. Joe Street and Henry Knight Lozano (University Press of Florida, n.d.).

46. Gay Talese, "Burly Sheriff Clark Is Selma Symbol of Racism," *New York Times*, March 16, 1965.

47. David Greenberg, "The Idea of 'The Liberal Media' and Its Roots in the Civil Rights Movement," *The Sixties: A Journal of History, Politics, and Culture* 1 (2008): 167–86.

48. SNCC, "Press Release," February 21, 1962, Series A.VII.3, Reel 13 Slide 757–85, SNCC Papers; SNCC, "Press Release," April 16, 1962, Series A.VII.3, Reel 13 Slide 786, SNCC Papers.

49. Mary King to Lisa Anderson, March 1964, Series A.VII.2, Reel 13 Slide 360–440, SNCC Papers.

50. Ralph J. Gleason, "SNCC and the New U.S. Image," *This World*, January 31, 1965, Series A.VIII.283, Reel 22 Slide 1070, SNCC Papers.

51. Carl T. Rowan, "Crisis in Civil Rights Leadership," *Ebony*, November 1966, 28.

52. Coffee in Grimes, "Debate," 126.

53. Leigh Raiford, "'Come Let Us Build a New World Together': SNCC and Photography of the Civil Rights Movement," *American Quarterly* 59 (2007): 1130–31.

54. Karl Fleming, *Son of the Rough South: An Uncivil Memoir* (New York: Public Affairs, 2005), 19; Harrison E. Salisbury, *A Time of Change: A Reporter's Tales of Our Time* (New York: Harper and Row, 1988), 56.

55. Ortiz et al., "Where Do We Stand?," 401.

56. Reed, "Alabama Police Use Gas and Clubs to Rout Negroes." For corroboration of this incident see: Raines, *My Soul Is Rested*, 202–3.

57. Joe Cumming, "Cumming Add One," March 1965, Newsweek Atlanta Bureau Records, 1953–1979, Box 43 Folder 13, Manuscript and Rare Books Library, Emory University.

58. Ibid.; Ben A. Franklin, "Top Entertainers in Alabama Tonight," *New York Times*, March 24, 1965; Paul L. Montgomery, "Band in Vanguard All the Way from Selma to Montgomery," *New York Times*, March 25, 1965.

59. Fleming, *Son of the Rough South*, 230.

60. Fred Powledge, *Free at Last?: The Civil Rights Movement and the People Who Made It* (Boston: Little, Brown and Company, 1991), 513.

61. William Cook to Peter Goldman, "Race Reporters," May 26, 1964, Newsweek Atlanta Bureau Records, 1953–1979, Box 10 Folder 10, Manuscript and Rare Books Library, Emory University. See also: Fleming, *Son of the Rough South*, 255.

62. Goldman interview.

63. Peter Goldman to Mark Joseph Walmsley, e-mail "Re: Your Time at Newsweek," May 27, 2013.

64. Goldman interview.

65. Fred Powledge, as cited in Vanessa Murphree, *The Selling of Civil Rights: The Student Nonviolent Coordinating Committee and the Use of Public Relations* (New York: Routledge, 2006), 59–60.

66. Jenny Walker, "A Media-Made Movement?: Black Violence and Nonviolence in the Historiography of the Civil Rights Movement," in *Media, Culture, and the Modern*

African American Freedom Struggle, ed. Brian Ward (Gainesville: University Press of Florida, 2001), 41–66.

67. John Herbers, "Woman Punches Alabama Sheriff," *New York Times*, January 26, 1965.

68. Bob Allison, as cited in Davies, *The Postwar Decline of American Newspapers, 1945–1965*, 73.

69. John Herbers, "The Reporter in the Deep South," *Nieman Reports*, April 1962, at http://www.nieman.harvard.edu/reports/article/102051/1962-The-Reporter-in-the-Deep-South.aspx (consulted March 22, 2017).

70. Eugene "Bull" Connor in Greenberg, "The Idea of 'The Liberal Media' and Its Roots in the Civil Rights Movement," 176.

71. Raines, *My Soul Is Rested*, 190–93.

72. Ibid., 196.

73. Ibid., 190–96.

74. Mark Allen Peterson, "Getting to the Story: Unwriteable Discourse and Interpretive Practice in American Journalism," *Anthropological Quarterly* 74, no. 4 (October 1, 2001), 201–11.

75. Herbert J. Gans, *Democracy and the News* (Oxford: Oxford University Press, 2003), 53.

76. Fred Powledge, "From Little Rock to Here and Now," *Life*, September 1, 1972.

77. "Integration: Who Won What?," *Newsweek*, January 1, 1962. See also: "Integration: Hotter Fires," *Newsweek*, July 1, 1963.

78. Joe Cumming, "Re Civil Rights," March 19, 1965, Newsweek Atlanta Bureau Records, 1953–1979, Box 43 Folder 13, Manuscript and Rare Books Library, Emory University.

79. Ibid.

80. "'An American Tragedy,'" *Newsweek*, March 22, 1965; "On to Montgomery," *Newsweek*, March 29, 1965.

81. Roy Wilkins, as cited in M. S. Handler, "Wilkins Says Black Power Leads Only to Black Death," *New York Times*, July 6, 1966, 1.

82. "Black Power: Negro Leaders Split Over Policy," *New York Times*, July 10, 1966, Sec. 4: The Week in Review.

83. Murphree, *The Selling of Civil Rights*.

84. Jeanne F. Theoharis, "'Alabama on Avalon': Rethinking the Watts Uprising and the Character of Black Protest in Los Angeles," in *The Black Power Movement: Rethinking the Civil Rights-Black Power Era*, ed. Peniel E. Joseph (New York: Routledge, 2006), 50.

85. John Lewis in "Ex-Chairman Quits 'Black Power' SNCC," *Washington Post*, July 1, 1966.

86. Valeriani, interview.

87. Hodgson, *America in Our Time*, 134–35.

88. Stuart Hall, introduction to *Paper Voices: The Popular Press and Social Change, 1935–1965*, ed. A.C.H. Smith (London: Chatto and Windus, 1975), 11.

89. Cate Matthews, "Photos From Ferguson And 1960s Protests Side By Side Make It Clear How Little Has Changed," *Huffington Post*, August 14, 2014, Sec. Black Voices, at http://www.huffingtonpost.com/2014/08/14/ferguson-civil-rights-photos-comparison_n_5678852.html (consulted March 22, 2017).

90. John McWhorter, "Ferguson Is the Wrong Tragedy to Wake America Up," *Time*, November 24, 2014, at http://time.com/3594636/ferguson-is-the-wrong-tragedy-to-wake-america-up/ [My Emphasis].

91. Ibid.

9

Sidelining Selma's Segregationists

Memory, Strategy, Ideology, and Agency

GEORGE LEWIS

On March 4, 2007, the two front-runners in the race for the Democratic presidential nomination traveled to Selma, Alabama, ostensibly to mark the forty-second anniversary of the city's voter rights campaigns. Both Hillary Clinton and Barack Obama draped themselves carefully in those campaigns' historical artefacts: Obama beat Clinton to the coveted podium of Brown Chapel A.M.E. Church, relegating her to First Baptist Church, which was geographically close but symbolically distant; they were careful to be seen with march veterans, Clinton linking arms with Congressman John Lewis whilst Obama was flanked by the Reverend Joseph Lowery and, at one stage, guided a frail Reverend Fred Lee Shuttlesworth across Edmund Pettus Bridge in a wheelchair; and they made constant and careful reference to the significance of the 1965 Selma marches in their speeches.

Aware of the need to dilute what might otherwise be interpreted as the brazen electioneering of their respective appearances, both candidates sought to explain their presence at Selma in personal as well as political terms. For Obama, that part of the narrative was easier to achieve, but Clinton was not prepared to cede ground to her main rival. In a bid to match Obama's attempts to cast himself as a minority candidate, and thus one who could draw direct capital from close association with the memory of Selma, Clinton took the more awkward route of highlighting gender rather than race to remind her audience that she, too, represented a minority. Where Obama defined his minority status in the same broad terms that had served to limit the political rights of nonwhite potential voters in Selma some four decades previously, New York's U.S. Senator was forced into finding a far narrower focus, choosing to define her minority status as that of a woman within the rarefied male pantheon of past presidential candidates.

Having an African father with American links may have offered Obama a smoother means of eliciting political leverage from attendance at the Selma commemorations, but even he was forced into some unwieldy contortions. At the same time as linking himself to the African American struggle in Selma, for example, Obama was keen to escape the "interest group" tag that had dogged previous minority candidates' attempts at winning widespread national approval. Furthermore, perhaps sensing that his political opponents were becoming increasingly adroit at playing upon his apparent alterity, he also demonstrated a particular sensitivity to one of the many lessons hewn from the collective memory of those activists who had participated in the original Selma campaign. It was one thing to run as a Washington outsider, but quite another to be labeled as an "outside agitator," a mantle that had been worn by civil rights movement volunteers so regularly that Obama was still quick to avoid it four decades later. He had been invited in to Selma by Alabama Senator Hank Sanders, he noted wisely, although perhaps less wise was Dallas County Commissioner Kim Ballard's remark when presenting a key to the city to Obama. In 1965, Ballard stated, Obama might have found the key useful "to get out of jail."[1]

Clearly, both campaign teams had to work at making their respective candidate's presence at Selma appear effortless. That, in turn, highlights the extent to which all sides recognized that there was substantial electoral reward to be gained from becoming closely associated with one of the focal points of the classical phase of civil rights activity. Viewed through that particular lens, the 2007 event revealed more about the candidates themselves than it did about the Selma campaign, for it cast light on the ways in which they wished their candidacies to be perceived and the parts of the electorate to whom they believed they could—and should—appeal.

It was during his appearance there, for example, that Obama gave a speech that became widely known for its development of the "Joshua Generation" idea and his attempts to position himself within longer traditions of African American history and campaigning. That speech has largely been interpreted not as an attempt to understand the Selma demonstrations per se, but rather as an attempt to understand Obama. In David

Remnick's words, the speech represented a strategic push by a candidate who had often been seen as separate from the African American struggle to win "the approval of his elders."[2]

While such analysis is telling in terms of the construction of one potential presidential candidate, and the way in which it was designed to help place Obama in voters' minds, it misses important elements of wider significance. In particular, such a narrow interpretation omits any analysis of the ways in which the content of Obama's speech also addressed wider issues, either explicitly or implicitly, including the central role that Selma has played in the development of historical memory of the Freedom Struggle, the construction of the American past, and broader American discourses of race and racism. As reporters at the 2007 event recalled, Obama used the Joshua Generation speech to remind his Selma audience that "if you had not endured the taunts and the torments and violence, I would not be in the halls of Congress. I stand on the shoulders of giants." These were giants, he elaborated, who "battled . . . on behalf of all America" and "battled for America's soul," and this event was therefore a commemoration of those who "shed blood . . . endured taunts and torment and in some cases gave the full measure of their devotion." In that sense, Obama held Selma to be not just a single, isolated historical event that deserved to be commemorated, but rather a signal point in the development of a national narrative that was both clear and equally clearly redemptive. By the terms of that narrative, the audience that had gathered at the commemoration was not simply celebrating victory at Selma, but also a victory for true Americanism.

Here, then, Obama was moving beyond a pointed political campaign message designed to align his candidacy with the interests of African American voters, emphasizing instead the fact that, in 1965, the ideology of Americanism had triumphed. That, in turn, allowed him to recast those protestors upon whose shoulders he claimed to stand not just as victors in a local civil rights struggle but as vessels for that wider victory of Americanism. The unsaid caveat from Obama's speech was that if those protestors' position was fixed as an emblem of Americanism, then the place of those who had opposed them was equally fixed. First and foremost, they were defined by their actions—"taunts," "torment," and "violence"—and not as actors—taunters, tormentors, and purveyors of violence—which immediately limited their capacity for individualism and agency. Second, by identifying them as having stood in opposition to forces that represented the ideology of Americanism, he was also effectively excising them from what it meant to be American.

Under those terms, Obama was contributing to a national narrative of racial redemption, which began with the complete victory of the civil rights movement, and, concomitantly, the total defeat of Jim Crow segregation. As a consequence of that defeat, segregationists were subsequently either written out of the narrative or forced to reside within particular, and particularly restrictive, roles. The most clearly established of those roles was that of public penitent, in which previously committed segregationists such as former Alabama Governor George Corley Wallace underwent an apparent damascene conversion and paid lip service to the constitutional basis of racial equality and, in emphasizing the truly American basis of that equality, tacitly highlighted the un-American nature of segregation. The obvious conclusion of that narrative was that, with a civil rights movement victorious and a color-blind Americanism ascendant, race was no longer an issue in the United States. In early 2007, even the possibility of an Obama presidency therefore opened a potential final chapter for that narrative, in which the election of a nonwhite president might herald a post-racial United States.[3]

The ability to sustain that redemptive narrative is heavily reliant upon the development of the historical memory of the civil rights movement, as a whole, and on a broader acceptance of the role that Obama assigned to Selma's segregationists in particular. In one of the final rich seams of civil rights historiography, scholars have begun to explore the complex curatorial processes that have defined the way in which the civil rights movement has come to be presented and represented in both public and political consciousness and memory. Historians of visual art and culture, for example, have returned to the apparently fixed images that archived the major civil rights clashes of the 1950s and 1960s in the public mind, to address the ways in which the iconic images of the movement were central both to contemporaneous understandings of the Freedom Struggle as it unfolded and to contemporary public perceptions of its content and character. In so doing, they have found considerable flexibility and nuance both in what those images purported to show and the ways in which they have subsequently been interpreted.[4] In particular, historians have argued that the precise ways in which African American protestors were depicted by press photographers at events such as Selma managed to evoke sympathy from a northern white liberal audience by freezing in place "images of legitimate leadership, appropriate forms of political action, and the proper place of African Americans within the national imaginary." They had to do so, it is argued, via images that conformed to the "selection, emphasis, and presentation" of particular, established "media frames" in order to be successful.[5]

The crux of that analysis centers on the need for African American protestors to be seen in relatively passive roles, with little or no agency, in ways that were not deemed to threaten the basis of white power overtly. Prominently here, Martin Berger has created what might be termed a taxonomy of images that were calculated to have held the interest and the sympathy of northern whites without troubling their sense of political or societal control. That taxonomy includes black children at its apogee, with women in the "middle ground" between children and men, and also members of the clergy. In terms of the specifics of the Selma campaign, images conforming to that taxonomy can be found readily in the *New York Times*' portrayal of nuns resting amidst an interracial crowd on the first leg of the Selma to Montgomery march, the *Los Angeles Times*' depiction of "Alabama bound" whites, including clergymen and a child, awaiting a plane eastward to join the march, the *New Yorker*'s image of a white clergyman craning for a view from within a clutch of African American boys, and *LIFE* magazine's consecutive images of Emily Taft Douglas, wife of Illinois Senator Paul Douglas, mixing with the march's leaders.[6]

Building upon a significant existing body of work that demonstrates the extent to which the movement's primary tacticians were all too aware of not only the power of such images but also the mechanics that were necessary in their creation, a reductive summary of what emerges is not far from a mathematical calculation leading nonviolent direct action's proponents to civil rights success: orderly, nonviolent protestors, their ranks swelled by representatives of Berger's taxonomy, sought clearly identifiable objectives and were caught on film enduring the taunts, torment, and violence to which Obama made mention; those images were reproduced in publications with a predominately northern, white, liberal readership; and the resultant pressure forced the federal government to intervene in individual states to ensure that the constitutional rights of all U.S. citizens were upheld equally.[7]

Such a calculation, however, misses crucial parts of the equation. The key ingredient that has allowed politicians in particular, and collective public memory more generally, to forget the segregationist proponents of opposition has been the very photographs that did so much to ensure the success of civil rights protests such as those at Selma.[8] In other words, the images that led to the construction of Berger's taxonomy also served a very different purpose, for they were pivotal in distilling the representation of southern segregationists into such a two-dimensional force that they fundamentally distorted viewers' comprehension of the opposition that faced protestors, and thus the scale of the task facing the movement. That, in turn, has had a significant and lasting effect on the public memory of Selma itself and the movement more generally, and as a result, on the narrative of post-movement racial politics that Obama was helping to craft.[9] An analysis of the ways in which Selma's segregationists appeared in—or, to use sociologist Todd Gitlin's term, were "framed" by—the iconic photographs of the Selma campaign allows for the development of a clearer understanding of the relatively short-term successes of the civil rights movement, the fragility of movement gains, the longer-term failures of the struggle for racial equality, the shape and tenor of historical memory, and the development of a "post-race" discourse at the turn of the twenty-first century.[10]

In overall terms, there were two significant shortcomings to the ways in which segregationists were depicted by the news media at Selma. First, of the many different forms taken by those segregationists who fought the movement under the banner of massive resistance, only one was represented, and was represented repeatedly. Second, the literal two-dimensional nature of reportage photography meant that, where segregationists were captured by a lens, they were also captured as figuratively two-dimensional. Whether in the images demanded by the hectic deadlines of national print dailies such as the *New York Times* or the *Los Angeles Times*, those taken by freelance contract photographer Charles Moore, or in the more measured production of color images in the photographic essays of magazines with a predominately northern, white readership such as *LIFE* and the *New Yorker*, when readers' eyes moved away from civil rights proponents to their segregationist foes, the images that greeted them were starkly similar: a single line or serried ranks of baton-wielding, uniformed resistance.[11] On numerous occasions, the blue hues of the Alabama highway patrol uniforms would undoubtedly have appeared as an almost insurmountable road block to the marchers themselves. To the reader's eye, however, they represented something unalterably different: the single line

Figure 9.1. State troopers block the way as voters protest. By permission of Associated Press.

Figure 9.2. Charles Moore, "State Police form a barricade as they wait for marchers on 'Bloody Sunday.'" Courtesy Steven Kasher Gallery, New York.

of resistance that defended Jim Crow. Once that line had been broken, the images symbolically suggested, the protestors' task would be complete. That completion was rendered all the more possible by the tantalizing glimpses of space beyond the serried blue lines, whether through the legs of the ranked patrolmen photographed at ground level, or more fully above and beyond them via Moore's lofted lens. The task that confronted marchers at Selma was clearly not easy, readers were conditioned to believe, but neither was it particularly complex. To break Jim Crow successfully, the protestors had to break the only line in its defense of which those images' viewers had been made aware.

Such a reading of those images was exacerbated by the lack of any alternative visual representations of segregation published in northern, white-oriented news outlets during the Selma campaign, in stark contrast to the rich portfolio of images available of civil rights activists. To some extent, that was the natural product of Southern Christian Leadership Conference (SCLC) strategy, for, as historians are now well aware, by Selma, the tactics of nonviolent direct action had been honed to such an extent that movement strategists both actively sought out such confrontations and identified the means by which members of the national press were certain to be on hand and in position to capture them. Thus, for example, when *LIFE* photographer Flip Schulke was faced with the possibility of capturing shots in just that vein in Selma when he witnessed Sheriff Jim Clark's possemen roughly manhandling children to the ground, but chose instead to put down his camera and intercede on the children's behalf, he remembers being berated—in person—by Martin Luther King. "'I'm not being cold-blooded about it,'" Schulke later remembered being told by King, "'but it is so much more important for you to take a picture of us getting beaten up than for you to be another person joining the fray.'" King reprimanded Schulke and reminded him of his "'duty as a photographer.'"[12]

By the time of the Selma campaign, those tactics had been so thoroughly refined that they produced catalogues of images reflecting both the individual agency of single activists and the collective agency of protestors, for they were framed in multifaceted roles ranging from marching constitutionally and determinedly in their finest churchgoing clothing, to kneeling in prayer, or choosing to sing joyous freedom songs with church spires symbolically pictured in the background, offering a shorthand to denote who it was, crucially, that marched with God on their side. These

Figure 9.3. Selma to Montgomery protesters. Photo by Steve Schapiro. By permission of Getty Images.

were not, as some analyses have perplexingly claimed, images positing African American protestors in frames that denied them agency at the expense of their white opponents, or which confined them to "appropriately passive roles."[13]

Re-reading those images with an eye not on the protestors themselves, but rather on their segregationist opponents, reveals that the framed agency of civil rights activists was juxtaposed with segregationists who were routinely represented as no more than faceless automatons. Often, they were facing away from the camera in scenes framed to catch the agency of many of their individual activist foes, or, equally, they were captured in an identical, uniformed dress that represented them not as individuals but as machines of the state, replete with the stamp of their state-begotten identity in sewn patches on their sleeves. Moreover, even when they were caught in full-face portrait, they were often rendered featureless and austere, with the details of their individual identities blocked either by shadow, mirrored aviator sunglasses, or, of course, by gas masks.[14]

The general strength of prevailing Cold War discourses in 1965 made it highly unlikely that viewers of those images would not have made instant links between those faceless automatons and the forces of totalitarian,

Figure 9.4. March across Edmund Pettus Bridge. Photo by Charles Moore. By permission of Getty Images.

Figure 9.5. Civil rights marchers kneeling in prayer. Photo by Flip Schulke Archives. By permission of Getty Images.

communist regimes. Given the images to which they were immediately linked, it is surely inconceivable. On March 5th, only two days before Colonel Al Lingo's horse-borne possemen were captured on film steaming into nonviolent protestors on Edmund Pettus Bridge, the front pages of the nation's newspapers covered equally visceral images of Soviet police cavalry ploughing into demonstrators in Moscow. By the time that coverage of Selma appeared in *LIFE* magazine, the juxtaposition of images might have come straight from one of Bayard Rustin's strategy playbooks.

On three consecutive pages, *LIFE* led its readers through a triptych of scenes: Soviet protestors; a Soviet cavalry charge into those protestors; and Selma's Sheriff Jim Clark, the upper half of his facial features blanked by the shadow of his helmet, but the identifying "SPD" insignia of his police force glinting in full sun.[15] The sense that the rhetoric of the Cold War hung heavy in the air during the Selma demonstrations was amplified by Federal District Court Judge Frank Minis Johnson's opinion in *Williams v. Wallace*, in which he noted that the tactics used by state troopers and Lingo's possemen "were similar to those recommended for use by the United States Army to quell armed rioters in occupied countries," not least in their combined use of tear gas, smoke canisters, and nausea gas.[16] In an allusion to the Soviet-style lack of rights and judicial due process meted out to Selma's protestors, journalists covering the campaign began to refer, only half-jokingly, to many demonstrators being jailed for "resisting assault," an idea that was conveyed directly to northern white liberals through the pages of the *New Yorker*.[17]

The casting of Selma's segregationists as agency-free automatons in sharp contrast to their activist opponents appears more deliberate still, given the existence of images of segregationists that framed them in different modes but which were not selected for publication nationally. *The Birmingham News*'s Spider Martin, for example, took a series of shots of white law enforcement officers passing outside Brown Chapel with their facial expressions clearly visible, and one of a Dallas County deputy with a face sufficiently close—and sufficiently unmasked—to allow viewers a glimpse of the concentration needed to deploy the tear gas gun that he held in one hand, while Student Nonviolent Coordinating Committee photographer Danny Lyon's image of Jim Clark, alongside relaxed deputies, some smoking, all with their helmets tilted to allow light rather than shadow on their facial features, captured the individuality of those lawmen as relaxed white southerners. None appeared in national news publications.[18] Although none were as deliberately and richly textured as the photographs that Alabama photographer Wayne Sides was able to take of Bill Wilkinson's Ku Klux Klan revival in the late 1970s, they were nonetheless images that, somewhere in the editorial production process, had been deliberately set aside.[19]

Thus, the consumption of images of Selma's segregationists as totalitarian automatons was the product of a number of contributors, from movement strategists who designed means of engineering particular photographic opportunities to the activists who were willing and able to put those strategies into place to the cameramen who were both present and willing to capture them and to the editorial staff who chose to print particular framings over others. At times, also, it was bolstered by the published prose of journalists, such as George B. Leonard, who began an article for the *Nation* by drawing parallels between Auschwitz, Belsen, Dachau, and Selma, but also by more subtle means that were designed to provide steep contrasts between segregation's automatons and civil rights' individual agents.[20]

The same strategic architects behind the images of segregation's totalitarian blue lines found ways to emphasize the difference between the two sets of protagonists further by constructing scenarios that, when reported, framed movement activists as truly American freethinkers, rather than machinelike un-American followers of a central power. In particular, they reported from inside a "closed strategy session" to which *LIFE* magazine's Henry Suydam was granted access, which showed a particularly animated Martin Luther King Jr. thrashing out possibilities with Hosea Williams, James Forman, Ralph Abernathy, and James Farmer. Not only did such a photoset highlight the extent to which movement activists were a proactive rather than a reactive force it also contradicted the long held ideological mantra of hard-line segregationists that blacks were inherently incapable of independent, intelligent thought.[21]

Elsewhere, those contrasts were sustained by images that continued to frame the forces of civil rights as the natural progenitors of a free, democratic Americanism, once again in contrast to segregationists' apparent totalitarianism. If the overall narrative of marching for voting rights did not make the point sufficiently, the imagery certainly did: thus, for example, the *New Yorker* captured one image of a marcher cocooned by the Stars and Stripes and another of Old Glory rising from the heart of

Figure 9.6. Man holding American flag during Selma civil rights march. Photo by Steve Schapiro. By permission of Getty Images.

a prone roadside supporter, but tellingly did not reproduce Spider Martin's image of a protestor with an inverted flag.[22] Where segregationists had been depicted as a sectional force of automatons that, with inward-looking figures on the outside of the Selma to Montgomery marches, had kept those marchers' dreams and ideals hemmed in, the national force of the United States Army was pictured giving its protective blessing to the marchers, looking out with them to promised horizons, and—literally—framing the March through the recently wiped windscreen of the metaphorical force of Americanism.[23]

The extent to which that simplistic and two-dimensional archetype of Selma's segregationists was a particular construct, in the building of which the northern white press had been actively complicit, is clear from the ways in which other sectors of the press offered an alternative view. John H. Johnson's black press, in particular, sought to belittle segregationists by lampooning them, which not only played to the Johnson Publishing Company's agenda of selling its readership a view of American life in

Figure 9.7. Onlookers at the Selma to Montgomery march. Photo by Stephen F. Somerstein. Courtesy of Getty Images.

which they were on at least an equal footing with the nation's whites but also appealed to those southern blacks who knew that, once the national spotlight had left Selma, they would have to endure ongoing daily contact with its segregationists and system of Jim Crow. Thus, for example, *Ebony* pictured the indignity of a middle-aged white man left with no defense of his way of life other than a raised middle finger, any possible menace diffused by the onlooker laughing at him as much as with him, as well as a cartoonish vehicle that, the caption tells us, "amused" rather than threatened its intended targets along the course of the Selma march and which simply "gave up when marchers refused to respond." Stephen F. Somerstein captured what he termed "a few rowdy white hecklers" at the edge of the march, but they, he recalled, were "playing to the camera" rather than delivering real menace. In *Jet*, a static Jim Clark was caught in a less than flattering triptych of images, juxtaposed with the animated fervour of C. T. Vivian, who, we are told for added emphasis, used his agency to make light of the sheriff.[24]

Lampooning from the white press was far more limited. Its main, albeit occasional, source was in the journalism of Renata Adler, whose parents had fled from Nazi Germany and who was one of the very few white reporters to allow segregationists any measure of wit. Thus, for example, Adler noted the way in which participants of the third, successful attempt to march from Selma to Montgomery found themselves leaving Brown Chapel not only to the expected soundtrack of "Dixie" being piped through loud speakers but also the strains of Ray Henderson and Mort Dixon's "Bye, Bye, Blackbird." Her treatment of roadside segregationist hecklers, a number of whom lined parts of the route of the march between Selma and Montgomery, was more equivocal, leaving readers to decide whether the hecklers' actions veered toward unexpected wit or a cruelty redolent of their uniformed peers. In particular, Adler reported on the progress of Jim Letherer, an amputee who became a feature of both photographic and written reportage of the march because of the way in which he determinedly finished the route on crutches, and whose framing contributed to the established narrative of marchers as true Americans via recurring images that were printed of him flanked by American flags, one held by a white supporter and one by an African American. As the one-legged Letherer passed by one group of segregationists, she noted, he was greeted by chants of "Left! Left! Left!"[25] In one of the very few images of segregationists to appear in northern magazines in a guise other than that of the automaton or the lampooned, a Steven Schapiro image for the *New Yorker* contained a cluster of four presumed segregationists fitting the image of comic book toughs, but their impact was significantly diluted by the ambiguity of their appearance in a biracial (if not desegregated) crowd shot, and the apparent ease of their immediate neighbours.[26] There were, to complete the contrast and to return to the basis of Berger's taxonomy, simply no published images of openly segregationist women, children, or members of the clergy.

The limited and two-dimensional depiction of segregationists that became emblematic of the coverage of the Selma campaign was responsible for a number of significant misrepresentations. More pressingly, it allowed an audience that relied on press accounts to come to an understanding of events that wholly misrepresented the strength and depth of white supremacy in the southern states, and, thus, the complexity of the task facing the movement. The intertwining latticework of obstruction

Figure 9.8. Selma to Montgomery onlookers. Photo by Steve Schapiro. By permission of Getty Images.

and obfuscation that was Jim Crow sustained a far more complex barrier to African American equality than that which was represented by the simplicity of a highway patrolman's cordon.

Even as Judge Johnson declared in the seminal *Williams v. Wallace* decision that the order restraining protestors from marching to Montgomery should be revoked, for example, he acknowledged just how close a call that decision had been. The defendants had played upon the particular constitutional complexities of the case so skillfully, in fact, that Johnson was forced to muse long and hard on the vagaries of the "constitutional boundary line" between the right to maintain law and order and the right to peaceful protest and petitioning that had first been propounded by the Fifth Circuit Court of Appeals in *Kelly v. Page*. Indeed, Johnson was only finally swayed not by the moral and constitutional rectitude of the movement's aims, but by the minutiae of the detailed blueprint for controlling the march that the plaintiffs had submitted.[27] The intricacies of the daunting voter registration processes facing blacks were also unrepresented by such selective and two-dimensional representations of Jim Crow, whether in terms of the "take a number" system, the dearth of available registrars—Walter L. Darby Sr. became the sixth registrar to resign from the three-member Montgomery County Board of Registrars in March 1965, and the sixth to cite "pay too low for amount of time required for work" in so doing—or the Supreme Court of Alabama's 1964 decision to allow the twelve questions asked of voter registration applicants to change every month, so as not to allow "Negro applicants to memorize the questions and answers at classes conducted by civil rights groups."[28]

Absent, too, was any representation of the economic intimidation, whether organized or ad hoc, that faced not only those who attempted to register to vote but also many of those who attempted to show any form of sympathy for the amelioration of racial inequality. Indeed, it is crucial here that it was in *Jet* magazine, rather than any publication that sought a national white readership, that representations of some of the wider issues of segregation appeared in visual form to flesh out the simplicities of segregation on show elsewhere. Thus, *Jet* captured King walking beneath a Coca-Cola advertisement that also carried the chimerical claim of Selma as "Progressive and Friendly," and a caption beneath a photograph of a roadside plaque advertising the presence of the Citizens' Council drew attention to the deceptive, race-free rhetoric of "States' Rights" that characterised an organization steeped in a region that was "Unwilling to bury [the] Confederacy."[29]

The often-hidden economic strategies of segregationists were particularly egregious, but again not depicted. As others had done across the South, Selma's segregationists had perfected the art of forcing the foreclosure of loans from the People's Bank and Trust Company of Selma to those suspected of supporting civil rights a decade before Bloody Sunday and reminded those local protestors who might have experienced a heightened feeling of security within the larger, Army-protected corpus of the third march that their longer-term prospects were fragile in the face of segregationist economic power. To that end, flyers were judiciously dropped by light airplane along the line of the Selma-Montgomery march bearing the words "An unemployed agitator ceases to agitate. Operation Ban. Selective hiring, firing, buying, selling." One reporter noted segregationist bystanders photographing the marchers as they passed, surmising correctly that this was a warning "that their faces would not be forgotten when the march was over."[30]

Essential here, too, is the fact that more mainstream conservative voices at the national level had already begun to point out the inadequacies of viewing segregationists in such limited terms. As early as 1956, for example, the *National Review* commented that the national and international press had "misconstrued Southern resistance," and that "To suggest that opposition to that ruling [*Brown v. Board of Education of Topeka, Kansas*] is in the hands of brute racists indulging an anarchic passion to smash an underprivileged race is worse than unreasonable; it is uncharitable." Nevertheless, it was still the case almost ten years later.[31] *National Review* proved to be incorrect in many things, not least the assertion made by one of its reviewers, having attended a lecture by King at Yale, "that Martin Luther King will never rouse a rabble; in fact, I doubt he could keep a rabble awake, if it were past its bedtime," but nevertheless by 1965, it had developed a series of positions that complicated the all too simple visual depiction of the freedom struggle at Selma almost beyond recognition, none of which were represented in its more prevalent visual imagery: that, in an early neoliberal foray, there were philosophical and economic arguments for maintaining segregation; that there were significant grounds for further explicating Judge Johnson's "constitutional boundary line"; that the freedom movement at its core included just as many true radicals as reformists; that there were significant legal issues yet to be teased out over the constitutionality of using federal force in the quelling of civil rights disturbances; that the movement should be held responsible for deliberately creating a "revolutionary environment" so as to cause a federal abrogation of States' Rights; that an "ideologized [*sic*] Supreme Judiciary" was working beyond its precise remit; and that King had misapplied the "just war" theory of St. Thomas Aquinas and had misappropriated and misunderstood St. Augustine's theory of divine law.[32]

The selective processes that delivered a two-dimensional, limited framing of segregationists to a predominately white, northern audience were central to the shaping of national, and indeed international, understanding of the clashes in Selma in 1965. As Julian Bond commented, photographs "froze the movement and its supporters and opponents into black and white."[33] That should not be taken to mean that such images have been frozen in their particular moment, however, for many have generated—and continue to generate—a significant impact long after their respective photographers' lenses snapped shut. In this particular case, the Selma images have had a longer-term impact by greatly facilitating the creation of a national redemptive narrative that, ultimately, allowed the idea of a "post-race" nation some purchase. By distilling their rendering of Selma's segregationists into only one form—that of the totalitarian blue line—those images allowed a national audience to believe that, once that line had been shattered by the Selma to Montgomery march, so, too, had segregation. The movement had been successful, and racism was overcome. The nation had redeemed itself.

Civil rights organizations were, therefore, complicit in the creation of that redemptive narrative. It was largely SCLC strategists, for example, who generated the situations that were framed by photographers and who found ways of depicting the metaphysical phenomenon of racism in physical terms. That they did so by managing scenarios in which white supremacy was represented via agency-free, violent instruments of the state, vividly juxtaposed with a vibrant collection of activist individuals seeking no more than constitutionally mandated democratic freedoms, was a significant and successful step toward their short-term goal of forcing federal intervention against Jim Crow. Indeed, there is widespread evidence of the extent to which movement tacticians' desire to frame segregationists in such simple terms went beyond the printed image. The president of the Alabama State National Association for the Advancement of Colored People (NAACP), for example, sent a telegram to George Wallace to denounce the "raw and sadistic force" arraigned against "citizens trying to exercise their constitutional rights," while Roy Wilkins and Bishop Stephen G. Spottswood used a press conference jointly to equate activists' plight to that of "people in Nazi-occupied Europe." The tactic appeared to have an impact. Angry citizens from beyond Alabama who sympathized with civil rights activists bemoaned state troopers who "deported themselves as unleashed vicious animals," and even wrote to President Johnson to argue that "No American citizen can tolerate these persistent inhumane atrocities."[34]

Jim Clark's role was, of course, also significant, with even his fellow southern lawman, Laurie Pritchett, identifying him as one of the two men most responsible for the passage of federal civil rights legislation, alongside Birmingham's Theophilus Eugene "Bull" Connor.[35] If Clark played the role of co-author for the prologue of that redemptive narrative, however, his failure to adhere to its prescribed contours thereafter by refusing either to apologize for his uncomplicated role in the Selma demonstrations or to undergo a Wallace-like conversion away from open segregation assured his disappearance from its later chapters. "Basically, I'd do the same thing today if I had to do it all over again," Clark said in a rare interview just over a year before his death in 2007. "I did what I thought was right to uphold the law," continued the man who himself served nine months in jail in 1978 for failing to do just that. Uncharacteristically, but true to the contours of the wider narrative in which Clark would have been recast had he repented, Andrew Young failed to find anything positive to say about the sheriff, even on news of his death. "He was a very, very mean man," Young mused.[36] Far more sensitive to what the plot ought to have been was Gay Talese, who in 1965 had been on the ground in Selma reporting for the *New York Times*. In 1990, Talese built a twenty-fifth anniversary report on the city around the successes of a succession of biracial marriages that had developed as a direct result of the protests. "Old Faces" but a "New Spirit," ran his headline.[37]

The production and then protection of that redemptive narrative offered mainstream white America a relatively simple route out of the complexities of the nation's racial issues. It is a narrative with particular traction in contemporary politics and particular resonance in historical memory, for it has allowed national and international audiences to believe that American racism has been overcome. Part of that construction has been in the way in which the civil rights movement and its key figures have long been represented during that movement's commemorative events. At Selma's fiftieth anniversary in 2015, for example, Obama remembered the movement in its most generous terms, choosing to note "the dream of a Baptist preacher" rather than the anti-war radical who came to Washington to cash a "bad cheque." The U.S. National Park Service, too, prepared for the opening of the Martin Luther King Jr. Memorial on Washington's Mall in similar terms, flagging up the possibility of a tour that would lead participants "In the Footsteps of a Dream."[38] The images not only just generated by Selma in 1965 but also selected from that portfolio for publication in white-read newspapers and photographic magazines were fundamental to the creation of that narrative: segregationists were denied agency; all but a handful of the most visible segregationists—performing their role "correctly"—were effectively erased from public memory; the complexities of segregation were dramatically reduced; and, as a result, segregation as a whole could claim to have been defeated in relatively simple—if still heroically brave—steps.

The creation and maintenance of that redemptive narrative meant that discussions of "post-racial America" were possible, but only because it allowed the existence of less visible, but no less pernicious, aspects of white supremacy to remain as far beyond that narrative's pages as it had been beyond those images' frames. A greater awareness within that narrative of the complexities of entrenched racism would have lessened the fractures felt by the reporting and the social, cultural, and political implications of the deaths of nonwhite citizens including Eric Garner, Trayvon Martin, Michael Brown, and Wenjian Liu that, effectively, forced the authors of the narrative to admit that they were at least one chapter short. Noticeably, too, new images in the light of those deaths played upon an image of a radical King, marching not for constitutional justice but against police brutality.[39] Interestingly, again, it has largely been the images of either those deaths or of the unrest that followed in their immediate aftermath that has forced that narrative's authors and adherents to rethink. Fifty years on from Selma, though, there is no curatorial hand from white picture editors, just the more democratic processes of social media.

Speaking on Edmund Pettus Bridge on the fiftieth anniversary of Bloody Sunday, Obama was forced to acknowledge that a new chapter needed to be added to that national narrative. Apparently reshaping the message that he had delivered at Brown Chapel only eight years previously, Obama told his fellow Americans that they had made progress, but his emphasis now was that considerably more remained to be done. Finding an American spin to place on the evidence of continued egregious acts of racism and racial violence, he asked "what greater form of patriotism is there than the belief that America is not yet finished?"[40]

Once again, agency remained central. To deny progress in civil, gender, economic, and gay rights "would be to rob us of our own agency," Obama argued, using "us" to denote Americans. At the same time, he strove to ensure that segregationists remained devoid of any agency of their own. Where civil rights activists were named as individuals, for example, Obama returned to the original redemptive template by describing segregationists not as living actors, but as the inanimate instruments of their oppression. Named protestors such as John Lewis were not met by people, but by "billy clubs and chastening rod; tear gas and trampling hoof," a construction that was eerily redolent of *LIFE* magazine's account fifty years earlier, which referred not to marchers' opponents as animated individuals but to "the tear gas, bull whips and billy clubs that Negro civil rights marchers endured."[41] In 2007, Obama celebrated the Selma centenary by claiming that "understanding our history and knowing what it means is an everyday activity." In 2015, white southerner Todd Kiscaden stayed away from the celebrations on Edmund Pettus Bridge, preferring instead to tend the grave of Confederate and suspected Klansman

Edmund Pettus himself, because, he noted in reference to the fiftieth Anniversary, "It's not my history."[42]

Notes

1. See, for example, Verna Gates, "Clintons, Obama Cross Paths in Selma," *TIME*, March 4, 2007, at http://content.time.com/time/nation/article/0,8599,1595866,00.html and a full transcript of both speeches, at http://edition.cnn.com/TRANSCRIPTS/0703/04/le.02.html. Hillary's claim to being a minority candidate based on gender was made via the absurdly reductionist "I know where my chance came from and I am grateful."

2. David Remnick, *The Bridge: The Life and Rise of Barack Obama* (London: Picador, 2010), 24.

3. As Obama went on to state, religion was also key to this narrative's development. See, http://edition.cnn.com/TRANSCRIPTS/0703/04/le.02.html.

4. For memory in general, see, for example, Renee C. Romano and Leigh Raiford, *The Civil Rights Movement in American Memory* (Athens: University of Georgia Press, 2006) and Emilye Crosby, *Civil Rights History from the Ground Up: Local Struggles, A National Movement* (Athens: University of Georgia Press, 2011); for images in particular, see Martin A. Berger, *Seeing through Race: A Reinterpretation of Civil Rights Photography* (Berkeley: University of California Press, 2011) and Leigh Raiford, *Imprisoned in a Luminous Glare: Photography and the African American Freedom Struggle* (Chapel Hill: University of North Carolina Press, 2011).

5. Raiford, *Imprisoned in a Luminous Glare*, 3; Todd Gitlin, *The Whole World Is Watching: Mass Media in the Making and Unmaking of the New Left* (Berkeley: University of California Press, 1980), 6-7. Garrow's empirical analysis of references to Bloody Sunday in the Congressional Record has also drawn attention to the sublimation of images over written accounts. See David J. Garrow, *Protest at Selma: Martin Luther King, Jr., and the Voting Rights Act of 1965* (New Haven: Yale University Press, 1978), 163.

6. Berger, *Seeing through Race*, 34-35, and 100; Garrow, *Protest at Selma*, 148; David J. Garrow, foreword to Berger, *Seeing through Race*, x. Images drawn from *New York Times*, March 22, 1965, 26; *Los Angeles Times*, March 9, 1965, 1; *LIFE*, March 19, 1965, 34. Steve Schapiro's images for the *New Yorker* now available at http://www.newyorker.com/project/portfolio/long-road. Interestingly, black-oriented magazines carried similar images. See, for example, *Ebony*, May 1965, 46, 58, and 60.

7. See, most notably, Garrow, *Protest at Selma*, especially on ideas of nonviolent "coercion," and Gene Roberts and Hank Klibanoff, *The Race Beat: The Press, The Civil Rights Struggle, and the Awakening of a Nation* (New York: Vintage Books, 2006).

8. Written accounts in news magazines had to alter the framework within which they reported the actions of Selma dramatically as the events of the campaign unfolded, but the images remained static. See Richard Lentz, *Symbols, The News Magazines, and Martin Luther King* (Baton Rouge: Louisiana State University Press, 1990), esp. 151-53.

9. Berger, *Seeing through Race*, 100.

10. Todd Gitlin, *The Whole World Is Watching: Mass Media in the Making and Unmaking of the New Left* (Berkeley: University of California Press, 1980), 6–7.

11. This Associated Press image, or variants on it from photographers standing shoulder to shoulder at the same vantage point, was published in the *New York Times*, March 8, 1965, 1 and March 10, 1965, 1, and in the *Los Angeles Times*, March 10, 1965, 1 and March 8, 1965, 26. The Charles Moore image is courtesy of the Steven Kasher Gallery, New York. For coverage in *LIFE*, see *LIFE*, March 19, 1965, front cover and 32, available online at https://books.google.co.uk/books?id=JUEEAAAAMBAJ&printsec=frontcover&source=gbs_ge_summary_r&cad=0#v=onepage&q&f=false. A similar image by Steve Schapiro for the *New Yorker* is available online at http://www.newyorker.com/project/portfolio/long-road.

12. Schulke recalled the exchange in an interview with the authors, Roberts and Klibanoff, *The Race Beat*, 383.

13. Berger, *Seeing through Race*, 34–35.

14. Such images appeared, for example, in *LIFE*, March 19, 1965, 33 and 37. The first of these images, by Steve Schapiro, is available to view at the *New Yorker*, now available at http://www.newyorker.com/project/portfolio/long-road. See also similar images by Spider Martin, a photographer for the *Birmingham News*, available at http://www.spidermartin.com/image-gallery/u2lpw5vi9uk8kd963uqg43o72fueso.

15. For images of the horse-borne Soviet attack on protestors, see *New York Times*, March 5, 1965 1 and *Los Angeles Times*, March 5, 1965, 1. For the triptych of images, see *LIFE*, March 19, 1965, 35–37, available online at https://books.google.co.uk/books?id=JUEEAAAAMBAJ&printsec=frontcover&source=gbs_ge_summary_r&cad=0#v=onepage&q&f=false.

16. *Williams v. Wallace*, 240 F. Supp. 100 (M.D. Ala. 1965). For a full transcript of Judge Johnson's opinion in *Williams v. Wallace*, see https://www.courtlistener.com/opinion/2145163/williams-v-wallace/.

17. Renata Adler, "Letter from Selma," *New Yorker*, March 27, 1965.

18. Spider Martin's images are now available at http://www.spidermartin.com/image-gallery/u2lpw5vi9uk8kd963uqg43o72fueso. For Lyon's image of Clark and his deputies, see Danny Lyon, *Memories of the Southern Civil Rights Movement* [The Lyndhurst Series on the South] (Chapel Hill: University of North Carolina Press, 1992), 102. It is also now available online at http://www.magnumphotos.com/CorexDoc/MAG/Media/TR2/6/a/3/a/NYC17759.jpg.

19. Wayne Sides, *Photographs by Wayne Sides* (N.p.: Thunderhouse, 1984).

20. George B. Leonard, "Midnight Plane to Alabama," *Nation*, May, 10, 1965.

21. *LIFE*, March 19, 1965, 35, available online at https://books.google.co.uk/books?id=JUEEAAAAMBAJ&printsec=frontcover&source=gbs_ge_summary_r&cad=0#v=onepage&q&f=false. A similar image of a different strategy session was reproduced in *Ebony*, May 1965, 53, available online at https://books.google.co.uk/books?id=NN4DAAAAMBAJ&printsec=frontcover&source=gbs_ge_summary_r&cad=0#v=onepage&q&f=false.

22. For the cocooning image, see http://www.newyorker.com/project/portfolio/long-road. For the image of the flag rising as if from a protestor's chest, see *New York Times*, March 25, 1965, 27. See, too, *Ebony*, May 1965, 62, available online at https://books.

google.co.uk/books?id=NN4DAAAAMBAJ&printsec=frontcover&source=gbs_ge_su mmary_r&cad=0#v=onepage&q&f=false. For Spider Martin's image of the African American protestor marching with an inverted flag, see http://www.spidermartin.com/ image-gallery/qsvtl0ohrkcmcov6elb5m1n8dhz6yn.

23. For the soldier gazing out onto far horizons, see http://www.spidermartin.com/ image-gallery/ne1uboenloh0ss65b8o6lyxwqu1ilu. For the marchers captured through the frame of a U.S. Army jeep windscreen, see *Los Angeles Times*, March 23, 1965, 2. Similar images appeared in the *New York Times*, for example March 23, 1965, 28.

24. For the *Ebony* and *Jet* images see *Ebony*, May 1965, 50 and 62, available online at https://books.google.co.uk/books?id=NN4DAAAAMBAJ&printsec=frontcover &source=gbs_ge_summary_r&cad=0#v=onepage&q&f=false, and *Jet*, February 25, 1965, 49, available online at https://books.google.co.uk/books?id=pcADAAAAMBAJ &printsec=frontcover&source=gbs_ge_summary_r&cad=0#v=onepage&q&f=false. For Somerstein's recollections, see https://www.theguardian.com/film/gallery/2014/ dec/17/1965-selma-montgomery-march-stephen-somerstein.

25. Adler, "Letter from Selma."

26. http://www.newyorker.com/project/portfolio/long-road.

27. Johnson opinion, *Williams v. Wallace*; *Kelly v. Page*, 335 F. 2d 114—Court of Appeals, 5th Circuit 1964.

28. Clipping, "Darby quits capital board of registrars," National Association for the Advancement of Colored Peoples White Reprisals and Resistance Papers [hereafter NAACP-WRRP], Reel 13, Frame 0845; clipping, March 12, 1964, "New Voter Questionnaire OK'd for state," NAACP-WRRP, Reel 13, 0858.

29. *Jet*, March 25, 1965, 7, available online at https://books.google.co.uk/books?id=j sADAAAAMBAJ&printsec=frontcover&source=gbs_ge_summary_r&cad=0#v=onepa ge&q&f=false.

30. Johnny Sims of Selma, for example, approached the NAACP for a $15 loan because the People's Bank of Selma demanded the immediate repayment of a loan on his farm "because they found out that I was a member of the NAACP." Sims letter to NAACP headquarters, August 31, 1956, NAACP-WRRP, Reel 13, 0844; Adler, "Letter from Selma."

31. "None So Blind . . ." *National Review* 1, no. 18 (21 March 1956): 5.

32. "A.B.H.," "The Two faces of Dr King," *National Review* 6, no. 18 (31 January 1959): 482 and 486; "Foul," *National Review* 1, no. 22 (18 April 1956): 6; William F. Buckley Jr., "Birmingham and After," *National Review* 14, no. 20 (21 May 1963): 397; L. Brent Bozell, "Alabama Goes to Court," *National Review* 14, no. 22 (4 June 1963): 445; Frank S. Meyer, "Principles and Heresies," *National Review* 14, no. 24 (18 June 1963): 496; "Mississippi," *National Review* 16, no. 28 (14 July 1964): 573; and Will Herberg, "A Religious 'Right' to Violate the Law?," *National Review* 16, no. 28 (14 July 1964): 579.

33. Julian Bond, Foreword to Lyon, *Memories of the Southern Civil Rights Movement*, 6.

34. Press Release, March 12, 1965, "NAACP Rallies Nationwide Support for Selma Drive," NAACP-WRRP, Reel 13, 0917; Bishop Stephen G. Spottswood and Roy Wilkins, Press Conference, Transcript at NAACP-WRRP, Reel 13, 0918; L. S. Hollowell telegram

to NAACP HQ, NAACP-WRRP, Reel 13, 0902; Stanley A. Rock letter to Lyndon Baines Johnson, [n.d.], Reel 13, 0936.

35. Laurie Pritchett quoted in Howell Raines, *My Soul Is Rested: Movement Days in the Deep South Remembered* (New York: G. P. Putnam's and Sons, 1977), 366.

36. Alvin Benn, "1960s Selma sheriff won't back down," *Montgomery Advertiser*, March 3, 2006, at http://archive.montgomeryadvertiser.com/article/20060303/NEWS/603030343; Associated Press, "Sheriff Jim Clark Segregationist Icon Dies," June 6, 2007, at http://www.nbcnews.com/id/19075327/ns/us_news-life/t/sheriff-jim-clark-segregationist-icon-dies/#.VFyfmlVyaUk.

37. Gay Talese, "Selma 1990: Old Faces and a New Spirit," *New York Times*, March 7, 1990, at http://www.nytimes.com/1990/03/07/us/selma-1990-old-faces-and-a-new-spirit.html?pagewanted=1.

38. Press release, "Remarks by the President at the 50th Anniversary of the Selma to Montgomery Marches," March 7, 2015, at http://www.whitehouse.gov/the-press-office/2015/03/07/remarks-president-50th-anniversary-selma-montgomery-marches. At the unveiling of King's memorial, that redemptive narrative was still a cornerstone of the story that the Park Service was trying to relay. See, for example, Jeanine Barone, "In the Footsteps of a Dream," *National Parks* (Fall 2010), 34–40.

39. Front cover, *New Yorker*, January 26, 2015, at http://www.newyorker.com/magazine/2015/01/26. For the image from which it closely draws, see http://www.charlotteobserver.com/news/local/article9261413.html.

40. Press release, "Remarks by the President at the 50th Anniversary of the Selma to Montgomery Marches," March 7, 2015, at http://www.whitehouse.gov/the-press-office/2015/03/07/remarks-president-50th-anniversary-selma-montgomery-marches.

41. Press release, "Remarks by the President at the 50th Anniversary of the Selma to Montgomery Marches," March 7, 2015, at http://www.whitehouse.gov/the-press-office/2015/03/07/remarks-president-50th-anniversary-selma-montgomery-marches; *LIFE*, March 19, 1965, 35.

42. Todd Kiscaden interviewed at http://www.theguardian.com/us-news/2015/mar/10/selma-alabama-march-confederate.

10

"Men and Women of God and Goodwill Everywhere"

Selma and the Role of Religion in Civil Rights Drama

MEGAN HUNT

"Surely the most commemorated social movement in American history," according to Scott Romine, the southern civil rights movement has remained a fascination for Hollywood since the release of Alan Parker's *Mississippi Burning* in 1988.[1] Cinematic interpretations of the struggles of the 1950s and 1960s have proven a marketable way for filmmakers to wrestle with more contemporary racial issues, and yet they have also helped construct and uphold dominant ideas of the movement and its legacy.

Scholarly investigations of the civil rights film genre have frequently critiqued its proclivity to prioritize white heroes at the expense of black activists, arguing that films such as *Mississippi Burning* and *Ghosts of Mississippi* (Rob Reiner, 1996) distort the public memory with their depictions of passive black martyrs unable to organize and liberate themselves.[2] Yet, while there is little doubt that Hollywood has consistently presented its civil rights stories as "white hero narratives," its specific tendency to pit dignified black Protestants against zealous Klansmen has seldom been discussed by scholars. Often a simplified battle of good versus evil, cinematic constructions of the civil rights movement frequently rely on popular preconceptions about religion in the American South.

More than simply a matter of regional identification, Hollywood's portrayals of southern religion often magnify racial, class, and educational distinctions. Put simply, while religion seemingly unites cinematic southern blacks in a dignified quest toward freedom, it is often used to indicate irreconcilable divisions of educational attainment, income, and racial attitudes among whites. The result is a continued conflation of white southern evangelicalism with reactionary, even racist southern politics and a consistent failure to acknowledge those white Christian and Jewish activists who were compelled by their faith to join the civil rights movement.

This chapter explores the legacy of religion in civil rights drama in order to show how Ava DuVernay's *Selma* (2014) exposes and expands the limited projection of religion in previous films. DuVernay's depiction of the 1965 voting rights campaign in Selma, Alabama, highlights a broad landscape of religious thought in the freedom struggle, as Martin Luther King Jr. (David Oyelowo) urges people of all faiths to march with him and other activists on their second attempt to reach Montgomery. In the film, as in reality, the response was both "rapid and astonishing;" a moment that New-Left journalists Warren Hinckle and David Welsh christened "The Charge of the Bible Brigade."[3] "Never in the history of the United States has organized religion collaborated to such an extent on an issue of social justice," Hinckle and Welsh wrote in 1965.[4] Thus, although *Selma* undoubtedly centralizes the role of black activists in the campaign—and rightly so—it acknowledges the ecumenical and racial solidarity crucial to its eventual success, making an essential narrative point about the universal morality of King's message, directed in the film to "men and women of God and goodwill everywhere."[5] In so doing, *Selma* is the first mainstream civil rights drama that uses religion to unite rather than divide its characters.

The unparalleled inclusivity of this religious vision has inspired numerous debates about religion in civil rights filmmaking and within the movement itself, from examinations of *Selma*'s use of spiritual music to questions about the omission of Rabbi Abraham Joshua Heschel, something that has angered many Jewish commentators.[6] *Selma* has also forced many white conservative evangelicals to question the absence of their forebears in King's "beloved community," reflecting the important role cinema plays in the construction of public memory. This chapter examines these debates, situating *Selma*'s presentation of religious diversity within the history of civil rights filmmaking.

Hollywood requires clearly delineated divisions when it wrestles with any period of social change, simplifying ideologies and personalities in pursuit of streamlined narratives. As a result, *Selma*'s predecessors in the civil rights drama were wholly committed to a depiction of the fanatic, violent, segregationist South best exemplified by the Ku Klux Klan, rather than contrasting this extremism alongside other, more moderate supporters of Jim Crow. Yet, although scholarly discussions of civil rights melodrama analyze the roles of white heroes and subjugated, silent blacks, the genre's construction of its segregationist villains rarely figures in the critical literature.[7]

In Rob Reiner's *Ghosts of Mississippi*, reconstructed southerner and Assistant District Attorney Bobby DeLaughter (Alec Baldwin) is directly contrasted with Byron De La Beckwith (James Woods), a rabid white supremacist who shows no remorse when convicted in the 1990s for the 1963 murder of National Association for the Advancement of Colored People (NAACP) field secretary Medgar Evers. While many reviewers criticized *Ghosts of Mississippi*'s focus on DeLaughter at the expense of the Evers family, most heaped praise on what the *New York Times* acknowledged as the "wily malevolence" of Woods's Beckwith.[8] Despite this attention, critics failed to acknowledge the intersections of Beckwith's extreme racial views with his vengeful religious preoccupations, which prove central to the film's attempts to communicate his evil and his distinctly southern, almost archaic identity.

Abandoning Methodism for the Christian Identity movement in the 1970s, the real Beckwith regularly espoused racist and anti-Semitic diatribes alongside biblical teachings.[9] Many of his words in the film are based on real interviews he gave in the 1990s. As such, it is hard to criticize *Ghosts of Mississippi*'s presentation of him. Rather, it is in its portrayal of DeLaughter that the film manipulates the religious leanings of its characters. DeLaughter has spoken openly about his faith and Reiner understood him to be "a very principled, religious man."[10] Myrlie Evers recalls praying with DeLaughter in her memoirs.[11] Yet, *Ghosts* only reflects Beckwith's religious preoccupations. Like so many other cinematic white southerners who prove to be significant, progressive characters in civil rights dramas, Hollywood's DeLaughter has abandoned the religiosity of his homeland, just as he has shunned its racism. DeLaughter's religion, it seems, would have compromised the film's secular morality, constructed through his opposition to Beckwith.

This nonreligious righteousness has proven critical to Hollywood's understanding of good and evil in the white South, rooted in popular ideas of white southerners as irrationally religious as well as racist. Despite

Mississippi's historically prominent religiosity, *Mississippi Burning* offers no local theological, social, or political alternative to the Ku Klux Klan, which is pitted solely against the secular, federal power of the FBI. Historians' and activists' accounts have shown that mainstream denominations might have been quietly complicit with segregation in the mid decades of the twentieth century, but they seldom supported Klan activity.[12] Instead of depicting a more liberal or even mainstream local religious or political organization alongside the Klan, *Mississippi Burning* ensures that its heroes and villains are starkly opposed, with little room for theological or political complexity. Therefore, like *Ghosts*, it does not simply celebrate white heroes at the expense of black activism, but rather creates divisions within whiteness along regional, class, and religious boundaries, projecting the idea that dominant, secular, consensus liberalism is stronger and more resilient than the values of an anomalous, religious, and racist region.

Unprecedented among civil rights cinema, *Selma* highlights mainstream white religious responsibility, as King chastises hypocritical white ministers who quote the Bible but "remain silent before their white congregations."[13] He equates these clergymen with politicians and law enforcement officers who blindly accept and enforce segregation and brutality. Later, following the horrific violence inflicted on marchers at the Edmund Pettus Bridge on March 7, 1965, King uses the media to appeal directly to white clergy. Yet, in highlighting the later murders of Boston Minister James Reeb (Jeremy Strong) and Detroit activist Viola Liuzzo (Tara Ochs)—both Unitarian Universalists—*Selma* suggests that these enlightened whites were likely to be northern and certainly not from the evangelical denominations that dominated the southern religious landscape.

While historians have long debated the roles—and absences—of various white religious congregations in the civil rights movement,[14] *Selma* is the first mainstream drama to do so, stimulating unprecedented debates among film critics and religious groups. Reflecting the discomfort many conservative evangelicals felt when faced with the conspicuous absence of their denominations in *Selma*'s depiction of the voting rights campaign, Southern Baptist pastor Jon Speed titled his review of the film "You Will Hate Selma But Should Watch It Anyway." "The people who tried to stop the march to Montgomery? They look like me," Speed writes. Although "it makes me cringe to type it," Speed concluded, many conservative evangelicals were probably "on the other side of the bridge. They were standing with the Alabama State Troopers. If they weren't standing with them in body, perhaps they were in spirit."[15]

Sharing Speed's anxieties, The Gospel Coalition (TGC), a high-profile "fellowship of evangelical churches," looked to religious historians for answers, publishing a series of specially commissioned articles from scholars working on segregation and religion in the twentieth-century South.[16] One historian, J. Russell Hawkins, revealed that the National Association of Evangelicals responded to King's call to clergy from Selma with the following dismissal: the association "has a policy of not becoming involved in political or sociological affairs that do not affect the function of the church or those involved in the propagation of the gospel."[17] In another post, historian Carolyn Dupont argues that "any suggestion that the religion of southern whites aided the civil rights struggle grossly perverts the past." She continues: "It is true that every major denomination in the United States embraced the Supreme Court's *Brown v. Board of Education of Topeka, Kansas*, decision that declared segregated schools unconstitutional. However, the picture looks very different at the local level, where southern evangelicals more often fought ferociously against any effort to dismantle the system of white supremacy."[18] It is clear, then, that *Selma* provoked difficult conversations for white evangelicals, who questioned their denominations' absence in the film's evocation of King's "beloved community." The fact that such a conversation occurred on TGC's website is testament to the skill with which *Selma* forces audiences to acknowledge those present at the marches but also ask questions of those who were not. In so doing, *Selma* contributes to the consistent reshaping of public memory, disrupting the popular assumption that no religious whites supported the civil rights movement without simply rewriting history to alleviate white guilt.

Yet, while *Selma* forced many white evangelicals to accept the absence of their denominational forebears in the civil rights movement, it stimulated a much more divisive debate among Jewish commentators about its muted presentation of Jewish activism. Shortly after the film's release, the political scientist Peter Dreier noted that, in contrast to *Selma's* suggestion, "Jews—secular and religious—were disproportionately involved" in white civil rights activism. He listed no fewer than twenty rabbis who marched on Tuesday, March 9, 1965, none of whom were featured in the film. Dreier drew specific attention to *Selma's* omission of Rabbi Abraham

Joshua Heschel, whose white beard and traditional Jewish garments made him particularly identifiable alongside King in photographs of the third march, which reached the Alabama State Capitol on March 25, 1965. "Heschel's absence from that scene in the movie could not be a simple oversight," Dreier argued, a complaint that was echoed by Heschel's daughter Susannah, and the journalist Leida Snow in the Jewish publication *Forward*.[19] "White contributions to the ongoing war against discrimination should be noted," Snow argued, going on to detail numerous rabbis, Jewish philanthropists, and students who gave their time, money, and sometimes even their lives in the pursuit of African American liberty.[20]

Snow's article inspired several responses from Jewish commentators, many of whom drew attention to what the historian Katie Rosenblatt recognized as Snow's "triumphalist version of black-Jewish relations." Rosenblatt concluded that "only a small proportion of Jews played significant roles" in the movement and that the deaths of white Jewish activists Andrew Goodman and Michael Schwerner in Mississippi in 1964 simply drew national attention to a cause that had already claimed the lives of countless African Americans.[21] Local Jewish leaders had attempted to persuade Schwerner to leave Mississippi, "frightened," in the historian Clive Webb's words, "for their own security."[22] For many southern Jews, isolated in the region, being associated with northern Jewish activists provoked fear of anti-Semitic attacks. Sarah Seltzer concurred, stating "*Selma* is not our story and it should not be our story." Seltzer argued that Snow's piece reflected the same white sense of entitlement that motivated critiques of the film's presentation of President Lyndon B. Johnson, the product of "white anxiety about being made secondary in a black story."[23]

Exposing dominant ideas that Jewish and black are mutually exclusive categories, concerns about the presentation of Judaism in *Selma* negate the experiences of nonwhite Jews. They also imply that white Jewish identity was distinctive from broader southern or American categories of whiteness, despite evidence that the majority of white Jews, particularly in the South, conformed with rather than rebelled against Jim Crow. King often praised the sacrifices of northern Jews, notably the sixteen rabbis arrested and abused in 1963 during campaigns in St. Augustine, Florida, and of course Schwerner and Goodman. However, King observed in 1967 "that there are Jews in the South who have not been anything like our allies in the civil rights struggle and have gone out of the way to consort with the perpetrators of the status quo."[24] When the American Jewish

Committee continued to publicly oppose segregation in the mid-1950s, the Jewish Federation of Montgomery withdrew its financial support, as Webb has shown, stating that: "The Jewish community in the South is a part of the white community in the South."[25]

While it is understandable that some Jews were disappointed not to see Rabbi Heschel alongside King in *Selma*, there were countless other marchers omitted, including key African American organizers such as Reverend Fred Shuttlesworth. A founding member of the Southern Christian Leadership Council (SCLC), Shuttlesworth petitioned both President Johnson and the U.S. Department of Justice to protect his fellow marchers in Selma. Identified next to Heschel in the original photographs central to Dreier's argument, Shuttlesworth receives no further mention in Dreier's article. Obviously, *Selma* could never encompass every aspect and figure of a broad coalition. Yet, while the focus of these debates often reflects specific, personal preoccupations, collectively they convey wider contentions about the role of race and religion in the civil rights movement and how best to remember it.

Unaccustomed to the cinematic presentation of black politicization within the church, some critics have disparaged DuVernay's attempt to project King's message of spiritual and political resistance. The religious scholar Ulrich Rosenhagen argues that religion in *Selma* "is often little more than a skeletal stage set to provide a little context or drama, and King's Christian language seems to be little more than the rhetorical flourishes of an artful political motivator." Despite showing King's appeal to religious people across the nation, their subsequent arrival in Selma and the spiritual nature of the second march (known as Turnaround Tuesday), *Selma*—according to Rosenhagen—"misses how a broad coalition of people of different faith traditions who shared a sense of accountability before their God carried the civil rights movement forward." Rosenhagen concludes that *Selma* "fails to communicate . . . this fusion of the spiritual with the political."[26]

Yet, while *Selma* shows King leading the protestors in a silent prayer on the Edmund Pettus Bridge before abandoning the attempt to reach Montgomery, it relies heavily on notions of King's spiritual preoccupations, denying the shrewd political maneuvering that actually produced this "symbolic" march. Evidence shows that King had already negotiated this outcome with the government, promising to lead the marchers to the bridge and then back to Selma in return for peaceful restraint from the police and Alabama state troopers.[27] Although *Selma* presents King in conversations with Assistant Attorney General for Civil Rights John Doar (Alessandro Nivola), these discussions are inconclusive. While DuVernay portrays the dissatisfaction many in the movement felt at the turnaround, she never provides the viewer with the evidence or even the suggestion of King's deal. In DuVernay's vision, James Reeb goes to his death in the film trusting that King was "tapped into what's higher, what's true." King, *Selma*'s Reeb averred, had "prayed to God and got an answer."

Although these scenes overemphasize the place of religion in King's decision-making, it is nevertheless important to acknowledge the moments in which DuVernay's presentation of King powerfully intersects political demands with deep spirituality. His first speech upon arrival in Alabama in *Selma* is met with a rapturous reception, the congregation united, not in a meek rendition of a hymn akin to the presentation of black churches in *Mississippi Burning*, but in their vocal, political demand: "Give us the vote! Give us the vote!" Although these scenes occur within the walls of a black Methodist church and are perhaps, therefore, not the interfaith vision that Rosenhagen had hoped for, this positioning of the black church as both religious and political site is central to *Selma*'s diversion from the white-centric narratives of previous civil rights melodramas, demonstrating the regularity with which King and others skillfully intertwined black and white evangelical traditions with contemporary political concerns within the walls of black Protestant institutions.

All too often, Professor Eddie Glaude has written, "the prophetic energies of black churches are represented as something inherent to the institution," rather than the result of the concerted effort of individuals.[28] Glaude writes of "a reductive historical narrative about African American religion," where internal theological and political differences are ignored and ideas about the African American "'public' (or 'publics')" become extremely limited.[29] Although Glaude does not mention film specifically, it is interesting to consider his understanding of outdated perceptions about the centrality of church to African American life alongside cinematic projections, where the black church is so often stripped of its political significance.

Many films have downplayed or even degraded black political activity within the walls of the church in favor of a more uniformed, unthreatening spirituality. *A Time to Kill* (Joel Schumacher, 1996), for example, is deeply cynical of black churches' involvement with organizations such as the NAACP, which is presented as a manipulative, self-serving group of elite blacks determined to raise their own profile. By contrast, *Selma* does not shy from the internal tensions—particularly between the Student Nonviolent Coordinating Committee (SNCC) and the SCLC—that, by 1965, threatened the movement's cohesiveness. The film confidently displays moments of division as part of a wider visualization of the African American freedom struggle as one of personalities with distinctive and sometimes opposing views. Constantly evolving and adapting, the civil rights movement depicted in *Selma* exists within a broad cultural and political landscape. The film's use of music is crucial to this presentation. Where previous films have relied on muted hymns offering the promise of eventual deliverance to soundtrack scenes of black suffering, *Selma* articulates the movement's commitment to earthly change through bold political action and profound religious witness, accompanied by a diverse musical selection that encompasses gospel, soul, and contemporary R&B/rap.

Morgan Rhodes, *Selma*'s music supervisor, argued on the film's release that because "you can't separate Dr King from his faith, nor can you separate the Civil Rights Movement from the faith that undergirded the Movement . . . it's very important to have gospel music and hymns in [the film], and certainly Negro Spirituals too."[30] Indeed, Rhodes's religious choices, like *Selma*'s narrative, reflect a more nuanced understanding of the role of African American religion in the movement than previous civil rights melodramas, celebrating rather than obscuring the political will displayed in the voting rights campaign. In selecting Martha Bass's rendition of the spiritual "Walk with Me," Rhodes hoped to communicate "generations of freedom fighters and generations of struggle."[31] The spiritual, as the theologian James Cone has recognized, can be "a vibrant affirmation of life and its possibilities." While "trouble is inseparable from the black religious experience . . . the spiritual is the people's response to societal contradictions. It is the people facing trouble and affirming, 'I ain't tired yet.'"[32] Backed by full choir, Bass's powerful delivery of the spiritual provides a composed yet mournful soundtrack to the chaos of the visual scene as marchers are battered and assaulted at the hands of Alabama law enforcement on what is now known as Bloody Sunday.

DuVernay's film puts audiences in the midst of the action, unlike television coverage of this march, which situated viewers as onlookers, as Aniko Bodroghkozy observes. Television audiences in 1965 "may [have been] encouraged to pity and sympathize with the victims," Bodroghkozy writes, but "DuVernay's film puts viewers right in the center of the violence as marchers choke on the gas, their bodies bludgeoned by state troopers' clubs. The film asks viewers to be with the marchers, sharing and participating in their brutalization."[33] Supplementing DuVernay's camera angles, the words of "Walk with Me," become more than just a plea for God's grace and deliverance. They force viewers to acknowledge their position among the marchers and the violence they are witnessing.

Rhodes claims that she was attracted to the words "tedious journey" in the song. "Nothing was more tedious than that journey across the Edmund Pettus Bridge," she continues; "you could describe it in a lot of ways: tedious, perilous, uncertain."[34] Although "tedious" may seem an unlikely description for an event that was surely terrifying, Rhodes understands the word here as synonymous with "wearisome," a reference to the sheer length of the journey: both physically, as it is over fifty miles from Selma to Montgomery, but also historically.[35] Selma's activists were building upon an African American struggle that began with the arrival of the first slaves. Progress had been incredibly slow. As a spiritual, the song "had travelled over the generations," Rhodes advocated, "from slaves singing it to now, this critical moment in civil rights history."[36]

With its specific references to the Book of Revelation, Sister Gertrude Morgan's up-tempo "I've Got the New World in My View" was another important religious choice for Rhodes, heard as protestors march to demand their right to register to vote. Advised by King that they "have clear avenues of approach to a defined battle zone," the marchers descend upon Selma's County Courthouse—"a citadel defended by fanatics . . . the perfect stage." As King's words fade into Sister Morgan's vision, her lyrics reflect the desire for change: "I got the new world in my view, On my journey I pursue, Said I'm running, Running for the city, I got the new world in my view."[37] "People were marching for rights that they did not yet enjoy," Rhodes explained, but they "had a vision of the world that they wanted."[38]

Even in her use of more mainstream popular music, Rhodes often maintains the sense that the Selma campaign was a spiritual mission. Immediately following King's first speech in Brown Chapel A.M.E. Church, the scene transition is accompanied by The Impressions's 1964 hit "Keep on Pushing," which echoes biblical ideas of transcendence in Curtis Mayfield's lyrics, "Hallelujah, hallelujah; Keep on pushing; Now maybe someday; I'll reach that higher goal."[39] Born and bred in the Chicago projects, Mayfield may have been geographically distant from the southern civil rights movement, but his music reflected his spiritual and political affinity with much of its rhetoric. "Keep on Pushing" exposed Mayfield's gospel roots, lending "lyrical and spiritual support to the civil rights movement," according to his biographer Peter Burns.[40] Musicologist Tammy Kernodle argues that "Keep on Pushing" reflects the transition of African American political thought in the mid-1960s, chronicling the "growing anger that exploded in 1964 and '65 with rioting in major cities across the country." Musically, Kernodle argues, "Keep on Pushing" is just one example of how "the freedom song [developed from] its beginnings as revamped spiritual and gospel song performed in call-and-response format to a secular individually performed song that reflected the feelings and aspirations of the larger community."[41]

Connecting mid-twentieth century gospel with contemporary R&B and rap, "Glory," the Academy Award–winning duet between singer John Legend and rapper Common, features a powerful, gospel-inspired chorus. Common's rap, NPR pop critic Ann Powers argues, is "preacherly," delivered like a sermon.[42] Reinforced by his role in the film as SCLC leader and preacher James Bevel, Common—an artist renowned for his social commentary and political activism—reinforces the film's attempts to make links between the past and the present. Referencing contemporary racial injustices as well as the high points of the civil rights movement of the 1950s and 1960s, "Glory" plays over the film's end credits, transporting audiences from the periodization of *Selma* back into the twenty-first century by encouraging them to examine more recent events and the limitations of North America's racial progress.[43]

The centrality of *Selma*'s soundtrack to its capacity to provoke deeper, more probing questions than its cinematic forbearers was evident from its original trailer, which featured "Say It like It Really Is," from Public Enemy's 2012 album *Evil Empire of Everything*. Writing for *Tribeca*, Mark Blankenship noted that while "you might expect a studio historical drama with obvious awards ambitions to score its trailer with period-appropriate music about racial equality," *Selma*'s first trailer featured "a furious, modern hip-hop song, pounding us with beats and the promise of a revolution."[44] Although Public Enemy is not used within the film's narrative, the use of its song to generate public interest surely reflects *Selma*'s commitment to an unflinching examination of the legacy of the civil rights movement, thus linking it with bold explorations of African American identity such as Spike Lee's *Do the Right Thing* (1989), which prominently featured Public Enemy's "Fight the Power." "Glory" urges the continued politicization of African Americans, contributing to a very different cinematic ending than those seen in earlier civil rights dramas, such as *Mississippi Burning* and *A Time to Kill,* in which the triumphant use of gospel music over closing credits often suggests that American racism has been overcome.

Rhodes was clear that her musical choices were intended to link *Selma*'s protestors to their collective history, reflecting the power of African American spiritual music across generations of struggle. DuVernay urged her to uncover "underground hits and B-sides" to soundtrack the film's action, rather than movement "classics" such as "We Shall Overcome."[45] Rhodes's only significant departure from these instructions comes at the conclusion of the film's credits, following "Glory." Here Rhodes inserts an audio recording of activists singing a medley of "This Little Light of Mine/Come by Here" at Jimmie Lee Jackson's funeral.[46] "I thought it was a good way to end," Rhodes recalls, "so that you remember that there was a time, a significant time in 1965 . . . [when] the core of this movement was also faith. It gets into your spirit and it just gives you chills, because you're transported back to that time."[47] However, it is questionable whether many audience members will have remained in their seats by the time the medley begins.

For Robert Darden, who has written extensively on the religious music of the civil rights movement, the inclusion of the gospel medley at the very end of *Selma*'s credits was simply not enough. Although Darden praises the writing, directing, and acting evident in *Selma*, he believed the film could have been improved by the inclusion of what he calls "the real sounds of its story." Through its omission of civil rights anthems such as "Ain't Gonna Let Nobody Turn Me Round" and "Woke Up this Morning with My Mind Stayed on Freedom," *Selma* denies "music its rightful place as a transformative change agent in the movement."[48] Ann Powers disagrees, arguing that *Selma*'s understated presentation of King and his followers in some of their most private moments meant it was unlikely that DuVernay would focus on the "big group sing-alongs and celebrity sightings weighing down our memories of King's crusades."[49] Indeed, DuVernay's instructions to Rhodes reveal that she deliberately avoided them.

Instead, King's interaction with spiritual music, like so many of his experiences in *Selma*, occurs privately, when he calls Mahalia Jackson (played by Ledisi Young) in the middle of the night, fearful of what awaits him and his friends in Alabama. "I need to hear the Lord's voice," King tells Jackson, who responds with a heartfelt, unaccompanied rendition of "Take My Hand, Precious Lord." Like the scenes in Selma's jail, where Ralph Abernathy (Colman Domingo) reminds his weary friend of the gospel's teachings on the ineffectuality of worrying, this moving evocation of King's personal spirituality is vital to the film's capacity to highlight Martin Luther King both as a powerful orator and leader, but also as a man who looked to his friends and his faith for guidance and inspiration.

Film critic Shannon M. Houston notes that the scene with Jackson "could have made for an incredible, musical film moment on a much grander scale," evoking the song's hallowed place within King's legacy. King's favorite hymn conveys weariness and longing and was performed at his funeral by Jackson herself and at a later memorial by Aretha Franklin. King had implored Ben Branch, the musical director of SCLC's Operation Breadbasket, to play the song "real pretty" at an upcoming rally just moments before he was assassinated on April 4, 1968.[50] Thus, it is through this song, Powers argues, that "King lived, died, and was spiritually resurrected."[51] Despite all this, DuVernay enshrines the song within a private moment, enabling the audience to hear the song as King would have heard it, without the symbolism it acquired upon his death. King may have needed "the headlines and the big names at the protests," Houston continues, but "in the midnight hour, so to speak, it's 'the voice of the Lord' (the voice of a woman) that allows him to keep his eyes on the prize."[52]

It is undoubtedly because of its connection with King that "Take My Hand, Precious Lord" has featured so prominently in civil rights filmmaking. Mahalia Jackson's version opens *Mississippi Burning*, while a searching rendition by the Jones Sisters soundtracks the most dramatic moments of *A Time to Kill*, as Carl Lee Hailey (Samuel L. Jackson) assassinates the men who raped his daughter on the steps of the courthouse as they make their way to their trial. Willing Carl Lee on through the shared power of the song, the words seem to reflect his frustration and desperation:

> Precious Lord, take my hand,
> Lead me on, let me stand,

I am tired, I am weak, I am worn,
Through the storm, Through the night,
Lead me on to the light,
Take my hand precious Lord, lead me home.[53]

Whereas black gospel music often soundtracks white violence inflicted upon innocent, peaceful African Americans, "Take My Hand" here accompanies scenes of black vigilantism and murder, potentially reflecting the limitations of nonviolent Christian patience.[54]

Throughout the film, Carl Lee is forced to contemplate the failure of the civil rights movement to change the hearts and minds of many white southerners. "America is a war," he concludes. By its conclusion, however, *A Time to Kill* elicits hope in a more positive future, as white and black families come together suggesting that the promise of the civil rights movement has been reborn in Canton, Mississippi. As the credits begin, a large choral rendition of "Take My Hand, Precious Lord" begins to play, at a faster tempo than the song's previous appearance in the film. This triumphant musical ending, in keeping with dominant tropes of civil rights filmmaking, creates the impression that America's racial turmoil has been laid to rest.

It is apparent, then, that the soothing image of black evangelicalism seen in *Mississippi Burning* and *A Time to Kill*, helps to depoliticize African Americans, but also to unite them in their intentions—not just at the height of the movement, but even in more contemporary narratives. Despite the transformations of the post–Jim Crow era, films such as these seem to long nostalgically for a past, mythologized black community that denies the complexity of African American religion (notably ignoring or compromising groups that are alternative to the mainline southern Protestant hegemony) and suggests little connection with the complex interests and experiences of contemporary African Americans. As the events and tensions of the 1980s and 1990s threatened what the media scholar Jennifer Fuller deems America's relatively recent "sense of itself as a successfully integrated nation," it is hardly surprising that popular culture attempted to replace the angry urban black of the present with his cinematic ancestor: the docile, deserving, poor southern black.[55] As an integral feature of southern black life, the church is central to a safe and comforting image of blacks that is readily absorbed by white audiences to this day in films as recent as *The Help* (Tate Taylor, 2011). *Selma*, while foregrounding the importance of the church to King's leadership and the movement's successes, does not deny the deeply political nature of the voting rights campaign and indeed the movement as a whole. Rather, it powerfully communicates the manner in which King and others used religion to inspire bold political action.

Willfully avoiding the more political functions of the black church during the civil rights movement and beyond, Hollywood consistently flattens the diversity of white involvement in civil rights discourse. More specifically, it denies the complex and disparate nature of white religious responses to the African American struggle for equal rights, from those who were inspired to join the movement, to those who expressed their commitment to segregation in a much more refined manner than through the Ku Klux Klan. By limiting its portrayal of progressive whites to the secular and pushing white religious expression in this period to the margins of segregationist society, Hollywood not only denies considerable white religious activism in the pursuit of civil rights but also overlooks what Carolyn Dupont recognizes as "the racial hierarchy's powerful but often subtle articulation by more polished religious leaders and prominent laymen."[56]

Selma, by contrast, confidently presents a range of white involvement in the voting rights campaign, while simultaneously relying on political rhetoric to convey the choking hold of American racism. In its presentations of Governor George Wallace (Tim Roth) and Sheriff Jim Clark (Sam Houston) among others, *Selma* acknowledges the deep-seated prejudice that marked political and legal structures, rather than relying on overused clichés about "white trash" that have so frequently marked the presentation of segregationist villains. Boldly asserting that those who blocked African American access to their full rights as American citizens were not poor, evangelical whites, but local and national politicians, DuVernay's film conveys religion as a powerful force that can unite people across racial and regional divides, but also provide political, even radical inspiration.

Notes

1. Scott Romine, *The Real South: Southern Narrative in the Age of Cultural Reproduction* (Baton Rouge: Louisiana State University Press, 2008), 132.

2. For example, see Kelly J. Madison, "Legitimation crisis and containment: The

'anti-racist-white-hero" film,'" *Critical Studies in Mass Communication* 16, no. 4 (1999): 399–416.

3. Warren Hinckle and David Welsh, "The Five Battles of Selma," *Ramparts Magazine*, June 1965, 36, republished in David Garrow, *We Shall Overcome*, vol. 2 (Brooklyn, NY: Carlson Publishing, 1989), 438.

4. Ibid.

5. King's actual words are copyrighted and licensed by his estate to another film project and so DuVernay effectively paraphrased many of King's speeches. See Jonathan Band, "Can You Copyright a Dream?: How the Martin Luther King estate controls the national hero's image," *Politico*, January 12, 2015, at http://www.politico.com/magazine/story/2015/01/selma-martin-luther-king-can-you-copyright-a-dream-114187.html#.VTu-zK1Viko (consulted March 22, 2017).

6. Peter Dreier, "*Selma*'s Missing Rabbi," *Huffington Post*, January 17, 2015, at http://www.huffingtonpost.com/peter-dreier/selmas-missing-rabbi_b_6491368.html; Susannah Heschel, "What Selma Meant to Jews Like My Father," *Forward*, January 18, 2015, at http://forward.com/opinion/212971/what-selma-meant-to-jews-like-my-father/ (consulted March 22, 2017; Leida Snow, "*Selma* Distorts History by Airbrushing Out Jewish Contributions to Civil Rights," *Forward*, January 5, 2015, at http://forward.com/culture/212000/selma-distorts-history-by-airbrushing-out-jewish-c/ (consulted March 22, 2017).

7. For the dominant reading of *Mississippi Burning* see Henry Bourgeois, "Hollywood and the Civil Rights Movement: The Case of *Mississippi Burning*," *Howard Journal of Communications* 4, no. 1–2 (1992); Robert Brent Toplin, "*Mississippi Burning*: 'A Standard to which We Couldn't Live Up,'" in *History by Hollywood: The Use and Abuse of the American Past* (Champaign: University of Illinois Press, 1996), 25–44.

8. Janet Maslin, "For a True Story, Dipping into the Classics," *New York Times*, December 20, 1996, at http://www.nytimes.com/movie/review?res=9F0DE7DF1431F93 3A15751C1A960958260; Margaret A. McGurk, "Mississippi Smouldering," *Cincinnati Enquirer*, date unknown, at http://enquirer.com/columns/mcgurk/010397b_mm.html (consulted March 22, 2017); Matthew Gilbert, "The Perfect Villain," *Spokesman-Review* (Spokane, WA), January 5, 1997, E3.

9. Michael Newton, *The Ku Klux Klan in Mississippi: A History* (Jefferson, NC: McFarland, 2010), 186.

10. Rob Reiner, quoted in Amy Dawes, "Making Film Emotional Trip for Rob Reiner," *Sun Sentinel* (Florida), January 3, 1997, at http://articles.sun-sentinel.com/1997-01-03/entertainment/9612310140_1_evers-killer-medgar-evers-myrlie-evers-williams/2 (consulted March 22, 2017).

11. Myrlie Evers-Williams (with Melinda Blau), *Watch Me Fly: What I Learned on the Way to Becoming the Woman I Was Meant to Be* (Boston: Little, Brown and Company, 1999), 205.

12. See Florence Mars (with Lynne Eden), *Witness in Philadelphia* (Baton Rouge: Louisiana State University Press, 1989).

13. This is a direct quotation from the film, which paraphrases King's eulogy for Jimmie Lee Jackson on March 3, 1965, in Marion, AL, quoted in Roy Reed: "Alabama Victim

Called a Martyr: Dr. King and Others Speak at Marion Funeral," *New York Times*, March 4, 1965, 23.

14. See, for example, Davis W. Houck and David E. Dixon, *Rhetoric, Religion, and the Civil Rights Movement 1954–1965* (Waco, TX: Baylor University Press, 2006); Andrew M. Manis, *Southern Civil Religions in Conflict: Civil Rights and the Culture Wars* (Macon, GA: Mercer University Press, 2002); David L. Chappell, *A Stone of Hope: Prophetic Religion and the Death of Jim Crow* (Chapel Hill: University of North Carolina Press, 2009).

15. Jon Speed, "You Will Hate Selma But Should Watch It Anyway," *Gospel Spam*, January 14, 2015, at http://gospelspam.com/selma-movie-review/ (consulted March 22, 2017).

16. Justin Taylor, "Jim Crow, Civil Rights, and Southern White Evangelicals: A Historian's Forum," *The Gospel Coalition (TGC)*, February 9, 2015, at http://www.thegospelcoalition.org/blogs/justintaylor/2015/02/09/jim-crow-civil-rights-and-southern-white-evangelicals-a-historians-forum-rusty-hawkins/#_ftn2 (consulted March 22, 2017).

17. "Memo for Dr. Taylor," March 12, 1965, National Association of Evangelicals Papers, Box 52, Folder "Civil Rights 1965," quoted by J. Russell Hawkins, "Jim Crow, Civil Rights, and Southern White Evangelicals: A Historian's Forum."

18. Carolyn Dupont, *TGC* "Historian's Forum," at http://www.thegospelcoalition.org/blogs/justintaylor/2015/02/10/jim-crow-civil-rights-and-southern-white-evangelicals-a-historians-forum-carolyn-dupont/ (consulted March 22, 2017).

19. Dreier, "*Selma*'s Missing Rabbi"; Heschel, "What Selma Meant to Jews Like My Father"; Snow, "*Selma* Distorts History."

20. Snow, "*Selma* Distorts History."

21. Katie Rosenblatt, "*Selma* Got It Right by Leaving Out Jews," *Forward*, January 9, 2015, at http://forward.com/opinion/212369/selma-got-it-right-by-leaving-out-jews/ (consulted March 22, 2017).

22. Clive Webb, "A Tangled Web: Black-Jewish Relations in the Twentieth-Century South," in *Jewish Roots in Southern Soil: A New History*, ed. Marcie Cohen Ferris and Mark I. Greenberg (Lebanon, NH: University Press of New England/Brandeis University Press, 2006), 201.

23. Sarah Seltzer, "White People Are Flipping Out Because *Selma* Isn't About Them," *Flavorwire*, January 9, 2015, at http://flavorwire.com/498002/white-people-are-flipping-out-because-selma-isnt-about-them/ (consulted March 22, 2017).

24. Martin Luther King Jr. to Rabbi Jacob M. Rothschild, September 28, 1967, quoted in Webb, "A Tangled Web," 192.

25. Jewish Federation of Montgomery, letter to the American Jewish Committee, quoted in Webb, "A Tangled Web," 200.

26. Ulrich Rosenhagen, "The People's Legs Are Not Praying—Why Selma Is Not the Interfaith Movie I Was Hoping For," *Huffington Post*, January 16, 2015, at http://www.huffingtonpost.com/ulrich-rosenhagen/the-peoples-legs-are-not-_b_6479070.html (consulted March 22, 2017).

27. David J. Garrow, *Bearing the Cross: Martin Luther King Jr. and the Southern Christian Leadership Conference* (New York: Open Road Media, 2015), E-book, 693–96.

28. Eddie Glaude, "The Black Church is Dead," *Huffington Post Religion Blog*, April

26, 2010, at http://www.huffingtonpost.com/eddie-glaude-jr-phd/the-black-church-is-dead_b_473815.html (consulted March 22, 2017).

29. Eddie Glaude, "Publics, Prosperity, and Politics: The Changing Face of African American Christianity and Black Political Life," in *Crediting God: Sovereignty and Religion in the Age of Global Capitalism*, ed. Miguel E. Vatter (Bronx, NY: Fordham University Press, 2011), 287.

30. Morgan Rhodes, quoted in Fredara M. Harley, "Musiqology Interview with *Selma* Music Supervisor, Morgan Rhodes," *Musiqology*, January 22, 2015, at http://musiqology.com/blog/2015/01/22/musiqology-interview-with-selma-music-supervisor-morgan-rhodes/#sthash.cecBCLnK.dpuf (consulted March 22, 2017).

31. Morgan Rhodes, interviewed by Alex Cohen and Jacob Margolis, "The music of *Selma*: scoring the civil rights movement," Take Two, Southern California Public Radio, January 9, 2015, at http://www.scpr.org/programs/take two/2015/01/09/41040/the-music-of-selma-scoring-the-civil-rights-moveme/ (consulted March 22, 2017).

32. James Cone, *The Spiritual and the Blues: An Interpretation* (Maryknoll, NY: Orbis Books, 1992), 31.

33. Aniko Bodroghkozy, "Oscars 2015: What *Selma* Got Right and Got Wrong," NBC Storyline, February 22, 2015, at http://www.nbcnews.com/storyline/oscars/oscars-2015-what-selma-got-right-got-wrong-n310361 (consulted March 22, 2017).

34. Rhodes, "The music of *Selma*" interview.

35. Rhodes clarified her understanding of "tedious" in a Twitter post, January 3, 2015, 3:11 p.m., at https://twitter.com/morganrhodes/status/683787883711299584 (consulted March 22, 2017).

36. Rhodes, "The music of *Selma*" interview.

37. Sister Gertrude Morgan, "I Got the New World in My View," *Selma-Music from the Motion Picture,* Paramount Pictures/Pathe Productions, Digital Download, 2015.

38. Rhodes, "The music of *Selma*" interview.

39. The Impressions, "Keep on Pushing," *Selma-Music from the Motion Picture.*

40. Peter Burns, *Curtis Mayfield: People Never Give Up* (London: Sanctuary Publishing, 2003), 29.

41. Tammy L. Kernodle, "'I Wish I Knew How It Would Feel to Be Free': Nina Simone and the Redefining of the Freedom Song of the 1960s," *Journal of the Society for American Music* 2, no. 3 (2008): 296.

42. Ann Powers, interviewed by Renee Montagne, Morning Edition, NPR, February 20, 2015. Listen at http://www.npr.org/sections/therecord/2015/01/15/377427650/how-one-of-gospels-essential-songs-gave-selma-its-soul (consulted March 22, 2017).

43. "The movement is a rhythm to us, Freedom is like religion to us. . . . That's why Rosa sat on the bus, That's why we walk through Ferguson with our hands up," Common and John Legend, "Glory," in *Selma: Music from the Motion Picture*, Paramount Pictures/Pathe Productions, Digital Download, 2015.

44. Mark Blankenship, "Can Public Enemy Make *Selma* Feel Modern?," *Tribeca*, November 7, 2014, at https://tribecafilm.com/stories/public-enemy-selma-trailer-song (consulted March 22, 2017).

45. Ibid.

46. Jimmie Lee Jackson was shot by a white Alabama state trooper during a peaceful protest in Marion, Alabama, on February 18, 1965. He was twenty-six years old. His murder is depicted in *Selma*, and proves central to the decision to march to Montgomery.

47. Rhodes, "The music of *Selma*" radio interview.

48. Robert Darden, "The Missing Songs of *Selma*," *On Faith*, January 16, 2015, at http://www.faithstreet.com/onfaith/2015/01/16/the-missing-songs-of-selma/35899 (consulted March 22, 2017).

49. Ann Powers, "How One of Gospel's Essential Songs Gave 'Selma' Its Soul," *The Record: Music News from NPR*, January 15, 2015, at http://www.npr.org/sections/therecord/2015/01/15/377427650/how-one-of-gospels-essential-songs-gave-selma-its-soul (consulted March 22, 2017).

50. Author unknown, Obituary: "Ben Branch, 59, Leader in Civil Rights, Business," Chicago Tribune, August 28, 1987, at http://articles.chicagotribune.com/1987-08-28/news/8703050549_1_mr-branch-ben-branch-southern-christian-leadership-conference (consulted March 22, 2017).

51. Powers, "How One of Gospel's Essential Songs Gave 'Selma' Its Soul."

52. Shannon M. Houston, "Violence and Glory in Ava DuVernay's *Selma*," *Paste*, January 5, 2015, at http://www.pastemagazine.com/articles/2015/01/violence-and-glory-in-ava-duvernays-selma.html (consulted March 22, 2017).

53. The Jones Sisters, "Take My Hand Precious Lord," written by Rev. Thomas Dorsey. *A Time to Kill OST*, Atlantic, 1996.

54. *Mississippi Burning* makes frequent use of black gospel music to soundtrack white racist violence, most notably during a scene in which a singing African American congregation is terrorized outside their church by Klansmen. The song they had been singing ("When We All Get to Heaven") is heard again, this time in a low-tempo solo.

55. Jennifer Fuller, "Debating the Present through the Past: Representations of the Civil Rights Movement in the 1990s," in Renee C. Romano and Leigh Raiford, eds., *The Civil Rights Movement in American Memory* (Athens: University of Georgia Press, 2006), 169.

56. Carolyn Renee Dupont, *Mississippi Praying: Southern White Evangelicals and the Civil Rights Movement, 1945–1975* (New York University Press, 2013), 6.

3

THE MYTH OF A COLOR-BLIND AMERICA

11

The Third Reconstruction

The Racial Wealth Gap in the Post–Civil Rights South

DEVIN FERGUS

"If Negroes could vote," Martin Luther King told some 700 courthouse picketers in Selma, February 1, 1965, "there would be no oppressive poverty directed against Negroes."[1] As the words of King, along with countless flyers, handbills, and other ephemera from Selma's Voting Rights Campaign make plain, voting was key to unlocking *both* political and economic mobility during the Second Reconstruction. The Second Reconstruction (circa 1954–1965), which largely helped to fulfill the constitutional goals left incomplete by the First Reconstruction (circa 1865–1877) has been largely successful in improving African Americans' access to the political and electoral system. Blacks in the South today have dramatically closed the electoral gap, closing the registration and voting disparities.[2] The number of black elected officials in the South has risen exponentially over this period as well. Prior to the Voting Rights Act of 1965 (VRA), a mere three blacks served in southern state legislatures. By 1985, 176 African Americans were serving in southern state legislatures, and by 2010, there were 313.[3] And while black electoral power has been blunted by a series of means since the 1960s, the U.S. Department of Justice's website touts the 1965 act as likely "the single most effective piece of civil rights legislation ever passed by Congress."[4]

But have these gains translated into greater black economic mobility, as King and other civil rights leaders imagined or hoped they would? Until recently, scholars of the civil rights movement have tended to overlook the interplay between the movement and economic justice during the Second Reconstruction. This has slowly been changing. Recent literature has documented the positive socioeconomic effects that the aggressive application of voting and other antidiscrimination laws have played in closing racial gaps in income, employment, education, access to government contracts and public services, and other spheres informing economic wellbeing in the U.S. South—where the plurality of African Americans reside today and where, historically, the sting of legal racism was felt most and feared unassailable.[5]

As economic historians like Gavin Wright have shown, black income growth relative to whites in the South has been impressive in the decades that followed the landmark civil rights legislation of the 1960s. While incomes grew throughout the South, the region's relative gain on the rest of the nation was mostly attributable to the dramatic increases in southern black family incomes. For example, from 1960 to 1972, the median black male income in the South relative to whites rose from less than 40 percent to nearly 60 percent.[6] Within a generation, median black income gains grew faster in the South than any other region.[7] By the end of the 1990s, southern black median income virtually equaled that of the median black income in the Northeast or Midwest, eliminating the regional income gap.[8] And by 2000, "black incomes relative to whites . . . were as high or higher in the South than elsewhere in the country."[9] The civil rights laws of the 1950s and 1960s have been instrumental to the rise of southern black wages since the 1980s. Laws like Title VII of the Civil Rights Act, which prohibited employment discrimination, fostered economic opportunities for most African Americans, paving the way especially for college-educated blacks in high-paying occupational sectors.

Also significant, civil rights legislation actually helped to spur the reverse Black Migration South. This migration started shortly after the passage of the Civil Rights Act of 1964 and continues to this day. The South's economic growth "coupled with its much improved racial climate, represents a far different context for the new generations of black migrants than the region their counterparts vacated in large numbers over 30 years ago," writes demographer William H. Frey of the Brookings Institution.[10]

The reverse Black Migration may well have benefitted African Americans across the country, as opening the South may have potentially alleviated existing "labor crowding" in the primary labor market (that is, jobs with high wages and greater security) in other regions. A supply-and-demand theory, labor crowding is thought to occur when a clutch of workers is "crowded" into a relatively small number of occupations, the

Table 11.1. Net migration into the South 1870–1880 to 2005–2010 (in thousands)

Years	White	African American
1870–1880	91	68
1880–1890	-271	88
1890–1900	-30	-185
1900–1910	-69	-194
1910–1920	-663	-555
1920–1930	-704	-903
1930–1940	-558	-408
1940–1950	-866	-1,581
1950–1960	-234	-1,202
1960–1970	1,807	-1,308
1970–1980	3,556	206
1980–1985	1,808	83
1985–1990	971	325
1990–1995	1,344[a]	358
1995–2000	1,127[a]	347
2000–2005	1,127[a]	318
2005–2010	731[a]	267

Source: Gavin Wright, *Sharing the Prize: The Economics of the Civil Rights Revolution in the American South* (Cambridge: Belknap Press of Harvard University Press, 2013), copyright © by the President and Fellows of Harvard College.
Note: a. Non-Hispanic white.

result of which is lower wages and reduced work incentive. While the impact of crowding is typically associated with the secondary labor market (low wage, insecure jobs), an often hidden racial result, according to urban economists Timothy M. Bates and Daniel Fusfeld, is "the payment of substandard wages to minority employees when they are able to get jobs in . . . high wage occupations."[11] Bates and Fusfeld argue that the "lack of alternative opportunities is the chief economic factor that preserves the process of crowding."[12] For educated blacks living outside the pre–civil rights South, labor crowding may well have resulted in limited job opportunities in the primary labor sector. The post–civil rights exodus of educated blacks to the southern United States may also have helped to obviate further wage stagnation in other regions, relieving "labor crowding" in the Northeast, Midwest, and West Coast, where this labor-and-supply dynamic may have served to (artificially) suppress wages outside the South.

Why Wealth, Not Income

Certainly, income is central in the telling of the socioeconomic impact of civil rights on the South, as earnings are a significant mechanism in black material advancement. Yet judging economic wellbeing and mobility through the prism of income leaves the impression that black economic progress in the South appeared too established and difficult to reverse by the 1980s, even while under policy assault by the Reagan administration to undo civil rights.[13] But is income—or other economic mechanisms so often used, like a college degree, minority business expansions, entrepreneurialism, or employment—the best metric to measure the economic success, prosperity, and wellbeing of a society?[14]

It may be useful to make the distinction between wealth and income. Although they are interrelated, "wealth is not income, spending, and consumption, but rather savings, investment, and the accumulation of assets," writes Michael Sherraden, a social work professor.[15] An income is one's salary, wages, or cash assistance from government at a particular moment in time.[16] By wealth, I mean financial assets (stocks, bonds, retirement accounts, mutual funds, certificates of deposit, et cetera) and nonfinancial assets (homes, other real estate, vehicles, jewelry, antiques, artwork, et cetera) minus debts. For the federal government, such as the Federal Reserve's Survey of Consumer Finances, wealth is meant to mean and is interchangeable with net worth. Wealth almost always generates income, whereas income does not necessarily create wealth. Wealth insulates individuals and families from economic shocks and disruption. Households without financial assets run a far greater risk of transforming a destabilizing circumstance such as sudden job loss, medical catastrophe, or some other life-altering event into bankruptcy, foreclosure, homelessness, or worse. Because wealth can be inherited, several studies suggest it plays an outsized role in determining the quality of education and economic and social opportunities parents are able to pass on to future generations.[17] Similar studies—one by the public policy organization Demos and the other, an unpublished report by researchers at Northwestern University—show that extreme wealth also translates into greater social and political influence.[18]

To stop short of addressing the racial wealth gap question, then, is to elide perhaps the most commonly cited metric used by scholars for measuring economic success and wellbeing. I do not mean to discount the value of income and income inequality but rather to emphasize the measurable impact of wealth on an individual and family's life chances. Elsewhere, I have collaborated with others describing the role income plays as a key mechanism historically in establishing household economic stability.[19] Here, the primary purpose is to place income within its larger context in terms of wealth.[20]

Beyond understanding how wealth differs from income, most experts tend to agree that today's racial economic gap is rooted in assets not income. As sociologist Thomas Shapiro explains in *The Hidden Cost of Being African American*, "When we look at assets rather than just earnings, [it] allows us to consider how the historical legacy of the past acts upon the present and, possibly, the future."[21] For African Americans in particular, metrics based on wealth since the 1980s may not only present a more accurate barometer compared to income, education, employment, or entrepreneurship but also might mean a less reassuring reading of the recent past. At the same time the racial *wage* gap was narrowing, the racial *wealth* gap expanded to three times its previous amount, according to a national report examining the post–civil rights period.[22]

In 1984, white households had a net value worth $85,000 more than black households. By 2009, the gap had steadily climbed, almost unabated since the early 1980s, to $236,000, or an increase of $152,000 over the last twenty-five years.[23] Nationally, the racial wealth gap during the 1990s and 2000s grew *despite* evidence revealing that blacks gained ground on whites in income and education attainment.[24] So a fundamental question lingers: If income does not adequately explain the $152,000 gap over the last generation, then what does? What is the primary pathway to wealth in America?

Researchers have concluded that homeownership is the single most important predictor that explains the "roots of the widening racial wealth divide," especially where one buys and how long one owns. Conducting a twenty-five-year longitudinal national survey from 1984 to 2009 of 1,700 U.S. households, the Institute on Assets and Social Policy (IASP) at Brandeis University found that homeownership "accounted for 27 percent of relative wealth growth between whites and blacks." This made homeownership the largest portion of the growing wealth gap—compared to

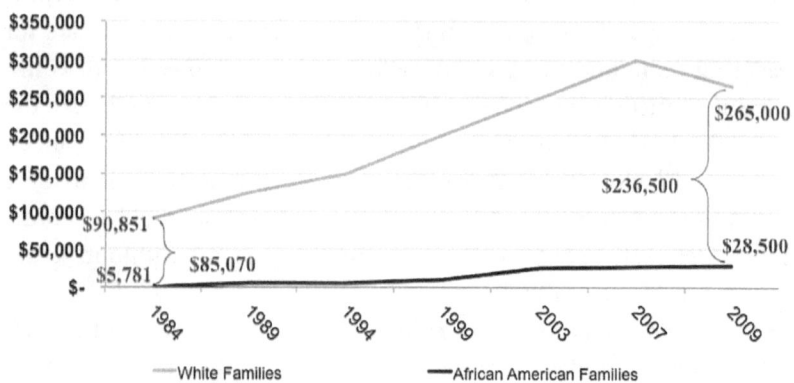

Figure 11.1. Median net worth by race, 1984–2009. Source: Institute on Assets and Social Policy, February 2013.

income (20 percent), unemployment (9 percent), college education (5 percent), and inheritance (5 percent).[25]

Such transformative assets as homeownership and inherited wealth hold a special place in the wealth calculus. Unlike income, jobs, or a degree, for example, transformative assets like a home can be bequeathed—or in the case of inheritance, be given to children of family to provide down payments and closing costs for first-time homebuyers, college tuition payments, large cash gifts, loans, and bequests at death.[26] Transformative assets also translated into a measurable racial wealth advantage. For example, from the 1980s to the 2000s, white Americans were five times more likely to receive an inheritance than blacks. In addition, among those receiving inheritances, whites received approximately ten times more in wealth than African Americans.[27] Finally, inheritance and preexisting family wealth have heightened in significance with the fraying of the social safety net in recent decades. These "in vivo" transfers of wealth buffer a family member from the financial shock experienced by a loss of employment, medical emergency, divorce, or the unexpected death of a family member—the most common reasons for bankruptcy.[28]

Moreover, because whites and blacks have such different starting places when it comes to net worth and assets, their wealth grows at vastly different rates. As the IASP-based table below indicates, even when the accomplishments, advances, or events are equal—a pay raise at work, family inheritance, or wedding and marriage—wealth grows far slower "for

Table 11.2. White and African American wealth accumulation

How Wealth is Accumulated?	White Wealth Growth	African American Wealth Growth
Each $1 increase in income yields	$5.29	$0.69
Each $1 increase in inheritance yields	$0.91	$0.20
Marriage	Significant Impact	No Significant Impact

Source: Institute on Assets and Social Policy, February 2013.

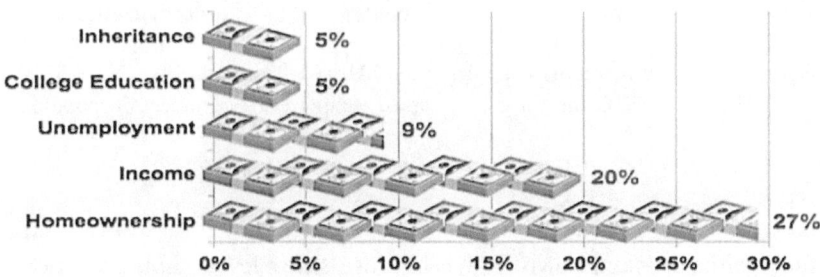

Figure 11.2. Factors contributing to the wealth gap between whites and blacks. Source: Institute on Assets and Social Policy, February 2013.

African American households who typically need to use financial gains for everyday needs compared to white households who are more likely" to put away for long-term savings or in assets.[29] These yields shrink considerably, though, when white and black wealth portfolios are similar.[30]

Why the South?

Region still matters. A poor child born in the 1970s, 1980s, or 1990s growing up in Charlotte, North Carolina, the financial capital of the New South, has only 4.4 percent probability of being a high income earner while that same poor child growing up in San Jose, California, has a 12.9 percent chance—or roughly the same chance as she would if she was raised in Denmark, according to the Equality of Opportunity Project, an intergenerational mobility study by economists of nearly 40 million tax returns from 1971 to 1993. While the project uses income tax returns to map the absence of social mobility for all Americans, the economic team authoring this study says almost nothing about race and wealth.[31] How

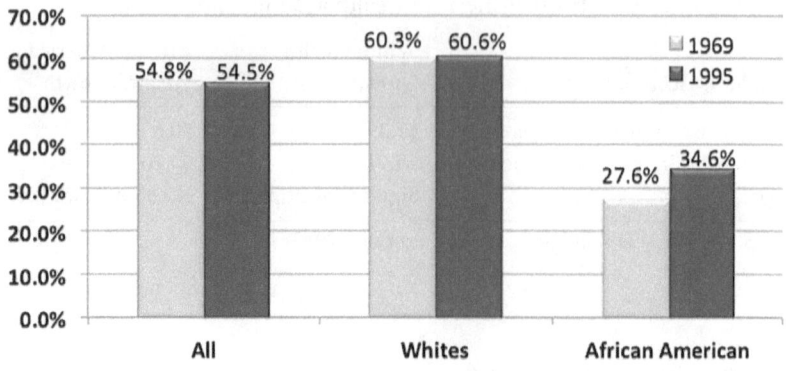

Figure 11.3. Percent of southern families in top 3 U.S. wealth quintiles by race, 1969 and 1995. Source: MDC, Inc. (originally named Manpower Development Corporation, Inc.).

much the South remains a statistical outlier when it comes to race and the wealth gap is unknown. That is because, save a few notable exceptions like the one above, regional studies have dissipated in the post–civil rights era—flattening not only distinctions between regions but also what scholars might be able to glean about material progress over time and space.[32] Among historians, the suburban synthesis school has been particularly adroit in deemphasizing regional variations.[33]

Despite the inescapable role of region in determining mobility over the last forty years, historians, political scientists, and sociologists, among other social scientists, have been at the fore of collapsing the regional distinctions between North and South.[34] This has certainly been the case with regard to studies of the racial wealth gap in the South. Poring over federal agency records and consulting individual and institutional experts in the field (for example, Closing the Racial Wealth Gap Initiative, the Research Network on Racial and Ethnic Inequality, and the Institute on Assets and Social Policy) has turned up scant systematic or longitudinal regional studies of race and the wealth gap in the post–civil rights South. And while promising analytical tools appear to be on the horizon that would enable future researchers to disaggregate assets data by the overlapping categories of race and region, at this point to date, nothing quite exists.[35]

That said, the little data known and accessible to this author suggests a divergence between income and wealth in the economic lives of southern blacks in the post–civil rights period. Between 1970 and 1996, the median family income for white southerners rose 20 percent while the median family income for black southerners rose 29 percent, according to a 1998 regional analysis of a population survey of the U.S. Census Bureau and Council of Economic Advisers report by MDC, a private research group headquartered in the North Carolina Triangle.[36] From 1969 to 1995, the southern racial wealth gap remained stubbornly unchanged, but the gap stayed relatively constant despite the impressive gains made in reducing the racial income gap and increases in the net worth of blacks and whites over this same course of time.[37] According to the MDC report's authors Timothy Smeeding and Edward N. Wolff:

> Even as the South makes historically significant economic gains, it is crucial that more Southerners be brought into the mainstream of the region's development. . . . It is a challenge that demands both "income" strategies and "wealth" strategies, because the two are interrelated. . . . Policies that lead to wider home ownership, for example, . . . represent a difficult, yet crucial, challenge to Southern policymakers who seek a higher quality of life and well-being for the people of the region.[38]

The limited research and evidence available, though incomplete, appears to reinforce the idea that disparate access and experiences of homeownership are key drivers of the growing racial wealth divide in the post–civil rights South. While there may be no statistical difference between the South and the rest of the nation regarding race and income, the same cannot be claimed about the more important predictor of wealth: homeownership. And because homeownership is the primary way families accumulate, pass on, and hold on to wealth, it seems like a reasonable place to start to begin examining the question whether the southern racial wealth gap has closed or spread in the post–civil rights era. This is particularly important given that blacks in the South are more likely to own their own homes than in any other region of the country.[39]

Race and the Lending Gap

By the 1980s, race and mortgage lending in the post–civil rights South seemed to be a decidedly mixed bag. During the 1980s, for example, black-white home loan rejection disparity in the South (13.9 percent) was only slightly above the national average (12.6 percent). Regionally, the gap in the South was wider than the West (10.7 percent) and Northeast (4.3 percent) but ahead of the Plains (18.3 percent) and Midwest (17.4 percent).[40] On closer examination, however, the South appeared to be spearheading a national trend of increasingly separate and unequal mortgage lending treatment. Nationally, between 1974 and 1988, the black-white lending gap effectively doubled in thirteen of the seventeen cities examined—with six of the thirteen cities in the South.[41]

Moreover, while the national lending gap was two times that of earlier gaps, it was three times wider in thirty of the fifty largest southern cities. Take, for example, metro Atlanta—whose self-styled moniker "Too Busy to Hate" did not necessarily mean the city's credit market was too busy to discriminate when it came to mortgage lending. Banks and savings and loans in metro Atlanta made five times as many loans to middle-income whites compared to middle-income blacks, despite evidence indicating that white homeowners appeared to pose a higher credit risk. In fact, the two black-owned banks making home loans almost exclusively in black areas not only possessed lower default rates on real estate loans than banks servicing white borrowers but also had the lowest default rates of any bank their size in the nation.[42]

Moreover, a lower-income white neighborhood was more likely (31 to 17 percent, respectively) to receive a loan than an upper-income black neighborhood. This included Atlanta mayor Andrew Young's own neighborhood of Cascade Heights, an upper crust, black enclave that had higher rejection rates and received far fewer bank mortgage loans than the typical white Atlanta neighborhood. Would-be prime borrowers of color had little choice but turn to the unregulated, high-cost market. For example, sixteen of the twenty of the homes purchased in Cascade Heights in 1986 were mortgaged by unregulated lenders. Excluded from bank loans, these middle-class blacks leaned heavily on unregulated lenders. These lenders of last resort often charged added-on fees and higher interest rates. So, yes, blacks may have been earning more, but there is also strong evidence to suggest that they were more likely to become targets of equity stripping.[43]

As another example of this systematic exclusion from lower interest, prime-rate mortgages in Atlanta, black applicants for home loans were rejected 2.2 times more often than white applicants of similar income. Atlanta's traditional lending industry would continue these same patterns of

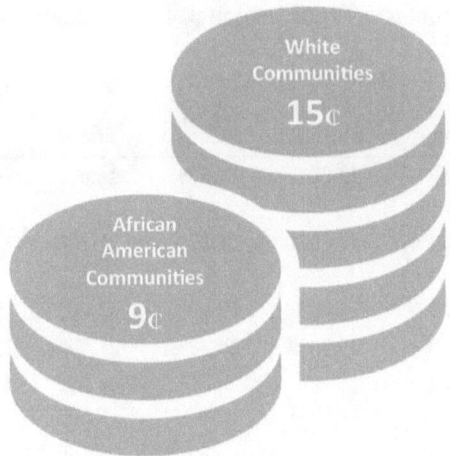

Figure 11.4. Savings and loans return investment in communities per dollar deposited. Source: *Atlanta Journal Constitution*.

mortgage credit discrimination well into the 1990s.[44] Despite this sizeable racial lending imbalance, Atlanta's lending practices were comparatively more racially equitable than three-quarters of the South and most of the nation—with Atlanta ranking thirty-seventh out of fifty southern cities in lending disparities and fifty-ninth out of the one hundred largest metro areas, respectively.[45] As this figure comparing local reinvestment illustrates, the gap in mortgage lending captured a larger, if hidden, transfer of wealth occurring in Atlanta, one in which banks and savings and loans returned sixteen cents of each dollar deposited by whites in home loans back to white communities compared to just nine cents of each dollar by blacks in home loans to black communities. Despite the apparent disparate treatment in lending, the 1980s came and went without bank regulators referring a single case of credit discrimination for prosecution to the U.S. Department of Justice from 1978 to at least 1989.[46]

Race, Subprime, and the Post–Civil Rights South

While homeownership in general is the main predictor of wealth, black families' wealth in the South is further diminished and made vulnerable by various discriminatory mechanisms, such as the recent racial discrimination charges exposed in the predatory lending scandal in which homebuyers who qualified for prime rates were steered to subprime mortgages.[47] Subprime mortgages are costlier for the borrower than prime or market-rate mortgage loans.

Table 11.3. Subprime lending as a percentage of state, regional, and U.S. markets by demographics, income, and location, 1998

Subprime Lending as a Percentage of...	Alabama	Arkansas	South Carolina	Georgia	South	U.S.
% of Total Lending Market	14.40%	15.60%	22.30%	14.80%	16.60%	10.70%
% of African-American Market	19.90%	28.00%	41.60%	21.70%	27.80%	18.60%
% of White Market	13.60%	12.30%	14.70%	10.40%	12.80%	9.90%
% of Low-Income Market	24.70%	25.20%	33.80%	26.40%	27.50%	13.20%
% of High-Income Market	9.40%	10.90%	11.60%	10%	10.50%	5.80%
% of Rural Market	20%	9%	17%	26.70%	18.20%	N/A
% of Urban Market	8%	7%	11%	12%	9.50%	N/A

Source: Housing Assistance Council.

Up until the 1990s, much of the lending research focused on blacks' lack of access to mortgage markets. Within this racially exclusive universe, the South tended to be only marginally more discriminatory than the rest of the nation. But when researchers shifted their attention away from lending exclusion (for example, redlining) to lending inclusion on high-cost terms (for example, reverse redlining), as occurred in the late 1990s, the South appeared far more likely to have engaged in predatory lending practices toward African Americans—charging blacks excessive rates and fees even when these borrowers were eligible for market-rate loans.

As table 11.3 shows, by the 1990s, African Americans in the South comprised the largest single share of the subprime mortgage market. A black southerner was far more likely to receive a high-priced, subprime loan than any other profile of borrower (for example, white, northern, western, low income, high income, rural, urban, et cetera) and more than any other part of the country, according to an analysis of the Home Mortgage Disclosure data by the Housing Assistance Council (HAC), which produced one of the few pre–Great Recession empirical studies of race, housing, and subprime in the South. Southern blacks were more than twice as likely as southern whites to buy from a subprime lender and three times more likely than whites nationally to borrow from a subprime lender.[48]

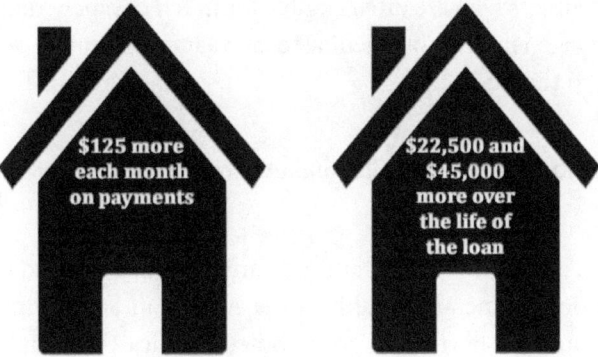

Figure 11.5. How much more does a subprime borrower pay compared to a prime rate borrower? Source: *Spartanburg Herald-Journal* and *Arkansas Business*.

In South Carolina, the primary focus of the HAC study, nearly 42 percent of all African Americans who took out a mortgage loan in 1998 (the year data for the study was collected) did so from a subprime mortgage lender, a figure four times higher than the national.[49] For the HAC study on South Carolina, for example, a subprime mortgage of $54,000 costs the borrower $125 more each month than an average bank loan.[50] Amortized over fifteen to thirty years, a subprime borrower in South Carolina would expect to pay between $22,500 and $45,000 more than a prime borrower over the life of their respective loan—dollars that black South Carolinians could save or put to other pressing financial concerns like one's retirement.

Too often overlooked, saving for retirement is nearly as important a determiner of wealth as home ownership, particularly given the dramatic decline of government and corporate pension programs (for example, defined benefit plans) along with the miniscule participatory rates in personal retirement accounts among African Americans and Hispanics who are the least likely among any category of worker to participate in IRAs and similar defined contribution plans. Others have shown that approximately 30 percent of subprime loan recipients at the time were eligible for much cheaper market-rate loans.[51] As the poorest people in one of America's poorest states, black South Carolinians could least afford to pay more. Yet, it was precisely the subprime borrower, disproportionately black in South Carolina, typically assuming a costly subprime loan. Such financial fracking—by which I mean the use of high-cost terms to extract financial resources from consumers who are often eligible for much cheaper credit products—in mortgage lending was facilitated by years of financial deregulation starting in the 1980s.

Financial Deregulation: Southern Policymakers and the Racial Wealth Gap

When the authors Timothy Smeeding and Edward N. Wolff concluded their MDC report on income and wealth in the American South, they closed by urging southern lawmakers to embrace policies that would expand home ownership to historically excluded peoples.[52] But what Smeeding and Wolff, along with many others, apparently missed at the time was the central role that many southern leaders, as legislative architects and advocates of subprime, had already played in opening up the lending markets. Neither MDC authors nor southern lawmakers appeared to ask what would be the cost of inclusion, however.

Southern lawmakers are central to the story of the making of financial deregulation that led to subprime lending. Most noticeably, southern members in the U.S. Senate and House were prominent and vocal supporters of the nation's first major financial deregulation law in 1980 called the Depository Institutions Deregulation and Monetary Control Act (DIDMCA).[53] This law was the gateway to subprime, as DIDMCA lifted the usury caps on mortgage loan products that made lending so profitable for lenders, brokers, and the secondary securities market. Southern support would be unremarkable had the legislation not had at its heart a clause requiring federal preemption of existing state laws. DIDMCA's preemption clause empowered the federal government to override existing state regulatory laws, including intervening state consumer financial protections, while lifting rate caps in states across the nation. While northern congressmen authored, sponsored, and voted for the bill, few if any had built their careers on a states' rights platform that DIDMCA fundamentally challenged, at least in the realm of regulation. Many of the same southern politicians, notably John Stennis (D-MS), Strom Thurmond (D-SC; R-SC from 1964 onward), Herman Talmadge (D-GA), who rose to prominence in the postwar decades to become national power brokers challenging federal interposition, would by the late 1970s and 1980s then cede state sovereignty (on consumer finance) to the federal government.

The irony of this did not escape all elected southern officials. Fearful that DIDMCA's preemption would erode both consumer protections and the principle of federalism, Senator Robert Morgan (D-NC) introduced an amendment that would strike the clause.[54] Without this amendment, Morgan admonished colleagues "we are preempting the rights of States to govern usury in their own States."[55] The Morgan amendment failed sixty-two to twenty—however, with as many southern lawmakers voting against it or staying silent as supporting it. The cognitive dissonance of fellow southern lawmakers did not escape Morgan. He would go on to chastise fellow southerners on the Hill who either voted against striking down the preemption amendment or voted for the actual law. "They want states rights and this goes to people of my home state, and then they want the federal government to move in and preempt State laws when it suits their convenience."[56]

With DIDMCA and its companion bill two years later in 1982 known as the Alternative Mortgage Transaction Parity Act (AMTPA), which once again overrode state laws to nationally codify adjustable-rate mortgages, prepayment penalties, and other creative mortgage instruments, southern congressmen would help erect the statutory architecture that made subprime possible. In fact, AMTPA's preemption was so one-sided and unequivocal regarding the federal supremacy of law as to act as a thoroughly effective deterrent; consequently, very few court challenges were ever mounted against it. Whether southern lawmakers were motivated by expediency over principle, as Senator Morgan would accuse them, is beyond the scope of my analysis. What DIDMCA and AMTPA does demonstrate, however, is southern legislators' willingness to privilege federal sovereignty when first principles of decentralization clashed with financial deregulation.

Financial deregulation created the legal and operational space for the rise of destructive mortgage instruments. Such instruments as balloon payments and other credit innovations—along with excessive liquidity (in the securities markets like credit default swaps), which was also fueled by deregulation—ultimately helped pave the way to subprime whose growth as part of the mortgage market share would play an outsized role in the larger mortgage meltdown and the 2007 global financial crisis.[57] Relative to the broader population, Black America has been particularly harmed by the greatest evaporation of wealth since the Great Depression. From the start of the mortgage downturn in 2006 to 2009, blacks lost 53 percent of their median household net worth compared to the 16 percent lost by whites, according to a Pew Research Center study based on 2010 Census data.[58] And because of the concentration of black wealth in homeownership, the collapse of the housing market contributed to an even further devaluation with the median household wealth gap between whites and blacks nearly doubling over this span of time, from 11:1 to 20:1.[59]

Conclusion

At the fiftieth anniversary of the Selma to Montgomery March in February 2015, President Barack Obama acknowledged the sacrifices of civil rights–era activists, "Because of campaigns like [Selma], a Voting Rights Act was passed. Political and economic and social barriers came down." Although President Obama added, "America is not yet finished," he was right on both counts.[60] Federal legislation, statutory decisions, and court rulings have been critical state mechanisms used to close racial gaps that existed in the Jim Crow South in voting, education, income, and employment. But, as the president readily conceded in previous speeches,[61] federal policymaking has been less effective in addressing the racial wealth gap, whose drivers are more likely to be subterranean than those that determine wages and employment opportunities.[62] Yet because so little has been researched, written, or published on the racial wealth gap in the South, it is difficult to draw unattenuated conclusions about black households in the region and the relative economic success longitudinally or vis-à-vis the rest of the nation.

This is not to suggest that economic and political gains in the post–civil rights South have not been made and that those gains have not been significant. At minimum, civil rights and voting rights laws of the 1950s and 1960s likely helped mitigate the harmful effects of racial discrimination—obviating school, employment, income, and residential segregation as well as lending discrimination in the South and North—a fact that even Federal Reserve Bank researchers pointed out in a 1981 report on one hundred cities writing, "Perhaps federal laws against racial discrimination have had their intended effect."[63] These and similar policies in subsequent years, such as the Equal Credit Opportunity Act of 1974 and the Community Reinvestment Act of 1977, have sought to expand credit and housing markets to racial minorities, women, and other historically excluded populations. Yet, as I've written elsewhere, a set of counter-mechanisms known as financial deregulation have emerged since the 1980s.[64] These counter-mechanisms would claim to open markets by removing or reducing oversight. As a result, financial deregulation in a post–civil rights era would produce a toxic alchemy: the expansion of high-risk lending that has opened housing and other credit markets to previously excluded populations without the accompanying watchful eye of the state to check potential consumer abuses.[65]

Historians and other scholars have been slow to recognize how financial deregulation has been a key driver of racial inequality. The literature has been too silent about how financial deregulatory laws—laws that are ostensibly unconcerned with race like DIDMCA—may also have a disparate racial impact. As a consequence, much of current post–civil rights scholarship is pervaded by a sort of deregulation exceptionalism—an exceptionalism that, for example, tends to treat financial regulatory enforcement differently from, say, civil rights, criminal justice, or voting enforcement. By bringing financial deregulation into the conversation of post–civil rights, scholars can begin to consider how, amid a putative golden age of color-blindness, a set of race-neutral economic policies starting primarily since the 1980s have drained pecuniary resources from communities of color, especially in the South.[66] Applying a "racial audit" to ostensibly color-blind laws, statutes, court decisions, and other social policy choices is a crucial step in ultimately making sense of the ongoing anomaly whereby the racial wealth gap continues to grow even when or at times that the racial wage gap has narrowed. Such an audit, according to its creators, captures "the unintended side effects" of policies "regardless of whether the policy has an explicit aim to affect wealth disparities."[67]

Hopefully, scholars of civil rights, as well as those of the American South, political economy, and late labor and capital might be encouraged to study financial deregulation and see how it might inform the most pressing issue left unfinished by the Second Reconstruction—the racial wealth gap—in the place where race has always mattered most: the American South.

Notes

I wish to thank Joe Street and Henry Knight Lozano for bringing together this important conference and volume. In addition, I would like to thank the following individuals for their comments, insights, and feedback: Eric Arnesen, Ishan Ashutosh, Anthony J. Badger, Rich Benjamin, Thomas Bynum, J. Mijin Cha, Simona Combi, Fay Lomax Cook, William Darity, Tamara Draut, Brett Gadsden, Lynn M. Itagaki, John L. Jackson,

University of Jena Department of English and American Studies faculty Joerg Nagler, Caroline Rosenthal, Andrew Kahrl, Anthony LaVopa, Stephanie Moulton, Derek Musgrove, Gail O'Brien, Molly Reinhoudt, Maya Rockeymoore, Thomas Schwartz, Thomas Shapiro, Nicole Smith, Brian Ward, and Gavin Wright, as well as the peer reviewers. This work benefitted, too, from the research assistance provided by Krista Benson, Shunichi Maruyama, Haley Swenson, and Bethany Varcho.

1. John Herbers, "Dr. King and 770 Others Seized in Alabama Protest," *New York Times*, February 2, 1965, 1.

2. For voter registration, from 1965 to 2004, based on compilation of Senate and House reports in 2006 of the six states (Alabama, Georgia, Louisiana, Mississippi, South Carolina, and Virginia) originally covered by Voting Rights Act of 1965, see Justice John Roberts Opinion in Supreme Court of the United States, No. 12-96, Shelby County, Alabama, Petitioner, v. Eric H. Holder, Attorney General et al., Certiorari to the U.S. Court of Appeals for the District of Columbia Circuit Court, June 25, 2013, 15 [print] or 18 [electronic]. For fuller analysis (e.g., entire south, registration, voting), see Hanes Walton Jr., Sherman Puckett, Donald R. Deskins Jr., *The African American Electorate* (New York: Sage Publications, 2012), 489-90, 616-17, 624-30, 827-28, 875-76.

3. Black voting power has nonetheless been curtailed by a series of factors such as southern whites' flight from state Democratic parties. Their electoral exodus from, first, the national and then state party has marginalized black elected officials who, starting in the 1990s, no longer found themselves in the party controlling state houses in the South. According to Bernard Grofman and Lisa Handley, the increase in southern black elected officials (BEO) is primarily "the result of the enforcement of the Voting Rights Act of 1965" than other factors like the "color-blind hypothesis" that posits southern whites in the immediate generation after the VRA were more willing to vote for black candidates. See Grofman and Handley, "Impact of the Voting Rights Act on Black Representation in Southern State Legislatures," *Legislative Studies Quarterly* 16, no. 1 (February 1991), 112-13; for post-1980s BEOs in South, see Thomas B. Edsall, "Decline of Black Power in the South," *New York Times*, July 10, 2013.

4. "Introduction to Federal Voting Rights Laws/CRT/Department of Justice: The Effect of the Civil Rights Act." The U.S. Department of Justice, at http://www.justice.gov/crt/introduction-federal-voting-rights-laws-0 (consulted March 17, 2015).

5. Elizabeth U. Cascio and Ebonya L. Washington, "Valuing the Vote: The Redistribution of Voting Rights and State Funds Following the Voting Rights Act of 1965," NBER Working Paper 17776, National Bureau of Economic Research, Washington, DC (January 2012).

6. Gavin Wright, *Sharing the Prize: The Economics of the Civil Rights Revolution in the American South* (Cambridge: Harvard University Press, 2013), 147; see also economic historian William J. Collins, "Race and Twentieth Century America Economic History," NBER Reporter: Research Summary (Winter 2006).

7. Wright, *Sharing the Prize*, 145.

8. Wright, *Sharing the Prize*, 146; "Income and Wealth in the South, A State of the South Interim Report," MDC, Inc., May 1998, at http://www.mdcinc.org/sites/default/files/resources/income.pdf (consulted March 17, 2015).

9. Wright, *Sharing the Prize*, 145.

10. William H. Frey, "The New Great Migration: Black Americans' Return to the South, 1965–2000," May 2004, Living Cities Census Series, 4, at http://www.brookings.edu/~/media/research/files/reports/2004/5/demographics-frey/20040524_frey.pdf (consulted March 17, 2015).

11. Timothy Bates and Daniel Fusfeld, "The Crowding Hypothesis," in *African Americans in the US Economy*, ed. Cecelia A. Conrad et al. (Lanham, MD: Rowman and Littlefield, 2005), 103.

12. Ibid., 106.

13. Wright, *Sharing the Prize*, 23.

14. For alternative evaluative approaches, see the Global Prosperity Index. First published by the Legatum Institute in 2007, the Prosperity Index measures 142 countries' prosperity against a broad set of metrics and describes itself as the only global index that measures both wealth and wellbeing. See http://www.li.com/programmes/prosperity-index (consulted March 17, 2015). See also the 2007–2008 Commission on the Measurement of Economic Performance and Social Progress (also known as the Stiglitz-Sen-Fitoussi Commission, after the economists who oversaw the inquiry). Critical of an overreliance of national income statistics like the GDP to measure the overall economic health of a nation, the commission measured the wealth and social progress of a country through metrics like health, household debt, and environment. For more on the Stiglitz-Sen-Fitoussi Commission, see http://www.insee.fr/fr/publications-et-services/dossiers_web/stiglitz/doc-commission/RAPPORT_anglais.pdf (consulted March 17, 2015).

15. Michael Sherraden, *Assets and the Poor: New American Welfare Policy* (New York: Routledge, 1992), 7.

16. Wealth vs. Income: What you own vs. What you made (in certain period).

17. Thomas Shapiro, *The Hidden Cost of Being African American* (New York: Oxford University Press, 2004), 155–82; Rucker C. Johnson, "The Impact of Parental Wealth on College Enrollment and Degree Attainment: Evidence from the Housing Boom and Bust," Goldman School of Public Policy Working Paper (January 2011).

18. Adam Lioz, "Stacked Deck: How the Racial Bias in our Big Money Political System Undermines Our Democracy and Our Economy," at http://www.demos.org/sites/default/files/publications/StackedDeck_0.pdf (consulted March 17, 2015); Fay Lomax Cook, Benjamin Page, and Rachel L. Moskowitz, "The Political Engagement of Wealthy Americans" (unpublished manuscript, November 2013).

19. Willie Elliott, Devin Fergus, and Terri Friedline, "What Are the Predictors of Economic Instability? Assets, Economic Instability, and Children's Human Capital: Building a Better Welfare System for the Poor," University of Kansas, last modified September 24, 2012, at https://assetsandedu.drupal.ku.edu/sites/assetsandedu.drupal.ku.edu/files/docs/Report%20II%20.pdf (consulted March 17, 2015).

20. For more about distinctions between wealth and income, see Arthur Kennickell, "Ponds and Streams: Wealth and Income in the US, 1989–2007," Finance and Economics Discussion Series, Federal Reserve Board, at http://www.federalreserve.gov/pubs/feds/2009/200913/200913pap.pdf (consulted February 24, 2015).

21. Shapiro, *The Hidden Cost of Being African American*, 10–11.

22. Thomas Shapiro, Sam Osoro, and Tatjana Meschede, "The Roots of the Widening Racial Wealth Gap: Explaining the Black-White Economic Divide," Brandeis University, February 2013, at http://iasp.brandeis.edu/pdfs/Author/shapiro-thomas-m/racialwealthgapbrief.pdf (consulted March 17, 2015).

23. Ibid.

24. Christine Crowell, "Brandeis Study Finds Racial Wealth Gap Growing," Brandeis University, December 9, 2013, at http://iasp.brandeis.edu/about/2013/12study.pdf (consulted March 17, 2015).

25. Shapiro, Osoro, and Meschede, "The Roots of the Widening Racial Wealth Gap."

26. Shapiro, *The Hidden Cost of Being African American*, 10.

27. Ibid.

28. See, for example, chap. 2 of Teresa Sullivan, Elizabeth Warren, and Jay Westbrook, *The Fragile Middle Class: Americans in Debt* (New Haven, CT: Yale University Press, 2001).

29. Shapiro, Osoro, and Meschede, "The Roots of the Widening Racial Wealth Gap," 4

30. Ibid.

31. For full report, see http://www.equality-of-opportunity.org/index.php/executive-summaries (consulted March 17, 2015). See also, "Mobility, measured," *Economist*, February 1, 2014.

32. For example, works like Matthew J. Countryman *Up South: Civil Rights and Black Power in Philadelphia* (Philadelphia: University of Pennsylvania Press, 2007) have tended to blur the racial boundaries between regions, while others like Byron E. Shafer and Richard Johnston, *The End of Southern Exceptionalism: Class, Race, and Partisan Change in the Postwar South* (New York: Oxford University Press, 2009), have blurred the racial politics of southern economic elites.

33. Kevin M. Kruse and Thomas Sugrue, *The New Suburban History* (Chicago: University of Chicago Press, 2006).

34. See Countryman, *Up South*; Shafer and Johnston, *The End of Southern Exceptionalism*. My first book, *Liberalism, Black Power and the Making of American Politics* (Athens: University of Georgia Press, 2008) also reflects this trend of regional conflation.

35. The IASP at Brandeis and Demos, an economic think tank, is in the developmental collaborative stages of a project designed to filter out and cross-reference asset and race- and region-based demographic information. While promising, this analytic tool is designed for current or pending legislation and will have very limited use for scholars engaged in actual historical study.

36. Timothy Smeeding and Edward N. Wolff, "Income and Wealth in the South: A State of the South Interim Report," MDC, Inc., May 1998, at http://www.mdcinc.org/sites/default/files/resources/income.pdf (consulted April 1, 2017).

37. Ibid., 13.

38. Ibid., 15.

39. Bill Dedman, "Racial Lending Gap Less in South than Midwest," *Atlanta Journal Constitution*, Color of Money Series, January 22, 1989, A1.

40. Gap in lending is based on author's calculation of Federal Home Loan Board statistics provided to Bill Dedman, "Blacks Turned Down for Home Loans from S&Ls

Twice as Often as Whites," *Atlanta Journal Constitution*, Color of Money Series, January 22, 1989, A1.

41. Dedman, "Blacks Turned Down for Home Loans," A1.

42. Ibid.

43. Unfortunately, there appears to be no longitudinal study of or report on black-white lending patterns in Atlanta. Per Bill Dedman's Color of Money series in the *Atlanta Journal Constitution*, at http://powerreporting.com/color.

44. Steven R. Holloway and Elvin K. Wyly, "The Color of Money" Expanded: Geographically Contingent Mortgage Lending in Atlanta," *Journal of Housing Research* 12, no. 1 (January 1, 2001): 55–90; Wyly and Holloway, "The Disappearance of Race in Mortgage Lending," *Economic Geography* 78, no. 2 (April 2002): 129–69.

45. Dedman, "Racial Lending Gap Less in South than Midwest," A1.

46. Dedman, "Blacks Turned Down for Home Loans," A1.

47. For example, see Bank of America, Wells Fargo, and Countrywide. See also "NCRC Files Civil Rights Complaints Against S&P," January 26, 2009, at http://www.ncrc.org/media-center/press-releases/item/388-ncrc-files-civil-rights-complaint-against-standard—poor%C3%83%C6%92%C3%86%E2%80%99%C3%83%E2%80%9A%C3%82%C2%A2%C3%83%C6%92%C3%82%C2%A2%C3%83%C2%A2%C3%A2%E2%80%9A%C2%AC%C3%85%C2%A1%C3%83%E2%80%9A%C3%82%C2%AC%C3%83%C6%92%C3%82%C2%A2%C3%83%C2%A2%C3%A2%E2%80%9A%C2%AC%C3%85%C2%BE%C3%83%E2%80%9A%C3%82%C2%A2s (consulted April 1, 2017); American Civil Liberties Union, "Justice Foreclosed: How Wall Street's Appetite for Subprime Mortgages Ended Up Hurting Black and Latino Communities," October 2012, at https://www.aclu.org/report/justice-foreclosed-how-wall-streets-appetite-subprime-mortgages-ended-hurting-black-and-latino-communities (consulted April 1, 2017).

48. Housing Assistance Council, "Run While You Still Can: Subprime Demand and Predatory Lending in Rural Areas," March 2004, 47, at http://docplayer.net/8111469-Housing-assistance-council-run-while-you-still-can-subprime-demand-and-predatory-lending-in-rural-areas.html (consulted April 1, 2017). This publication was sponsored by HUD and based on HAC's analysis of (1998?) HMDA data. HAC is a non-profit corporation founded in 1971 to provide technical assistance for low income, rural housing development.

49. Ibid., table 22.

50. Southern Rural Development Initiative Report; see also Associated Press, "Minorities, Poor Pay More for Home Borrowing," *Spartanburg Herald-Journal*, February 23, 2000, A9.

51. "Study Shows Low-Income Minorities Use High-Interest Lender to Buy Home," *Arkansas Business*, April 3, 2000, at http://www.arkansasbusiness.com/article/65333/study-shows-low-income-minorities-use-high-interest-lender-to-buy-a-home (consulted April 1, 2017).

52. Smeeding and Wolff, "Income and Wealth in the South" MDC, Inc., May 1998, 15, at http://www.mdcinc.org/sites/default/files/resources/income.pdf (consulted December 17, 2016).

53. For the Depository Institutions Deregulation and Monetary Control Act, see

https://en.wikipedia.org/wiki/Depository_Institutions_Deregulation_and_Monetary_Control_Act (consulted December 17, 2016).

54. Cathy Lesser Mansfield, "The Road to Subprime 'HEL'* Was Paved with Good Congressional Intentions: Usury Deregulation and the Subprime Home Equity Market," *South Carolina Law Review* (Spring 2000): 51 S.C. L. Rev. 473, 488.

55. Compilation of the Housing and Community Development Amendments of 1979, Senate Floor Debates, July 12–13, 1979, 668.

56. Senator Robert Morgan Speech, Congressional Record 1980, 7069.

57. Michael Mah-Hui Lim, "Old Wine in a New Bottle: Subprime Mortgage Crisis—Causes and Consequences," Working Paper, Levy Economics Institute of Bard College, no. 532, 2008; Mansfield, "The Road to Subprime 'HEL'* Was Paved with Good Congressional Intentions," 51.

58. Paul Taylor, Rakesh Kochhar, Richard Fry, Gabriel Valesco, and Seth Motel, "Twenty-to-One: Wealth Gaps Rise to Record Highs Between Whites, Blacks and Hispanics," Pew Research Center, July 26, 2011, at http://www.pewsocialtrends.org/files/2011/07/SDT-Wealth-Report_7-26-11_FINAL.pdf (consulted December 17, 2016).

59. Ibid.

60. Barack Obama, "Remarks by the President at the 50th Anniversary of the Selma to Montgomery Marches," March 7, 2015, at https://www.whitehouse.gov/the-press-office/2015/03/07/remarks-president-50th-anniversary-selma-montgomery-marches (consulted April 1, 2017).

61. Barack Obama, "Remarks by the President on Economic Mobility," Office of the President, White House, December 4, 2013, Washington, DC, at http://www.whitehouse.gov/the-press-office/2013/12/04/remarks-president-economic-mobility (consulted April 1, 2017); "President Obama on Jobs and the Economy," C-Span Video Library, December 4, 2011, at http://www.c-span.org/video/?316620-1/president-obama-delivers-remarks-economy (consulted April 1, 2017).

62. Frederick Harris and Robert Lieberman, introduction to *Beyond Discrimination: Racial Inequality in a Postracist Era* (New York: Russell Sage Foundation, 2013).

63. Bill Dedman, "Atlanta among 20 Worst Cities in Loan Inequities," *Atlanta Journal-Constitution*, Color of Money Series, July 27, 1988, A9.

64. Devin Fergus and Tim Boyd, "Introduction: Banking without Borders: Culture and Credit in the New Financial World," *Kalfou* 1, no. 2 (2014): 8, 25–26.

65. Ibid.

66. Perhaps the best example from the post-1970s era is the Gramm-Leach-Bliley Act of 1999. GLBA enabled and expanded banks' ability to underwrite riskier subprime loans via securitization while simultaneously restricting regulatory supervision of these very same lenders. For more on this history, especially in the 1990s and 2000s, see Final Report of the National Commission on the Causes of the Financial and Economic Crisis in the United States, January 2011, at https://www.gpo.gov/fdsys/pkg/GPO-FCIC/pdf/GPO-FCIC.pdf (consulted March 17, 2015). Post-recession legislation to curb these lending abuses was part of the 2010 Dodd-Frank Wall Street Reform and Consumer Protection Act (Dodd-Frank). For current efforts to chip away at Dodd-Frank, see Gary Cohn, Trump administration White House National Economic Council director, interview

with Bloomberg Television at https://www.bloomberg.com/news/articles/2017-02-03/wall-street-hope-revived-by-trump-plan-to-roll-back-crisis-rules (consulted February 10, 2017]. For Obama-era judicial efforts, see https://ecf.dcd.uscourts.gov/cgi-bin/show_public_doc?2011cv2146-69 (consulted December 15, 2016).

67. See the Racial Wealth Audit™ at https://iasp.brandeis.edu/pdfs/2014/RWA.pdf (consulted December 15, 2016).

12

How the Rise of Color-Blind Racism Opened the Door for the Supreme Court Decision in *Shelby County v. Holder*

BARBARA HARRIS COMBS

The Voting Rights Act of 1965 (VRA), which was designed to address the systemic and often violent nearly hundred-year disavowal of the franchise to African American and other minority groups, has been hailed the "crown jewel" of the Civil Rights movement, and while its legacy is clear, its future is uncertain.[1] The brutal beating on March 7, 1965, of peaceful civil rights protesters on the Edmund Pettus Bridge in Selma, Alabama, which came to be known as Bloody Sunday, ushered in swift passage of the VRA.[2] This landmark piece of legislation contains permanent provisions that bar the usage of voting devices and practices that discriminate against minority voters, and it contains temporary provisions—most notably Section 5 of the VRA—that require federal "preclearance" or approval before covered jurisdictions (that is, those identified with a proven history of enacting continuing measures with the purpose or effect of restricting minority voting rights) can enact even mundane changes in their voting practices and procedures.[3]

However, the June 25, 2013, U.S. Supreme Court decision in *Shelby County, Alabama v. Eric J. Holder, Jr.,* Attorney General, could be a substantial step toward a rollback in the voting rights protections afforded U.S. minorities under the VRA.[4] In fact, according to Carol Anderson, it reflects one of the myriad attempts by some whites to neutralize black gains through actions she terms "white rage."[5] Anderson argues that white rage "is cloaked in the niceties of law and order, but it is rage, nonetheless."[6] This chapter argues that the *Shelby County v. Holder* decision is one of a series of purportedly "color-blind" efforts that are in fact part of a sometimes subtle but often overt attempt to minimize the influence and import of minority voters and push them back in place—a marginal, liminal space in society where their presence is exploited for the gain of other actors (political and otherwise) but independent thought/action on the part of these minority voters is neither encouraged or, in some cases, tolerated.

To explain this concept, I advance a theory—Bodies Out of Place (BOP)—and test the extent to which it is useful to explicate the discourse utilized in several key voting rights decisions as indicative of one or more of the four frames of color-blind racism sociologist Eduardo Bonilla-Silva outlines in *Racism without Racists: Color-Blind Racism and the Persistence of Racial Inequality in America*, now in its fourth edition.[7] Bonilla-Silva's four frames are: (1) abstract liberalism (this frame uses ideas associated with liberalism to argue against race-based programs—for example, using the idea of "equal opportunity" to argue against affirmative action citing the latter as a preferential treatment program); (2) naturalization (this frame explains race-based outcomes by arguing that the same are natural phenomenon—for example, using homophily to explain persistent segregation practices); (3) cultural racism (this frame uses culture and cultural references to explain race-based outcomes—for example, suggestions that as a group, Mexicans do not value education or have too many babies); and (4) minimization of racism (this frame makes arguments such as "but things are so much better now" in order to suggest that racism no longer limits the life chances of minorities).[8] These color-blind frames act as a veneer that allows members of society to hold on to the fiction that they do not see color (that is, that they are color-blind).

BOP has eight basic tenets:

(1) Growing numbers of whites perceive that the social ills in society (that is, racism, sexism, homonegativity, et cetera) are not endemic or structural, but isolated incidents performed by a few bad actors.
(2) The growth of color-blind frames is partially sustained because members of society falsely perceive physical integration and/or proximity with social integration.
(3) Those who utilize color-blind frames often view the gendered, classed, and racial/ethnic patterns discernible in employment,

housing, education, religion, political and other arenas as the natural order and then work to maintain that equilibrium (that is, status quo) often under the guise that this order is what is best for society.

(4) Racism begins on a micro level but operates on a macro level.
(5) BOP theory is relational. Bodies need not be out of place per se as much as they *are* out of place relative to the individual position of the person opposing (sometimes called "the opposer") the heightened (that is, seemingly "out of place") status of the nonnormative (in this case black or brown) body. Additionally, the opposition may come about because the black or brown body seems displaced relative to the position of an individual in a group to which the opposer belongs or is affiliated with through strong kin or friendship ties.
(6) The opposer's feeling that a person is out of place posits a reaction or response, which is evidenced through an almost compulsory and provoked verbal or non-verbal reaction to the perceived displacement. The only requirement is that the displacement must produce a response. Responses may range from the benign to the malevolent. The important thing to consider is that the displacement is so disconcerting to the opposer that some response seems obligatory.
(7) When utilized through discourse, opposers often use seemingly race-neutral language, which is laden with race-based attitudes.
(8) BOP is necessarily intersectional in its nature and applicable across social structures.

The tenets of BOP operate as both a method and an analytical framework. As an analytical framework, BOP both complements and is distinguishable from other frames. For example, BOP employs aspects of color-blind racism and other theories, including Critical Race Theory (CRT), which posits that racism is not only a central but also an endemic aspect of U.S. society.[9] BOP not only complements CRT, but it also adds an important missing layer. Like CRT, BOP recognizes that color-blindness and white property rights have been embedded into the U.S. legal structure—and therefore ingrained in U.S. consciousness—for some time.[10] But, as I suggest in "No Rest for the Weary," while "CRT deals well with the macro level... a void is left in understanding how individual actors contribute to the social processes through which disadvantage is sustained, supported, and maintained. BOP fills that space of 'betweenness.'"[11]

This chapter posits that BOP is the unspoken epistemological lens through which historically rooted ideas about race relations and racialized ideologies about where certain groups belong get maintained. The theory explains or understands continuing acts of political and/or physical violence against certain bodies as an attempt to sanction the counterhegemonic form and push him or her back into place.[12] By way of example, across the United States numerous individuals and groups decried the election of America's first African American president, with over 30 percent of whites admitting they were "troubled" by the prospect of imagining Obama as president.[13] To those "troubled" by the premise, Barack Hussein Obama (in the role of president) represented a body out of place. In the time following the first election of Obama, a substantial amount of legislation was enacted to make it more difficult to vote.[14] Carol Anderson explains such legislation thusly: "[It is] white rage [the kind which] carries an aura of respectability and has access to the courts, police, legislatures, and governors who cast its efforts as noble, though they are actually driven by the most ignoble motivations."[15]

Despite prevailing ideologies prominent in U.S. society that suggest the contrary (such as the notion that Justice is blind), race has always played a central role in U.S. politics, economics, and cultural life. In fact, the concept of bodies out of place is not only applicable to this current moment in voting rights history but also can be seen as a thread running through past efforts. The presidential election of 1936 provides an excellent case study. Scholars agree that by the election of 1936, the movement of African Americans from the Republican Party (the party of the Great Emancipator, Abraham Lincoln) was almost complete—at least on the presidential election level.[16] When Franklin Delano Roosevelt (sometimes hereafter referred to as FDR) first took office in March 1933, the National Association for the Advancement of Colored People (NAACP) requested a meeting with him, and he refused.[17] Roosevelt indicated he wanted to help Americans as a whole and not single out any group; over time, the benefits of the New Deal programs would trickle down to some African Americans.[18]

African Americans voted for FDR because his programs improved their financial position.[19] In fact, Harvard Sitkoff observes that the Work Progress Administration (WPA) was singly responsible for raising "the economic floor for the whole black community in the 1930s, rivaling both agriculture and domestic service as the chief source."[20] But despite large-scale black allegiance to FDR, his commitment to black equality was both complex and sometimes contradictory. FDR failed to support anti-lynching legislation, but he implemented Executive Order 8802, which resulted in the formation of the Fair Employment Practices Committee.[21]

In the 1936 election, both the Democratic and Republican parties actively sought the black vote.[22] The courting of the black vote was not because large sections of either party felt that blacks were fundamentally equal to whites. Instead, each party sought to garner a large section of the black vote so that they could win the election.[23] Black participation in the Democratic Party occurred largely through a separate vehicle from the party itself called the Good Neighbor League Colored Committee.[24] This auxiliary group functioned on behalf of the Democratic Party but was separate from it.[25] In this respect, the African Americans whose votes they wooed remained in the party but not a part of it. This idea is consistent with BOP tenet 2, which states that physical integration is disparate from social integration.

The tokenism involved in previous large-scale attempts for blacks to take advantage of the constitutional principle of one-man, one-vote made the grant of equal protection under the law contained in the VRA unprecedented. In fact, in some ways the fact that the VRA has remained in-tact for almost fifty years is itself representative of a cultural shift, but the VRA has always had its detractors, especially in the South.[26] The first serious challenge came in early 1966—just months after it was signed into law. The test came in the form of the case of *South Carolina v. Katzenbach*.[27] The southern state of South Carolina brought the action, and, in a rare move, the Supreme Court agreed to hear the case as a matter of original jurisdiction (instead of requiring the action to come to it from the lower courts); the court wanted to resolve the matter before the upcoming congressional election.[28]

South Carolina, a Section 5-covered jurisdiction, sued U.S. Attorney General Nicholas Katzenbach, seeking declaratory judgment stating that certain sections of the VRA were unconstitutional. Other covered states joined the action.[29] The petitioners sought an immediate injunction to prevent the attorney general from enforcing certain parts of the act.[30] The Katzenbach Court held that the Voting Rights Act—including the "strong medicine" of the Section 5 preclearance requirement—was a valid exercise of Congress's power as identified in the enforcement clause of the Fifteenth Amendment to the U.S. Constitution.[31] The *South Carolina v. Katzenbach* decision states, "The Act's voluminous legislative history discloses unremitting and ingenious defiance in certain parts of the country."[32]

The *Katzenbach* decision was written by Chief Justice Earl Warren, who is best known for his opinion in the landmark school desegregation case of *Brown v. Board of Education of Topeka, Kansas*, and whose leadership is often credited for helping the Brown Court arrive at a unanimous decision.[33] That case was the first time that the Supreme Court relied upon social scientific data and cited it in an opinion.[34] The Brown Court noted that Kenneth and Mamie Clark's doll experiment was influential in its determination that separate but equal was inherently unequal.[35] Twelve years later, in *South Carolina v. Katzenbach*, Chief Justice Warren again relied on social scientific evidence. The opinion he authored provides a rich description of the sociohistorical context that gave rise to the dispute under examination: "The Voting Rights Act was designed by Congress to banish the blight of racial discrimination in voting, which has infected the electoral process in parts of our country for nearly a century."[36]

The majority opinion in *Katzenbach* clearly paints the broader historical context for the voting rights struggle. In doing so, the *Katzenbach* decision outlines a century of discrimination in voting. In unveiling this record, the court engages in a pointed historical discussion about the petitioner, South Carolina. The examination seems to suggest that the petitioner does not have "clean hands."[37] Mention is made of the South Carolina Constitutional Convention of 1895. Chief Justice Warren's opinion quotes statements made by U.S. Senator Benjamin Tillman of South Carolina at the convention. Tillman, a former Democratic governor of the state of South Carolina, is held to be the unquestioned leader of the post-Reconstruction movement to disenfranchise black citizens.[38] In a 2006 article appearing in the *South Carolina Law Review* describing the same, law professors Luis Fuentes-Rohwer and Guy-Uriel E. Charles note that during the 1895 South Carolina Constitutional Convention Tillman defined the goals of the new state literacy test thusly: "'The only thing we can do as patriots and as statesmen is to take from [the "ignorant blacks"] every ballot that we can under the laws of our national government.' [Later] On the floor of the United States Senate, Tillman offered similar sentiments: 'We took the government away. We stuffed ballot boxes. We shot them.

We are not ashamed of it."[39] Senator Tillman's comments make it clear that the efforts he and others employed to deny blacks the franchise were accomplished "under the laws of our national government." Consistent with BOP tenet 6, the black gains made during Reconstruction were met with rejoinder by Tillman and other southerners whose efforts pushed blacks back into a place of subordination. According to Carol Anderson, such efforts seek to neutralize black gains.[40]

In arriving at its holding, the majority *South Carolina v. Katzenbach* decision considered the deep legacy of contempt for black suffrage present in the South. A number of vehicles were employed to curtail the black vote. One of the many ways utilized to minimize black electoral power was simply to exclude blacks from the most powerful political party in the South—namely the Democratic Party.[41] Southern states and local jurisdictions included literacy tests and understanding tests that were facially universal (that is, on the books as applicable to all), but had a discriminatory effect on blacks (as the judgment as to whether you passed the test or not would often be delegated to the hands of racist local officials). The decision outlines how such tests and devices were administered in a way that favored whites. Nowhere was this clearer than when whites sought to register and were given simple tests and devices (and help answering those questions) and blacks were given complex ones. The decision also outlines how blacks who brought litigation to challenge being blocked from the voting rolls would face district judges that were hostile. Those who challenged the rulings might win on appeal to the federal court, but that required more time and money. Such successes brought with them the fear of reprisal from powerful, racist whites. This fear helped to maintain a system of black voter suppression. The record was so compelling that even Justice Hugo Black, the lone dissenter, concurred in part of the decision.[42]

As BOP tenet 4 posits, racism begins on a micro level but can operate on a macro level. Individual actors were necessary in order to administer the tests and devices used to exclude blacks, and the collective action of these individuals institutionalized a racist structure. It was against this social backdrop that the Katzenbach Court held the Voting Rights Act, including the "strong medicine" of Section 5, was a valid exercise of congressional power.[43]

From Katzenbach to Shelby

Between the *South Carolina v. Katzenbach* and *Shelby County v. Holder* decisions, there were numerous challenges to the VRA, but the first serious challenges came in the wake of the 2008 election of Barack Obama as U.S. president. Minorities—including racial/ethnic communities of color and female voters—played a substantial role in the election of America's first president of color.[44] Despite a discernible increase in state and local legislative measures anticipated to have a negative impact on the group, minority voters again influenced Obama's re-election.[45] While voter turnout is always higher in presidential election years, the historic rates of minority voter participation in 2008 and 2012 were taken by many as evidence that widespread race-based discrimination in voting no longer existed.[46] A utility district in Texas, a covered jurisdiction, made such a claim.

Northwest Austin Municipal Utility District No. 1 (MUD) in Austin, Texas, a covered jurisdiction, filed suit challenging the constitutionality of the VRA.[47] The case was heard on the one hundredth day of President Obama's first term. The utility district cited the election of Obama as affirmative proof that Section 5 was now unnecessary. The MUD Court rejected the plaintiff's claim, but the very holding of the decision includes language that suggested that later challenges might be successful. The court writes:

> The historic accomplishments of the Voting Rights Act are undeniable, but the Act now raises serious constitutional concerns. The preclearance requirement represents an intrusion into areas of state and local responsibility that is otherwise unfamiliar to our federal system. *Some of the conditions that the Court relied upon in upholding this statutory scheme in South Carolina v. Katzenbach, 383 U.S. 301, and City of Rome v. United States, 446 U.S. 156, have unquestionably improved* [emphasis added]. Those improvements are no doubt due in significant part to the Voting Rights Act itself, and stand as a monument to its success, *but the Act imposes current burdens and must be justified by current needs. The Act also differentiates between the States in ways that may no longer be justified* [emphasis added].[48]

The MUD Court upholds Section 5 of the Voting Rights Act, but hints future challenges to the constitutionality of the act might be successful due to a purportedly changing social landscape.

Unlike the Katzenbach Court, the majority opinion in *Shelby County v. Holder* seems unwilling to find (or even consider) the potential that voting laws today might be administered unequally. Yet many civil rights groups suggest that the various and multiple legislative responses—state, local, and federal—that followed the election of President Obama, including prolific voter identification laws, amount to second generation barriers. Advocates for tougher voting laws often cite a need to protect against widespread voter fraud; however, a report by the Brennan Center for Justice at New York University School of Law states, "Fraud by individual voters is both irrational and extremely rare."[49] As the response is not logical, it is reasonable to assume that something else is fueling it.

Pursuant to BOP tenet 6, opposers in society feel a need to respond to bodies that they perceive as being out of place. The response is an attempt to restore social order. The most rigorous study on voter ID and turnout to date found that stricter voter ID requirements depressed turnout, particularly among less educated and lower income populations.[50] Despite this compelling evidence of the great harm stricter voter identification laws and other restrictive measures pose to the American project of democracy, proponents of these laws argue they not only know what is best but they are doing what is necessary to prevent unsubstantiated but alleged wide voter fraud (see BOP tenet 3).[51]

During oral arguments in the *Shelby* case, Justice Antonin Scalia made several remarks that framed the VRA as an insidious and incendiary racial entitlement program. His language ignores a nearly one-hundred-year denial of the franchise and suggests that the protections afforded by the Voting Rights Act are a handout. Once again, we can see how BOP—specifically tenet 7—can be useful to explicate this discourse. In a series of questions, more conservative members of the court seem to suggest that the "strong medicine" of Section 5 of the VRA may no longer be necessary. Again, the implication seems to be that the utility of Section 5 has been outlived because the 1965 enactment of the VRA for the purpose of addressing entrenched racial discrimination in voting has either been met or is no longer justified. Therefore, those who continue to cry out for its protections want a handout, not a hand up.

While the history of voting discrimination did not factor prominently into the majority opinion in *Shelby County v. Holder*, another history did. As stated earlier in this chapter, Justice Black wrote a separate opinion in *South Carolina v. Katzenbach* where he in part concurred and in part dissented.[52] Much of the spirit of Black's dissent appears in the majority decision in *Shelby*. In his lone dissent in *Katzenbach*, Black writes:

> One of the most basic premises upon which our structure of government was founded was that the Federal Government was to have certain specific and limited powers and no others, and all other power was to be reserved either "to the States respectively, or to the people." Certainly, if all the provisions of our Constitution which limit the power of the Federal Government and reserve other power to the States are to mean anything, they mean at least that the States have power to pass laws and amend their constitutions without first sending their officials hundreds of miles away to beg federal authorities to approve them.[53]

Almost fifty years later, the majority opinion in *Shelby County v. Holder* invokes the Tenth Amendment to suggest that states should be viewed as sovereign entities (not subject to unnecessary intrusion from the federal government) and treated equally. This, too, is a form of color-blindness as it fails to recognize that the states differ in very real respects that fall within the purview of the federal. One of these areas is with respect to race. The distribution of racial/ethnic and language minorities (groups protected by the VRA) are not equal throughout the states. Further, the Voting Rights Act of 1965 was a remedial measure, and as such, it need not apply equally to the states. Instead, its aim was to remediate the ill. This means that the court's outcries that the equal sovereignty of the states is under attack ring false.

Tenet 2 of BOP says that physical integration often masks as social integration. According to the 2010 Census, 55 percent of the black population of the United States resides in the American South.[54] As more than half of U.S. blacks live in the South, some U.S. jurisdictions are far more diverse than others. The United States as a whole may be integrated, but large sections of it are not. As a result, whether through preference or residual effects of past discrimination, minorities seem to belong in some jurisdictions and be out of place in others.

Discourse often has express political purposes and conveys ideological stances, and these separate ideological stances are unveiled in both the majority *Shelby County v. Holder* opinion and the dissent. While the majority opinion focuses on a "changed South," the dissent challenges that assertion. Justice Ruth Bader Ginsburg argued that, if things have changed in the American South and the other covered jurisdictions, it is because of Section 5, and that continuance of the "strong medicine" would guard against backsliding.[55] Oral arguments revealed the same sharp distinctions in ideological stances. Justice Sonia Sotomayor commented that if things had changed in the South, they had not changed in Shelby County (this was a reference to Calera, Alabama, a city in Shelby County with a recent history of disfranchisement of black voters).[56]

Whereas the Katzenbach Court seemed obsessed with social scientific data, the *Shelby County v. Holder* majority largely ignores the same. For example, the lower court record in the *Shelby* case clearly establishes that voting discrimination is not a thing of the distant past. Between 1983 and 2004, the U.S. Department of Justice filed more objections to voting law changes it deemed discriminatory than it did in the period from 1965 to 1982.[57] The lower court record establishes that a majority of the Justice Department objections included findings of discriminatory intent.[58] The changes blocked by preclearance were said to be "calculated decisions to keep minority voters from fully participating in the political process."[59] Most of these are included in the nearly 15,000-page record Congress amassed during the congressional reauthorization hearings in 2006. The same report states that "discrimination [in voting] today is more subtle than the visible means used in 1965 . . . but the effect is the same."[60]

Herein, BOP tenet 7 is implicated. Just because the tactics and discourse of discrimination have changed, does not mean discrimination no longer exists. Instead, the congressional record makes it clear that, while less visible, discrimination in voting persists. The absence of blatant references to voters as niggers, coons, et cetera has been used to suggest that discriminatory purposes must be absent, too, but even if we accept that proposition, we are left with a congressional record that suggests a discriminatory effect still exists.

Since the Supreme Court's decision in *Shelby County v. Holder*, momentum for the movement to curtail minority voting rights has grown more resounding, and the color-blind racial frame of minimization has enabled much of this growth. There is no doubt that progress has occurred, but progress can occur amid setbacks. Additionally, progress does not mean that victory has been won. A June 26, 2013, article in the *New York Times* stated, "Tate Reeves, the Republican Lieutenant Governor of Mississippi, said he was pleased by the [Shelby County] decision . . . [as] preclearance 'unfairly applied to certain states should be eliminated in recognition of the progress Mississippi has made over the past 48 years.'"[61] That "progress" included a 1995 attempt to revive a dual registration system "initially enacted in 1892 to disenfranchise Black voters" and a 2001 decision by officials in the town of Kilmichael to cancel an election after "an unprecedented number" of African Americans registered to run for office.[62] The NAACP Legal Defense Fund reported that, within two hours of the *Shelby* decision, Texas Attorney General Greg Abbott announced that the state's voter identification law, previously rejected by federal court as the most discriminatory measure of its kind in the country, would go into immediate effect. The law was enacted without revision despite an earlier federal court finding that some citizens would have to drive as many as 250 miles to obtain the required Election Identification Certificates (EICs) available to those without required IDs.[63] The dissent's conclusion is stark: "[This discriminatory] history did not end in 1965."

For most of North American history, race has operated as a caste system. Despite the elimination of de jure segregation, de facto segregation persists. This continuing segregation impacts education, housing, and employment, resulting in a system where large members of racial and ethnic groups in U.S. society continue to operate essentially separate lives in the midst of what appears to be an integrated society. The threat comes when people move outside of those patterns. Just as the Roosevelt coalition brought together a diverse group of voters to give power to the Democratic presidential candidate, the Obama coalition did the same. This shift, along with the projected browning of America, has invoked a response. The rise of the Latino (brown) population and their relative voting power threatens the established racial order; this threat incites fear in some.[64]

Since the *Shelby County v. Holder* decision, a number of states with large and/or growing minority populations have enacted voting law changes that would likely have been blocked by Section 5. For example, a group of litigants in Texas has brought an action challenging the current map used by the state to draw Senate districts.[65] According to the 2014 American Community Survey, 38.6 percent of the population of Texas identifies as Latino. The litigants challenge the constitutionality of the map, arguing that it should be drawn based on the number of eligible voters, not on the total number of people in the district.⁶⁶ Specifically, they claim that up to half of Latinos in Dallas and Austin are not citizens.⁶⁷

The Texas response is broader than the Evenwel case. The same group of Texas litigants who brought the *Evenwel v. Abbott* action has supported the dismantling of Affirmative Action at the University of Texas.⁶⁸ In the wake of the *Shelby* decision, Texas also enacted a restrictive photo identification law. The law allowed gun licenses as an acceptable form of state identification, but it would not accept college identification cards. Considering the state's history of discrimination against Prairie View A&M University students, this action seems to have both the intent and effect of discriminating against them.⁶⁹ According to the Brennan Center for Justice: "A federal judge found 600,000 registered Texas voters do not have acceptable ID. Testimony showed African-American and Hispanic registered voters are two to four times more likely than white registered voters to lack photo ID."⁷⁰ Arriving at intent is a complicated matter, but in the post-*Shelby* climate, dismantling effect has proven equally onerous. Still, legitimate inferences can be made that even absent the intent to discriminate against minorities, the effect is present.

This paper argues that the voting rights struggle has been full of successes and setbacks and views the setbacks as attempts to put black and other minority voters back in a subservient place. While some states and jurisdictions have passed laws to make voting less restrictive, a number of locales have made voting harder. Alabama initiated a redistricting plan that "packed" black voters into a few districts. At the behest of the Alabama Legislative Black Caucus, the Supreme Court agreed to hear appeals on the case.⁷¹ In 2015, as a reported cost-saving measure, the state of Alabama was planning to close most of the offices where citizens can obtain a driver's license.⁷² As the state recently enacted a restrictive photo identification law, this closing is expected to have a great impact on the elderly, the economically disadvantaged, and racial/ethnic minorities.

Alabama is not alone in its efforts to limit voting rights; efforts in Arizona and North Carolina have been identified as some of the most officious. In 2013, Arizona Attorney General Tom Horne issued an opinion that voter registrations for all those who filed forms provided by the federal government would be declared invalid unless those individuals also provided satisfactory proof of U.S. citizenship.⁷³ Later, Horne stated that such individuals could vote in federal but not state elections and that such individuals would not be permitted to sign petitions for ballot initiatives or candidates, but the Supreme Court struck down Arizona's law requiring proof of citizenship to register to vote.[74] While the Arizona dispute seems settled, restrictive measures in North Carolina have not. The voting changes proposed by North Carolina are considered by many to be the most restrictive in the nation. The Brennan Center for Justice again notes, "In North Carolina, data showed African Americans used early voting and same-day registration at much higher rates than whites."[75]

The contemporary voting rights struggle seems mired by advances and retreats. The Advancement Project in Wisconsin brought a successful challenge to block Wisconsin's voter ID law, which the *New York Times* called "one of the strictest in the nation," as an unconstitutional violation under Section 2 of the VRA; however, the Seventh Circuit Court of Appeals reversed that decision, and the Supreme Court declined to hear the matter, so the law stays in place.[76] In the last year, the Brennan Center for Justice reports that there has been some leveling in the passage of laws that frustrate access to the vote.[77] In a post-*Shelby* society, covered jurisdictions are effectively free to make changes to election law or district maps without preclearance from the Justice Department.[78]

The text of the 5–4 *Shelby County v. Holder* decision acknowledges that "voting discrimination still exists; no one doubts that," but, consistent with one of the oft-articulated frames of color-blind racism, the majority opinion declares, "nearly 50 years later, things have changed dramatically."[79] The Supreme Court's attack on the coverage formula instead of Section 5 itself avoids the need to reconcile the inconsistencies its own majority opinion unearths or address the continuing role voting barriers play in the systemic racism experienced by minority communities in U.S. society. This failure to discuss continuing racial oppression in America, including second generation acts of political violence, is a form of racism that sociologist Eduardo Bonilla-Silva terms "colorblind racism."[80]

Since the Supreme Court's decision in *Shelby County v. Holder* struck down the coverage formula in Section 4 of the Voting Rights Act of 1965, a number of restrictions that might have formerly been considered racially discriminatory have been implemented.[81] However, a range of these rollbacks began long before the *Shelby* decision.[82] These include curtailments and constraints on absentee and early voting, closing of polling places, felony disfranchisement (sometimes permanent), restrictions on the rights of students to vote, and a barrage of other tactics, but the most pervasive of these strategies is the institution of photo identification laws.[83]

In fact, years before the historic *Shelby* decision, Congressman John Lewis of Georgia called the rise in voter identification laws since 2010 "a poll tax by another name."[84]

Considerable research supports the claim that these restrictions will have a disproportionate effect on certain segments of the potential voting population. One finding says as many as 25 percent of African-Americans lack valid photo ID, but disproportionate impacts are also anticipated for other groups protected by the Voting Rights Act of 1965.[85] For example, as amended, the act offers protections for language minorities. From the 2000 to 2010 Census, the Latino population in Alabama, a Section 5-covered jurisdiction, grew by 145 percent. Data shows that in some cases, Latinos are as much as 46 to 120 percent more likely than whites to lack a photo ID.[86]

Conclusion

Since its inception, the VRA has been subject to continuing challenges; however, other well-known pieces of civil rights litigation have not. For example, Title II of the 1964 Civil Rights Act has never been amended. Title II entitles persons "to the full and equal enjoyment of the goods, services, facilities, and privileges, advantages, and accommodations of any place of public accommodation . . . without discrimination or segregation on the ground of race, religion, or national origin."[87] Jim Crow legislation has been widely repudiated. As a result, our societal contempt for discrimination in public accommodations is a fight that has been largely won, but as BOP tenet 2 advises, physical integration is not the same as social integration. As a society, the United States is committed to the principle of equality, but this commitment, like the ideological belief in colorblindness, is more theoretical than practical.

The ability to elect the candidate of your choice still matters, and it has ripple effects in the ability to prevent civil unrest. The aftermath of the 2014 shooting death of Michael Brown, an unarmed black teenager, in Ferguson, Missouri, by a white police officer, unveils the true power of the ballot. The Justice Department report on the shooting revealed that the Ferguson Police Department engaged in "a pattern or practice of conduct that violates the First, Fourth, and 14th Amendments of the Constitution."[88] The Justice Department report also states that the Ferguson Municipal Court, an elected body, was complicit in the process. A September

16, 2014, letter from the NAACP Legal Defense and Educational Fund to potential donors urged, "The events in Ferguson have made it clear that voters of color desperately lack a voice in the nation's political system, and this is largely because of structural barriers to the polls. 67% of Ferguson is Black, yet 5 out of 6 council members and the mayor are white. It's no wonder that Ferguson's Black community had to take to the streets to be heard."[89]

This paper introduces a theory—Bodies Out of Place—that helps to elucidate our understanding of color-blindness and post-racial ideology today.[90] These color-blind ideologies abound and paint a picture of a post-racial America that does not exist and possibly never will. This belies the argument that America is beyond race. Structural barriers persist in the election of black politicians, and black (and brown) representation is still largely dependent upon the maintenance of black and brown voting districts.[91] The recent city council elections in Ferguson, Missouri, illustrate this point. In spring 2015, Ferguson elected two new African Americans to their six-member city council, thereby raising the composition of that city council to one-half African American.[92] The election of these candidates was largely made possible by a significant rise in minority candidates and minority voter turnout.[93]

Despite severe restraints on the voting rights of blacks in the South and other minority groups in the West, blacks played a substantial role in the presidential election of 1936. Since that time, both major parties have courted the minority vote without substantially changing the racial/ethnic composition of the leadership of the parties. There were some gains. In 1967, Carl Stokes was elected as the first black mayor of a major U.S. city, and in the time since, a number of cities have done the same.[94] In 1971, the Congressional Black Caucus formed,[95] but despite these gains, no racial/ethnic minority candidate was ever a substantial contender for the elite role of president of the United States. This paper argues that the gains on the local and congressional district-level represent spaces ceded to the minority community—albeit sometimes grudgingly—and that the election of Barack Obama as president (largely at the hands of a minority coalition) acted as kind of attitudinal temporal shift wherein some members of the majority society seek to again curtail the voting rights of minorities.

A great deal of the contemporary and historical legislative restrictions on the franchise can be understood as an attempt to put minority voters back in their place. But it is important to understand these as one of multiple representations of white rage that has recurred throughout history, and, along with Carol Anderson and others I opine that "Obama's election and reelection . . . unleased yet another wave of fear and anger."[96] This manifestation of white rage utilizes the imperceptibly subtle tool of "law and order" to do its bidding, thereby making the racial undertone almost imperceptible. In this way, it mirrors the Southern Strategy (that is, methods often used in the South, designed to appeal to racial resentment and white solidarity).

The Southern Strategy became part of Nixon's playbook for using white anger over advances like the Civil Rights Act of 1964 and the Voting Rights Act for political gain, and by the 1990s, the Republican Party surged to majority status in the formerly Democratic South.[97] Comments later attributed to Republican strategist Lee Atwater reveal that an important element of the strategy was the use of abstract ideas and concepts to represent politically incorrect ideas such as the use of terms like nigger.[98] Atwater's revelations suggest that ideological and theoretical assertions of color-blindness are a farce.

At the same time as the United States began to profess its "color-blindness," the U.S. Latino population began to grow exponentially. According to the 2010 Census, 16.3 percent of the U.S. population was of Latino or Hispanic origin (of any race).[99] The same Census revealed 13 percent of the U.S. population was foreign-born and originating from varied regions including not only Latin America and the Caribbean but also Africa, Asia, Europe, North America, and Oceania.[100] This reveals that color-blind racial frames began to grow at a time when America's racial/ethnic composition became more diverse than ever.

In many ways, the VRA has become the victim of its own success. The very preclearance requirements that prevented some of the most egregious and discriminatory voting law changes from ever going into effect at all created the foundation for the plaintiffs in *Shelby County v. Holder* to argue that discrimination in voting has been substantially reduced. The American democratic experiment has resulted in the expansion of the franchise to African Americans, racial ethnic minorities, language minorities, women, and youth. However, the contraction of that right to vote will have a disproportionate chilling impact on minority voters. Research shows that irrespective of political party affiliation, racial animosity is the biggest predictor of individuals' likelihood to support voter ID laws.[101]

The construct of place can be instructive for understanding how racial hierarchy, which is at the very core of systemic racism, operates and is maintained. I utilize Bodies Out of Place—to highlight the role individual actors play in the maintenance of systemic racism. BOP explains "how raced-based attitudes (a necessary precursor to racism) continue to flourish in society despite overt legislation to the contrary."[102] BOP proffers that, despite advances, vestiges of the Jim Crow system still operate in society and play a substantial role in limiting the life chances for minorities.[103] The theory is useful to explain or understand continuing acts of political and/or physical violence against certain bodies as an attempt to sanction the counterhegemonic form and push him or her back into place.

BOP illustrates that despite assertions of color-blindness, opposers (albeit sometimes unwittingly) become agents of the racist order. We are not color-blind, and yet the curtailment of the franchise is happening under the seemingly color-blind narrative of eliminating voter fraud. It is, however, the elaboration of a racial agenda over political matters without using direct racial references, as suggested by BOP tenet 7. Bodies Out of Place, both as a theoretical and methodological framework, explains how threatened individuals respond to perceived or future risk to their social status and identify and seek mechanisms (like legal restrictions on the franchise) to restore order today. This response is a manifestation of lingering white rage against both black progress and black protest against issues of police and other state-sanctioned violence against black bodies. These black protests are represented in the media as black rage, but Carol Anderson notes that while black protests get represented as rage, "the real rage smolders in meetings where officials redraw precincts to dilute African American voting strength."[104] The Supreme Court's ruling in *Shelby County v. Holder* is but one of the latest "law and order" attempts at the social control of a population that purports to be color-blind but is arguably neither color-blind in its purpose or effect.

Notes

1. Barbara Harris Combs, *From Selma to Montgomery: The Long March to Freedom* (New York: Routledge, 2013), 14, 110.

2. Ibid, 11, 49, 111–12.

3. "The Voting Rights Act of 1965," in *Student's Guide to Elections*, ed. Bruce J. Schulman, (Washington, DC: CQ Press, 2008), 301–8.

4. 570 U.S. (2013). Syllabus. The case, which challenged the constitutionality of Section 5 of the Voting Rights Act of 1965, was brought by Shelby County, Alabama, a covered jurisdiction. The court issued no holding on Section 5 itself, but ruled the coverage formula (established under Section 4 of the Voting Rights Act of 1965 as amended) unconstitutional. The coverage formula is used to determine which states and/or jurisdictions would be subject to the preclearance requirements (under Section 5) before voting law changes could be instituted. The act required covered jurisdictions to preclear voting changes as mundane as the change of polling places to complex matters of redistricting.

5. Carol Anderson, "Ferguson Isn't about Black Rage against Cops. It's about White Rage against Progress," *New York Times*, August 29, 2014.

6. Ibid.

7. See Eduardo Bonilla-Silva, *Racism without Racists: Color-Blind Racism and the Persistence of Racial Inequality in America*, 4th ed. (New York: Routledge, 2014), 76–77.

8. Ibid.

9. See Barbara Harris Combs, "No Rest for the Weary: The Weight of Race, Gender, and Place Inside and Outside a Southern Classroom" (forthcoming, *Sociology of Race and Ethnicity*). In this article, I argue that while BOP makes several basic assumptions about society as set forth in earlier theories such as Critical Race Theory, Standpoint Theory, and Social Identity Theory, it distinguishes itself from the others in the attention it pays bodies, context (i.e., place whether as a geographical or social construct), and to how micro level interactions contribute to the maintenance of inequality on the macro scale. Published online before print, December 1, 2016, at doi: 10.1177/2332649216680101.

10. Ibid.

11. Ibid.

12. The rage that Carol Anderson aptly discusses in both the newspaper article (see note 5, above) and book (see Carol Anderson, *White Rage: The Unspoken Truth of Our Racial Divide* [New York: Bloomsbury, 2016]) is but one manifestation of this pushback.

13. David Redlawsk, Caroline J. Tolbert, and William Frank, "Voters, Emotions, and Race in 2008: Obama as the First Black President," *Political Research Quarterly* 63, no. 4 (2010): 877–80.

14. Barbara Harris Comb, "Black (and Brown) Bodies Out of Place: Towards a Theoretical Examination of Systematic Voter Suppression," *Critical Sociology* 42, nos. 4–5 (2016): 535–49.

15. Anderson, "Ferguson Isn't about Black Rage against Cops."

16. Nancy J. Weiss, *Farewell to the Party of Lincoln: Black Politics in the Age of FDR* (Princeton: Princeton University Press, 1983).

17. Ibid.

18. James M. Sears, "Black Americans and the New Deal," *History Teacher* 10, no. 1 (November 1976): 89–105.

19. Ibid.

20. Harvard Sitkoff, *A New Deal for Blacks: The Emergence of Civil Rights as a National Issue: The Depression Decade* (Oxford: Oxford University Press, 2008), 71.

21. David M. Kennedy, *Freedom from Fear: The American People in Depression and War, 1929–1945* (New York: Oxford University Press, 1999).

22. Sitkoff, *A New Deal for Blacks*.

23. Weiss, *Farewell to the Party of Lincoln*.

24. Thomas T. Spencer, "The Good Neighbor League Colored Committee and the 1936 Democratic Presidential Campaign," *Journal of Negro History* 63, no. 4 (October 1978): 307–16.

25. Ibid.

26. Alexander M. Bickel, "The Voting Rights Cases" (1966), Yale Law School, Faculty Scholarship Series, Paper 3962, at http://www.digitalcommons.lawyale.edu/fss_papers/3962 (consulted March 22, 2017).

27. See South Carolina v. Katzenbach, 383 U.S. 301 (1966).

28. Bickel, "The Voting Rights Cases."

29. Ibid.

30. See South Carolina v. Katzenbach. The case was filed directly to the Supreme Court. The court heard the case prior to the 1966 elections. It was argued January 17–18, 1966, and decided March 7, 1966.

31. Davis S. Tatel, Shelby County v. Holder (No. 11–5256, United States Court of Appeals for the District of Columbia Circuit, May 18, 2012), 28. Available at https:///www.cadc.uscourts.gov/internet/opinions.nsf/D79C82694E572B4D85257A02004EC903/$file/11-5256-1374370.pdf (consulted July 25, 2017).

32. Ibid, 303.

33. Jim Newton, *Justice for All: Earl Warren and the Nation He Made* (New York: Riverhead Books, 2006).

34. Ludy T. Benjamin Jr. and Ellen M. Crouse, "The American Psychological Association's Response to Brown v. Board of Education: The Case of Kenneth B. Clark," *American Psychologist* 57, no. 1 (January 2002): 38–50.

35. Brown v. Board of Education of Topeka, 347 U.S. 483 (1954).

36. South Carolina v. Katzenbach, 308.

37. The legal doctrine of clean hands is a rule of law that a person coming to petition the court for redress must be free from misconduct (i.e., he or she must have "clean hands") in regard to the subject matter of the claim. States, however, have been held not to be persons.

38. Bickel, "The Voting Rights Cases."

39. Luis Fuentes-Rohwer and Guy-Uriel E. Charles, "Preclearance, Discrimination, and the Department of Justice: The Case of South Carolina," *South Carolina Law Review* 57 (2006): 827–58, 831.

40. Anderson, *White Rage*.

41. J. Morgan Kousser, *The Shaping of Southern Politics: Suffrage Restriction and the Establishment of the One-Party South, 1880–1910* (New Haven: Yale University Press, 1974); Samuel Issacharoff, Pamela Karlan, and Richard Pildes, *The Law of Democracy* (Westbury, NY: Foundation Press, 1998).

42. See South Carolina v. Katzenbach, 355–62, re concurring and dissenting opinion.

43. Ibid.

44. Combs, "Black (and Brown) Bodies Out of Place."

45. Ibid, 4.

46. According to the U.S. Department of Justice's website, jurisdictions were included in the Section 4 coverage formula if

> on November 1, 1964, the state or a political subdivision of the state maintained a "test or device" restricting the opportunity to register and vote. The Act's definition of a "test or device" included such requirements as the applicant being able to pass a literacy test, establish that he or she had good moral character, or have another registered voter vouch for his or her qualifications.
>
> The second element of the formula would be satisfied if the Director of the Census determined that less than 50 percent of persons of voting age were registered to vote on November 1, 1964, or that less than 50 percent of persons of voting age voted in the presidential election of November 1964.

Available at https://www.justice.gov/crt/section-4-voting-rights-act (consulted July 25, 2017)

47. Northwest Austin Municipal Utility District No. 1 v. Eric Holder, 557 U.S. 193 (2009).

48. Ibid, Syllabus, 1.

49. Justin Levitt, "The Truth about Voter Fraud," Brennan Center for Justice at New York University School of Law, 2007. Available at www.brennancenter.org/publication/truth-about-voter-fraud (consulted March 22, 2017).

50. R. Michael Alvarez, Delia Bailey, and Jonathan N. Katz, "An Empirical Bayes Approach to Estimating Ordinal Treatment Effects," *Political Analysis* 1, no. 19 (2011): 20–31.

51. Levitt, "The Truth About Voter Fraud." Allegations of voter fraud have been widely discounted. In fact, upon investigation, most fraud allegations have been found to be clerical error.

52. Justice Hugo Black was a former member of the Ku Klux Klan, Congressional Senator, and was later appointed to the Supreme Court by President Franklin Delano Roosevelt.

53. See South Carolina v. Katzenbach, 301, 355–62, re concurring and dissenting opinion.

54. Sonya Rastogi, Tallese D. Johnson, Elizabeth M. Hoeffel, and Malcolm P. Drewery Jr., "The Black Population 2010" (Washington, DC: Census, 2011). See *2010 Census Briefs*, C2010BR-06, at www.census.gov/prod/cen2010/briefs/c2010br-06.pdf (consulted March 22, 2017).

55. Justices Ruth Bader Ginsburg (writing), Stephen Breyer, Sonia Sotomayor, and Elena Kagan joined the dissent to the Shelby decision.

56. Combs, "Black (and Brown) Bodies Out of Place."

57. Shelby dissent, Shelby County v. Holder.

58. See 679 F 3d, at 867, Shelby County v. Holder.

59. See H.R. Rep. 109–478, 21.

60. Ibid, 6.

61. Jackie Calmes, Robbie Brown, and Campbell Robertson, "On Voting Case Reaction from 'Deeply Disappointed' to 'It's about Time,'" *New York Times*, June 25, 2013.

62. David S. Tatel, Shelby County v. Holder, 28.

63. NAACP Legal Defense and Educational Fund, *Defending Democracy: Confronting Modern Barriers to Voting Rights in America* (Baltimore, MD: NAACP, 2011), at http://naacp.3cdn.net/67065c25be9ae43367_mlbrsy48b.pdf

64. Mark Hugo Lopez, "The Latino Electorate in 2010: More Voters, More Non-Voters" (Washington DC: Pew Hispanic Center, 2011), at http://pewhispanic.org/files/reports/141.pdf (consulted March 22, 2017); and Paul G. Bain, Matthew J. Hornsey, Renata Bongiorno, and Yoshihisa Kashima, "Collective Futures: How Projections about the Future of Society are Related to Actions and Attitudes Supporting Social Change," *Personality and Social Psychology Bulletin* 39, no. 4 (2013): 523–39.

65. The Supreme Court heard oral arguments in Evenwel v. Abbott on December 8, 2015, Docket No. 14–940. The issue before the court is whether the three-judge district court correctly held that the "one-person, one-vote" principle under the Equal Protection Clause allows states to use total population and does not require states to use voter population, when apportioning state legislative districts.

66. Ibid.

67. Adam Liptak, "Supreme Court Agrees to Settle Meaning of 'One Person One Vote,'" *New York Times,* May 26, 2015.

68. In a 4–3 decision, the Supreme Court ruled the University of Texas's admission policy constitutional. See Fisher v. University of Texas at Austin et al., 579 US ___ (2016).

69. Combs, *From Selma to Montgomery*, 20, 128–9.

70. Vishal Agraharkar, "50 Years Later, Voting Rights Act under Unprecedented Assault," Brennan Center for Justice at New York University School of Law, August 2, 2015, at https://www.brennancenter.org/analysis/50-years-later-voting-rights-act-under-unprecedented-assault (consulted March 22, 2017).

71. Jess Bravin, "Supreme Court Casts Doubt on Alabama Redistricting Plan," *Wall Street Journal,* March 25, 2015, at http://www.wsj.com/articles/supreme-court-blocks-alabama-voter-redistricting-plan-1427296385 (consulted March 22, 2017).

72. See Adam Gitlin and Christopher Famighetti, "Closing Driver's License Offices in Alabama," Brennan Center for Social Justice Center at New York University School of Law, October 7, 2015, at https://www.brennancenter.org/blog/closing-drivers-license-offices-alabama (consulted March 22, 2017). This report discusses Alabama's intention to close 31 of its part-time division of motor vehicle (DMV) offices in largely minority counties. Democrats quickly condemned the measure as one with either the purpose or effect of curtailing the voting rights of poor and minority voters in Alabama's rural counties. By late October 2015, Alabama's Republican governor Robert J. Bentley announced he would reopen the DMV offices slated for closure for one day out of each month. See Bryan Lyman, "Alabama Will Reopen Closed DMV Offices in Black Counties," *Tribune News Service,* October 20, 2015, at http://www.governing.com/topics/politics/drivers-license-offices-will-reopen-on-limited-basis.html (consulted March 22, 2017).

73. State of Arizona Attorney General Thomas Horne Opinion No. I13–011 (R13–16), State of Arizona, Office of the Attorney General. October 7, 2013, at https://www.azag.gov/sites/default/files/I13-011_0.pdf (consulted March 22, 2017).

74. Arizona et al. v. Inter Tribal Council of Arizona. Inc., et al., slip op. No. 12–71 (opinion) U.S. Supreme Court, June 17, 2013.

75. Agraharkar, "50 Years Later."

76. Adam Liptak, "Wisconsin Decides Not to Enforce Voter ID Law," *New York Times,* March 23, 2015, at http://www.nytimes.com/2015/03/24/us/supreme-court-rejects-challenge-to-wisconsin-voter-id-law.html (consulted March 22, 2017). Note: Wisconsin agreed not to enforce the law in the upcoming April 2015 elections, but said it would in later elections. Wisconsin governor Scott Walker and former candidate for the GOP nomination to the 2016 presidential election has championed the law.

77. "States with New Voting Restrictions Since 2010," Brennan Center for Justice at New York University School of Law, 2007, at http://www.brennancenter.org/new-voting-restrictions-2010-election (consulted March 22, 2017).

78. In January 2014, a bipartisan congressional group introduced the Voting Rights Amendment Act of 2014, but lacking widespread support, the amendment received little forward movement. While Section 2 challenges can still be brought, the effect of a crippled Section 5 is that fewer legal resources are available to challenge discriminatory voting practices.

79. Shelby County v. Holder, Syllabus, 2.

80. Bonilla-Silva, *Racism without Racists.*

81. See Wendy R. Weiser and Lawrence Norden, "Voting Law Changes in 2012," Brennan Center for Justice at New York University School of Law, 2011; William D. Hicks, Seth C. McKee, Mitchell D. Sellers, Danel A. Smith. "'A Principle or A Strategy? Voter Identification Laws and Partisan Competition in the American States'." 2014: 1-16.

82. For a discussion of the growing number of voter identification laws and their effect, also see Barbara Harris Combs, "Black (and Brown) Bodies Out of Place."

83. Jaime Fuller, "How Has Voting Changed since Shelby County v. Holder?" *Washington Post,* July 7, 2014, at http://www.washingtonpost.com/blogs/the-fix/wp/2014/07/07/how-has-voting-changed-since-shelby-county-v-holder/ (consulted March 22, 2017).

84. Lewis was one of the leaders of the Student Nonviolent Coordinating Committee (SNCC), and he was one of the leaders of the first Selma to Montgomery march, which has come to be known as Bloody Sunday. In one of the most iconic images of Bloody Sunday, Lewis is seen lying prostrate on the ground while a policeman strikes him in the head with a club; and John Lewis, "A Poll Tax by Another Name," *New York Times,* August 26, 2011.

85. Weiser and Norden, "Voting Law Changes in 2012."

86. Letter from Thomas E. Perez, Assistant Attorney General, U.S. Department of Justice, to Keith Ingram, Director of Elections, Office of the Texas Secretary of State, March 12, 2012, at http://brennan.3cdn.net/fe6a21493d7ec1aafc_vym6b91dt.pdf (consulted March 22, 2017).

87. See U.S. Statutes at Large 78 (1964): 241.

88. U.S. Department of Justice, "Justice Department Announces Findings of Two Civil Rights Investigations in Ferguson, Missouri," News Release, Department of Justice, March 4, 2015, at http://www.justice.gov/opa/pr/justice-department-announces-findings-two-civil-rights-investigations-ferguson-missouri (consulted March 22, 2017).

89. Personal correspondence.

90. Note Nirmal Puwar introduces a similar concept in *Space Invaders: Race, Gender and Bodies out of Place* (New York: Berg, 2004). In her analysis, Puwar focuses on the related concept of space, not place.

91. Bonilla-Silva, *Racism without Racists*, 39, 29.

92. Matt Pearce, "Ferguson Voters Turn Out to Elect 2 More Black City Council Members," *Los Angeles Times*, April 7, 2015, at http://www.latimes.com/nation/la-na-ferguson-election-20150407-story.html (consulted March 22, 2017).

93. Ibid.

94. J. Phillip Thompson, *Double Trouble: Black Mayors, Black Communities, and the Call for a Deep Democracy* (Oxford: Oxford University Press, 2005).

95. Christina Rivers, *The Congressional Black Caucus, Minority Voting Rights, and the U.S. Supreme Court* (Ann Arbor: University of Michigan Press, 2014).

96. Anderson, "Ferguson Isn't about Black Rage against Cops."

97. Alexander P. Lamis, *Southern Politics in the 1990s* (Baton Rouge: Louisiana State University Press, 1999).

98. Ibid., 8.

99. Because Hispanic or Latino is an ethnic classification, not a race, Americans can identify as any racial classification (for example Hispanic white or Hispanic nonwhite).

100. Elizabeth M. Grieco, Yesenia D. Acosta, G. Patricia de la Cruz, Christine Gambino, Thomas Gryn, Luke J. Larsen, Edward N. Trevelyan, and Nathan P. Walters, "The Foreign-Born Population in the United States: 2010, American Community Survey Reports," 2012, ACS-19, at www.census.gov/prod/2012pubs/acs-19.pdf (consulted March 22, 2017).

101. Bonilla-Silva, *Racism without Racists*, 39.

102. Combs, "No Rest for the Weary," 493.

103. For a fuller understanding of the concept of Bodies Out of Place, see Combs, "Black (and Brown) Bodies Out of Place."

104. Anderson, "Ferguson Isn't about Black Rage against Cops."

13

The Racial Laundering of Equality after *Shelby County v. Holder*

LYNN MIE ITAGAKI

The contentious 5–4 *Shelby County v. Holder* Supreme Court decision (2013) invalidated the coverage formula, one of the centerpiece accomplishments of the 1965 Voting Rights Act (VRA) that Congress had most recently reauthorized in 2006 to last another twenty-five years. The *Shelby* decision dismantled the VRA's Section 4 and Section 5 preemptive regulatory powers that could evaluate discriminatory voter laws *before* they went into effect rather than *after* an election was conducted with illegal procedures. The Supreme Court ruled on the VRA amid a series of controversial judgments allowing more money in politics and fewer restrictions on the amount an individual donor and what kind of donor could contribute.[1]

This essay considers the impact of the majority and concurring justices' opinions on current conceptions of citizenship. I contend that the Shelby Court asserts certain assumptions about democratic participation that presumes all voters experience equal treatment across jurisdictions, approximating what sociologist Michael Schudson has identified as a "trust-based public life."[2] While ostensibly building on pro-social values and civic virtues such as trust and belonging, the justices of the *Shelby* majority have a much more restrictive notion of who constitutes deserving, meritorious participants in the political community. These implicit notions end up having the effect of the continued exclusion and discrimination against those who cannot be trusted and who do not belong: non-investors, noncorporate speakers, and now individual voters who are unlucky enough to live in jurisdictions that in the past have actively disenfranchised and can now effectively attempt to disenfranchise or dilute their votes without preclearance.

Less acknowledged in the discussion of the *Shelby County v. Holder* majority opinion is the context of racial profiling, a national conversation sparked by the fatal shooting of black teenager Trayvon Martin on February 26, 2012, by a self-appointed law enforcer, mixed-race Latino George Zimmerman. Oral arguments for *Shelby* began almost exactly one year after Martin's death, and the majority opinion was announced two weeks into Zimmerman's trial for second-degree murder. I analyze *Shelby* through the notion of racial laundering, or the process by which the terms of determining access to or the distribution of resources not only further racial inequality but are also deracialized, promoted as race-neutral, and posited as the result of color-blind practices. I deliberately invoke the disturbing connotations that racial laundering elicits to emphasize the all-too-often minimized or ignored unconstitutionality of the repeated inadvertent failure to treat people equally and foster mostly equal outcomes in resource distribution such as access to K-16 education, career opportunities, wealth accumulation, healthcare, and quality of life, to name just a few.

Racial laundering identifies the process by which illegal actions and their ill-gotten gains are transformed into legal processes and outcomes: making illegal racist intent into legal race-neutral reasoning and ostensibly fair outcomes. I use the concept of racial laundering to identify ways in which the long, ignoble, and inhuman history of slavery, racial apartheid, and their continuing aftermath are ignored. The brief opinion for *Shelby* makes its analyses and rationales even more legally and politically potent.

Racial laundering is a fundamental strategy of the post–civil rights era, and *Shelby County v. Holder*'s landmark dismantling of historic civil rights legislation deploys racial laundering in one of the many repeated, increasingly successful attempts to either repeal, make ineffective, or sidestep civil rights protections like the VRA.[3] Basing its reasoning on core post–civil rights era assumptions, the Shelby Court can then convincingly ignore a voluminous history of voter dilution, disenfranchisement, and intimidation and assert in its stead a legal principle of equal sovereignty that develops from the blatantly racist exclusion and exploitation of descendants of African enslaved persons from state and national political communities and legal rights. Moreover, the Shelby Court focuses on gains of black voting in the South in order to exclude the expanding constituencies of "language minorities" that later amendments to the VRA sought to protect. This exclusionary focus is another feature of the post–civil rights era in terms of racial triangulation: to valorize one nonwhite constituency in order to obscure the devaluation of another to preserve white hegemony.[4]

Despite the increasing visibility of the adjective "post-racial," especially during Barack Obama's campaign and two-term presidency, I read post-racialism as primarily a repackaging of strategies of the post–civil rights era. I argue that it is crucial not only to recognize the continuation so as to use all the anti-racist tools at our disposal to accurately identify and combat the confluence of what scholars have isolated as post–civil rights and post-racial strategies.

Racial Laundering in the Post–Civil Rights Era

Racial laundering usefully analogizes the application of racial neutrality and its deceptive simplicity that has proven so effective in weakening support for policies equalizing outcomes or remedying past injustices for differently racialized populations. In the post–civil rights era, the vast majority across the political spectrum agrees that racial discrimination violates the equal protection clause of the Fifth and Fifteenth Amendments as well as the Constitution. However, racist intent is much more difficult to identify and prove as the motivation behind everyday, ostensibly racially neutral choices by the average individual. A society and state upholding slavery and white supremacy has easily explained for centuries unequal racial outcomes through discourses of religion, science, morality, and anthropology that sought to protect the interests of white citizens and slaveholders over that of enslaved, immigrant, and indigenous peoples.

I use racial laundering with its illegal and criminal definitions. Laundering money earned from illegal activities first separates the money from the criminal; second, uses a variety of financial transactions to make the illegal origins hard or impossible to trace; and third, returns the money to the criminal in the form of legitimate goods and investments. Analogously, racial laundering first separates racist intent from individual and institutional actors that deploy intentionally or unintentionally racist policies. Second, it uses a variety of racially neutral explanations to justify these policies and their racially unequal outcomes.[5] Third, racial laundering returns or redistributes resources to the racial elites or intended beneficiaries of these actions; it purges both the skewed process and recipients of their discriminatory intent and unfairly allocated resources.

Racial laundering also occurs in how critics characterize the contemporary moment and historicize the past: because legal remedies currently prohibit people and institutions from perpetuating discrimination, racism has occurred in the past and not the present. If, however, inequalities persist, then these outcomes naturally or fairly result from equal treatment and opportunity. Or an individual's taste-based or preference discrimination are normalized as just the way people are and the government cannot regulate these kinds of interpersonal behaviors and private choices. Just as money laundering makes it difficult to find the "dirty" origins of illegal gains, so too racial laundering makes it difficult to find the racist intent of racially neutral policies. Moreover, as in money laundering, the beneficiaries of these resources tainted by illegal processes are also analogously illegitimate and unworthy.

Racial laundering deracializes processes, purges them of their racist intent and illegality, and promotes a race-neutrality that initiates and results from color-blind practices. Racial laundering reveals the interconnection between what scholars have distinguished as separate: the post–civil rights and post-racial eras. Elsewhere I have argued that the post–civil rights era marks the shift from formal, legal forms of discrimination to informal, yet still legal, ones.[6] Community historian William Chafe explains this shift from overt to hidden racism: "Inequality and discrimination still suffuse our social and economic system, buttressed by informal modes of social control even more powerful than the law. Although the means of keeping blacks in their place may now be implicit rather than explicit, they too often are just as effective as in the past."[7] In the relationship between political and social equality, the difference in the civil rights era was the state's explicit use of political and legal mechanisms to try to lessen social and economic inequalities. These state mandates contrast to preceding and following historical periods in which policymakers and power elites promote and even rely on existing social and racial inequalities to preserve or worsen political and economic hierarchies.

Both critical race theorists Sumi Cho and Ian Haney-López identify a changing discourse of color-blindness that marks what they see as a distinctly post-racial era. For Haney-López, post-racialism does acknowledge the racial injustices and injuries of the recent and far-reaching past, unlike color-blindness, which demands a kind of forgetting and exoneration of past injustices in order to embrace a racially neutral future. However, both post-racialism and color-blindness depend on the belief that only color-blind practices would have prevented past inequalities and will prevent present and future ones.

Haney-López criticizes post-racialism for its universalist demands in that we should now deploy practices to help all people, regardless of race:

> Post-racialism reduces racism to individual, unreconstructed bigotry. It rejects the argument that racism also describes structural practices, deeply entrenched cultural beliefs among whites, or political efforts to mobilize the electorate to vote its racial fears. By truncating the meaning of racism, post-racialism helps diffuse our moral responsibility to directly challenge these dimensions of race as well as the persistent inequality they protect and produce. Instead, like colorblindness, if for very different reasons, post-racialism tells us to eschew the divisive politics of race-conscious efforts, and instead urges that we throw our weight behind universal solutions to the nation's ills.[8]

What Haney-López identifies as our diffusion of moral responsibility, Sumi Cho identifies post-racialism as reaching a new, expanded constituency for those left of center whereas the "inequality activism" of the post–civil rights era appealed mostly to constituencies from right of center to the far right. Cho defines the civil rights era as one of "racial remediation" and the post–civil rights era as "getting beyond race to colorblindness" and moving away from remediation or correction in U.S. society and government, evidenced in civil rights protections such as the legislative mechanisms institutionalized by the 1964 Civil Rights Act, 1965 Voting Rights Act, and 1968 Fair Housing Act, and the landmark decisions of the liberal Warren Court (1953–1969).[9]

Political scientist Howard Winant identifies Jim Crow segregation as a "racial dictatorship" and for him and sociologist Michael Omi, the civil rights era marks the shift to the "racial hegemony" of the post-civil rights era, largely through a racial hierarchy established through consent not coercion.[10] This notion of a racialized hegemony importantly explains the discursive shift in the post-rights era over who constitutes the ruling majority and the subordinate minority, or, if not plausible in terms of sheer numbers, who holds the majority of power and resources and who receives the lesser share. For example, white supremacy instantiates the white majority as a governing and economic elite. The advent of persuasive discursive strategies such as "reverse racism," "equal treatment," and even "equal opportunity" have undergirded shifts in policy and public opinion; these phrases have shaped interracial antagonisms most prominently in debates over affirmative action. Opponents of racial equality rhetorically switched whites as the victimized, deserving minority and people of color as the victimizing, undeserving majority.

The post–civil rights era is characterized by what critical race theorist Kimberlé Crenshaw has called "racial retrenchment" through the culture wars, anti–affirmative action referenda, Supreme Court decisions, the militarized policing of urban neighborhoods, and the encroachments on Fourth Amendment search and seizure protections facilitated by the so-called War on Drugs.[11] What geographer Neil Smith has called "revanchism," this kind of racial revenge against historically vulnerable populations has rendered them even more vulnerable.[12] What Omi and Winant have mapped in the transitions from racial despotism to racial hegemony appears in relationship to the emergence of the carceral state: the use of the criminal justice system and expanding prison-industrial complex to discipline and kill people of color, especially black and brown young men and women. Despite the shift from the U.S. state's racial dictatorship to a racial hegemony as Omi and Winant have detailed, repeated instances of anti-black and anti-immigrant violence from police and "self-appointed law enforcers"—security guards, neighborhood watches, citizen councils, lynch mobs—exemplifies the persistence of racial terror from the antebellum era to the present.

The framework of the post–civil rights era has continuing salience. Historian Jacqueline Dowd Hall has identified "the Long Civil Rights Movement" that encompasses Bloody Sunday at Selma and the passage and implementation of the Voting Rights Act among many other landmark events;[13] I posit analogously the *long* post–civil rights era that swallows up not only the racial retrenchment of the Reagan Revolution but also the putative end of the Cold War; the aftermath of 9/11; the imperial wars in the Persian Gulf, Iraq, and Afghanistan; the lingering effects of Hurricane Katrina; the Great Recession; and the publicized numbers of murders of black men, women, and children by police and self-appointed law enforcers.

Thus, despite the prominence of post-racialism superseding the post–civil rights era, I think it crucial for audiences to recognize the continued applicability of many of the frames and analytics used to understand the post–civil rights era are also necessary to grasp present conditions. While pundits have often heralded the 2008 election of President Barack Obama as the inaugural post-racial moment, the racial strategies deployed by those Cho calls "inequality activists" continue the "civil racism," "retreat from race," and "racial retrenchment" of the post–civil rights era.[14] I posit Cho's and Haney-López's post-racial strategies as retooled ones falling under the post–civil rights era. Connecting the post-racial strategies identified by Cho and Haney-López with the post–civil rights frames of sociologist Eduardo Bonilla-Silva is the basic desire to launder racist motivations into race-neutral or color-blind policies and structures so as to make their harmful, injurious, and unequal outcomes fair, just, and natural. Although the texture of the discourse might change, the fundamental logic behind the strategies remains unchanged: redistribution of resources to the top of the racial hierarchy. But I think it is important to note that many of the same strategies that effectively diminished or dismantled civil rights legislation continue to be effective for audiences as broad as those in national politics to ones as intimate as those in everyday conversations.

The Strange Career of Equality

For the Roberts Court, privileging existing economic elites emerges as its signature form of racial laundering. The state protections for the "investor class" racially launders economically privileged classes under the guise of racial neutrality. In post–Great Recession forms of economic citizenship that restrict and even foreclose our political imagination, the shareholder citizen and corporate donor supplants the human voter and noncorporate speaker in the recent campaign finance reform Supreme Court decisions such as *Citizens United v. FEC* and *McCutcheon v. FEC* that have grounded the long-term vision of the Roberts Court. Upholding the electoral power of the "investor class," the valorization of the elite donor and shareholder reaffirms the financialization of the economy and big money in politics by encouraging the supremacy of shareholder, owner, and consumer over the voter and citizen. The economic recovery after 2009 has disproportionately gone to shareholders benefitting from the stock market's historic highs; however, for those whose assets and wealth are pegged to housing and wages, largely people of color and women, their economic outlook has not "recovered" as much. The intersection of politics and economic prerogatives facilitates and establishes de facto citizenship hierarchies that again are largely white, male, and propertied at the top, historically echoing the "free white male" property owner of the notoriously exclusionary 1790 Naturalization Law and requirements for voting during the early decades of the Republic.

Political and legal equality under the Roberts Court has enjoyed a tortured interpretation or has been abandoned altogether for noncorporate, human speakers (*Citizens United*), non-donor class voters (*McCutcheon*) and non-covered jurisdictions under Section 4 of the VRA (*Shelby County*). The Roberts Court majority deems these categories of people as experiencing putative privileges and protections, and uses this designation of their unduly elevated, preferred, or extraordinarily protected status to raise up and equalize the privileges and protections given to corporate speakers, donor class campaign contributors, and formerly covered jurisdictions, respectively, that historically disenfranchised black voters before 1964 or had low percentages of nonwhite or language minority voters before 1972.[15]

One of the most notable assertions of the court in *Shelby County v. Holder* is the unprecedented interpretation of the "equal sovereignty" principle. The court's constitutional concern for the equal treatment of states can be provocatively juxtaposed to their lack of constitutional concern for human speakers and voters in formerly covered VRA jurisdictions. Significantly, the political equality rationale dropped completely out of any discussion of campaign finance reform in any of the Roberts Court campaign finance reform cases such as *Citizens United* or *McCutcheon*. It perhaps expectedly drops out of the conservative majority opinion, but surprisingly also disappears from Justice John Paul Stevens's eloquent dissent in *Citizens United*. For some court observers, political equality is dead before the Roberts Court.[16]

But it is dead only if you are an individual, noncorporate (read: human) speaker and voter. Instead, the concern for inequality or unequal treatment goes to the wealthy donors, the shareholder, the corporation, the states formerly covered by the VRA Section 5 that had more per capita VRA litigation (still covered under Section 2), at the expense of the noncorporate speaker, the racial or language minority voter, or the millions of voters outside the elite donor class. The latter is represented by post–*Citizens United* Super PAC million-dollar corporate contributors or by the Alabama millionaire businessman Shaun McCutcheon who wanted to contribute more to Republican candidates' election campaigns than the existing aggregate campaign limits would allow, or $117,000 to candidates, PACs, and parties in the 2011–2012 campaign cycle. In the logic of the Citizens United and McCutcheon Court majorities, election laws discriminate against corporate speakers and wealthy donors because of their inability to contribute without restrictions to political parties: in essence, their freedom to participate in electoral politics should be commensurate with their desire to donate.

The increasing salience of the post–civil rights era appears in *Shelby County v. Holder*. In this startlingly brief opinion with unprecedented applications and interpretations of precedent and doctrine, the conservative majority dismantled one of the cornerstone legislative gains of the modern civil rights movement in such a way that court watchers anticipate future attacks if not the complete evisceration of the VRA. Election law scholar Richard Hasen scathingly indicts the *Shelby* decision as "an audacious opinion which ignores history, declines to engage the dissent's powerful argument that the VRA's bailout provisions solve any constitutional problem, and rejects the Roberts Court's stated commitment to judicial minimalism in its treatment of facial challenges and severability," calling out the Roberts majority for creating an "illusion of minimalism."[17] In this way the most egregious instance of racial laundering in the *Shelby County v. Holder* was not its cursory citation and breezy dismissal of the voting proposals that federal judge panels or examiners rejected or were voluntarily withdrawn by covered jurisdictions in recent years submitted to the Congressional Record as the reasons for the VRA's renewal for twenty-five years in 2006. Rather, the majority opinion exhibited such extreme minimalism that it ignored the long-standing historical precedent for its main argument of equal sovereignty: the justification for slavery.

In Chief Justice Roberts's stated attempts to make governance more efficient in brief opinions and to limit government's intrusion by reducing its regulatory oversight in court decisions, minimalism has proven a useful strategy to remove or diminish racial remedies. The same logic operates to delegitimize claims of racism and other forms of discrimination by minimizing the effects of racism and thus minimizing or doing away with governmental efforts to equalize racial outcomes. The *Shelby* opinion was so abbreviated it notably failed to provide the judicial precedence supporting the majority argument's main justification for deeming the coverage formula unconstitutional: the equal sovereignty principle. As put forward in the earlier, almost unanimous, decision *Northwest Austin Municipal Utility District No. 1 (NAMUDNO) v. FEC* (2009), Roberts's 8–1 majority opinion warned that the VRA "imposes substantial federalism costs" and "differentiates between the States despite our historic tradition that all the States enjoy 'equal sovereignty.'"[18] Roberts's assertion of a "historic tradition" of the equal sovereignty principle that begins with *NAMUDNO* was criticized variously as a "newly invented idea" and a work out of the "conservative imagination."[19] Yet the legal history of this principle is so baffling that federal appellate judge (and one of the most prolific legal scholars) Richard Posner argues that the principle has no precedence except through Roberts's *NAMUDNO* majority opinion, the most recent challenge to the VRA.

However, civil rights attorney James Blacksher and critical race scholar Lani Guinier argue that the decision's equal sovereignty principle goes back even farther than this century, back to the mid-nineteenth century antebellum period, in fact. Far from having no precedent, the equal sovereignty principle is deeply enmeshed in the landmark antebellum case that cast African Americans entirely out of U.S. citizenship, preserving slavery through the 1857 *Dred Scott v. Sandford* decision. According to Blacksher and Guinier, the equal sovereignty principle "revitalizes the oldest and most demeaning official insult to African Americans in American constitutional history."[20]

In returning to this case and Chief Justice Roger B. Taney's notorious majority opinion, Blacksher and Guinier note the fuller, pernicious contexts of Chief Justice Roberts's resuscitation of the equal sovereignty principle even if his majority opinion omitted it: first, "just as the Court did in *Dred Scott*, the Court in *Shelby* held that 'equal sovereignty' of the State of Alabama takes precedence over Congress' exercise of its explicit constitutional power to enforce the voting rights of the descendants of slaves"; and second, that "black persons—slave or free—were not citizens, as they were not members of the sovereign people who founded the United States and enacted the Constitution."[21] Blacksher and Guinier detail the centuries of the court's tortured interpretations of Article IV, the Fourteenth and Fifteenth Amendments of the Constitution, specifically those of the "privileges and immunities" clause in order to keep freed African American men from voting.

Blacksher and Guinier track how voting citizenship has come to indicate sovereign citizenship although the two have had different legal rights and protections in U.S. history.[22] Sovereign citizenship, in Chief Justice Taney's words, derives from the "people of the United States," synonymous with citizens and "both describe the political body who, according to our republican institutions, form the sovereignty, and who hold the power and conduct the Government through their representatives."[23] Taney's interpretation of the Constitution was founded on the new nation's deliberate exclusion and subordination of nonwhites, and blacks were not intended to be included as sovereign citizens who had the collective power of governance:

> They ... can therefore claim none of the rights and privileges which that instrument provides for and secures to citizens of the United States. On the contrary, they were at that time considered as a subordinate and inferior class of beings, who had been subjugated by the dominant race, and, whether emancipated or not, yet remained subject to their authority, and had no rights or privileges but such as those who held the power and the government might choose to grant them.[24]

Unlike inalienable or natural rights accorded to the "people of the United States," Taney reasserts the racism of the drafters of the Constitution to accord alienable rights to African Americans among others, subject to the state governments that may "choose" to protect or take them away.

While first-generation voting restrictions were racially neutral in their language such as that found in the grandfather clause, literacy tests, good character vouchers, and poll taxes and excluded some poor, illiterate whites from voting, their passage and implementation targeted and disenfranchised black voters who white elites continually argued, along the lines of Chief Justice Taney, were "a subordinate and inferior class of beings."[25] This racism blatantly animated the various strategies used to disenfranchise and denationalize African Americans since the debates of the Constitutional Convention. In the civil rights era, police and "self-appointed law enforcers" reinforced the "first-generation barriers" of outright vote denial with terror and intimidation; in the post–civil rights era, "second-generation barriers" more regularly resulted in "vote dilution" in the forms of gerrymandering, redistricting, and selective annexation. Essentially, the Roberts opinion deems that protecting the equal treatment of states outweighs protecting the equal treatment of individual voters. The argumentation of the *Shelby* opinion relies upon an implicit logic of trust and merit: those who belong can trust legal systems to recognize their merit. This logic works both ways: those who have merit can trust legal systems to recognize that they belong; those that belong are thought to have merit.[26]

To reanimate the equal sovereignty principle from this case also resuscitates the deeply racist logic that once validated slavery's hierarchies of white over black and justified the differences between some U.S. citizens who have inalienable rights and others who have none except those that the state government, and by extension the political subdivision, *grant* the right and privilege to vote in however way election officials determine. Through the equal sovereignty principle, the Supreme Court superintended the creation of different classes of citizens: those who are enfranchised individual state and sovereign citizens (white adult men with or without property according to state laws); those who are individual state and sovereign citizens with no political power (women, minors, and in some states, men without property); and those who are absolutely not sovereign citizens ("free blacks and mulattoes" who might have voted in local and state elections and were state citizens depending on the jurisdiction since five states allowed black suffrage by that time).

The Model Minority Right to Choose One's Leaders

While accusing Congress of relying on a coverage formula from forty years ago, the Shelby Court bases its decision on the absence of voting restrictions that were prevalent and necessitated the 1965 VRA. They are considered "first-generation barriers"—literacy tests, good character requirements, vouchers, and poll taxes, for example—and which the VRA largely made impossible for covered jurisdictions to implement through the preclearance process. The *Shelby County v. Holder* majority implies that if Congress had changed the coverage formula as well as the criteria for voting rights violations, then it may have found Section 4 constitutional, stating that Congress's use of forty-year-old data is "irrational" since this specific mechanism of vote denial—tests—is no longer present.

"If Congress had started from scratch in 2006, it plainly could not have enacted the present coverage formula. It would have been irrational for Congress to distinguish between States in such a fundamental way based on forty-year-old data, when today's statistics tell an entirely different story. And it would have been irrational to base coverage on the use of voting tests forty years ago, when such tests have been illegal since that time. But that is exactly what Congress has done."[27] The court appears to rely on voting barriers being illegal as an effective enough deterrence from their being implemented, or that the preclearance oversight is not crucial to these devices' continuing absence.

While the voting tests of the Jim Crow era are no longer in use, it is precisely the ingenuity of voting commissions to create new barriers to voting that resulted in the first and subsequent amendments to the VRA and the fifteen categories identifying areas of concern for U.S. Department of Justice objections beyond the specific category of tests. The court majority uses the success of the VRA in eradicating these first-generation barriers to justify dismantling the coverage formula and the covered jurisdictions, and this argument has led many critics of the opinion such as author of the *Shelby* dissent Justice Ruth Bader Ginsberg to argue that the VRA is victimized by its own success.[28]

With the logic of Chief Justice Roberts's majority opinion, I posit this success in terms of the model minority paradigm. Most often used to praise and criticize Asian Americans, the model minority functions to criticize other racial minorities or obscure their particular needs or barriers to equality; provide the justification for dismantling or defunding affirmative action, welfare, and other social safety net programs; and furnish these "inequality activists" anti-racist cover by casting the failures of other groups on cultural reasons or naturalizing justifications as just the way people are rather than intentional discrimination. The fact that a racial minority can putatively succeed while others seem to "fail" or are less successful emerges as a rationale to dismantle or weaken policies aiding other minority groups without appearing to have racist intent. In other words, if Asian Americans ostensibly succeed without the specific policies targeting African Americans and Latina/os, then something is wrong with these latter groups that state remedies will never fix. This blame can then be used to dismantle programs such as affirmative action, and these motivations are cleansed of their anti-black or anti-brown racism, rather than forcing an evaluation of whether something is wrong with the policies that appear to help some racial minorities rather than others.

Pundits and policymakers have often referred to Asian Americans as a model minority of above average educational attainment and household incomes in order to avoid accusations of racism since elites can now use this racial group's socioeconomic successes to advocate for fewer or scaled-back racial remedies. This process creates new racial hierarchies, privileging some groups by assigning moral or intellectual abilities to physical characteristics, thus scaling the effects of ideological racism. In political scientist Claire Jean Kim's conception of racial triangulation, she explains the model minority thesis for Asian Americans through this kind of relative valorization: educational success, hard work, and strong family bonds.[29] But Asian Americans, construed as "forever foreigners" from their long legal history as aliens ineligible for citizenship in the United States, face "civic ostracism" in contrast to African Americans' claim on American citizenship and identity.[30]

As both forms of comparative racialization, racial triangulation reveals racial laundering. Comparative racialization analyzes the ways in which the state and power elites position differently racialized individuals and groups in relation to one another, often establishing racial hierarchies that concentrate more resources and rights at the top and with each subordinate level accorded fewer resources. Comparative racialization identifies how elites force different racial groups to compete with one another for resources such as education, jobs, or even citizenship protections; use the putative successes of a particular racial group to demean the abilities, morals, or values of other groups; and promote the success of one racial group in order to dismantle governmental programs or policies that attempt to create equal outcomes for other racial groups.

The VRA's success creates a new model minority, a new racial group that is used to criticize other racial groups and marshal public opinion against racial remedies such as the VRA itself. The *Shelby County v. Holder* opinion identifies African American voters in the six southern states covered under the VRA formula as a model minority of voters, and thus the voting successes of this group emerges as the reason to dismantle the VRA. As many critics of *Shelby* have already noted, the Roberts Court uses the success of the VRA in achieving or even exceeding parity in black and white voter registration to dismantle a coverage formula and preclearance mechanism that enabled its success in the first place. *Shelby* cites Senior Circuit Judge Stephen F. Williams's dissenting opinion of the federal appeals court that upheld the VRA and decided against the plaintiff Shelby County in 2012 in which he correlated inclusion under the coverage formula to higher black registration or turnout as well as more black elected officials. Moreover, the judge compared what he determined the "five worst uncovered jurisdictions" to have worse records than eight of the covered jurisdictions.[31]

This argumentation oddly implies that the parity achieved by state, county, and local election commissions was voluntarily achieved rather than resulting from Section 4 and 5 enforcement that Roberts's opinion deems extraordinary measures. Thus, *Shelby County v. Holder* identifies a deracialized model minority in terms of institutions: the successful group is in fact, none other than the voting commissions of the formerly covered states and districts who created this parity in white-black voter registration and eligibility. In this way, Roberts's majority opinion racially launders the initial conditions that forced these states into coverage in the first place. Moreover, the *Shelby* majority makes no mention of parity for Native American, Asian American, and Latina/o voter registrations with white or black numbers. In 1975 the VRA was reauthorized and amended to include language minorities, which brought additional states and voting districts into coverage beyond the original six states already addressed by the 1965 VRA. These language minorities would also be affected by the *Shelby* decision.

Given that the percentages of registered voters to eligible voters when compared with whites activates the coverage formula, this benchmark resulted in entire states and voting districts with substantial indigenous and Latina/o populations brought under the coverage of the VRA and with Asian and language minority voters such as New York and California to become "bailed-in" and subject to preclearance. Furthermore, because the identity of the New South is shifting due to its changing racial demographics, the numbers of Asian Americans and Latinas/os are increasing in the original southern states that fell under the coverage formula in the early years of the VRA. The *Shelby County v. Holder* opinion's specific reference to "tests" also reveals that the majority's understanding of the VRA appears stuck forty years in the past: the opinion ignores the VRA reauthorization and amendments of 1975 that extended the original language of "tests and devices" to also mean English-only ballots and election materials and created the protected voter category of "language minorities" whose low registration and turnout could also trigger Section 5 coverage.

In this way, the Roberts Court narrowly focuses on black-white comparisons and gives cursory mention of how the VRA continues to help nonblack racial and language minority voters through the coverage formula. The *Shelby* majority, in its largely singular attention to comparisons between white and black voters and officeholders, presumes that progressive gains of the civil rights movement only affected African Americans, despite its having a much broader impact. Even Congress, for its voluminous records of voter suppression targeting various racial groups and its eventual passage of the twenty-five year extension to the VRA, also initially emphasized the recognition of black civil rights heroes, evident in the "short title" of the VRA reauthorization and amendments passed in 2006: the Fannie Lou Hamer, Rosa Parks, and Coretta Scott King Act, which was then retitled by a 2008 amendment to include African American House Representative Barbara Jordan (D-Texas) as well as Chicano civil rights leaders Cesar E. Chávez, William Velásquez, and Dr. Héctor Garcia.[32]

The Voting Rights Act commemorates not only the extraordinary lives of these civil rights leaders but also the thousands of others who had given or jeopardized their lives for the right to vote. Senator Patrick Leahy (D-Vermont), in introducing this bill, argued that the change in the short title "is overdue recognition of the importance of the Voting Rights Act to Hispanic-Americans" and connects African American civil rights struggles to those of Latinas/os who, "like minorities of all races, faced major barriers to participation in the political process, through the use of such devices as poll taxes, exclusionary primaries, intimidation by voting officials, language barriers, and systematic vote dilution."[33] Specifically mentioning Chávez, Senator Leahy argued it was "an important recognition of the broad landscape of political inclusion made possible by the Voting Rights Act."[34]

However, this after-the-fact inclusion is a telling example of how other racial and language minorities such as Latinas/os are viewed as an afterthought to the VRA even by its supporters and not one of its target populations, despite their experiences with voter suppression and low percentages of registered to eligible voters that have triggered the Section 5 coverage in the states of Arizona, Florida, and Texas and counties in

California and New York.[35] Both anti-racist and inequality activists inadvertently promote this narrow understanding of the civil rights movement and its broader impact on multiple racial groups and language minorities.

The Shelby Court majority deems second-generation barriers of vote dilution—racial gerrymandering, selective annexation, or at-large elections, for example—more of a problem of "electoral arrangement" rather than the abridgment of the right to vote. As such, the court majority concentrates on the barriers to casting one's vote rather than how one's vote might be counted. To return to the stated intent of President Lyndon Johnson in his speech on the passage of the Voting Rights Act, the right to choose one's leaders is "the most basic right of all," and going on to explain: "Many of the issues of civil rights are very complex and most difficult. But about this there can and should be no argument. Every American citizen must have an equal right to vote. There is no reason which can excuse the denial of that right. There is no duty which weighs more heavily on us than the duty we have to ensure that right."[36] Despite this sentiment, the *Shelby* majority, with Justice Clarence Thomas concurring, contends that voting disparities are not as bad as the "extraordinary" circumstances that warranted the 1965 VRA. Although the percentage of eligible and registered African Americans compares favorably with white voters, other racial and language minority voters such as Latina/o, Asian American, and indigenous do not.

Just as the Shelby Court argues Congress's Section 4 coverage formula has not evolved to address the contemporary moment, so does the majority fail to recognize ever-changing voter restrictions. The decision effectively continues to allow the exclusion of these voters under second-generation barriers, but the court majority uses the time-honored, if little-acknowledged strategy of the post–civil rights era: racial competition and triangulation, most often manifested as the model minority thesis that has been used to explain Asian American success. The Shelby Court dismantled the VRA by using the successful increases in African American voter registration to obfuscate the disparities in voting for other vulnerable groups that also include disenfranchised black voters in non-covered jurisdictions. The court majority effectively purges fifty years of preemptive mechanisms and regulatory oversight that has produced these favorable comparisons as if they were created voluntarily by the inexplicably racially enlightened and equality-motivated largesse of formerly discriminatory jurisdictions. This logic drives Justice Ginsberg's criticism:

"throwing out preclearance when it has worked and is continuing to work to stop discriminatory changes is like throwing away your umbrella in a rainstorm because you are not getting wet."[37]

DWR or Driving While Redheaded

Both Chief Justice Roberts's majority opinion and Justice Ruth Bader Ginsberg's dissent use plainspoken analogies to encapsulate their opposing arguments and make their reasoning toward different outcomes commonsense for their audiences. While these analogies might be perceived as minor offhand remarks, both are so memorable that they have been repeated in news coverage, editorials, and scholarship as the essence of the right or wrong of either side's argumentation. Justice Ginsberg uses the umbrella and rainstorm analogy mentioned above to expose that the coverage formula and oversight it triggered was so effective people like the justices in the court majority now believe these conditions without voting barriers are achievable without VRA mechanisms. Chief Justice Roberts responds with his own analogy that attacks Justice Ginsberg's assertion that the covered Shelby County plaintiff and other political subdivisions like it have no legal ground to "complain" because they could have "bailed-out" of coverage with a clean record that evidenced parity in racial and language minority voting. Chief Justice Roberts compares the complainants, the allegedly unfairly burdened covered jurisdictions with long histories of violations, to automobile drivers who are charged with additional offenses after they are initially profiled and stopped by police: "But that is like saying that a driver pulled over pursuant to a policy of stopping all redheads cannot complain about that policy, if it turns out his license has expired."[38] Because the state of Alabama was one of the original covered states in the 1965 VRA, the *Shelby County v. Holder* opinion likens preclearance to a kind of guilty-until-proven-innocent judgment that seems anathema to the ideal of presumed innocence allegedly foundational to the U.S. legal system and ostensibly the same logic that governs police profiling, in this case, of drivers with red hair.

Chief Justice Roberts's analogy also relies on the dissent's anticipated rejection of racial profiling. For the Shelby Court, if stop and frisk or search and seizure based on one's racial identity are unconstitutional, covered jurisdictions are victimized like these racialized subjects. This analogy is particularly resonant as an instructive example of racial laundering that defines black and brown experiences. I posit that this analogy functions to parody concerns of racial (and language) minority groups, issues that daily threaten the security and safety of black and brown bodies under perpetual surveillance.

The analogy also alludes to the racial terror perpetrated by the police since Jim Crow: the violent, sometimes fatal ways police prevented African Americans from voting to police stops of black drivers, male and female, that have resulted in their murder on the spot or death under suspicious circumstances while in police custody. The absurdity of the profiling of red-haired people only works because it relies on an assurance that red-headed drivers would never be pulled over via profiling; yet if the statistical evidence bears it out, then red-haired black and brown drivers, along with drivers of all hair colors from these racially marked groups would be disproportionately pulled over. Thus, Roberts's seemingly racially neutral physical marker of hair color is a racial sign of whiteness as well as a long-standing ethnic identifier of Scots-Irish descent, when these white ethnicities were once racialized in the United States.[39]

The Supreme Court justices in the majority provocatively spit in the eye of voting rights advocates by likening the federal government's forcing some states into preclearance to the hypothetical arbitrary traffic stops targeting drivers with red hair who might then face fines for having expired licenses. The court majority uses this multilayered analogy to invalidate the dissent's claims that covered jurisdictions are hardly deserving of being released from federal oversight such as the plaintiff in the case, Shelby County, have no right to complain about their allegedly unequal treatment given their pre-1965 histories of racially skewed voter registration. Moreover, these VRA-covered jurisdictions have been unable to bail out of these provisions because they could not prove ten years of nondiscriminatory voter registration.

This awkward and misleading analogy has spawned numerous improvements on the hypothetical by legal critics such as Richard Hasen who argues a more appropriate one would have been if drivers convicted of DUIs were forced to drive with stickers on their cars and thus were pulled over at higher rates and the voting rights lawyer and scholar Samuel Spital's scenario in which a twelve-year-old driver could challenge the sixteen-year-old age requirement by saying fifteen-year-old drivers are safer than ninety-eight-year old ones, alluding to covered jurisdictions being "safer" for voters or having fewer restrictions on historically marginalized voters than non-covered ones, respectively. Rather than improving Roberts's flawed analogy, I am more interested in the commentary it reveals in the *Shelby* majority's historicization of the modern civil rights movement, its legislative and judicial achievements. Most important, the Roberts Court deploys a particular legal memory of the movement's continuing legacy that justifies the preservation or dismantling of state mechanisms that counter racial discrimination and inequality.

The brevity of this quip is consistent with the rest of the majority opinion. The inappropriateness of this analogy is stunning not only because the conservative court majority has reanimated equal sovereignty without acknowledging this principle's roots in justifying slavery through states' rights but also because it has flippantly transmuted driving while black and brown—racial profiling in which human and financial costs are disproportionately borne by communities of color—into the implausible and ostensibly racially neutral red hair color as signaling discrimination. Just as the court uses this flippant analogy to ignore racialized populations that have been made historically vulnerable to racist policing and vigilante terrorism in driving and, here more specifically, in voting, the court also conspicuously ignores how difficult it has been for civil rights organizations and the Justice Department to deter racial profiling and prevent the escalation to deadly force, even if redheaded drivers had a collective grievance, much less the more aggrieved racial minority drivers.

Moreover, these daily, hourly, occurrences of racially imbalanced ticketing and traffic stops have been cited as one of the long-standing frustrations black residents have felt in Ferguson, Missouri—the disproportionate monetary burdens of traffic ticket revenue from African American drivers that support the tax base of the town itself, in addition of the police officer shooting of Michael Brown in August 2014 that sparked worldwide protests. Furthermore, second-generation barriers of at-large elections have diluted the majority-black population of Ferguson and resulted in the overwhelmingly white city leaders who were elected prior to the international attention from Brown's death.[40]

The Shelby Court's racial laundering obscures black and brown vulnerability to traffic stops. Racial laundering not only minimizes the harm faced by some populations but also in its ostensible absurdity, ridicules the concerns of individuals and communities victimized by disproportionate traffic citations, harassment, injury, or even death. Roberts's *Shelby County v. Holder* opinion relies on the apparent obviousness that it would be absurd for white drivers, albeit with the offending hair color, to be treated in this manner, yet by not using the more controversial, long-standing issues of Driving While Black and Driving While Brown, the omission implies that it is not absurd for black and brown drivers to be treated this way.

Racial Laundering, with No Umbrella

If voting truly is the most cherished right of citizenship, then it would follow that any measure to prevent this central form of democratic participation would fall under strict scrutiny: these protections must be narrowly tailored to produce the intended outcome. However, the Voting Rights Act had some flaws that the Shelby Court exploited. I posit several ways the Supreme Court justices in the majority engaged in acts of racial laundering that rationalize and minimize the effects on vulnerable, racialized populations that go beyond the common explanations for their motivations, deregulation, and small government.

In terms of trust, voters might believe that local and state lawmakers would only create reasonable and nondiscriminatory laws and restrictions. Elected by the people, the expectation is that these officials will be voted out of office if they do something against the law or popular will. In terms of merit, voters might believe that people who are prevented from voting either do not deserve to vote or are not meeting the standards for voting that the state or jurisdiction maintains. In this logic, those denied the franchise are expected to be able to fulfill the additional requirements for a voter identification, which may mean driving the 250 miles to apply or affording the costs of a driver's or concealed-gun licenses that could serve as approved identification.

That the covered jurisdictions such as Shelby County were not eligible for bailout when the decision was handed down in 2013 should have given the court pause. In essence, the majority opinion implies that we should trust voting districts and election boards that have not merited bailout with a clean record and, in comparing the worse registration and voting records of some non-covered jurisdictions, that either these non-covered areas should also be trusted, should not be brought into coverage, or that all voting districts should be brought into coverage instead of none, *Shelby*'s default outcome. Because trust and merit are often the standards and measures implicitly or explicitly applied to individual plaintiffs in cases under equal protection jurisprudence, determinations of trust and merit are often racially laundered terms. Shelby County and other covered jurisdictions had not merited bailout in the forty years since the VRA had been amended to provide the bailout and bail-in provisions, meaning that this voting jurisdiction among many others had continued to violate the VRA with repeated attempts to implement discriminatory voting changes (of which the dissent provided some of the most flagrant ones), or otherwise failed to earn a clean record for ten years.

Of course, in *Shelby County v. Holder*, the Roberts Court majority had to overlook the proliferating and inventive twenty-first century derivatives of first-generation barriers: requiring voter ID, purging voter rolls, using inaccurate databases such as SAVE (Systematic Alien Verification for Entitlements) and the Interstate Cross-Check Program, making polling places more inaccessible, or reducing numbers of polling places, and restricting voting hours. In essence, the majority opinion uses a post-racial amnesia in a post–civil rights context. Yes, the VRA is a victim of its own success, but success the Shelby Court and its supporters have defined in very narrow, racially laundered terms.

Notes

I thank Krista Benson, Nick Cobb, Anna Lunsford, Trina Thomas, Hannah Tuschman, and Quinn Vela for research assistance. For their suggestions, I thank Devin Fergus, Jennifer Gully, and the organizers: Brian Ward, Henry Knight Lozano, and Joe Street, as well as the participants of the *Shadow of Selma: Selma and the Voting Rights Act, 1965–2015* symposium at Northumbria University.

1. In the 2010 Citizens United v. Federal Election Commission (FEC) decision, Justice Anthony Kennedy, writing for the majority, posited specific notions of citizenship through his articulation of the rights of corporate and noncorporate (human) speakers, viewing human speakers as unjustly preferred over disfavored corporate ones. This controversial, landmark decision would soon be followed by the campaign finance reform rulings of the 2011 Arizona Free Enterprise Club's Freedom Club PAC v. Bennett and 2014 McCutcheon v. FEC that would more firmly cement the foundation of the Roberts Court's interpretation of free speech, voting rights, and corporate personhood. For a more detailed discussion of economic definitions of citizenship in recent Supreme Court campaign finance reform decisions, see Lynn Itagaki, "United States, Inc.: *Citizens United* and the Shareholder Citizen," *Kalfou: A Journal of Comparative and Relational Ethnic Studies* 1, no. 2 (Fall 2014): 114–37.

2. See Michael Schudson, *The Good Citizen: A History of American Civic Life* (Cambridge: Harvard University Press, 1998).

3. Racial laundering is similar to what sociologist Eduardo Bonilla-Silva has called color-blind racism and identified abstract liberalism as its foundational frame that "involves using ideas associated with political liberalism (e.g., 'equal opportunity,' the idea that force should not be used to achieve social policy) and economic liberalism (e.g., choice, individualism) in an *abstract* manner to explain racial matters"; Eduardo Bonilla-Silva, *Racism without Racists: Color-Blind Racism and the Persistence of Racial Inequality in the United States* (Lanham, MD: Rowman and Littlefield, 2003), 28, original emphasis.

4. Elsewhere I have discussed the relationship between national belonging through membership in political communities and who is perceived as civil and thus meriting full citizenship and full humanity; see Lynn Itagaki, *Civil Racism: The 1992 Los Angeles Rebellion and the Crisis of Racial Burnout* (Minneapolis: University of Minnesota Press, 2016) for more detailed discussion.

5. Some strategies that obfuscate racist intent are those that Bonilla-Silva identifies as frames: abstract liberalism, naturalization of racist outcomes, minimization of racism, and cultural racism. Critical race scholar Sumi Cho identifies four features of post-racialism: racial progress and transcendence, race-neutral universalism, moral equivalence, and distancing moves. See Bonilla-Silva, *Racism without Racists*; Sumi Cho, "Post-Racialism," *Iowa Law Review* 94 (2008–2009): 1589–1649.

6. See Itagaki, *Civil Racism*, 1–36.

7. William H. Chafe, *Civilities and Civil Rights: Greensboro, North Carolina, and the Black Struggle for Freedom* (Oxford: Oxford University Press, 1981), vii–viii.

8. Ian F. Haney-López, "Is the 'Post' in the Post-Racial the 'Blind' in Colorblind?," *Cardozo Law Review* 32, no. 3 (2011): 829–30.

9. Sumi Cho, "Post-Racialism" *Iowa Law Review* Vol. 94 (2008–2009), 1589–1649.

10. Howard Winant, *Racial Conditions: Politics, Theory, Comparisons* (Minneapolis: University of Minneapolis Press, 1994), 39; and Michael Omi and Howard Winant, *Racial Formation in the United States*, 3rd ed. (New York: Routledge, 2014), 132.

11. See Kimberlé Williams Crenshaw, "Race, Reform, and Retrenchment: Transformation and Legitimation in Antidiscrimination Law," *Harvard Law Review* 101 (1988): 1331–87.

12. See Neil Smith, *The New Urban Frontier: Gentrification and the Revanchist City* (New York: Routledge, 1996).

13. See Jacqueline Dowd Hall, "The Long Civil Rights Movement and the Political Uses of the Past," *Journal of American History* 91 (March 2005): 1233–63.

14. Elsewhere I have discussed the beginning of the post–civil rights era with the passage of the 1968 Fair Housing Act and the assassination of Dr. Martin Luther King Jr; see Itagaki, *Civil Racism*, 1–36. Cho posits a later beginning to the era marked by the conservative Rehnquist Court from 1986, and the post-racial era beginning with the landmark case Parents Involved in Community Schools v. Seattle School District No. 1 handed down in 2007. In addition to Crenshaw's term "racial retrenchment," I also cite here Dana Y. Takagi, *The Retreat from Race: Asian-American Admissions and Racial Politics* (New Brunswick, NJ: Rutgers University Press, 1992).

15. Congress not only reauthorized the VRA before it expired in 1975 but it also expanded the original meaning of "tests and devices" to incorporate English-only ballots

and election materials for language minorities, American Indian, Alaskan natives, Asian, and Spanish heritage.

16. Richard L. Hasen, "*Citizens United* and the Illusion of Coherence," *Michigan Law Review* 109 (February 2011): n178.

17. Richard L. Hasen, "Shelby County and the Illusion of Minimalism," *William & Mary Bill of Rights Journal* 22, no. 3 (2014): 714.

18. Northwest Austin Municipal Utility District No. 1 v. Holder, 557 U.S. 193 (2009), 7, 8. Available at https://www.supremecourt.gov/opinions/08pdf/08-322/pdf.

19. Eric Posner, "John Roberts' Opinion on the Voting Rights Act Is Really Lame," *Slate*.com (June 25, 2013) (consulted March 22, 2017); Richard A. Posner, "The Voting Rights Act Ruling Is about the Conservative Imagination," *Slate*.com, June 26, 2013, at http://www.slate.com/articles/news_and_politics/the_breakfast_table/features/2013/supreme_court_2013/the_supreme_court_and_the_voting_rights_act_striking_down_the_law_is_all.html (consulted March 22, 2017).

20. James Blacksher and Lani Guinier, "Free at Last: Rejecting Equal Sovereignty and Restoring the Constitutional Right to Vote: *Shelby County v. Holder*," *Harvard Law and Policy Review* 8 (2014): 39.

21. Ibid., 39–40.

22. In addition to the denial of voting rights, black freedmen and women were often denied the right to bear arms, to have freedom of speech, and to travel.

23. Dred Scott v. Sandford, 404–5.

24. Ibid.

25. Ibid., 404–5.

26. See Stephen J. McNamee and Robert K. Miller Jr., *The Meritocracy Myth*, 3rd ed. (Lanham, MD: Rowman and Littlefield, 2014).

27. Shelby County v. Holder, slip op. at 23–24.

28. The concern for political equality returns in Justice Ginsberg's dissent: "The grand aim of the Act is to secure to all in our polity equal citizenship stature, a voice in our democracy undiluted by race. As the record for the 2006 reauthorization makes abundantly clear, second-generation barriers to minority voting rights have emerged in the covered jurisdictions as attempted *substitutes* for the first-generation barriers that originally triggered preclearance in those jurisdictions. But the court disregards what Congress set about to do in enacting the VRA. That extraordinary legislation scarcely stopped at the particular tests and devices that happened to exist in 1965" [original emphasis]; Shelby County v. Holder, slip op. at 66.

29. See Claire Jean Kim, "The Racial Triangulation of Asian Americans," *Politics and Society* 27, no. 1 (March 1999): 105–38.

30. See Mia Tuan, *Forever Foreigners Or Honorary Whites?: The Asian Ethnic Experience Today* (New Brunswick, NJ: Rutgers University Press, 1998); and Kim, "The Racial Triangulation of Asian Americans," 107.

31. Of course, such data could be interpreted that either those uncovered jurisdictions need to fall under a newer, stringent coverage formula, or that preclearance should apply to all states and political subdivisions in the nation. In dismissing these arguments, Judge Williams uses an analogy of his own: "Of course sometimes a skilled dart-thrower can

hit the bull's eye throwing a dart backwards over his shoulder." It is his dissent and the Shelby Court majority that have turned their backs on history.

32. The first black woman from the South to be elected to the U.S. House of Representatives, Barbara Jordan introduced the VRA amendment in 1975 to add language minorities under the jurisdiction of the legislation. Cesar Chávez was an internationally renowned labor leader of the United Farm Workers in central California. William Velásquez was the founder of the Southwest Voter Registration Education Project that facilitated get-out-the-vote campaigns throughout the southwestern United States. Dr. Héctor Garcia was a World War II veteran who founded the American G.I. Forum to advocate for Mexican American veterans and fight segregation in Texas.

33. Senator Leahy, speaking on S. 188, 110th Cong., 1st sess., Congressional Record Volume 153, Number 29 (Thursday, February 15, 2007): S2115–S2116.

34. Ibid.

35. Senator Leahy notes that the bill's sponsor, Senator Ken Salazar (D-Colorado), did not want to interfere with the passage of the original amendment in 2006 and so did not push to change the title then (ibid). While the 2008 legislation is just a name change in which the reauthorization and amendments remain the same, the spirit of recognition and symbolism that marks the titling of this amendment is significant.

36. Lyndon B. Johnson, "Speech Before Congress on Voting Rights," Miller Center (March 15, 1965), at http://millercenter.org/president/speeches/speech-3386 (consulted March 22, 2017).

37. Shelby County v. Holder, slip op. at 33.

38. Ibid. at 22.

39. See Matthew Frye Jacobson, *Roots Too: White Ethnic Revival in Post–Civil Rights America* (Cambridge: Harvard University Press, 2006) for a discussion of how white supremacy has been superseded in the post–civil rights era by white "primacy," or the focus on white ethnic identities alongside nonwhite racialized ones within a multicultural paradigm.

40. "Race and Voting Rights in Ferguson," *New York Times*, January 4, 2015, at https://www.nytimes.com/2015/01/05/opinion/race-and-voting-rights-in-ferguson.html?_r=0 (consulted March 22, 2017).

CONTRIBUTORS

Tony Badger is professor in American history, Northumbria University. He is Emeritus Paul Mellon Professor of American History, Cambridge University. He has written extensively on the New Deal and on the post-1945 South. He has just completed a biography of Albert Gore Sr.

Alma Jean Billingslea Brown is professor emerita at the Department of English, Spelman College. She is the author of *Crossing Borders through Folklore: African American Women's Fiction and Art* and has published on black women's fiction and civil rights biography.

Aniko Bodroghkozy is professor of media studies at the University of Virginia. Her books include *Equal Time: Television and the Civil Rights Movement*, *Groove Tube: Sixties Television and the Youth Rebellion*, and an anthology, *A Companion to the History of American Broadcasting*. Currently she is completing two book projects: *#birmingham #selma #charlottesville* and *Black Weekend: Television News and the Kennedy Assassination*.

Barbara Harris Combs is associate professor in the Department of Sociology and Criminal Justice at Clark Atlanta University in Atlanta, Georgia. Her research focuses on the role place (as a geographical, social/cultural, and class construct) has on modern identity formation and human relations, especially race relations. She is the author of *From Selma to Montgomery: The Long March to Freedom*. She has published in many academic journals and is completing a book project titled *Blackout: The Continuing Assault against Black Bodies*.

Devin Fergus is associate professor of African American and African studies at Ohio State University. His research focuses on the historical mechanisms driving contemporary inequality. He is the author of *Land of the Fee: Hidden Costs and the Decline of the American Middle Class* and *Liberalism, Black Power, and the Making of American Politics, 1965–1980*.

Benjamin Houston is senior lecturer at Newcastle University, teaching modern U.S. and civil rights history. He is the author of *The Nashville Way: Racial Etiquette and the Struggle for Social Justice in a Southern City*.

Megan Hunt is teaching fellow in American History at the University of Edinburgh. She is working on her first monograph, *Southern by the Grace of God: Religion, Race, and Civil Rights in Hollywood's South*, having previously published on films such as *Mississippi Burning*, *The Help*, and here, *Selma*. She has also conducted research into the African American freedom struggle as taught in the UK, and developed teaching materials and resources for schools.

Lynn Mie Itagaki is associate professor in the departments of English and Women's, Gender, and Sexuality Studies at Ohio State University. Her recent book, *Civil Racism: The 1992 Los Angeles Rebellion and the Crisis of Racial Burnout*, examines literary and filmic representations of multiracial urban violence in the post–cold war and post–civil rights eras.

George Lewis is head of the School of History, Politics, and International Relations at the University of Leicester. His work focuses on race relations, civil rights, white supremacy, and American radicalism, antiradicalism, and anticommunism. He is the author of *Massive Resistance: The White Response to the Civil Rights Movement* and *The White South and the Red Menace: Segregationists, Anticommunism, and Massive Resistance*.

Peter Ling is professor of American studies at the University of Nottingham. His work combines history, sociology, cultural studies, and memory studies. He is the author of acclaimed biographies of John F. Kennedy and Martin Luther King Jr. and coedited *Gender in the Civil Rights Movement* with Sharon Monteith.

Henry Knight Lozano is senior lecturer in American history at the University of Exeter. His research focuses on race, environment, expansion, and regional identities in American history. His first book, *Tropic of Hopes: California, Florida, and the Selling of American Paradise, 1869–1929*, won a Florida Book Award Gold Medal and was joint winner of the British Association for American Studies's Arthur Miller Center First Book Prize.

Mark McLay is lecturer in history at the University of Glasgow. He is the author of the forthcoming book *The Elephant in the Room: The White House, the Republican party, and the War on Poverty*. His work has been published in the *Journal of Policy History* and the *Historical Journal*, and he is the co-host of the popular *American History Too! Podcast*.

Joe Street is associate professor in history at Northumbria University, Newcastle. He is the author of *Dirty Harry's America: Clint Eastwood, Harry Callahan, and the Conservative Backlash*; *The Culture War in the Civil Rights Movement*; and numerous articles on African American radicalism in the 1960s.

Mark Walmsley is lecturer in the humanities at the University of East Anglia and received his PhD from the University of Leeds in 2016. His academic research examines the impact that news production had on social activism in the 1950s and 1960s and how this has affected our understanding of the black freedom struggle and gay liberation in particular.

Clive Webb is professor of modern American history at the University of Sussex. His publications include *Forgotten Dead: Mob Violence against Mexicans in the United States, 1848–1928*; *Rabble Rousers: The American Far Right in the Civil Rights Era*; and *Fight against Fear: Southern Jews and Black Civil Rights*.

INDEX

Page numbers in *italics* refer to figures or tables.

Abbott, Greg, 251
Abernathy, Ralph, 64, 182, 208
Adler, Renata, 185
Advancement Project in Wisconsin, 252
Affirmative Action, 276
African Americans, 9, 279; elected officials, 96–97, 109, 217
Alabama, 86, 97, 107, 108, 124, 252; legislative black caucus, 252; State Legislature, 160; state troopers, 22, 23–24, 51, 66, 68, 70, 72, 87, 117, 124, 133, *135f*, 136, 138, 140, 141, 142, 146, 176, *177f*, 178, *179f*, *180f*
Albany, Georgia, 58, 155, 157
Allison, Bob, 161
Alternative Mortgage Transaction Parity Act, 231
American Civil War, 6, 16–17, 26, 71
American Jewish Committee, 201–2
Arizona, 252–53, 279
Asian Americans, 276–77, 278. *See also* Model minority
A Time to Kill (Schumacher), 203, 207, 208–9
Atlanta, Georgia, 226–27
Atwater, Lee, 255
Austin, Texas, 79, 247, 252

Baker, Ella, 19
Baker, Wilson, 60–61, 64, 103
Ballard, Kim, 172
Bevel, James, 43–44, 50, 62, 67; in *Selma*, 206
Birmingham, Alabama, 155. *See also* Southern Christian Leadership Conference
Birmingham News, 181

Black, Hugo, 249
Black Lives Matter movement, 2–3
Black Panther Party, 154
Black Power, 38, 58, 73, 153, 158, 163–64
Black press, 183–84
"Bloody Sunday," 5, 7, 42, 48, 66, 87–88, 89, 113, 269; international response to, 117, 124; media representation of, 8, 16, 23–24, 25, 31, 37, 68, 101, 133–34, *135f*, 136, 138–39, 140, 146, 157, 159–60, *177f*; in *Selma*, 136, *137f*, 146, 204
"Bodies Out of Place," 10, 246, 247, 248–50, 255, 257, 258n9; definition of, 241–43
Bond, Julian, 28, 155, 188
Boynton, Amelia, 38, 40, 61, 87; in *Selma*, 136, *137f*, 144
Boynton, Sam, 38
Brennan Center for Justice, 248, 252–53
Brown, Michael, 2–3, 139–40, 191, 254, 283
Brown Chapel AME Church, Selma, 48, 64, 68, 70, 171, 181, 185, 205. *See also* Selma campaign
Brown v. Board of Education of Topeka, Kansas, 39, 47, 80, 153, 188, 200, 245
Bush, George H. W., 109
The Butler (Daniels), 143, 144
"Bye Bye Blackbird" (song), 185
Byrd, Harry, 102

Califano, Joseph A., 15, 20, 86, 144
California, 278, 280
Campaign finance, 10, 271–72
Capell, Arthur, 61
Carmichael, Stokely, 71
Carrier, Jim, 151
Carter, Hodding, III, 97

Carter, Jimmy, 108
CBS, 161
Charlotte, North Carolina, 223
Chávez, Cesar E., 279, 288n32
Chestnut, J. L., Jr., 39, 42, 47, 52
Citizens' Council, 187
Citizenship, 246–47, 273–74, 286n4; corporate/shareholder, 270–71
Citizens United v. FEC, 270–71, 285n1
Civil disobedience, 3
Civil Rights Act (1957), 18–19, 81, 97, 98, 101–2
Civil Rights Act (1964), 7, 45, 58, 62–63, 78, 79, 81, 82, 84, 85, 88, 102, 108, 120, 147, 254, 268; Albert Gore and, 97–100, 101–2; Community Relations Service, 61, 64, 69–70; Title VI, 98, 99–100; Title VII, 103, 218
Civil Rights Act (1968), 78, 101, 268, 286n14
Civil rights movement. *See specific topics*
Clark, Jim, 7, 42, 43, 45, 48, 51, 59, 60–62, 64–65, 66, 68–69, 73, 86, 103, 145, 156, 158, 161, 178, 181, 184; in *Selma*, 142, 210; unrepentance of, 189–90
Clark, Kenneth, 245
Clark, Mamie, 245
Clinton, Hillary, 147, 171
Clinton, William J., 109
Cold War, 113, 121, 179, 181, 269
Color-blindness, 10, 233, 241–42, 249, 255–57, 267–68. *See also* Post-racialism
Common, 1, 2, 206
Community Reinvestment Act, 232
Confederate States of America, 6
Congressional Black Caucus, 255
Congress of Racial Equality, 28, 155
Connor, Eugene "Bull," 7, 59, 161–62, 189
Cook, William, 161
Cooper, Annie Lee, 7, 46, 61–62, 146, 161; in *Selma*, 144–46, 145f
Council of Economic Advisers, 225
Crawford, Kenneth, 157
Critical Race Theory, 242–43, 269
Cullors, Patrisse, 3
Cumming, Joe, 160, 163

Dallas County deputies, 23–24
Dallas County Voters League, 38, 40, 46, 61
Daniels, Jonathan Myrick, 25–26, 31, 71–72
Darby, Walter L., Sr., 186

De La Beckwith, Byron, 198
DeLaughter, Bobby, 198
Democratic Party, 109, 246
Demonstrations. *See specific locations and campaigns*
Demos, 220, 236n35
Department of Justice, 37, 51, 68, 87, 140, 254, 260n46
Depository Institutions Deregulation and Monetary Control Act, 230–33
Detroit, Michigan, 153
Dirksen, Everett, 63, 68, 84, 98
Disfranchisement, 18
"Dixie" (song), 185
Doar, John, 203
Donovan, Hedley, 150
Dorn, Williams Jennings Bryan, 96–97
Do The Right Thing (Lee), 207
Douglas, Emily Taft, 141, 175
Douglas, Paul, 141, 175
Dred Scott v Sandford, 273–74
DuVernay, Ava, 1–2, 5, 15, 77, 92, 133, 136–37, 141–46, 150, 207

Ebony, 184
Economic mobility of African Americans, 217–24, 232–33
Edmund Pettus Bridge, 3, 4, 27, 68, 70, 72, 87, 113, 121, 133, 139, 162, 181, 205, 240; depicted in mass media, 135f, 180f; as metaphor, 16, 20–21, 25, 31–32; in *Selma*, 136, 137f, 150, 199, 202; as site of memory, 22–24, 171, 191
Elliott, Osborne, 152
Equal Credit Opportunity Act, 232
Equality of Opportunity Project, 223
Equal Sovereignty Principle, 271, 273–75
Evenwel v. Abbott, 252, 261n65
Evers, Medgar, 42, 198
Evers, Myrlie, 198

Fair Employment Practices Committee, 244
Fair Housing Act (1968). *See* Civil Rights Act (1968)
Farmer, James, 182
Fauntroy, Walter, 64
Federal Bureau of Investigation, 199. *See also* Hoover, J. Edgar
Federal government, 97

Ferguson, Missouri, 2–3, 4, 139–40, 165, 254–55, 283
Fifteenth Amendment, 17, 245, 266, 273–74
"Fight the Power" (song), 207
Financial crisis (2007), 231, 269, 270
Financial deregulation, 10. *See also* Racial inequality
First Baptist Church (Selma), 171
Fleming, Karl, 160
Florida, 279
Forman, James, 69, 71, 90, 160, 182
Forrest, Nathan Bedford, 17
Foster, Marie, 39, 40
Fourteenth Amendment, 273–74
France, 8, 113–14, 121–24, 126–27; media response to Selma, 123–26
Frankel, Max, 152
Franklin, Aretha, 208

Gandhi, Mahatma, 4, 59
Garcia, Héctor, 279, 288n32
Garner, Eric, 191
Garza, Alicia, 3
Ghosts of Mississippi (Reiner), 143, 196, 198–99
Ginsberg, Ruth Bader, 250, 276, 280–81, 287n27. *See also Shelby County v. Holder*
Gitlin, Todd, 153, 154, 176
Gleason, Ralph J., 158
"Glory" (song), 206
Goldman, Peter, 152, 156–57, 161
Goldwater, Barry, 63, 79, 105
Goodman, Andrew, 201
Good Neighbor League Colored Committee, 244
Gore, Albert, Sr., 96, 97–101, 105, 108
Gospel Coalition, The, 200
Grassroots organizing, 16, 20, 21, 38–42, 49–52; schoolchildren's activism, 42–49
Great Britain. *See* United Kingdom
Guihard, Paul, 122, 162

Hamer, Fannie Lou, 279
The Help (Taylor), 143, 209
Henderson, Roy, 185
Herbers, John, 161
Herron, Matt, 28–30
Heschel, Abraham Joshua, 197, 200–202
Hinckle, Warren, 197

Hispanics. *See* Latinos
Holloway, Frank, 43
Hollywood, 9, 92; "white savior" films, 142–43, 147, 196. *See also specific films*
Homeownership, 221–22, 227–30. *See also* Mortgages; Racial inequality
Hoover, J. Edgar, 77
Horne, Tom, 252–53
Housing Assistance Council, 228
Humphrey, Hubert, 82, 86, 98–100, 124
Hurricane Katrina, 269

Immigration and Nationality Act (1965), 126
Impressions, The, 205
Income, 9, 217–23; and mortgages, 225–31, 227t, 228t, 229t, 238n66; and region, 217–28; and wealth, 9–10, 217–30, 222t, 223t, 224t. *See also* Segregation
Institute on Assets and Social Policy, 221–22, 224, 236n35
Iraq War, 269
"I've Got the New World In My View" (song), 205

Jackson, Jesse, 3
Jackson, Jimmie Lee, 7, 44, 48, 50–51, 66, 70, 72, 87, 141, 142, 148n19, 162, 214n46; in *Selma*, 141–42, 145, 207
Jackson, Mahalia, 208
Jet, 184, 187
Jewish Federation of Montgomery, 202
Jim Crow. *See* Segregation; Segregationists
Johnson, Frank Minis, 181, 186, 188
Johnson, John H., 183
Johnson, Lyndon Baines, 7, 15, 23, 37, 62, 67, 70, 77–92, 101, 126, 147, 189; and George Wallace, 88–89; international opinion of, 117–18, 119–20, 124–25; and Dr. Martin Luther King Jr., 63–65, 81, 84–87, 90–91, 92n2; in *Selma*, 2, 77, 83, 84–86, 92, 141, 142, 143, 144, 147, 201; as Senate majority leader, 81, 98; and the Southern Manifesto, 80–81; as vice president, 81; and voting rights, 16, 19–20, 25, 58, 63–65, 70–71, 78, 83–91, 98–99, 101, 126, 280
Johnson Publishing Company, 183
Jordan, Barbara, 279, 288n32
Judgment at Nuremberg (Kramer), 68, 134, 136

Katzenbach, Nicholas, 84–86, 89, 90, 124, 244–45
"Keep on Pushing" (song), 205–6
Kennedy, John F., 60, 64, 81, 97–98
Kerner Commission, 152
Kilmichael, Mississippi, 251
King, Coretta Scott, 3, 279
King, Dr. Martin Luther, Jr., 4, 16, 18, 19, 20, 24, 59, 72, 113, 125, 147, 188; and Jewish activists, 201–2; "Letter from Birmingham Jail," 60, 73, 81; and Lyndon B. Johnson, 63–65, 78, 81, 84–87, 89, 90–91, 124; and nonviolence, 58–61, 63, 65, 71–73; media focus on, 138, 141; memorialization of, 22, 23, 106–7, 190; Nobel Prize, 62, 85, 119; opposition to the Vietnam War, 58; radicalism of, 191; in *Selma*, 1–2, 77, 84, 85, 141–42, 144, 146, 155, 202, 207–8, 210; during the Selma campaign, 5, 6–7, 25, 32n4, 37, 43, 61–62, 64–71, 73, 86–87, 90–91, 101, 139, 146, 155–56, 178, 217; on voting rights, 217–18
King, Mary, 158
King, Rodney, 2
Knights of the White Camellia, 18
Ku Klux Klan, 9, 17–18, 30, 49, 71, 104, 107–8, 159, 182, 199, 210

Labor Crowding theory, 218–19
Lafayette, Bernard, 18, 67, 37–43, 46, 49, 50, 52–53
Lafayette, Colia, 18, 43, 44
Language minorities, 249, 254, 256, 266, 271, 278–82, 286–87n15, 288n32
Latinos, 251–52, 254, 255, 256, 263n99, 276, 278, 279–80. *See also* Language minorities
Leahy, Patrick, 279, 288n35
Lee, Spike, 207
Legend, John, 1, 206
Leonard, George B., 182
Letherer, Jim, 185
Lewis, John, 5, 26, 44, 90, 151, 164, 191, 254; in *Selma*, 136, *137f*, 144; during the Selma campaign, 67, 68; at Selma memorial events, 3–4, 23, 24, 171
Liberalism, 9. *See also* Johnson, Lyndon Baines
Liberals, well-meaning, 21. *See also specific figures*
LIFE magazine, 176, 178, 181, 182

Lingo, Al, 66, 68–70, 181
Literacy tests, 10
Little Rock, Arkansas, 115, 122, 161
Liu, Wenjian, 191
Liuzzo, Viola, 71, 90, 141–42, 199
Long, Russell, 102
Long, Worth, 44, 49
Los Angeles. *See* Watts Rebellion
Los Angeles Times, 175, 176
Louisiana, 97
Lowery, Joseph, 64, 171
Lowndes County, Alabama, 16, 25–27, 31, 50, 51, 67, 68, 71, 73
Lyons, Danny, 181

Malcolm X (Lee), 2
Manpower Development Corporation, Inc., 225, 230
Mants, Bob, 23
Marion, Alabama, 7, 45, 66, 87, 162
Martin, Spider, 181, 183
Martin, Trayvon, 2–3, 164, 191, 265
Mass media, 16, 201
McCulloch, William, 63
McCutcheon, Shaun, 272
McCutcheon v. Federal Election Commission, 270–71
McKee, Don, 160–61
Memorials, 16–17, 22, 31–32
Memory, historical, 15, 21–22, 24–25, 37, 174, 190–92
Memory, public, 15, 16–17, 24, 27–28
Memphis, Tennessee, 58
Meredith March Against Fear, 58, 163
Migration, 9, 218, *219t*
Mississippi, 82–83, 86, 97, 108, 122; civil rights activism, 63, 65, 73, 103–5; Mississippi Freedom Democratic Party, 62, 81–82. *See also* Student Nonviolent Coordinating Committee
Mississippi Burning (Parker), 142–43, 144, 149n25, 196, 199, 203, 207, 208, 214n54
Model minority, 275–78
Montgomery, Alabama, 66–67, 71
Moore, Charles, 176–78
Morgan, Robert, 231
Mortgages, 9–10, 225–31, 238n66. *See also* Racial inequality

Nash, Diane, 15, 16, 20, 32n1, 144
Nashville, Tennessee, 15
Nation, The, 182
National Association for the Advancement of Colored People, 28, 30–31, 39, 63, 155, 243; Alabama chapter, 189; in *A Time to Kill*, 203–4; Legal Defense and Educational Fund, 251, 254–55; tensions with SCLC, 63, 73
National Association of Evangelicals, 200
National Review, 187–88
National Voting Rights Museum, 27
Native Americans, 278
Naturalization Law (1790), 271
Newark, New Jersey, 153
New Deal, 79–80, 243–44
Newsweek, 152, 156, 157, 160, 161, 163
New York (state), 278, 280
New Yorker, 1, 176, 181, 182–83
New York Times, 1, 151, 152, 157, 160, 175, 176, 185, 190, 198, 250–51
Nixon, Richard M., 101, 105, 255; Southern Strategy of, 109, 256
Nonviolence, 8, 16, 58–60, 65–68, 73, 74nn2,6
North Carolina, 96, 97, 107–8, 223, 252–53
Northwest Austin Municipal Utility District No. 1 v. FEC, 247–48, 273

Obama, Barack, 22–24, 108–9; and Bodies out of Place, 243, 255; and fiftieth anniversary of Selma, 4, 5, 22–23, 31, 171–75, 190–91, 232; and minority voters, 247; and post-racialism, 270
O'Dell, Jack, 18, 20–21, 25
"Ole Miss" (University of Mississippi), 162
Orange, James, 44, 50
Oyelowo, David, 1–2

Parker, Alan, 196
Parks, Rosa, 279
Police oppression, 4, 9, 10, 191, 269, 274, 282
Post–civil rights era, 10, 268–70, 272, 274–75, 280, 286n14, 288n39; and financial deregulation, 233; and racial laundering, 265–66; and racial wealth gap, 221, 224–25; and subprime mortgages, 227
Post-racialism, 255, 266–68, 270, 285

286nn5,14; Obama and, 174, 191, 266; Selma campaign and, 188–90
Powledge, Fred, 160, 161, 163
Presidential election (1936), 243–44, 255
Pritchett, Laurie, 189
Public Enemy, 206–7

"Race beat" journalism, 151–65
Racial inequality, 9–10, 109–10, 217–33, 240–43; in education, 10; and financial deregulation, 230–33; incarceration, 10, 269
"Racial laundering," 10, 264–67, 270, 277, 283–85, 286n3
Racial profiling, 265, 281–83
Racial triangulation, 277
Reagan, Ronald, 109, 220, 269
Reconstruction, 16, 17–18, 21, 217, 246
Reeb, James, 51, 70, 87, 141, 199, 203
Reed, John Shelton, 96–97, 109
Reed, Roy, 150, 159
Reese, Frederick, 41, 46
Reeves, Tate, 251
Reiner, Rob, 196, 198
Religion, *180f*; Christianity, 9; evangelicalism, 196–97, 200; Hollywood depictions of, 196–210; Judaism, 200–202; and Dr. Martin Luther King, 59
Representations of the civil rights movement, 22, 23, 28, *29f*, 31, 62, 113, *135f*, 137–38, 142, 174–75, *179f*, *180f*, *183f*, *184f*, *186f*. See also "Bloody Sunday"; King, Dr. Martin Luther, Jr.; Selma campaign
Republican party, 109–10, 255
Rhodes, Morgan, 204, 205, 207
Roberts, Justice John, 10, 272–73, 275, 276, 281–83
Roberts Court. *See Shelby County v. Holder*
Rolling Stone, 158
Roosevelt, Franklin Delano, 243–44, 251
Russell, Richard, 102
Rustin, Bayard, 181

Salazar, Ken, 288n35
Sanders, Hank, 26–27, 172
"Say It Like It Really Is" (song), 206
Scalia, Antonin, 248
Schapiro, Steven, 185
Schulke, Flip, 178

Schwerner, Michael, 201
Segregation, 6, 7, 8, 16, 38, 52, 97, 106, 108, 174; and business community, 102–3
Segregationists, 9, 97, 174–92; media coverage of, 9, 176–92, *184f*. *See also* Selma campaign
Selma (DuVernay), 1–5, 7–9, 15, 77, 83–85, 150, 197; representation of Lyndon B. Johnson, 2, 77, 83, 84–86, 92, 142, 144, 201; representation of Martin Luther King Jr., 1–2, 77, 84, 85, 141–42, 144, 146, 197, 202–3, 207–8; representation of Selma campaign, 133, 136, *137f*, 141–47, 199–200, 202–3, 204, 210; soundtrack of, 204–9
Selma, Alabama, 3–7, 16–18, 31, 84, 86; civil rights activism prior to 1965, 18–19, 37–43; as site of memory, 22–24, 26–27, 30–31, 70
Selma campaign, 3–8, 9, 15–16, 18, 24–25, 28, 38, 46, 51, 97, 100, 110, *179f, 180f, 183f*; commemorations of, 3–5, 16, 22–23; federal intervention in, 46, 69–71, 73, 88, 89, 90, 121, 124; general media coverage of, 20, 68, 140, 147, 151–52, 174–76, *177f*; international response to, 113–15, 117–21, 123–26; Lyndon B. Johnson and, 63–64, 78, 85–87; Marion protests, 66, 162; and Dr. Martin Luther King Jr., 58, 60, 64, 65–67, 73, 86–87, 90–91, 100, 139, 182, 217; as media event, 133, 139, 150–51, 154–60; night marches, 44, 50–51, 65, 66; print media coverage of, 8–9, 61–62, 64, 70, 134, 136, 140–41, 145, 147, 156–61, 176–77; schoolchildren in, 44–49, 64–65; SCLC tactics and strategy in, 40, 46, 61, 64–69, 72, 108, 117, 126, 139, 155–57, 178, 189; Selma to Montgomery march, *29f*, 37, 51, 66–67, 71, 87–88, 90, 124, 126, 160, 183–85, *184f, 186f*, 187; and surrounding locality, 49–51; television coverage of, 8, 37, 61–62, 65, 68, 72, 134–36, 140, 141, 142, 145–46, 147, 148n17; as threshold moment in American history, 19–21, 31, 78, 133–34; "Tuesday Turnaround," 66, 69–70, 72, 146; violence in, 58–62, 64–67, 73, 145–46, 159–60, 199. *See also* "Bloody Sunday"; Edmund Pettus Bridge
Selma to Montgomery National Historic Trail, 27
Shelby County v. Holder, 9–10, 30–31, 247, 256–57, 258n4, 264–66; criticism of, 272, 273, 277–78, 282–83; dissenting opinion, 250, 276, 280–81; and equal sovereignty, 271–73, 275; majority opinion, 248–50, 253, 264–65, 272–73, 275–76, 278–79, 280–85; and "model minorities," 277–78; oral arguments, 248, 250; responses to, 250–53
Shuttlesworth, Fred Lee, 171, 202
Sides, Wayne, 182
Slavery, 10, 17
Smitherman, Joseph, 39, 60, 61, 64, 68
Somerstein, Stephen F., 184
South Carolina, 39, 86, 96, 97, 108, 229, 244–46
South Carolina v. Katzenbach, 244–49
Southern Christian Leadership Conference, 6–7, 15, 18, 27, 28, 39, 51, 158; Albany campaign of, 58; Birmingham campaign of, 7, 43–44, 58, 62, 64, 65, 72, 113, 138, 146; Chicago campaign of, 58; Crusade for Citizenship, 18–19; Poor People's Campaign, 58; Selma campaign of (*see* Selma campaign); St. Augustine campaign of, 58, 62, 65, 201; tensions with SNCC, 43, 46, 50, 59, 72–73, 147, 155, 163; tensions with the NAACP, 40, 63, 73
Southern Manifesto, 80–81, 96, 97, 99, 101, 102, 107
Spottswood, Stephen G., 189
States' rights, 187, 188, 230, 231, 283
Stennis, John, 105, 230
Stevens, John Paul, 271
Stokes, Carl, 255
Streator, George, 152
Student Nonviolent Coordinating Committee, 15, 17–18, 26, 28–29, 37, 43, 44, 49–50, 51, 71, 158; and nonviolence, 67, 71; in Selma campaign, 6–7, 45, 46, 47, 65, 73, 85, 155; 1964 Summer Project ("Freedom Summer"), 61, 62, 73, 103–4, 163; tensions with SCLC, 40, 43, 46, 50, 59, 63, 65, 67, 69–70, 71–73, 147
Subprime mortgages. *See* Mortgages; Racial inequality
Supreme Court, 10, 244–45. *See also specific Supreme Court decisions*
Suydam, Henry, 182

"Take My Hand, Precious Lord" (song), 208–9
Talese, Gay, 190
Talmadge, Herman, 230
Taney, Roger B., 273–74
Tennessee, 17, 84, 97–101, 105, 108
Tenth Amendment, 249
Texas, 251–52, 279
"This Little Light of Mine" (song), 207
Thomas, Clarence, 280
Thurmond, Strom, 230
Tillman, Benjamin, 245
TIME magazine, 150, 164
Turner, Albert, 23, 162

United Kingdom, 8, 113–17, 119–21, 126–27; press response to Selma, 117–19, 126

Valeriani, Richard, 142, 150
Varela, Maria, 39, 45
Velásquez, William, 279, 288n32
Violence against African Americans, 18, 25, 26, 42, 45–46, 48, 61–62, 64–68, 71, 72. *See also* "Bloody Sunday"; Clark, Jim; Selma campaign
Vivian, C. T., 184
Voter discrimination, 10, 64, 217, 244–46, 271, 274–75, 278–79, 284–85; gerrymandering, 275, 280
Voter identification laws, 248, 251–54, 256–57, 261n72, 285; after *Shelby County v. Holder*, 250–55, 256–57, 264–65, 275–76, 278; in Selma, 186–87
Voter registration, 91, 108, 251; African American elected officials, 96–97, 109, 217. *See also Shelby County v. Holder*; Voting Rights Act (1965)
Voting rights, 10, 217, 240–44, 284–85, 287n28
Voting Rights Act (1965), 5, 26, 30–31, 51, 72, 102, 124–25, 240, 247–49, 264, 268, 271–72, 286n15; Albert Gore and, 100–102; congressional support for, 7, 78, 101–2; legacy of, 9–10, 23, 103–8, 217, 232, 234nn2,3, 240, 255, 277, 279–80; opposition to, 103, 105, 107, 244–48, 254; relationship with African American unrest, 91–92; Section Two, 253, 271; Section Four, 253, 265, 271, 275, 278, 280; Section Five, 240, 244–45, 248, 250, 251, 253, 264, 271, 278, 279; in *Selma*, 77, 84; Selma campaign and, 6, 18, 19, 25, 38. *See also* Johnson, Lyndon Baines
Voting Rights Amendment Act (2014), 31, 262n78

"Walk With Me" (song), 204
Wallace, George, 3, 61, 66, 67–69, 71, 73, 107, 108, 136, 146, 174, 189; and Lyndon Johnson, 88–89, 90; in *Selma*, 210
Warren, Earl, 245, 268
Watts Rebellion, 72, 91, 127, 153, 156, 164
Welsh, David, 197
"We Shall Overcome" (song), 207
White backlash, 97
White Citizens Council, 31
Wilkins, Roy, 63, 73, 163, 189
Wilkinson, Bill, 182
Williams, Hosea, 23, 45, 68, 182; in *Selma*, 136, 137f, 144
Williams v. Wallace, 181, 186
Winfrey, Oprah, 3, 144–45
Wisconsin, 253, 262n76
Works Progress Administration. *See* New Deal

X, Malcolm, 67, 119

Young, Andrew, Jr., 64, 68, 85, 190, 226

Zimmerman, George, 265